Contesting Security

Contesting Security investigates to what extent the "logic of security", which underpins securitization, can be contained, rolled back or dismantled.

Featuring legitimacy as a cement of security practices, this volume presents a detailed account of the "logic" which sustains security in order to develop a novel approach to the relation between security and the policies in which it is engraved. Understanding security as a normative practice, the contributors suggest a nuanced, and richer take on the conditions under which it is possible, advisable or fair to accept or roll back its policies.

The book comprises four parts, each investigating one specific modality of contesting security practices: resistance, desecuritization, emancipation, and resilience. These strategies are examined, compared and assessed in different political and cultural habitats.

This book will be of much interest to students of critical security studies, securitization theory, social theory, and IR in general.

Thierry Balzacq is Scientific Director of the Institute for Strategic Research (IRSEM) at the French Ministry of Defence and Tocqueville Professor of International Relations at the University of Namur, Belgium. He is also Honorary Professorial Fellow at the School of Social and Political Science at the University of Edinburgh, UK.

PRIO New Security Studies

Series Editor: J. Peter Burgess, PRIO, Oslo

The aim of this book series is to gather state-of-the-art theoretical reflection and empirical research into a core set of volumes that respond vigorously and dynamically to the new challenges to security scholarship.

Contesting Security

Strategies and logics

Edited by Thierry Balzacq

Routledge
Taylor & Francis Group

LONDON AND NEW YORK

First published 2015
by Routledge
2 Park Square, Milton Park, Abingdon, Oxon, OX14 4RN

and by Routledge
711 Third Avenue, New York, NY 10017

Routledge is an imprint of the Taylor & Francis Group, an informa business

British Library Cataloguing in Publication Data
A catalogue record for this book is available from the British Library

Library of Congress Cataloging-in-Publication Data
Contesting security : strategies and logics / edited by Thierry Balzacq.
    pages cm. – (PRIO new security studies)
    Includes bibliographical references and index.
    1. Public safety – Social aspects. 2. Internal security – Social aspects.
    3. National security – Social aspects. 4. Security, International – Social
    aspects. I. Balzacq, Thierry, editor of compilation.
    HV7431.C6678 2015
    363.1–dc23   2014022757

ISBN: 978-0-415-64386-3 (hbk)
ISBN: 978-0-203-07985-0 (ebk)

Typeset in Times New Roman
by HWA Text and Data Management, London

Contents

Illustrations

Figures

Tables

Contributors

Mika Aaltola is the Director of the Global Security Research Program at the Finnish Institute of International Affairs, Finland.

Claudia Aradau is Reader in International Politics, the Department of War Studies at King's College London, UK.

Thierry Balzacq is Scientific Director of the Institute for Strategic Research (IRSEM) at the French Ministry of Defense and Tocqueville Professor of International Relations at the University of Namur, Belgium.

Florent Blanc is a Program Manager for the Peace Program in Grenoble, France.

Philippe Bourbeau is Temporary University Lecturer in the Department of Politics and International Studies at the University of Cambridge, UK, and Research Fellow in the Tocqueville Chair in Security Policies at the University of Namur, Belgium.

Sara Depauw is Research Fellow at the Flemish Peace Research Institute, Brussels, Belgium.

Rita Floyd is Birmingham Fellow in Conflict and Security in the Department of Political Science and International Studies at the University of Birmingham, UK.

Lene Hansen is Professor of International Relations at the University of Copenhagen, Denmark.

Sarah Léonard is Senior Lecturer in Politics at the University of Dundee, UK.

Matt McDonald is Senior Lecturer in International Relations at the University of Queensland, Australia.

Gary T. Marx is Emeritus Professor of Sociology at the Massachusetts Institute of Technology (MIT), United States of America.

João Nunes is Lecturer in International Relations at the University of York, UK.

Pierre Piazza is Maître de Conference at the University of Cergy-Pontoise, France.

Peter Rogers is Senior Lecturer in the Department of Sociology at the Macquarie University, Australia.

Juha A. Vuori is Senior Lecturer in International Relations at the University of Turku and Adjunct Professor at the University of Tampere, Finland.

Preface

The issue that presents itself as crucial for scholars of critical approaches to security (CAS) is the extent to which the "logic of security", which is said to underpin security practices, can be contained, rolled back or dismantled. For a critical researcher, the issue is central because it is difficult to study security policies and practices without dealing, for instance, with the following questions: what should people do in face of a securitizing move that they deem inappropriate? How should they act when an issue has been securitized? What strategies should they deploy when they live within a securitized site? Are the strategies of equal strength, merit and ethical status? Thus, the overriding objective of this volume is to clearly map out the different ways in which a dominant register of meaning that shapes a specific security formation is debased.

Specifically, the book pursues the following aims: to rethink the meaning of emancipation, desecuritization, resistance and resilience, *as they relate to* security; to examine when and how these concepts interact; when they are complementary and when they compete; to show the linkages between social and political theories, IR, security studies, political psychology and the development of practices, which challenge security's logic; to provide a dedicated sample of empirical cases in which the contours of each modality of contesting security demonstrate their practical application, in relation to others; to evaluate how compatible are the policies that they sustain and/or embody.

Two caveats. First, it has been the tendency of CAS to deal with desecuritization, emancipation, resilience, and resistance as more or less isolated strategies, as practices that could conceivably operate by themselves. It is true that different strategies apply to different issues and yield contrasting results depending upon the culture, the political regime, and the power of those who activate them. Yet, it is not uncommon that two or more of these strategies would overlap or, alternatively, come to clash. Second, the book is normatively agnostic toward security. Indeed, not all authors of this volume would hold that security pronouncements are necessarily negative, in all situations (Elbe, 2006; Wæver, 2000). Rather, contributors are united in the view that, in many instances, security practices and policies have detrimental effects on the political and on social relations. Thus, developing strategies that make for inclusive register of meanings, poses one of the greatest challenges to critical security scholars.

In this book, those strategies are examined, compared and assessed, in different political and cultural environments.

This book has benefited from the contribution of many colleagues. My greatest thanks go to the contributors who accepted embarking on this project and offered generous comments to chapters they had to read before and after the workshop. I owe them a lot, as some of them shelved their own projects in order to produce original pieces for this specific volume. I am glad to report that interactions generated during the workshop have led to fruitful collaborations between some of the participants. A preparatory workshop was held at the Finnish Institute of International Affairs in 2012. I would like to thank Mika Aaltola who made this possible, providing us with a very friendly environment. I thank Stephane Baele for his crucial help with the bibliography. My special thanks are to Lene Hansen who was a careful reader of all the chapters. She has been very generous with her support. Peter Burgess, Annabelle Harris, and Andrew Humphreys, were helpful editors, unstinting in patience. The preparation of the book and my working on it, occurred when I was a Fellow at the Institute for Advance Studies (programme for "outstanding research"), at the University of Edinburgh. My warmest thanks go to Christina Boswell, Xavier Guillaume, Juliet Karboo, Andrew Neal, and Anthea Taylor, who provided me with a very friendly environment and made my sabbatical not only an intellectual but also a human experience that I wish others could enjoy. Anonymous reviewers from Routledge provided extremely useful insights, which enabled me to enrich the contents of the book.

Thierry Balzacq
Marcq-en-Baroeul, France

1 Legitimacy and the "logic" of security

Thierry Balzacq

Introduction

The choice between critical and traditional approaches to security is often treated as one between a constructivist and a realist ontology, between the conviction that security follows one unique script, and the view that security is a derivate property (CASE Collective 2006). In other words, security is either a given or a constructed state of affairs; either immutable or variable. The debate boils down, I argue, to whether security has a "logic" or none or, alternatively, admits to a plurality of logics, whose meaning depends on context, and whose effect is indeterminate. For Jef Huysmans (1998a) there is a logic of security, which can be seen in the fact that security pronouncements often produce a specific social order. Cai Wilkinson (2011), on the other hand, is less enthusiastic about the existence of such a logic. Be that as it may, the discussion on security's logic presupposes if anything else that there is an agreement on the content of the word "logic." This is far from the case, however. Yet only when this has been done can we properly capture the logic of a particular practice. My view is that before we start enumerating the number of logics that would underpin security, a basic, that is, preliminary enquiry has to be undertaken: what do we mean when we say that security has "a" logic?[1]

To answer this question, I want to make a slight detour. It is now a commonplace not only of security studies but also of IR that security is a social practice. Yet, as simple as it is, this claim has stronger implications than it might first appear. That is, what is often referred to as "the logic of security" is, in essence, an attempt to ascribe a logic to an abstract concept. However, the logic I have in mind is not of this sort. Instead, if anything, the logic of security is always already the logic of a concept as expressed by, or engraved in various practices. Huysmans (1998a: 232) argues, for instance, that the logic of security is "an ensemble of rules that is immanent to security practice and that defines the practice in its specificity." In other words, the logic of security is parasitic upon security practices. Therefore, in this chapter, I use the "logic of security practices" to delineate both the scope and horizon of my investigation. In this respect, I deliberately sacrifice the economy of expression to the precision and, hopefully, clarity of the argument. Drawing on Glynos and Howarth (2007: 136), I argue that the logic of security practices articulates two main elements: the "rule or grammar of the practice," on the one hand, and the "conditions which make the practice both possible and vulnerable," on the other hand.

Constitutive features of the "logic" of security

Theories of security differ over their understanding of this logic, its demands and effects. For instance, a realist rendition of the logic of security practices would hold that military rules inform the characteristic grammar of security practices and the concept of "existential threats" provides the background condition, which enables the different components of security practices to operate in a distinctive way. Securitization theory, in particular Ole Wæver's formulation, has adopted this view of the logic of security, while attempting to nest security pronouncements in a constructivist ontology (Wæver 1995). However, the constructivist influence has stopped at the doors of the realist logic of security practices. It is as if the construction of security remains impervious to the social conditions which allow security practices to discharge their meaning and function. Thus, in this version of securitization theory, the logic of security practices is reduced to the rules and grammar of the practices; conditions that surround the practice are dropped out of the framework. If they were introduced back into the equation, the constitutive parts of the logic would have to be clothed in a decisively constructivist fabric (Buzan and Hansen 2009: 215).

Other scholars working within critical studies on security take a different tack. Felix Ciúta (2009: 311–314) argues, for instance, that the contextual thickness of security practices undermines Wæver's logic of security practices (cf. also Bubandt 2005: 276, 291). In this sense, both the rules and circumstances that hold security practices are contextually bound. In many ways, I have some sympathy for this proposal. However, the most disturbing problem with Ciúta and Bubandt otherwise compelling readings of securitization's shortcomings is that, they seem to follow, in various modulations, the path well trodden by many contextualists who tend to argue that context exhausts the rules of a practice (DeRose 2009). This is bizarre. The point is not that I subscribe, let alone defend, the logic of security laid out by the initial formulation of securitization theory (Balzacq 2011b: 11–15). Instead, I only want to argue that the rules of security practices are not reducible to the features of specific empirical contexts. To imagine a contextual influence on security practices, is one thing; to drain rules from content because context matters, is quite another. In fact, one does not lead to the other.

To some extent, this only restates the problem, but does not solve it. Thus, in order to better appropriate the status of "logic" in securitization theory, I propose to build my reasoning on one assumption, from which I derive two sets of arguments. The assumption is that security practices result from securitization. No security practices without a prior securitization. Though security practices can, in turn, generate new securitization patterns, I postulate that securitization predates security practices. For practices to be acknowledged as "security" practices, there needs to be an intersubjective assent on the fact that they bear on "security"; that is, they call for a form of securitization. Of course, when I investigate security practices, the concern is with practices which happen within a securitized site and that, as such, either sustain or transform securitization.

Now, the two arguments I want to extract from this assumption take the following schematic forms. First, security practices somewhat negotiate their content and meaning with the context and other practices therein. Second, security practices owe their logic to processes of securitization. If we understand this move in relevant terms, the question becomes, therefore, what (if any) is the logic of securitization? To start, it is often argued that the aim of securitization is to transform the "status function" of a problem into a security issue (Searle 2009: 19). Securitization is a moment of political agonism, out of which a security problem is instituted (Balzacq forthcoming; Williams forthcoming). Security practices that result from securitization remain socially binding so long as they respond to commonly accepted values. That is, so long as they are regarded as legitimate. In other words, the logic of securitization comprises a specific grammar or rules of the political and the principle of legitimacy, that is, a necessary (not sufficient) condition by which security practices are sustained and without which they lose their moral grips on the subjects. As Juha Vuori (2008: 68) puts it, "security is a strong legitimator." In turn, I posit, arguments for contesting security are closely related to justifications of legitimacy.

Legitimacy and the silos of security practices

Security practices draw their efficacy from legitimacy, as legitimacy confers them a normative status. People may have many ideas about security practices, but only those deemed inappropriate or illegitimate would be contested. I do not claim, obviously, that legitimacy is the sole basis for enduring security practices. Indeed, naked coercion can equally sustain a body of security practices. Take Robert Mugabe's Zimbabwe. If security practices are so effective there, it has less to do with their legitimacy than with the ability of Robert Mugabe to muster a range of coercive means to crack on any attempt to challenge his policies. In this respect, I argue that the greater capacity leaders have in generating and maintaining the legitimacy of security practices, the less opposition these will encounter. This means that the very existence of a security practice depends on a sufficient number of people believing that it is the most appropriate way to secure what they commonly value. I understand, of course, that "sufficient number" remains open to a diverse range of interpretations. The idea I want to convey, however, is that a number is insufficient to the extent that it is unable to fundamentally undermine a policy. In this light, "number" should not be read in terms of sheer arithmetic; instead, it is a matter of the quantum of "alienative motivational elements" that the contesting group is able to concentrate around critical points of disagreement (Parsons 1951: 521). "Conscientious objection can become politically significant", says Hannah Arendt, "when a number of consciences happen to coincide and the conscientious objectors decide to enter the marketplace and make their voices heard and public" (Arendt 1971: 219–220). On the face of it, the erosion of security practices' legitimacy would weaken their power to oblige people to conform to their prescriptions. In this sense, then, legitimacy is an important factor for both the effectiveness and survival of sets of security practices, though its impact on outcomes takes "complex causal forms" (Gilley 2007: 145). I follow Robert Dahl who holds that legitimacy "is not any more reliable and durable than naked coercion but it also enables rulers to govern with a minimum of political resources" (Dahl 1984: 54).

In other words, it is possible to explicate demands for emancipation, desecuritization, resilience, and resistance, by resorting to the operation of legitimacy. However, the relation between resilience and legitimacy is a bit more complicated. While resilience might be sponsored by a state as a complement to traditional measures of security policies, resilience can also be regarded as state's recognition that existing mechanisms of ensuring security are not the most appropriate or are potentially ineffective. One of the results is to undermine the belief in the legitimacy of those extant security practices. I spell out the distinctive relationship between legitimacy and the constitutive components of this book, under the different "editor's introductions."

My argument on legitimacy extends the current effort within critical studies on security to redeem the concept of security (Gjørv 2012). In fact, the reactionary impulse of its origins led a sizable number of critical scholars to entertain an ambiguous if not negative relation with the concept of security (Browning and McDonald 2013). Confusing security and securitization, it became a fairly common place to assume that security necessarily released negative outcomes. Not only do such attitudes elevate one kind of potential result of a practice to the rank of unavoidable rules of security, they also somewhat made more difficult the dialogue with traditional approaches to security. In this light, some of the reactions raised by Rita Floyd's (2011) attempt to establish a just securitization can be understood in the context of a negative attitude toward security. While an important point of Floyd's view has been to provide a more sophisticated basis to Elbe's (2006) argument, I want to interpret the criticism leveled at it in two ways. The first line of argument, which is important but not entirely justified, is that Floyd subverts the original idea of securitization theory, which did not admit of any "objective" threat (de Wilde 2012; Wæver 2011). Probably, the main bone of contention rests with the specific understanding of the word "objective." If objectivity refers to the positivist separation between subject and object, critics have a point. However, if by "objective threats" Floyd means the intersubjective solidification of a social fact, then the ground for quibble considerably shrinks (Neufeld 1995; Kompridis 2006). The second, less outspoken aspect of the reservation raised by Floyd's proposal might be that her thesis makes room for conceiving of securitization as a process that can rightfully instantiate security problems, under certain circumstances. In this respect, it has, so to speak, a positive relation with security. To me, the most important insight I retain from this discussion is that critical approaches to security should never have departed from the view that security is neither positive nor negative, a priori. Leaning on either side deprives one from developing a non-biased critical examination of security. Understanding security in exclusively negative terms amounts to a cheap ethics, of sorts, as it puts critical security scholars on the rather defensive position of having to resist anything that looks like a security practice. If this were so, then, critical approaches to security would become dogmatic security studies.

The concept of legitimacy enables us to determine the conditions under which security practices are likely to obtain or fail. Does it lead to the ethical argument that a legitimate security practice is necessarily a good security practice? No, but to a certain degree it would countenance the view that good security practices are legitimate. For the analyst, however, there are many problems with adjudicating that a security practice is legitimate. Political contexts, for instance, can modify what is treated as legitimate. In addition, the legitimacy of security practices is not a matter of all or nothing; in fact, it is more productive to characterize security legitimacy as a continuum. Therein lies the organic vulnerability of security practices, whatever the conventions of a specific context.

The texture of legitimacy

In social sciences, the study of legitimacy is peculiarly tied to the work of Max Weber (1978: 213) who, to put it succinctly, defined it as "the belief in legitimacy." Translated in our terms, a security practice is legitimate if people concerned believe it to be so. It is because people who partake in security practices hold these to be legitimate that they are. This definition raises several difficulties for the analyst. It tends, for instance, to treat legitimacy as a given phenomenon in which people can believe or not. That is, legitimacy is seen as an article of faith. Moreover, Weber's legitimacy principles (charismatic, rational-legal, traditional) also rely on the subjective belief of people in each of them as they constitute the basis of three separate types of legitimacy: the belief in tradition, is the basis of a traditional legitimacy; the belief in rules and procedures sustains rational-legal kind of legitimacy; and the belief in charisma offers grounds for charismatic legitimacy (Beetham 1991: 24–25).

I spend some time on Weber's account of legitimacy because it is probably the most influential; it is often, indeed, the background against which alternative approaches to legitimacy are gauged. For all its appeal, however, it is misleading. This claim might sound presumptuous, but it is an argument that, I hope, is worth taking a moment to appreciate. To start, Weber's typology does not tell us how to aggregate the three kinds of legitimacy into a coherent understanding of legitimacy. In fact, we are left we three distinct *kinds* of legitimacy, each operating under a different rationale. Further, the definition of legitimacy as a subjective belief in one of the three principles obscures the different elements that provide the basis for this belief. But of what do these elements consist? A review of the literature returns three main features constitutive of legitimacy: legality, justification, and consent (Beetham 1991: 16–21; Gilley 2007: 6–8; Coicaud 1997: 10–25). In what follows, I briefly discuss the three principles in the light of security practices.

Legality. It is the starting point of discussions about legitimacy pointing, as it were, to the original meaning of the word legitimacy as it first surfaced in medieval documents (Merquior, 1980: 2). Security practices draw a parcel of their legitimacy from the fact that they are adopted and played out in ways that conform to the legal rules of the political system, which provides them with their normative conspectus. Specifically significant, of course, is the view that not all rules are strictly formalized; but the most important idea is that, in general, political leaders try to make security practices that they promote look legal. When a security practice seems to run counter existing rules, leaders are tempted to resort to transforming the legal order within which new security practices can thrive. Societies with strong formalized rules tend to have an ultimate authority that adjudicates between competing interpretations of the legality of a policy prescription. Nonetheless, the matters become complex if security practices conflict with the existing legal order to such an extent that it puts its validity at stake. Here, however, we come close to the edge of exceptionalism. Rules – whether exceptional or not – are not legitimate uniquely by virtue of their enactment. Arguing otherwise would suggest that any rule adopted and applied in accordance with the legal order is legitimate. Obviously, this is not true. The legal hierarchy of many modern societies does not mean that legality should be equated with legitimacy. Sometimes, rules are not enough; and people might be skeptical about their function and rightfulness. In other words, rules need to be justified (Onuf 1989).

Justification. Legitimacy belongs primarily to a constructivist analysis of compliance. Here, it is a willing acceptance of security policies for reasons other than structural constraints, physical or psychological violence that is the main vector of influence. In my view, this also means that politics (as a field of contestation) contributes to the textures of legitimacy. This is because without justification of why some practices of security should be followed, any measure the elites propose would probably face skepticism if not strong defiance. I have shown above that Vuori (2008), for instance, has conceptualized securitization as a form of legitimacy, that is, a process whereby security practices (and sometimes the elites who defend them) draw their political support from justificatory arguments. That is, justification is the mechanism that creates and sustains security practices. Put otherwise, the support of the public is acquired precisely through justificatory processes, and not exclusively from the legality of security practices. Leaders make security practices essentially by arguing their case that X counts as a threat. The mechanism of justification enables the public to weight the claims put forward by the political elites, in terms of the community's shared values and norms. It is at this particular juncture that the meaning and legitimacy of security practices are fixed. That is, the process of justification is legitimacy's political core (Unger 1976: 62). The success of justificatory claims depends, to a large extent, on the leaders' ability to persuade the public that security practices "contribute in a credible way to the achievement of society's values" (Coicaud 1997: 23). Once the acceptance is secured, two consequences follow. First, security practices acquire their collective nature. They are no longer a fact decided by a securitizing actor; instead, they express a kind of shared agency. Second, political leaders obtain the right to liberate deontic powers in order to curb the threat – duties, obligations, derogations. It is possible to see in this creation of deontic powers signs that the ultimate aim of justification is to establish a form of consent. In other words, the legitimacy of security practices depends on the extent to which consent allows the community to resolve the tension around the status function of security problems and the appropriate methods to address them.

Consent. Security practices are authoritative to the extent that they rest with a foundational consent. This consent is a necessary condition for legitimacy. Yet, it is worth noting that consent has consequences both for the elite and the general public. On the one hand, consent accords the political elite the right to develop policies that ensure the protection of the object upon which agreement has been reached. For the public, on the other hand, consent means the duty to comply with the deontic powers granted to the elites. Consents are at once what permits rights and duties to be established. Duties and rights continue to hold so long as the consent upon which they are grounded persist. In this sense, consent has an integrative function, which legitimacy conveys. Eloquently, David Easton (1965: 278) substantiates this point, arguing that "the most stable support (in favor of the authorities) will derive from the conviction on the part of the member that it is right and proper for him to accept and obey the authorities and abide by the requirements of the regime."

Consent injects both a moral and a symbolic dimension into security practices. On the one hand, when people conduct themselves in accordance with the security practices established thanks to deontic powers, they contribute to the maintenance of normative consent toward those practices. This is the moral aspect of consent. On the other hand, actions that manifest consent are carried out in public, which means that third parties, whether acting in the same way or not, can indeed testify that the actors conform to prescribed security practices. This is the symbolic aspect of consent.

However, when I argue that there is a moral and a symbolic dimensions to consent, I do not hold that people always agree with the security practices they are engaged in. Instead, I suggest that any action that conforms to security practices expresses a commitment and a public consent to the security practices. There is nothing inferred about the degree of consent; my examples only apply to the object of consent: security practices.[2] However, it is also at this point that consent takes us back to legality, as security practices in our model are deployed in a legal framework. People consent because they want to abide by the rules. But in order to produce its effects, people need to act in accordance with what the rules prescribe. Consent is thus a constitutive condition of security practices' effectiveness and stability. Moreover, consent provides us with the intrinsic vulnerability of security practices. Indeed, if subjects qualified to give consent loose confidence in the rules, they could resist or oppose security practices, and, ultimately, undermine their effectiveness. As Gilley (2007: 152) puts it, "if legitimacy best explains citizen compliance with the policies, then the opposite is also true: illegitimacy is the best explanation of citizen unwillingness to obey." Legitimacy soothes opposition to security practices; conversely, lack of legitimacy renders contestation possible and likely to be successful (compare Gurr 1970: 183–92; Goldstone 1991).

However, security practices could lack legitimacy in three different ways at least. In the first place, security practices could be the product of an illegal procedure or they can themselves, even though adopted legally, take illegal tracks and shapes. In this context, it is best to speak about the *illegitimacy* of practices, in the sense that they breach the legal order of a political system. Second, security practices can suffer from a *deficit of legitimacy*. That is, when the shared beliefs that used to justify both their existence and operation weakens. Third, security practices are subjected to a process of *delegitimation* when the consent that sustains them erodes.[3] Taken together, these three forms of legitimacy problems are, in their peculiar way, crisis of legitimacy, as they raise important challenges for the existence of the practices attacked. Security practices endure to the extent that they do not encounter demands that undermine their essential rules. In contrast, according to Lipset (1970: 40), "a crisis of legitimacy is a crisis of change." In other words, crises of legitimacy express those occasions when security practices are disrupted, transformed or, even radically, dismantled.

Overview of the volume

This is a book of reflections on the contents, shapes and effects of contentious politics around security thought and practice. It explores the degree to which different crises of legitimacy get hooked up with the evolution of security practices. The crisis of legitimacy of a security practice often takes place against the background of other ideals or principles, which undermine that security practice's legitimacy. This book brings different approaches that aim to counter security practices to confront one another and substantiate their respective analytical value, for the most part through empirical evidence. To do so, it maps out the different ways in which a dominant register of meaning, legality and/or consent, which shapes a specific security formation, is challenged, debased or extinguished.

The book comprises four sections, each investigating one specific modality of contesting security: resistance, desecuritization, emancipation, and resilience. Each part starts with an editor's introduction. However, I want to give a broad presentation of their flow therein. In part I, "Resistance," we investigate one specific type of resistance, i.e., resistance against oppressive politics and policies of security. In other words, it does not study the resistance of domineering forces to emancipatory impulses. Further, Derrida, Deleuze and Foucault seem to hold, for instance, that resistance is "contextually bound to the social and psychological structures that are being resisted" (Hoy 2004: 3). In this light, the challenge that confronts contributors of this section is to think out resistance schemes that are not shaped by the social features that are being resisted.

Part II, focuses on both the theoretical and empirical purchase of "Desecuritization". This is not easy. Some argue that de-securitization is logically impossible, because of the "normative dilemma" which irremediably cripples those who speak about, or write on security (Roe 2004). Others say that desecuritization should be thought of as a matter of degrees, not as a political end point (Jutila 2006). Finally, a range of scholars claim that desecuritization should be seen as a "strategy" that can take various forms (called "tactics") such as repoliticization, rejudiciarization, and even emancipation, resistance, or resilience (see, in particular, Chapters 3, 5, 7). This section asks whether desecuritization is the "master signifier" which subsumes and gives meaning to cognate concepts that aim to unmake or transform security's logic. It does so by assessing whether the ethical concerns that desecuritization raises are distinct from those brought by emancipation, for instance.

Of the four concepts examined in this book, emancipation is perhaps the one that has generated most discussions and criticisms. In Part III, authors investigate both the universalist inclination of emancipation and the day-to-day and local practices of emancipation. Part III attempts to determine whether emancipation can overcome the risk of exclusion inherent in claims of universality that pervade it. In other words, the contributions examine the relative merits of various approaches to emancipation (politics within or politics outside of security). They are intended to situate emancipation in relation to resistance, resilience, and desecuritization.

Finally, Part IV, "Resilience," studies two types of resilience, "societal" and "organizational/infrastructure" resilience. The basic idea of resilience, drawn from social psychology, is that communities and organizations cannot prevent every threat from materializing. This means that the greatest asset of communities and organizations is to be able to adapt and manage threats. Put differently, a community is resilient, for instance, if it can cope with what cannot be prevented or can recover from a setback. As resilience does not aim to transform security, but the way it is dealt or lived with, it would be investigated primarily in relation to resistance and emancipation, arguing that resilience can go in either direction depending on whether it aims to escape the fear of threat or absorb the shock provoked by a security problem. The thrust of Part IV is to determine when and why resilience takes one form instead of the other, and the implications this might have on the referent object of security.

In addition to this broad presentation of the book's contents, I have written a short introduction for each section. Given the different strands within each strategy, I thought this way of proceeding had the potential of helping the reader to navigate the materials more smoothly.

Notes

1 I am grateful to Matt MacDonald who advised that I should put a stronger emphasis on the largely undertheorized concept of the "logic" of security.
2 On the degree and object of consent, see Webber and Macleod (2000).
3 I draw these three forms of crisis of legitimacy from Beetham (1991: 20).

Part I
Resistance

Editor's introduction

I

From Aristotle to Georges Sorell, through Plato, John Locke and Karl Marx, political theorists have long inquired into the morality, instruments, and conditions of possibility of resistance. In the seventeenth century, for instance, Luther and Calvin were pressed to clarify their position as regards the resort to violence as a means for resistance (Bell, 1973: 19–21). However, the study of resistance in social sciences takes it roots back a scant forty years. In fact, it was not until the so-called cultural turn of the 1980s that resistance became a consistent and dynamic field of study. For its part, IR has not remained untouched by the concern with resistance. Initially, however, research emphasized how resistance subverts a dominant discourse, by examining the goals and strategies of social movements (cf. Lynch, 1999; Keck and Sikking, 1998; Amoore, 2005). Similarly, in a tightly argued work, Roland Bleiker (2000) investigated how popular dissent unfolds in the context of transversal politics.

Whatever their focal point, however, IR scholars have broadly regarded resistance as a counter-politics against an oppressive/a dominating power or discourse. This is a sensible way of approaching resistance; perhaps it is the most convincing. Yet, it is certainly not the only one. For it assumes, among other things, that resistance is essentially, if not exclusively, captured by the binary opposition between rulers and ruled, those who dominate and those who resist. The problem, however, is that this tends to attribute power to one part of the binary opposition: the dominant force or the ruler. Importantly, moreover, resistance is conceptualized outside domination. That is, resistant subjects operate within an autonomous space or create one that remains out of the gaze of the dominant power (Scott, 1985). Finally, power is seen therein in primarily destructive terms.

Yet, such a reading reduces power to an exclusive substance or to a zero sum game. Michel Foucault posits that there is a complex relation between resistance and power. According to him, indeed, "where there is power there is resistance" (Foucault, 1976: 125). Put otherwise, there cannot be domination without resistance any more than there can be resistance without domination. In addition, it is now widely known that for Foucault, power is dispersed and has a productive nature, in the sense that power constitutes subjects of a specific blend. That is, "neither dominating power nor resisting power are total, but rather both are fragmentary, uneven and inconsistent to varying degrees" (Sharp et al. 2000: 20). This is not to claim that power does not often concentrate on institutions, thus creating an unbalance between the latter and the general public. Instead, it means that resistance and power always already embody the trace of the other, which is constitutive of its very nature and limits (Guillaume, 2011).

II

In Chapter 1, I argued that security practices reach their main limit when their legitimacy is debased. The causes of the erosion of security practices' legitimacy are numerous, but the outcome is virtually the same: cracks appear in their fabric. Depending upon the intensity and constraints exercised on security practices, the latter eventually collapses. In other words, the thickness of security practice depends upon the balance of power that prevails within a given context. The units (individuals, groups, states) and level (structures) might vary; but the underlying mechanism – power relations – enables us to understand the conditions under which security practices disintegrate.

The chapters under this Part examine resistant thought and action, by unpacking lines of security policy that sustain certain forms of domination. In their respective contributions, Gary T. Marx, Juha Vuori, Pierre Piazza and Florent Blanc argue that resistance often surface in "state's own internal operations" (Sharp et al., 2000: 20). In particular, Chapter 2 discusses different strategies for neutralizing surveillance. Expanding on his previous work on resistance and security (cf. Marx, 1988) Marx argues that technologies of surveillance are not only resisted from the outside, but also internally, as they contain their own possibility of contestation. The chapter investigates in detail how subjects attempt to beat surveillance technologies by developing strategies of counter-neutralization, which enable them to renegotiate if not to safeguard their margin of liberty for action. While Marx's chapter offers a set of cross-contextual insights, the remaining three chapters have a strong empirical wing, which also provides them with fertile terrains for conceptual design. In Chapter 3, Vuori investigates attitude against securitization attempts in post-Mao China. Testing a distinction that runs throughout the volume – contestation versus resistance – he proposes to reserve contestation to counter actions stemming from formal institutions and resistance to the movement of non-official or non-institutionalized groups. The student democracy movement (1989) and the events around the Falungong (1999) are discussed around the two interacting poles (i.e., contestation and resistance). In Chapter 4, Piazza emphasizes resistance to biometric identifiers in France. He analyzes not only the vector of resistance (Internet, cartoons, etc.), but also the sites of resistance (e.g., schools) as well as its objects (CCTV, DNA sampling, etc.). The chapter therefore offers a minute picture of how repertoires of resistance operate, while assessing their intrinsic frailty. In like manner, Chapter 5 focuses on the strategies of resistance after 9/11 in the US. But Blanc displaces the discussion onto the rationale behind the choice of different types of strategies. His study of the American Library Association (ALA) is organized around concepts such as "public" or "hidden transcripts". However, when he turns to evaluating the role of the Center for Constitutional Rights (CCR), Blanc is able to show how the "legimating blocs" of a security policy can be dismantled "piece by piece". For Blanc, then, in both cases, resisting national security measures means re-politicizing them or desecuritizing them. In this light, resistance is an instrument for desecuritization. However, as contributors to Part II will make clear, the enactment of desecuritization is neither necessary explicit nor conscious. That is, while resistance usually involves the use of power "over" others in an attempt to subvert a dominant situation, desecuritization can deliver its effects in a more benign way or can be effected without a tactical or strategic intention (Brown, 1996). To resist is to deliver a counter-force; to desecuritize is not to securitize in reverse. Resistance depends on a conception of security policy as consciously enlisted power relations. In other words, desecuritization may relate to resistance, but not as a sufficient condition: resistance to security policies can lead to other security policies; and not every form of desecuritization depends on resistance.

2 Security and surveillance contests

Resistance and counter-resistance

Gary T. Marx

> It may well be doubted whether human ingenuity can construct an enigma of the kind which human ingenuity may not, by proper application resolve.
>
> (Edgar Allen Poe, The Gold Bug)

Introduction

A major way of meeting the goal of security is through the means of surveillance. Security studies and surveillance studies have their own distinctive linguistic and epistemic communities. The former emphasizes the state, while the latter gives additional attention to the behavior of non-state actors such as employers, merchants and private police and of mixed public-private activities such as mega entertainment and sports events. Scholars such as Buzan and Weaver (2003), Burgess (2010) and the political scientists in this volume have broadened the field of security taking it beyond strictly military concerns and raising critical questions, while sociologists give increased attention to the diffusion of practices from business to government and the reverse. Both groups share an interest in studying common individual activities such as travel, consumption, employment and banking as these intersect with the rules and interests of states and international organizations. For several of the authors in this volume and the co-editors from the two fields of a volume on borders (Zureik and Salter 2005) the fields fuse.

Both groups view information technology as a major means of guarding against threats –wherever they may be located and however new and expansive they have become in crossing traditional public-private and national-international borders. This concern is seen in students of security (e.g., the work of Didier Bigo and his colleagues involved in the journals *Culture et Conflicts* and *International Political Sociology*) and of surveillance (e.g., those involved in journals such as *Surveillance and Society* and in a recent issue of the *Canadian Journal of Sociology*, Lyon *et al.*, 2012).

Security and Surveillance illustrates aspects of the fluidity of contemporary society (Bauman and Wood 2012). Thus fluidity is seen with respect to who is threatened and who does the threatening. As Thierry Balzacq notes in the introduction some in the securitization tradition appropriately ask the question Howard Becker posed so well in 1963, "Says who?" In this case security for whom and judged by what standards? Noting how the conventional answer is often tied to inequality and its perpetuation and to culture conflict between nations, there is a humane call for emancipation and resistance. For some analysts in the "who" and for "whom" tradition the world is conveniently divided into the powerful and powerless and insiders and outsiders. But those borders are fluid as well. Persons perform a variety of roles and this changes with the situation and life cycle.

In many ways a tool is just a tool to be used by whoever possesses it. The material or ideological interests of those marketing resources for resistance may transcend the easy language of social stratification, throwing a wrench into the machine of the hegemons. The *same* organization can benefit from providing services for both control and challenges to it – however unpatriotic this may appear to those in the maelstrom. Some businesses peddle an indiscriminate panoply of offensive and defensive means and services (e.g., for drug testing and drug detoxifying, radar detectors and radar guns, bugging and debugging, weapons and armor to protect against it). As they say, business is business, even if some of it is best preceded by the adjective *monkey*.

But the question must also be asked – emancipation for whom, – resistance to what? The thwarting responses this chapter identifies are in a sense equal opportunity tools – available to terrorists, corrupt politicians, identity thieves and malicious hackers, as well as to social movement activists, whistle blowers, muckrakers, consumers and electronically monitored and drug tested employees. The moral meaning of resistance lies in the context not the act –sometimes being heroic and sometimes despicable. This saw cuts in more than one direction.

This chapter deals with resistance but does not restrict its attention only to the disadvantaged struggling against tools seen as unfair. Rather, it begins with a more neutral look at the kinds of tools for resistance available to anyone seeking to avoid the scrutiny and control of others. Here we see another type of fluidity, or at least some shaking up of traditional expectations, as individuals and groups move back and forth between being subjects and agents of surveillance. Within the logic of prevention and categorical suspicion (Marx 1988), everyone is both a potential offender (at least until proven to the contrary) as well as a potential victim. With new technologies and their trail leaving, as well as trail blazing, we see an ironic twist. In some ways it is often the most powerful who are the most tracked given the electronic records they need and droppings they leave (computers, GPS, cell phones, etc.).

Those working within an emancipatory tradition identify the material and hierarchical factors that drive securitization. Consideration of such causes and their correlates is necessary. But it is not enough to ask, "Why?" We also need to ask "why not?" in the sense that, given the factors pushing toward ever greater securitization (whether in breadth, depth, intensity), what factors hold it back or limit it?

Consistent with Bourdieu's (1984) broad conception of a field and as elaborated in Bigo's analysis of the pursuit of global security (2006), we see the merging of security and commercial sectors into national and transnational fields of security and control. These are constantly changing and expanding under the sway of technology, but also acting back upon it.

There is also shifting in how and where the threat lines are drawn depending on current events and the expansion or contraction of resources for collecting, analyzing and acting on information. Beck's (1992) work emphasizing attention to threats posed by environmental risks has been vastly expanded to include many other sources (Ericson and Haggerty 2007). Risk management models shape, but also depend, on their environments. A nice early example of this *fluid threshold effect* was the American Puritans whose identification of the number of witches was related to the amount of resources available to process them (Erikson 1966).

Control systems are rarely as effective and efficient as their advocates claim, and they often have a variety of unintended consequences. Cultural values often conflict and fear of resistance and bad public relations can modulate practices. Most surveillance systems have inherent contradictions, ambiguities, gaps, blind spots and limitations, whether structural or cultural, and if they do not, they are likely to be connected to systems that do. The individual is often more than a passive and compliant reed buffeted about by the imposing winds of more powerful persons and institutions. Humans are wonderfully inventive at finding ways to beat control systems and avoid observation. As Goffman (1961) notes in his study of the under-life of organizations, challenges abound when individuals feel that surveillance and the controls associated with it are wrong. The kinds of behavioral techniques of neutralization this chapter discusses are a major means for mounting such challenges.

The enduring aspects of almost any control setting limit effectiveness. Yet with contemporary information control new limits appear even as new powers appear. The progenitor of many contemporary practices lies in nineteenth-century physically based, centralized, hierarchical organizations and juridically defined national borders. Traditional practices were inspired by a rather mechanical spirit of rationality and with a clear distinction between insiders and outsiders.

Yet many current forms are tied to neither a physical locale, nor face-to-face presence, involve horizontal rather than vertical ties, and share, merge or blur the roles of watcher and watched. As Dupont (2008) observes, the "rock and mortar architecture of the prison" is distinct from the structure of the internet built on wire and bits. The latter, with its open and connecting architecture, can offer a buffer against the control efforts of the more powerful and can also be turned against them. Horizontal networks that are independent of a central source may distribute rather than concentrate power (Lessig 2007). These changes radically break with traditional forms and bring new possibilities for resistance. The pluralism within democratic societies also supports challenges as Blanc (2012) notes in the retrenchment that took place in the United States after the hasty passage of the Patriot Act under the activism of lawyers and librarians.

The advantages of technological and other strategic surveillance developments may be limited and success (if present) short-lived – the same holds for new developments to defeat surveillance. New technologies rarely enter passive environments of total inequality. Instead, they become enmeshed in complex, pre-existing systems (often with weak heels and flies circling the ointment). They are as likely to be altered as to alter. Professional associations, oversight organizations, and political and social movements affect this, as do the new markets that control technologies create for counter-technologies.

Many factors inhibit the full unleashing of surveillance: logistical and economic limits, competing values, the interpretive and contextual nature of human situations, system complexity and interconnectedness and the vulnerability of those engaged in surveillance to be compromised. Particularly in liberal democratic societies, there is space for resistance, irony and surprise.

Accompanying these changes are calls by some to maximize surveillance and control; while others fear that unleashing surveillance technology will destroy what liberty exists in an age of blurry and fluid borders of so many kinds. However, whether the issue is seen as violence between or within states, drugs and money laundering, immigration, disease, or threats to the economy or the environment, both advocates and supporters share a belief in the efficiency and effectiveness of the tools. Partly this reflects the self-interest of product and moral entrepreneurs, but it also reflects a failure to look at the empirical record. Rhetorical claims must be tempered by empirical analysis of actual capabilities and consequences. Just because something positive or negative could happen, does not mean that it must happen. We need to consider factors tending toward or away from predicted outcomes. The response of those to be controlled is a key factor here.

Yet another aspect of fluidity is seen in dynamic, temporal developments wherein resistance by surveillance subjects is in turn met by the counter-responses of agents and this is matched by new responses by subjects in a seemingly endless spiral. This chapter suggests concepts to encompass *surveillance neutralization* and *counter-neutralization.*

This book's title *Contesting Security* implies not only questioning and challenging – but the idea of a contest or a game with competitors. The strategic actions of both watchers and the watched have an emergent quality and can be thought of as moves in a game, although unlike traditional games, the rules may not be equally binding on all players and may not be much fun. The dynamism of reciprocal innovations can keep the game fresh. The fluidity of these activities serves as a way to organize the concerns of this chapter as it offers concepts to encompass the major forms of *neutralization* and *counter-neutralization.*

Developments over time with respect to anti- and pro-surveillance actions require a natural history model. Such an approach involves a series of logically and temporally linked, yet distinct activities called *surveillance strips* that occur within a broad field. These are *creation, adoption, data collection* (including the behavior of subjects as well as of agents), *analysis* and *interpretation, application,* and *fate of the data* (and eventually the tactic) (Marx, forthcoming). Resistance and support can be studied in many empirical and analytical places. When viewed in relation to the stages of surveillance they are most likely at the data collection, analysis and interpretation strips.

Those attentive to societal heterogeneity, complexity, conflicts and ambiguity will not be surprised to observe that the rise of the surveillance society with its emphasis on control through information technology has been accompanied by a set of oppositional practices. In looking across institutional contexts (such as the military, police, employment, markets and families) in North America and Europe, I have identified a common set of neutralization and counter-neutralization efforts in response to surveillance.

Individual resistance as only one type

The spread of the new surveillance has been accompanied by organized political and legal challenges from established civil liberties, consumer and worker organizations as well as by new organizations. The politics of surveillance can even involve one level of government resisting another within a state. For these challenges, the emphasis is on stopping or regulating a broad strategy or a particular tactic within it, not a given application.

Resistance may involve a subject acting alone, or an interest group or social movement acting in cohort. Individual responses may be collective in the sense that many persons respond the same way to the same stimulus; however, they need not be organized by a group or a leader. Yet even if they are not formally organized, such actions may be linked, as when protest movements grow out of or encourage individual resistance and provide education, models, resources and legitimation.

The interplay and various links between individuals, small groups and more organized politics, particularly those that are contentious and rancorous and involve social movements facilitated by the internet is a vital new topic for research. The hydra-headed decentralized features of computing (e.g., the virtual advocacy networks for publicizing surveillance practices and challenging authority (Gibbons and Introna 2009, Earl and Kimport 2011) illustrates an intermediate form between individual and group protest. Individuals can send and receive information without the need for a directing authority. The decentralized organization of computing (Martin *et al.* 2009) illustrates how some resistance to, and support for, surveillance goes beyond the more easily seen subject-agent relationships.

The vast majority of individual forms of resistance are solitary rather than communal. They are distinct from the efforts of advocacy groups to educate the public, create awareness and offer alternative sources of data (whether general or directed at a particular action). The guerrilla theatre presentations of the New York surveillance players, the Big Brother Awards, artists and satirical and critical offerings on the internet including newsgroups documenting surveillance (e.g., the eye witness video project) are illustrative, as are the many French examples offered by Piazza in this volume.

The generality of the neutralization types suggested below cuts across a citizen concerned with protecting personal privacy, a criminal seeking to avoid detection and a control agent protecting his or her information. In spite of the obvious moral differences across motives and groups, there are behavioral similarities and equivalent structures, contingencies and processes in the moves to protect and discover personal and other forms of information.

While a variety of resistance activities fit within a broad anti-surveillance tent, here I emphasize individual instrumental responses in the data collection stage. A number of types of resistance with cross-cutting dimensions can be noted. Here my concern is primarily with 12 types of individual resistance I have inductively identified based on my observation and interviews. These *individual, strategic* tools contrast with the sheer contrariness to authority that Foucault (1977) identifies – that is, "a certain decisive will not to be governed." They also differ from the everyday forms of resistance noted by Scott (1985) such as "foot dragging, dissimulation, false compliance, pilfering, feigned ignorance, slander, arson, sabotage," Foucault's and Scott's forms of symbolic and/or non-instrumental behaviors express indignation and rebellion. Yet the contumacious are not necessarily strategic.

The resistance actions an individual takes to defeat a given application are often covert in order to maximize effectiveness and/or avoid suspicion and sanctioning. Moreover, the goal is to defeat a given application not to abolish it. Direct resistance or avoidance of this kind contrasts with a broad strategic response such as challenging a law or encouraging a boycott.

Neutralization may be direct or indirect. It may seek to effect the data offered (or taken from) the subject, the identity or location of the subject, the conditions under which data collection occurs, or it may directly engage the instruments of data collection and analysis. As to further variations, it may involve neutralization with regard to the subject's body or materials from it or aspects of the surveillance tool itself. And a natural process may lead to the agent's discovery of the neutralization, or it may remain unknown.

Twelve easy moves

Let 'em flutter me. I know how to pass a polygraph.

(W. Casey, Former CIA Head)

The number of *repertories of surveillance neutralization* and *counter-neutralization* is limited, even though the specifics and settings for surveillance vary greatly. This limit reflects the directive power of culture as well as commonalities in the nature and structure of surveillance contexts and resources. But much thwarting space remains.

Lance Armstrong ("I am the most tested person who ever lived") was able to beat the anti-doping system for many years. While his story involves sports, it demonstrates some generic forms of resistance to authority and the fluid nature of securitization and surveillance efforts. These forms are discussed next.

Twelve types of neutralization move are shown in Table 1: (1) discovering, (2) avoiding, (3) piggy-backing, (4) switching, (5) distorting, (6) blocking, (7) masking (identification), (8) breaking, (9) refusing, (10) cooperating, (11) explaining and (12) counter-surveillance. These moves emphasize visible behavior, although

Table 2.1 Twelve neutralization moves

Neutralization technique	Action
Discovering	Find out if surveillance is in operation, and if it is, where, by whom and how
Avoiding	Choose locations, time periods and means not subject to surveillance
Piggy backing	Accompany or be attached to a qualifying object or person
Switching	Transferring an authentic result to someone or thing it does not apply to
Distorting	Altering input such that a technically valid result appears but the inference drawn from it is invalid
Blocking	Eliminating or making data inaccessible
Masking	Blocking but with deception regarding factors such as identity and location
Breaking	Rendering the surveillance device inoperable
Refusing	Ignoring the surveillance and what it is meant to deter
Explaining and contesting	Accounting for an unfavorable result by reframing it in an acceptable way or offering alternative data and the claims of rival experts, making rights and procedural violations claims
Cooperating	Making collusive moves with agents
Counter-surveillance	Reversing roles, so that subjects apply the tactics to agents; taking advantage of the double-edged potential of tools

some inferences are drawn about presumed motives of subjects. Given the space limits these are offered in a summary fashion below (more detail is in Marx, forthcoming).

Each move can be seen as a rib within a broad umbrella of resistance or non-compliance. Thus the refusal move in its extreme form literally involves saying "no," as when the surveillance is overtly rejected or ignored – whether out of principle or strategic calculation that it will fail. Most of the other moves involve a more subtle and partial refusal to fully cooperate, even as cooperation may be feigned. Each move also refers to a distinct empirical element. In most cases, however, they are not mutually exclusive and can be systematically related. Several types may be simultaneously present, as when a person wearing gloves to block fingerprints also masks the true prints by leaving items containing another's fingerprints. The moves may also be temporally and logically linked, as when discovery leads to avoidance.

Neutralizing neutralization and beyond

The observer, suspecting that what he might have treated as an unwitting move actually or possibly an obfuscation or misrepresentation, suspecting that what appears to be ingenious in fact could be shot through and through with a gamesman's manipulation and design, suspecting this, he can attempt to crack, pierce, penetrate, and otherwise get behind the apparent facts in order to uncover the real ones. The observer performs an uncovering move.

(Erving Goffman, Strategic Interaction)

This book's title *Security in Contention* implies challenging it – but it also conveys the idea of a contest or a game with competitors. As noted, the strategic actions of both watchers and the watched can be thought of as moves in a game. The 12 moves noted above provoke counter-responses such as the uncovering moves Goffman identifies in opening quote. Agents serious about their work must eternally wonder if the reality they see is the reality it appears to be. As the countless examples of neutralization suggest, human ingenuity is often richer than the possibilities that can be anticipated and built into the machine. In conflict settings, the flexible and creative hum.an spirit so far has some advantages over "dumb" machines with a limited number of programmed responses (at least the first time around). Yet machines are quick learners, just as some subjects are.

Neutralization is a dynamic adversarial social dance involving strategic moves and counter-moves. It has the quality of an endless chess game mixing old and new moves. Those in the surveillance business respond to neutralization efforts with their own innovations which are then responded to in a re-occurring pattern. Whether for agents or subjects, innovations may offer only temporary solutions.

The cat and the mouse continually learn from each other and reiteratively adjust their behavior in the face of new offensive and defensive means. For example the Department of Defense through its Polygraph Institute offers a 40-hour course to prepare examiners to deter, detect and prevent polygraph countermeasures. The quality of play might improve or become more sophisticated, but this is within a broad moving equilibrium in which advantages from an innovation are not constant, particularly over time. This is one reason why "the war on ..." rhetoric with the idea of final victory which characterizes securitization efforts in fields far from traditional military battlegrounds is so often inapplicable to today's security efforts. A better military analogy lies in escalation and a kind of surveillance arms race captured by "the see-saw principle" of new developments balanced by counter-developments.

Several agent moves mirror those of subjects and equivalent tools may be used. Thus the uncovering moves noted by Goffman are examples of discovery. Cooperative moves with exchanges beneficial to both parties may be initiated by either party. But some distinct forms are also present. These result from the frequent power and other resource differences between agents and subjects as well as their divergent goals.

Some other major counter-neutralization moves are: technological developments, the creation of uncertainty through repetition, randomization and deception, the use of multiple means and the creation of new rules and penalties.

Table 2.2 Four counter-neutralization moves

Technological enhancements
Creation of uncertainty through repetition, randomization and deception
Multiple means
New rules and penalties

This reflects the traditional engineering model of relying on technical innovation. The counter-neutralization technologies (along of course with neutralization technologies) become more powerful, penetrating, broader in reach and "smarter." They also have become softer, in some cases to intentionally by-pass the subject's knowledge and consent (Marx 2006). Most drug tests now immediately take temperature readings – a reading less than 90 degrees is presumed to indicate dilution or substitution. Automated fingerprint access systems also now often have a temperature sensor. A "drugwipe" test claims to "pick-up where standard drug testing leaves off." It identifies drug residue on a desktop or other items. Or, "after the workers have gone home," a vacuum-like device can be used on computer keyboards to "surreptitiously check for illegal drugs."

X-ray machines can produce images of anything between a traveler's clothing and skin, making it harder to hide items. X-rays may be used in traditional ways to look within the body e.g., in a search for swallowed balloons containing drugs. Requiring school uniforms helps identify outsiders. Clothes without pockets and a requirement that shirts be tucked in (so it is harder to hide weapons) are advocated as ways of reducing school violence. Paper, explosives, typewriters and printing presses, and more recently, computer printers and copy machines, may carry unseen identifiers. These can be seen as counter-neutralization means to a subject's implicit avoidance in assuming anonymity.

Screening moves (which might also be called front-end exclusionary moves) seek to deny neutralizers the chance even to try. Bar code and other scanners are programmed to recall cancelled or suspect identities and patterns. Profiling and data bases are an effort to extend historical memories and avoid risks. The bad apples are to be stopped before they get into the barrel, even at a cost of excluding some good apples.

Randomization, repetition and deception

These strategies seek to counter the opportunity structures for neutralization. Such opportunities can be related to the impossibility of continually scrutinizing every. one all of the time and to the strategic advantage that may come from observing predictable agent patterns. Surveillance may appear at unpredictable times, places and forms. The goal is to create uncertainty. The possibility of surprise is intended to deter, or if not, to lead to discovery. Trickery is used to pierce informational borders.

For both agents and subjects, as a customs official said, "when you do it all the time, it's predictable. If you have a predictable regimen, it can be exploited." The random application of surveillance cannot be as easily "gamed." Consider the search of air travelers or those at borders based not on anything suspicious, but on a table of random numbers. Roving inspections on subways that rely on an honor system for ticket purchases and the mobile inspections that appeared within the internal borders of the European Union are other examples.

Subjects may encounter repeated applications of the same means. To maximize deterrence, they may be told that there will be repetition, but not when and where. Or, when the emphasis is on apprehension, nothing is communicated. Consider checking the tickets of skiers at the top of a hill to be sure that they did not send their entry ticket down the hill to be used by someone else. To prevent drinking after a car has been started, the ignition interlock device required of those convicted of drunk driving can be programmed to require periodic tests, beyond that initially required.

Deception, in creating concern that persons and objects are other than they appear to be, is another form of uncertainty. Informers and undercover tactics are the classic deceptive examples of breaking informational borders. Hidden bugs and disguised surveillance cameras in everyday objects such as clocks, smoke detectors, towel dispensers and even Bibles are other examples. Video cameras with flashing red lights invite evasive and blocking efforts. But the visible cameras may be inoperable or not the only cameras.

Multiple means

With the piling on of means a subject who successfully neutralizes one form may be unaware of, or unable to affect another. The use of multiple means may increase .confidence in results and create greater uncertainty and resource costs for challenging subjects. It also offers a backup system should there be a failure and can provide different kinds of data – note video-cam dogs patrolling borders trained to bark at intruders.

The ratcheting up of identity and eligibility verification often follows the discovery of chicanery. To lessen switching and masking through having another's identity tokens or knowledge, several access measures may be required. Biometric measures such as facial recognition, voice and finger prints and retinal scans are ways of excluding those who may otherwise beat the system with unauthorized tokens or knowledge (e.g., of access codes) and fake identity. Comparing an individual's voice, retinal, fingerprint, facial or DNA patterns to those in a data base, along with requiring the possession of passwords and documents offers a much higher degree of certainty, than when just the latter or a single biometric is used. Tying certification directly to the person's body lessens problems such as stolen identification and passwords. Video cameras aimed at computer users offer an additional means of identification (assuming a mask is not worn or the camera blocked), as do typing patterns.

Procedures, rules and penalties

Where it is not possible to defeat neutralization via any of the prior strategies, law and policy may comb.at it by controlling information about tactics, prohibiting and penalizing activities and artifacts, offering rewards or legally compelling cooperation. Required standards for tools and agents may be designed to minimize successful neutralization.

Keeping information about tactics secret through classification systems and non-disclosure agreements is a natural strategic response. There are efforts to restrict and even criminalize communication about some neutralization means. It is difficult to prevent motivated individuals from purchasing radar detectors and jammers, or to stop those under judicial supervision from the removal of an electronic monitoring device. Yet such behavior may be made less likely by applying criminalization moves in which neutralization leads to prison or fines and, as in the case of the anti-radar devices, confiscation. Some states have laws prohibiting the production, distribution, and use of products intended to falsify drug tests.

Some workplaces prohibit employees from encrypting their private email and phone communications. These are equivalent to anti-masking laws and signs requesting bank patrons to remove hats and dark glasses before entering. The U.S. government initially tried to ban forms of encryption that it did not control and encouraged organizations to voluntarily adopt a government provided encryption standard. It failed in this, but legislation was passed increasing penalties if encryption is used in a crime (just as penalties are greater when a weapon is used).

False reporting or failure to answer questions honestly can be grounds for legal sanctioning involving fines, imprisonment and other restrictions and/or denial of a benefit such as employment, security clearance, insurance, credit, welfare or a loan. Cooperative moves may be engendered in the form of a more direct reward (being paid for an interview, frequent "something" awards, guaranteed amnesty or immunity). The coercive power of government may be applied as with the subpoena and testimony before a Grand Jury.

Standards for how a technology is to be manufactured and applied can involve efforts to counter neutralization. The 1994 United States' Communications Assistance for Law Enforcement Act ("CALEA") requires industries and organizations involved in telephone and internet communication to use equipment manufactured so it is readily amenable to the wiretapping of digital telecommunications switches.

The game of course never ends. The resistance of subjects is met by innovations of agents which in turn are met by the new moves by subjects which are met by … Consider examples such as the fact that in response to police use of lasers for traffic enforcement, an anti-laser stealth coating can be painted on headlights which is said to reduce the targeting range for determining speed, giving the driver more time to slow down. Sellers of anti-drug products claim continual updates (e.g., heat strips for powdered urine to pass the temperature test). In response to aerial surveillance, marijuana growers in national parks have turned to strains that are shorter and grow well in shaded areas, making them less vulnerable to discovery.

Varieties of acceptance and resistance

The above concepts for organizing types of resistance and response can permit the systemat.ic analysis of variation for questions such as, "What are the correlates of the various forms of neutralization and counter-neutralization? What are the major interaction processes when neutralization and counter-neutralization are viewed sequentially?"

Yet resistance offers only part of the story. It is one end of a continuum of behavioral responses to surveillance. At the other end is acceptance. A central problem for the field should be exploring factors associated with acceptance or rejection. This effort also in turn needs to take account of the frequent gap between attitudes and behavior. The 12 neutralization tactics above emphasize behavioral rather than attitudinal responses. The varied relations between attitudes and behavior, between internal feelings and what is publicly presented should be eternally problematic for students of interaction and social order. Neutralization responses are more likely to involve a "feigned" conformity and covert resistance, than direct overt resistance. More common than either of the above is acceptance (whether gladly or out of resignation, ignorance or indifference). David Lyon (2007) captures the ubiquity and centrality of compliance:

> we tend to take-for-granted certain kinds of surveillance. … People key in their PINS, use their passes, scan their RFID entry cards, give out their Social Insurance numbers, swipe their loyalty cards, make cell-phone calls, present their passports, surf the internet, take breathalyzer tests, submit to face iris scans and walk openly past CCTV cameras in routine ways. … If people did hesitate, let alone withdraw willing cooperation, everyday social life as we know it today would break down.

Concepts for organizing types of conformity are also needed. Where individuals are aware and have the potential to respond, rarely will anyone be categorically accepting or rejecting.

The variety of surveillance means and contexts, distinctions between attitudes and behavior, overt and covert actions and crossing personal borders by taking from or imposing upon a person can be studied for acceptance or rejection. This complexity makes sweeping generalizations unwelcome. Analyzing distinct means (e.g., video, drug testing, biometric ID, location monitoring, surveys and application forms and web activity) would likely yield stronger associations than the search for general orientations. None-the-less there are likely patterns that can be studied more systematically. Robert Merton's (1957) distinction between attitudinal and behavioral conformity can be useful here. If we differentiate attitudes from behavior and accepting from resisting responses, and ignore

Table 2.3 Attitudinal and behavioral responses

True conformists	Persons who attitudinally and behaviorally accept the surveillance
Intimidated	(or at least lacking resources for neutralization) conformist persons who attitudinally reject, but behaviorally accept, the surveillance
True rebels	Persons who attitudinally reject the surveillance and overtly try to neutralize it
Closet rebel	Persons who attitudinally reject the surveillance and covertly try to neutralize it

ambivalence and fluidity, we have a fuller picture yielding four types of response for any given tool (Table 2.3).

This table refers to subjects of surveillance. But surveillance agents, too, show a variety of attitudinal and behavioral responses – varying from loyal agents who believe in what they do and do it conscientiously, to ritualists who do not believe in what they area doing but need the work, to closet rebels who perform with indifference and even outright cooperation (if hidden) cooperation with subjects. A surveillance agent as true rebel is rare and will likely be out of a job if discovered. A next step is to measure the distribution and correlates of these responses across surveillance types and settings and to seek explanations for the observed patterns.

Group resistance

What are the connections between individual and collective responses? The processes and social and political implications of such individual forms are relatively unstudied. That is also the case for social movements and quasi-movements challenging surveillance. The kind of rich description offered by Piazza in this volume on responses to biometrics in France can be put in an explanatory and comparative framework.

What are the connections between strategic and non-strategic responses? How does the presence of a social movement affect individual response and vice versa? Just how individually inventive are these forms of resistance? They often reflect the social currents Blumer (1957) identifies within the ethos of a broader social movement. When do they serve as a form of consciousness raising and pre-politicization in which individual resistance eventually leads to more organized political challenges? And when do they simply remain individualistic responses that inhibit such organized challenges? Are they alternatives or complementary and, when linked, what sequences are likely?

Data on the prior (and subsequent) political behavior of surveillance resistors and their interaction with social movements and policy changes, can shed light on these issues. The point of view of those involved in the actions needs to be understood and compared to that of the outside observer. What is the impact of individual responses? In what ways are they "political"?

The existence of resistance does not imply it will be successful and some may even be tolerated as a way of denying other realities. The silent and often nonconsensual spread of technological control and personal data collection to so many areas of life means that neutralization is often not an option (or available only at very disproportionate costs). Even where possible, what does choice mean in an increasingly mechanized world? When should one be able to legitimately just say "no"?

The question of how security and related forms of control *are* responded to is of course distinct from how they *should* in a moral sense be responded to. The issue is profound and goes to the core of liberty, freedom and wellbeing in contemporary society.

3   Contesting and resisting security in post-Mao China[1]

Juha A. Vuori

Introduction

The study of China has had an important role in the development of key notions within the field of resistance studies[2] (e.g., Scott 1987, 1990). The possibilities of civil society and state bureaucracies to resist securitization moves of elites in various types of Asian political orders, has also been examined within the securitization studies literature (Curley and Wong 2008). Accordingly, when the contestation of, and resistance to securitization is investigated, the Chinese political order is an appropriate setting to reflect on such possibilities.

It is important to examine the contestation of and resistance to security and securitization in a variety of political orders, as their features matter for the social construction of security, and concomitantly for moves against it: security means different things to different societies, as the core fears of any group or nation are unique and relate to vulnerabilities and historical experiences (Wæver 1989: 301). Indeed, political orders, their grammars of legitimacy, and the means of policing they deploy inform which kinds of grievances motivate resistance, which kinds of (and how) opportunities become present, and which kinds of means for resistance are available or common (see e.g., Shue 1994; Porta 1996). The stakes and costs of resistance can vary greatly from one political system to another, and also from one time to another within the same system.

In this chapter, I focus on post-Mao China from the vantage point of contestation and resistance to securitization moves by authorities. This examination reveals how 'security' works as a reservoir of socio-political capital that can become a site of contest, and can have severe political repercussions. The Communist Party has a set of institutionalized master signifiers of securitization (Vuori 2011b: 225–227), which also inform grammars of protest and the possibilities for 'rightful resistance' (O'Brien 1996).

I begin this examination with a general discussion of contestation and resistance in regard to security, and why it makes sense to make a distinction between contestation and resistance. These general views are then focused on China with a brief examination of how securitization informs the possibilities of protest and social mobilization, and their subsequent suppression. The chapter moves further into the particular as the focus shifts to two instances of securitization and resistance in post-Mao China: the Student Democracy Movement (1989), and the Falungong (1999). Conclusions from these two cases draw the chapter to a close.

Contestation and resistance in regard to security

If securitization (Buzan et al. 1998; Balzacq 2011) is taken as the (authoritative) construction of an issue of security that bears on social and political relations and situations, desecuritization is viewed here as a means of contestation and resistance in regard to such processes (cf. Balzacq et al.'s chapter in this volume). Securitization then, in Searle's (2011: 9) terms, is a 'status function declaration', which brings about deontic powers such as 'rights, duties, obligations, requirements, permissions, authorizations, entitlements, and so on'; to contest and resist security through desecuritization is to question either these deontic powers in total or their applicability to particular situations. Beyond desecuritization, counter-securitization moves can be a form of resistance too, which questions the power of the securitization on the other side of the political struggle. Security can be contested and resisted in a variety of other ways (see Marx's contribution to this volume), but the focus here is placed on desecuritization and counter-securitization moves.

In view of the political processes of securitization and desecuritization, the question of social capital (Bourdieu 1991) and positions of power is of major importance for the approach deployed in this chapter. The notion of contestation is reserved for the kinds of political actors which potentially have the capacity to affect securitization processes as 'top dogs' or actors with sufficient social capital or a position of power in matters of security. Resistance on the other hand is reserved for political positions that do not have such resources, i.e., for 'underdogs' or positions which are usually subjected to security rather than wield it.

It is useful here to make some distinctions between these concepts, and the various ways they have been deployed elsewhere. In terms of the desirability of security, I do not want to present a view on what security should be. Instead, the examination here focuses on what security does in the particular instances under investigation. Yet, in ethical terms, how security is contested and resisted by the political actors in question suggests a preference for an 'escape' from security rather a desire for more security (see McDonald's chapter in this volume). Indeed, rather than viewing security and emancipation as 'two sides of the same coin' (Booth 1991: 319), the two sides of the coin in the instances studied here seem to be closer to security and oppression instead (Neocleous 2008: 4–5).

When security appears here as 'oppression', this already suggests emphasis of certain aspects or understandings of power, which do not close all other aspects or understandings of power off, but merely focus the line of investigation here. Indeed, the way resistance is conceptualized here underlines the view of power as subordination, superordination or even suppression/repression/oppression.[3] In view of theories of hegemony, the effects of power may be taken on voluntarily, i.e., power may not always be explicitly coercive but subordinate positions may be taken up even enthusiastically. From such a viewpoint to power, resistance becomes the kind of actions which dissolve, undermine, question or challenge such subordination – and ultimately, produce non-subordinate relations. Indeed, for Vinthagen and Lilja (2007) resistance is a subaltern response to power; a practice that challenges and may undermine power, irrespective of intentions or political consciousness.

The difference between resistance and contestation is then about the issue of subordination: the way contestation is viewed here means that the positions are not hierarchical but potentially equal. Indeed, even in Leninist parties, like the CCP, there can be political contestation within the party on the horizontal levels of government (Lieberthal 2004). Yet, when such contests are decided, the minority should yield to the majority, and no longer question the adopted line of the party. Securitization, then, can be contested among top dogs, and resisted by underdogs. The added value of this conceptual distinction is that it allows us to identify and examine the variation of political dynamics when security is a site of contest within authorities or between authorities and subordinates.

In accordance with the terminology adopted for this chapter, the focus here is on instances where securitization is contested by 'public actors', or actors with formal authority, and resisted by actors who do not have formal authority. A similar distinction has been made by de Wilde (2008: 596–597), who has made a division between private and public securitizing/desecuritizing actors: private actors aim to pull public attention towards or away from claimed threats, while public actors aim to legitimize security measures or set priorities among issues on the agenda, or to take issues away from it altogether. Consequently, the empirical contests of securitization and desecuritization moves examined here are viewed as though they were moves in an interactive game (Vuori 2011a; 2011b). This kind of approach allows for the omission of questions of sincerity and intentionality, which chimes with Foucault's critique of the modern subject (Mitchell 1990): the moves manifest and can be detected regardless of whether the 'subject' exists within or without them, or whether the subject can 'own' the moves or not. Indeed, it is important to note that both securitization and its contestation can be unintentional, and that both can have unintended consequences. Just as in the general 'security dilemma', securitizing and desecuritizing actors have to deal with the ambiguity of their speech acts and actions.

In regard to such games or contests, securitizing actors and contesters or resisters of securitization can be on various social levels, and the power to securitize or contest securitization may be dispersed even on a single level. Foucault (1979b: 85) puts power into a perspective which consists of (a) a commanding head or ruler, and (b) the obedient subject: 'the formal homogeneity of power in these various instances corresponds to the general form of submission in the one who is constrained by it. […] A legislative power on one side, and an obedient subject on the other.' If Foucault's idea of the individual as a 'relay' of power is followed and power is viewed as productive, then the modern subject of power (or the subject of modern power) has historically been produced, which then also reproduces the fundamental mechanisms of power. The same form of power exists at all levels, including 'state to family, from prince to father, from the tribunal to the small change of everyday punishments from the agencies of social domination to the structures that constitute the subject himself' (Foucault 1979b: 84–85). Both power and resistance, then, produce subject positions, and possibly referent objects of security too.

Although contestation and resistance can be unintentional, like for Scott (1987), who resists, what, and how are important aspects of resistance. All of these aspects are relevant for securitization as well: who is speaking in the name of what or whom when security is spoken has been identified as a key feature of securitization (Wæver et al. 1993). Scott's (1987) major contribution was to point out that resistance can take on many forms, all of which are not in the public sphere, but 'Infra-politics' instead. His famous typology leads to six types of resistance: resistance exists in public as public declared resistance (e.g., open revolts, petitions, demonstrations, land invasions) against material domination, as assertions of worth or desecration of status symbols against status domination, and as counter-ideologies against ideological domination; resistance exists in disguised forms (e.g., low profile, undisclosed, or 'infra-politics') as 'everyday resistance' (e.g., poaching, squatting, desertion, evasion, foot-dragging), or direct resistance by disguised resisters against material domination, as hidden transcripts of anger or disguised discourses of dignity against status domination, and as dissident subcultures (e.g., millennial religion, myths of social banditry, class heroes) against ideological domination. Discourses and practices of security too can be resisted in these kinds of manners.

The plurality of power and resistance must be kept in mind when resistance and suppression are considered: civil society is often understood as being a more authentic site of social organization, and also as being an opposing force to the state i.e., an authentic site of resistance. But civil society can also be a site of conservatism, and civil society can be co-opted by the state, as is frequently the case in East Asia in general, and in China in particular (Callahan 2006: 99, 109); for example, NGOs are more often than not government organized NGOs in China. One should thus not see the relationship between the state and civil society as a binary position, for neither the state nor civil society is monolithic: scholars should not surrender to the 'Westphalean straitjacket' (Buzan and Little 2001; Wilkinson 2007). In the context of East Asia it may actually be more helpful to consider New Social Movements (the emphasis being on the plural) rather than a singular civil society, as based on European assumptions of social organization (Callahan 2006: 117, 122).

While disciplinary power also draws lines, or rather is a practice of limitation and exclusion, it goes beyond the power of the sovereign and manifests itself in a variety of practices (Foucault 1979a, 2007). Just as different geometries or diagrams of power create different positions of dominance, they create different forms of resistance as well. Resistance is never in a position of complete exteriority in relation to power. There is no single locus of 'great refusal', no soul of revolt, source of all rebellions, or pure law of the revolutionary. Just as there is a plurality of techniques of government, there is a plurality of resistances to them. As William A. Callahan (2006: 108) notes: 'The relation between power and resistance is not clean or pure, but sticky.'

Contestation and resistance in Post-Mao China

Political orders as institutionalized diagrams of power have a bearing on forms, contents, and possibilities for resistance. Thereby it is important to get a sense of both the political order and the socio-political context beyond it in order to comprehend real processes of securitization and its contestation. Important here are the prominent fears and vulnerabilities of the order, but also the mechanisms through which both politics and government are engaged.

In regard to how security operates in specific contexts, in order for an issue to be securitized or for it to follow the logic of security, the word 'security' itself does not always have to be used. Certain words or concepts (e.g., terrorism) automatically allude to the logic of danger, vulnerability, and fear and therefore the necessity to combat them does not need to be argued each and every time. The use of such watchwords, or institutionalized securitization as Buzan et al. (1998: 27–29) term the phenomenon, reduces the need for elaborate arguments on the securityness of specific cases. Indeed, the continuous use of watchwords (like 'counter-revolution', 'socialism', or 'terrorism') can be seen as an indicator of a successfully institutionalized securitization. For example, the word 'counter-revolution' was institutionally securitized in Mao's China: by using it as a label, its target was automatically considered a threat to national security; for example, the phrase 'counter-revolutionaries have sneaked into the party' meant 'certain people should be eradicated from the party (and we are justified in doing so).'

The transition from Mao's China to post-Mao China may be viewed as a transition from revolution to the state i.e., from constitutive power to constituted power. Despite being at times mere lip-service or 'autocommunication', official ideology is still crucial for the legitimacy of a post-totalitarian[4] political order, and its control over society. The body of these fundamental principles, universal truths and official norms, involves a small number of core elements that define the order's 'essence' and play a major role in its unification. This core has to be sustained in order to maintain the order's 'essence', i.e. to legitimize the leadership of the authorities, and their proclaimed historical mission (Paltemaa and Vuori 2009). To label social movements, forms of behaviour or even individuals as threats to the core principles of the political order is a very powerful tool to constrain and suppress political opponents, religious practices or dissident movements, since after the successful securitization of an issue, the full brunt of the action can be brought to bear on whichever issue is deemed as a threat.

In a totalitarian system, all issues are politicized. Everything is within the purview of the state, but not all issues are securitized, and not all politics is about survival (Vuori 2008). There are also qualitative differences between how authorities respond to protest and other forms of social mobilization, even in terms of which of these are securitized in a spectacular manner by leading politicians and which are allowed to happen, or are left for everyday policing. Social protests, or mass incidents as they are called in China, number in the tens of thousands in the contemporary PRC (Tanner 2004). Indeed, protest activities are commonplace in the PRC. It seems that the transition from Mao to post-Mao

China has also resulted in a transition from a desire for complete discipline to the deployment of security practices in Foucault's (2007) sense of the term: security 'lets things happen' (Foucault 2007: 45). Indeed, as long as protest activities do not pass certain thresholds of the permitted, they can be allowed to continue. Yet, Chinese security officials keep modulating the limits of freedom and discipline, which produces a panoptic effect of governance. Certain protests can also become the target of securitization of the highest level of government, when the everyday security practices are not deemed to suffice.

Even in post-Mao China, ideology will still set some aspects of the public transcript (Scott 1990) of the 'powerful' as it binds what they can and what, conversely, the powerless sometimes must do and say. The post-totalitarian order aims for harmony and peace, the obedience of its subjects in the system, without overt use of coercion; the post-totalitarian order relies more on 'symbolic violence' (Bourdieu 1977). Thereby, to defy or otherwise exceed the expected conformity and discipline will be regarded as an attack on the system itself i.e., on the core values of the system which define its nature. The forms and limits of the landscape of conformity may change, with top leaders defining the broad strokes and 'security professionals' modulating the limits of the allowed. In this case, citizens do not have to believe in the system, but merely comply with it to a degree that will not jeopardize the 'official truth' which remains rhetorically committed to the original ideology of the totalitarian order. Such 'rituals of complicity' become more important than the ideological zeal that may have driven the initial totalitarian stage. At this stage, the political order will no longer actively control all that it can, but it is sufficient to control what is necessary to perpetuate the system (cf., Foucault 2007). In China's post-Mao era, this has translated as 'maintaining stability and unity', 'upholding the four cardinal principles', and more recently, striving for a 'harmonious society'.

The possibilities and means of resistance, together with the use of identities in the mobilization of protest has been extensively covered in some of the research on protest and social mobilization on the Chinese mainland (see e.g., Perry and Selden 2003; Paltemaa and Vuori 2006). In autocratic settings of domination, resistance may also take forms beyond mass mobilization; discursive or symbolic resistance may be more effective in these circumstances (see e.g., Thornton 2002). For example, Kevin J. O'Brien (1996) has developed the term 'rightful resistance' to describe the nature of typical low-key protest in contemporary China, whereby protesters usually draw on various existing sources of legitimization for their protest, such as the legal code, CCP proclamations, social values and moral codes, that they hope will help to deflect repressive actions taken by the authorities.

As Williams (2007: 69–70) notes, identity narratives are not private constructions but social and relational. Narrative resources available to an actor are historically and socially constructed and contained, and depend on recognition and acquiescence by others. Mere identity imputations or avowals are insufficient as they must also be acknowledged by others as legitimate. As such, the frames through which social movements are presented can have significant effects, and the frame of national security is a powerful one in China. To be labelled a revisionist, a running dog of capitalism, or a counter-revolutionary has had drastic consequences for the bearers of these labels (cf., Koselleck 2004: 155–157). But if social activities are framed according to the set objectives of the authorities, the likelihood of their suppression will diminish. Even criticism against the authorities may be tolerable, if presented through the correct frame. For example, criticism of Chinese authorities through a patriotic or nationalist frame is far more tolerated by state authorities than many other frames of critique. In accordance with O'Brien's (1996) concept of rightful resistance, protesters/activists are usually compelled to frame their identities and goals in accordance with the stated goals of the political order. Even in the initial stages of collective action, the knowledge of past protests and their means of suppression can guide activists in framing their movement's collective identities and objectives in a pre-emptive manner. Thereby, in non-democratic settings, such as the PRC, securitization and desecuritization provide a possible logic to legitimize repression and resistance respectively, while the vocabulary of both of these is drawn from the resonant values, myths, laws and proclamations of the authorities.

The question of social capital (Bourdieu 1991) is also related to identity framing. It would seem that social movements, almost by definition, lack the socio-political capital needed to achieve desecuritization, capital which the authorities have stored in their formal positions. The desecuritization of the movement is nevertheless something that movements must try to effect when confronted with soft repression (denial of their identity frames by the authorities for example) in the form of securitization (imputations of negative identities thereto). Indeed, to charge those who hold critical views with negative labels such as treason, or counter–revolution, does not necessarily aim to question the credibility of the views held, but rather the credibility of those voicing them (Butler 2006: xix). To counter such moves, direct appeals to various audiences through the use of resonant collective and activist identities that carry moral authority and therefore endow their carriers with socio-political capital, such as popular support and approval can be made.

Two instances of resistance to securitization in the post-Mao period

The initial image of non-democratic political orders such as the PRC may appear to suggest that all protest is securitized, and that there cannot be contestation of security issues. Yet, when we take a closer look, it becomes apparent that there are forms and issues of protest, which are considered 'rightful', and which may even be promoted by the central leadership. Indeed, the vast amount of protest in contemporary China illustrates how things can be allowed to happen as long as they do not jeopardize certain core values. Two examples of when protest and social mobilization has been securitized and thereby presented as threats to the core values of the political order are examined here. Counter to the initial image of protest in China, even in these spectacular instances, we can find both contestation of and resistance to the securitization arguments of authorities.

The student democracy movement

The student democracy movement of 1989 was a culmination of the student activism of the 1980s (Han and Hua 1990). The reform period that had begun in 1978 had not shared out its fruits evenly in Chinese society, and students and intellectuals were concerned about their future and the corruption that seemed to be chronic in the CCP. The continuation of economic reforms was under threat from leftist conservatives, while many proponents of the economic reforms also advocated reforming the political system. Student activists were already prepared for political activity, when the sudden death of deposed reformist CCP general secretary Hu Yaobang[5] provided them with a chance to begin protest activities early. The authorities' initial tolerance of the mourning cum protest gave the students a political opportunity to widen their activities, which then spread quickly from the campuses to Tiananmen Square in Beijing and to other cities and provinces (Nathan et al. 2001). The perceived and actual split within the leadership provided the possibility of keeping the momentum of protest going. As the months of protest went on, millions of people from almost all walks of life took part in or supported the protest movement.

In the securitization process of the student democracy movement as eventually a 'counter-revolutionary rebellion', premier Li Peng's[6] conservative faction, and eventually Deng Xiaoping[7] (Nathan et al. 2001: 94–96) too, interpreted the protests as a conspiracy designed by a small group which aimed to reject the Communist Party and the socialist system at the deepest possible level:

> A tiny minority is exploiting the students; they want to confuse the people and throw the country into chaos. This is a well-planned plot whose real aim is to reject the Chinese Communist Party and the socialist system at the most fundamental level.

The whole issue was presented as being one about the core values of the Chinese political order: the Four Cardinal principles, the socialist system, the state and the government, were all presented as being under threat from a 'counter-revolutionary rebellion' and 'bourgeois liberalism'. Integral to this view was that without socialism and the leadership of the party, the People's Republic would certainly fall and China would once again suffer the oppression of foreign powers. Furthermore, Deng linked the 'turmoil' with events that had occurred in Poland (i.e., the rise of Solidarity), and derived a lesson from them: 'concessions lead to chaos.'

The securitization of the student movement evolved as the events unfolded, and the initial functions of the securitization had failed: from the initial moves for legitimacy and control the securitization evolved into a declaration of martial law and eventually the post hoc maintenance of the initial legitimization (Vuori 2008). This shows how actual securitization processes are not always clear-cut, or uncontested. There were several securitizing actors that used securitizing moves with various functions and multiple audiences. Initially, there were securitization moves where the Standing Committee and the party elders were the relevant audience. Here, Li Peng was the most important securitizing actor; party secretary Zhao Ziyang[8] contested Li's line until the end, but failed to garner support within the party and concomitantly failed to convince the students to cease their protest. As the moves to raise the issue onto the agenda succeeded, the issue became central on the agenda and the party elders eventually took charge. While formal decisions, such as the declaration of martial law were signed by Li, the de facto authority emanated from Deng and the other party elders.

Some of the securitization moves were a type of deterrence strategy that aimed to dissuade the activists from any further action through the threat of severe punishments. However, this proved to be an utter failure. The culmination of unprecedented social activism is also evident in the contestedness and resistance that took place both within the party leadership and on the streets. Some PLA forces refused to follow orders and many party members even participated in the demonstrations themselves. Beijing residents resisted the declaration of martial law and the deployment of troops.

The protesters' resistance was encouraged by the parallel contestation of Li's line by Zhao, although he failed to convince either Li's faction, Deng, or the students on the Square. In a public speech to the Asian Development Bank, Zhao (Han and Hua 1990: 132–134) stressed that 'the basic slogans of the student demonstrators are "uphold the Communist Party", "uphold socialism", "uphold the constitution", "uphold the reforms", "advance democracy", and "oppose corruption". [...] They are not opposed to our basic system.' This division among the leadership effectively worked towards the escalation of the conflict, and provided an opportunity to voice grievances. Within the party, Zhao's contestation was even more apparent than in his public statements. For example, Zhao (Nathan et al. 2001: 134–143) noted that 'If the party does not hold up the banner of democracy in our country, someone else will, and we will lose out.' The securitization of the protest was reactive and worked as part of factional politicking.

On the part of the student, from the outset, they resisted the securitization of their activities (Han and Hua 1990: 50):

> What right do you have to label the actions that students rightfully take to show their concern for the welfare of the country and its people 'illegal activities incited and participated in by a small handful of bad people who aim to destroy the stability and unity of our country?'

Security speech became the battleground for the legitimacy of both the authorities and the protest on the streets, as the protesters made desecuritization and even counter-securitization moves: protesters claimed that rather than them, it was nepotism among high-ranking cadres which would throw China into 'great turmoil' (Han and Hua 1990: 60–61). However, the students were also unsuccessful, both in their attempts to deflect the securitization with desecuritization arguments, and in getting their reverse-securitization through.

In his memoirs, Zhao (2009) presents the political developments within the top leadership in a way which illustrates how 'petty politicking' can have major repercussions. Factions within the leadership were jockeying for the greater prize of the future line of reform and, ultimately, the direction of Chinese society. The social foment of the demonstrations would seem to have provided an opportunity to make a move against Zhao and his position. There was even a precedent for such a move that had proved successful: Hu Yaobang had been demoted a few years before, under similar conditions. This time, however, the social situation was dramatically different from that of early 1987. The 'Golem' of securitization was let loose via the party-political tactics that provided a chance for unprecedented autonomous social mobilization. Indeed, while decision-makers may lack broader horizons, their intentions may be inconsequential in regard to the actual politics they produce. In 1989, both the securitization of the student movement and the counter-discourses contesting or resisting it had counterproductive effects, even internationally. June the fourth 1989 is the severest and most enduring contemporary blemish on China's international image. It illustrates the possible costs of securitization on inter-unit affairs: even though the securitization was a domestic affair in terms of the use of force, the 'Golem' may nonetheless wreak international havoc.

The Falungong

The events of 1989 were followed by a patriotic education campaign, and the CCP began to emphasize patriotism overall (Hughes 2006). In the early 1990s, the party supported the practice of qigong,[9] which was viewed as an apolitical activity together with other traditional folk-beliefs, such as fengshui (landscape positioning). The Chinese origin of qigong also meshed well with the calls for patriotism and nationalism. It is no wonder then, that qigong-masters rose to celebrity status during the 'qigong fever' that gripped China at the turn of the decade (Palmer 2007). The popularity of qigong can also be attributed to the reforms of state owned enterprises which left elderly women in particular without solidarity networks and social benefits that the work-unit had provided. A turn to traditional values and social organization became popular in this situation.

During the qigong fever, several new styles of qigong appeared. Li Hongzhi[10] was the master of the qigong-group that claimed to be the largest in China. He introduced a new qigong-system called Falungong or Xiulian Falun Dafa (great method for practising the Wheel of Law) in 1992. Although Li and his followers have denied having any worldly political goals, the banning of Li's works was not taken favourably by its practitioners. Protests were organized against the defamation of the Falungong. With the 'qigong fever' beginning to subside in the official line of the CCP by the mid-1990s, the FLG increased its resistance to the denunciation of Li and his doctrine and FLG activists seemed to become increasingly bolder in their protests. The watershed protest for FLG occurred April 25 1999 when some 10,000 practitioners made a peaceful protest and petitioned for the release of previously imprisoned practitioners in the vicinity of the headquarters of the CCP in Beijing.

It seems that there was no particular need for continued arguments for 'raising the issue onto the agenda' in the process of securitizing the FLG: while Falungong had been investigated by public security officials for several years, it would seem that there were no major moves to securitize it. Thereby, the securitization of the FLG appears to have been a reactive rather than a proactive process, and to have been initiated only after the protest of 25 April 1999. This suggests that it was the 'spectacularity' of the sit-in in the vicinity of the Zhongnanhai compound that garnered the attention of the premier leadership. With this act, the FLG had overstepped the threshold of permitted autonomous social mobilization, and rightful resistance.

In this instance, unlike a decade earlier, it would seem that there was no clear division on the issue among the party leadership. Jiang Zemin (Zong 2002: 62–63)[11] took the lead to transform the issue into one of security: 'If we fail to see its political essence and do not take firm, appropriate, and prompt action to resolve the issue, we will be committing a mistake of historical proportions.' While all Standing Committee members may not have deemed the issue of the FLG to be as dire as it was presented, they do not appear to have contended the label of security. The various sensitive anniversaries that fell due in 1999 might have concomitantly made the issue seem more sensitive than in other situations; had the securitization not occurred a decade after the 1989 process, where the issue of securitizing the student movement had effectively split and paralyzed the party, the issue might well have been contested to a greater degree. As such, there was no repeat of history in 1999: Jiang mobilized the party and its security apparatuses in prompt fashion.

Most of the securitization moves that have become available for study (Zong 2002) seem to have been for control and deterrence, while the politics of the securitization more broadly provided opportunities for positive identity avowals and the reproduction of discipline (人民日报 24.7.1999):

> The generation and spread of Falungong is a political struggle launched by hostile forces both in and outside the country to contend with our party for the masses and for battle positions. [...] We shall consciously resist and fight them, and with concrete action safeguard social and political stability

Moves for control were directed at party members and state bureaucracies, but those for deterrence were directed at FLG practitioners.

The same grammatical structures were used as in 1989, with the omission of the vocabulary of counter-revolution, but the threat was qualitatively different. The FLG was not presented as a danger emanating from within the party. The FLG was not a form of revisionism, nor a movement for restoring capitalism. The FLG was presented as superstition that threatened Marxist science and the health of individual people: Li Hongzhi and his doctrine were a threat to the core values of the political order from outside the party. Not only that, the group and its activities were presented as the tools of foreign anti-China forces.

In terms of contestation of and resistance to the securitization of the FLG, the analysis suggests the latter. While there does not seem to have been much contestation within the party, the targets of securitization resisted. Li and his disciples had used identity frames in their avowals in a manner that can be described as 'pre-emptive desecuritization' already before the anti-FLG campaign began. This was evident even during the 25 April 1999 demonstration where the representatives of the FLG denied any interest in politics; in an initial meeting that dealt with the issue of the FLG, Luo Gan[12] (Zong 2002, 61–62) noted that:

> At the scene of the incident, Falungong believers repeatedly professed that they did not participate in political matters, were not interested in politics, would not hinder government affairs, would not disturb state order, and would not create uncleanliness and confusion.

Similarly, as the suppression of the FLG began, Li (1999) continued to use the types of identity avowals that strived towards defusing the sense of threat and danger that the securitization moves of the party represented: 'I, Li Hongzhi, unconditionally help practitioners improve human morality and keep people healthy, which stabilizes society. [...] Isn't this bringing good fortune to the people in power?' Initially, then, the FLG's activities conformed with 'rightful resistance', but after the soft repression by the authorities began in earnest, Li (2007) was forced to engage in clear-cut desecuritization moves in his identity framings: 'The crux of the matter, it would seem, is that a cultivator's motive is to stop the persecution, and not to "get political" for the sake of gaining human political power'. As this desecuritization failed and the authorities turned to hard repression, Li (2001) launched his counter-securitization moves, identifying the CCP as the tool of evil that threatened the paradise of his disciples, and indeed, by extension, the entire world:

> If the evil has already reached the point where it is unsavable and unkeepable, then various measures at different levels can be used to stop it and eradicate it. Going beyond the limits of forebearance is included in the Fa's principles.

All in all, Li and his followers have used a mixture of desecuritization, reverse-securitization and counter-securitization moves in their resistance to the CCP.

Beyond the FLG having been 'decimated' on the mainland by the anti-FLG campaign, Li's counter-securitization has had major impacts on his doctrine and the practice of FLG. Li's declaration of a period of 'fa-rectification' seems to equal an existential threat for faith itself. In such a securitized situation, FLG practitioners are allowed to go 'beyond forebearance' and 'actively engage the evil' beyond personal cultivation. Such a change in Li's doctrine can be attributed to the anti-FLG campaign, and thus to the interactive nature of securitization processes. In terms of doctrine, it even seems that Li's securitization moves entailed more drastic measures than the CCP's securitization moves, although the practical activities suggest the exact opposite. Indeed, while Li claims to battle 'evil' in other 'dimensions', the CCP has sent FLG practitioners to mental hospitals and labour re-education camps without trial (Seymor 2005).

Conclusions

Security brings with it deontic powers of usually major significance. It is therefore not surprising that securitization moves become sites of contest, or even resistance. It makes sense to make a distinction between the dynamics of contention among political actors who have the possibilities to wield security and its deontic powers, and the dynamics of resistance between positions of such power and those who are subjected to, yet question it.

At the same time, security and its discourses is a vital avenue of investigation for students of social mobilization and its suppression. Although issues of mobilization and suppression are a larger group than issues of security, security is one of the most powerful tools of legitimization, and concomitantly resisting it can bear the greatest costs. The examination of processes of securitization and its contestation also allows the study of both mobilization and its suppression through one framework from both sides of the struggle. To do such investigations means that students of securitization, resistance, and social mobilization should be sensitive to both the features of the political order, where such processes take place, and to the interaction between authorities and social groups. The combination of securitization/desecuritization with frame theory can provide a set of means for taking these factors into account in the study of security and its contestation, also from comparative perspectives.

As the case of the PRC suggests, even in political orders that are non-democratic, we can still find dynamics of securitization, its contestation, as well as resistance to being labelled as a security threat. Like many other political settings, China has its own set of institutionalized master signifiers of security, which may change over time. Yet, the logic of security seems to resist change in the token referents and threats that make up security discourse. Security discourse seems to serve a variety of functions in the PRC. In Mao's China, it was often used to foment social unrest and to legitimize changes in party leadership. In post-Mao China, it has also been used as a means of control and deterrence, both to mobilize bureaucratic systems and to quell autonomous social unrest.

Spectacular instances of securitization seem to be perennial tools in factional party-politicking. At times, this politicking has resulted in the 'Golem' of securitization breaking loose and resulting in negative political results. Here, it seems that if the contestation of securitization becomes public, and thereby feeds into resistance of it, the likelihood of the 'Golem' breaking free increases. Public contestation then can provide opportunities for resistance, and this may produce a feedback loop into the original contest by raising its stakes. Such dynamics means that there is an added value in making a distinction between contestation and resistance in regard to securitization.

Still, political security is powerful as a means to compel bureaucracies to toe the line of the leadership, and it is useful in the production of a bond between the 'people' and the 'party': security provides the party with opportunities to present itself in a positive light as the guardian of all good in Chinese society against those who would do it harm, whether those be revisionists, counter-revolutionaries, foreign powers, or religious fundamentalists. As the referents of security are among the most valued in society, to contest the need of their protection can raise the stakes of political contests. The same applies to resistance dynamics. Prolonged resistance tends to raise the stakes on both sides of the political struggle. This also means that the strategies and logic of contesting security should be studied closely.

Notes

1 This chapter is based on a larger study. More detailed analyses of the cases here can be found in Vuori (2011a; 2011b, 2014).
2 Resistance studies have established a network of scholars working on similar themes. See http://resistancestudies.org/.
3 Repression is understood here as 'any action by another group which raises the contender's cost of collective action' (Tilly 1978: 100). These actions that raise the contender's costs, can further be divided into hard and soft forms. Myra Marx Ferree (2005) argues that states engage in hard repression through use of force, and in soft repression when they try to limit and 'exclude ideas and identities from the public forum' in non-violent ways. Such soft repression is specifically directed against movements' collective identities and ideas that support 'cognitive liberation' or 'oppositional consciousnesses.' In non-democratic systems like China, the use of soft repression (e.g., labelling) is an integral part of hard repression (e.g., sending dissidents to labour camps). Both are used in unison, with soft repression preceding hard repression.
4 For post-totalitarianism, see Havel (1992). For applications to analysis of Chinese politics, see Lai (2006) and Paltemaa and Vuori (2009).
5 Hu Yaobang was deposed from the position of the party secretary in 1987, formally because of his lenient stance towards student protests. He retained his position with the politbureau, and was considered to be a member of the liberal faction.
6 Li Peng was the leading cadre of the conservative faction and promoted a hard line in regard to how the protests should be handled. Li remained as the premier after the protests were suppressed with the use of force.
7 Although Deng Xiaoping did not have formal positions beyond the Military Commission, he was the de facto leader of the party in the 1980s. Deng's approval was necessary to mobilize the Chinese security apparatus in an extraordinary fashion.
8 Zhao Ziyang was the party secretary during the protests. He was a proponent of liberal economic policies, and for example press freedom. He championed a lenient line towards the protests, and was eventually deposed from all positions from the party and placed under house arrest until his death in 2005.
9 Qigong means the cultivation of qi- or cosmic energy, and is a general label for various styles of breathing exercises that often include esoteric beliefs.
10 Li's biographical information is disputed. The party presents Li as a dangerous charlatan who deceives gullible people, and a common soldier and worker before

he engaged in qigong in the late 1980s. The Falungong claims Li is a higher being with supernatural abilities, apparent since childhood when he was taught in ancient practices by monks. Li emigrated to the US in 1995, which affected his teachings (Ownby 2008).

11 Jiang Zemin became the party secretary after Zhao Ziyang was deposed in 1989. In 1999 he was beginning to canonize his political legacy for the forthcoming party congress.

12 Luo Gan was a member of the Central Secretariat which is the top executive and policy-coordination body of the party, and he was placed in charge of the anti-FLG campaign.

4   Rebelling against biometrics in France

Pierre Piazza

Ever since the eighteenth century at least, the French state has been manufacturing identities through an accumulation of knowledge, know-hows, and processes that have enabled the authorities not only to define and establish individual identities with greater certainty, but also to increase their hold over people's actual living experiences through the collection, formatting, and exploitation of growing amounts of personal data whereby operations of categorization, classification, sorting, etc., can be carried out to rearrange the social reality (Denis 2008; Heilmann 1991). Government-issued identification devices – in particular because they tend to establish unheard-of identity codes and involve new obligations for the targeted populations (red tape, registrations, checks and controls, etc.) – thus gradually came to shape personal habits, behaviors, and life experiences to serve the purpose of idiosyncratic government logics.[1]

However, far from having been imposed upon amorphous, passive, powerless individuals subjected to a Leviathan state system or some almighty "Big Brother," these systems and devices came to be institutionalized and have taken shape – exactly which shape they took depended on the historical context – precisely because they have been at stake in a variety of power struggles (About and Denis 2010; Noiriel 2001). Historically, as a matter of fact, attempts at identity allocation have always generated protests, refusals, and avoidance, bypass, or individual adjustment strategies,[2] as well as more institutionalized protests targeting the very logics underpinning the attempts.[3]

The significance of these various manifestations of a hostility and resistance should therefore not be underestimated, as they often have a direct influence on the design of specific government-led identification schemes, as well as on the objectives underlying the implementation of public policies. Substantial examples of this abound in French history. For instance, in September 1921, when Paris Prefect of police Robert Leullier decided to establish, in the Seine department, the very first ID card for French nationals ("Carte d'identité de Français"), which was connected to a central registry storing assorted data on the bearer (name, place and date of birth, a photograph, fingerprints, etc.), he sparked a major protest campaign in the national press against the all-encompassing "embertillonnage" of the population which forced him to revise his objectives – possession of the ID became optional, for instance (Piazza 2004, 2011). More recently, EDVIGE

(Exploitation documentaire et valorisation de l'information générale), a police database established by decree on 27 June 2008, raised such an outcry from so many actors in civil society after the CNIL (the French data protection authority) commented on the project on 16 June, and the protest was so quickly and efficiently relayed by most of the media and political sphere, that the Ministry of Interior ultimately had to alter the content and operating mode what was intended as a support tool for the reorganization of intelligence services (i.e. the creation of the DCRI, the new central domestic intelligence agency) (Piazza 2009).

Over the last few years, most actors in the field of security appear to have been convinced of the virtues of an incontrovertible new technology which seems to dramatically improve reliability in the identification of individuals – namely, biometrics (Ceyhan and Piazza 2010). The idea is to convert personal physical or physiological characteristics (fingerprints, palm prints, the iris, the retina, facial recognition, etc.) into a digital print that will allow for the unmistakable identification of the person. Biometrics are increasingly popular with public, semi-public, and private institutions, which use them to control access to their facilities and monitor people flows, but they are also finding their way into "secure" ID and travel documents (passports, residence permits, visas), and being drawn upon to feed DNA[4] and fingerprint repositories.[5] In France, such initiatives have triggered a resistance movement that has only been growing for the last few years, with a whole galaxy of associations, unions, Internet activist organizations, etc., which are all too eager to unite into collectives and joint committees: "Oblomoff, IRIS (Imaginons un Réseau Solidaire[6])," "Pièce et main d'Œuvre,"[7] Halte aux puces !,[8] Souriez, vous êtes filmés!,[9] Brigades Activiste des clowns,[10] "Coordination contre la biométrie," "Collectif George Orwell,"[11] "Collectif refus ADN,"[12] "Collectif pour la défense des libertés fondamentales," "Big Brother Awards France,[13]" "Mouvement pour l'abolition de la carte d'identité," SM (Syndicat de la magistrature – professional magistrates union),[14] Panoptique,[15] "LDH" (Ligue des Droits de l'Homme – Human Rights League[16]), etc.

The purpose of this chapter is to examine this little-studied movement, with a particular focus on some of the aspects of this movement that have been thus far under-studied, that is, the modalities of resistance (discourses and registers of oppositions) to the biometricization of identities. It then goes on to analyze the main forms of mobilization that three biometric dispositifs have raised: biometric national ID and passports, the introduction of biometric dispositifs in school settings and DNA sampling.

Resistance: why and how?[17]

Though the industrial sector is sometimes reprimanded for promoting high-tech dispositifs for purely commercial reasons, a vast body of the discourse of those who oppose biometric tools targets state's arguments in favor of a stronger reliance on technology for curbing security challenges that are presented as acute: the fight against identity theft, terrorism, irregular migration, etc. In this sense, resistance does not only entail saying "no" to the underlying logic of security practices, but also pointing to its consequences. In fact, rather than being absolute necessities that respond to the demands for security, the calls for biometry are primarily legitimating discourses, which conceal the real dangers raised by the new forms of persons' identification.

Opponents express themselves through a wide number of material and electronic media: graffiti and posters appear on the walls of the city; leaflets and brochures on "best practices" to follow are handed out on the street or during meetings; banners with instructions on new mobilizations at symbolic sites are deployed; contesting websites are set up, etc. They also come in distinctive iconographies of various forms and formats (caricatures, stickers, photographs, numeric images, etc.), which enable the recognition of networks of activists that, though different in their focus, share a basic ethos of contestation.[18] These iconographies have two additional roles. First, they are utilized to raise awareness or impact on public opinion in order to create circumstances that are conducive to mobilization. They are, therefore, "sensitizing dispositifs."[19] Second, it is through these iconographies that actors come together.[20] In this light, they may be seen as instruments of identification and coordination.

Those who oppose biometry often rely on four main types of arguments. First, humor is used in an attempt to discredit biometry or to denounce states' policies of recording the biometric data of individuals. This sometimes takes the form of satirical drawings posted on activists' websites. At other times, activists resort to spectacular public performances and iconography in order to condemn what they call "techno-policing biometric." These are often carried out by special brigades of clowns.[21] For instance, in 2006, after a high school of the twentieth arrondissement of Paris authorized the use of a biometric identification system to access the restaurant, the activists made a cardboard door in the form of a sheep. Above it, they wrote "controlled freedom of origin."[22] Students were invited to pass through this door like sheep.

However, the main vector of the creativity of those who resist biometric identification is the Internet. For instance, movie posters are parodied in a humoristic way in order to decry the government's decision to carry out DNA tests in the field of family reunification. In 2007, the then French Minister of Interior, Brice Hortefeux, was represented as Superman in a movie entitled *Hortefeux and the Mystery of DNA*. Other visual materials are designed from a variety of sources, with the aim of subverting the official message. For instance, the sentence on cigarettes boxes "smoking damages your health seriously" is turned into "data collection damages freedoms seriously." By the same token, activists utilize hoaxes to get their messages across. In 2005, for instance, many carefully designed but fake leaflets were distributed in mailboxes in Grenoble. They were promoting, in a very official tone, a new initiative which they called "Liberties," that is, a new biometric ID. The strategy aimed to deride and discredit the Ministry of Interior's project of developing such biometric ID. They used the same approach in high schools. This time, the fake card was called "Scolaris." It had all the necessary biometric features, and was presented as a government initiative in order to simplify students' life. Here, they turned the arguments promoting biometric technology upside down, emphasizing the elusive virtues of speed, simplicity and ease of use (Bérard, 2008: 47–50).

The second main mechanism used by activists is to draw on history in order to frame their anti-biometric messages (Snow *et al.*, 1986: 464–481; Goffman, 1991; Mathieu, 2012). References are numerous, but Alphonse Bertillon's (*Bertillonnage*) techniques and tools enjoy a prime place in the process (photographs; pair of compasses, caliper, etc.). Bertillon (nineteenth century) was a pioneer in using the body in order to identify individuals as clearly as possible. This is what is known as anthropometric science, that is, the science of measuring the individual and manipulating the body. In particular, opponents to biometric portray it as a kind of "computerized anthropometric." The reference to Bertillon's techniques has a deeper objective, however. Its aim is to incite an emotional reaction by drawing attention to the initial rationale of technologies of identification. In fact, they were primarily geared towards deviant or stigmatized people. Now, however, or so the argument goes, they are targeting indiscriminately the privacy of the whole population. However, the fact that they embody a type of "soft violence" enables them to be misleadingly easily tolerated.

Another historical event that is often cited by the opponents to biometry are the Luddite uprisings in nineteenth-century Britain (Binfield, 2004; Hobsbawm, 2006; Bourdeau, 2006). In the 1810s, the technological transformations brought by the industrial revolution threatened to leave many workers jobless. The workers thus retaliated by destroying the machines in different parts of the country (Leicestershire, Derbyshire, etc.). In this context, visual artifacts represent biometric devices as machines that endanger human existence (microchips, optical scanning, sensors, etc.). They are marked with a cross to show that their use should be stopped (Crettiez, 2006; Mathieu, 2011). On other posters, pictures are accompanied by slogans such as "sabotage is necessary against biometry! And the rest …." The message often indicates that biometric machines are transforming individuals into cyborgs.

Finally, Nazism is the third major historical event that is drawn upon in order to warn of the disastrous consequences that techniques of identification can have in terms of surveillance, control and discrimination, within genocidal contexts. For example, there are drawings illustrating "a generalized centre of surveillance" within which "compulsory biological samples are taken" on all sections of the population. At times, pictures showing forearms tattooed with a bar code are displayed, digital images of an eye (which means surveillance), the swastika and the "SS" symbols are affixed to the French flag. The objective is to show that the current biometric trend is as dangerous as the Nazi regime's practices. It therefore calls for a moral disapproval of equal strength.[23]

The third mobilization dispositif essentially creates an effective link with the public, through the constant distribution of images of babies and children. As a symbol of innocence and purity, babies are often presented as defenseless toys at the disposal of evil forces. For instance, the following shocking images have been used: the body of a dead baby is kept in a jar of formalin permanently scrutinized by pairs of eyes; faces of babies tattooed with bar codes; a young girl is made to say "I do not want to be part of a police record for my entire life, I oppose biometry and I act"; a child intimidated by a human-robot police officer, fully equipped with the latest technological devices, etc. The iconic creativity of activists is here put to one very specific use: making everyone responsible for the lives of children that are no longer protected in a world which is described as absolutely inhuman and utterly brutal.

Here, biometry is primarily presented as a new step in the growing hold of the state on our physical bodies (Dubey, 2008: 263–279). Many images concentrate on the heavy constraints that states put on our bodies through the new technologies of identification: a hand that is trapped in a biometric scanner for instance. Other images are activated in order to express the state's absolute will to control that comes to bear on biometricized bodies, which are thus reduced to mere commodities that can be continuously traced in time and space. For instance, bar codes represented on different parts of the body, are reminiscent of the cruel practices of the "judicial mark" that characterized the sixteenth century (Denis, 2010: 42–4). Opponents also condemn the violation of individuals' privacy through body searches. The visual aspects of these practices are conspicuously telling: cotton buds put in people's mouths in order to take DNA samples. One also finds another graphic register of meaning, which emphasizes the dehumanization of the person. In this light, the person is reduced to what certain features of her/his body can reveal, in particular those characteristics that can be retrieved thanks to computer programs by police forces (e.g., hand shapes, irises, fingerprints, etc.). A related argument is that biometrics comes with a kind of eugenicist ethos, as DNA is stored, compared, and retrieved at will. Biometry is therefore rejected through very rich visual images associated with strong words ("the rape of the intimate self"; "the dispossession of the self," etc.). In many ways, these images and slogans are meant to attack one of the most pervasive negative consequences of these new technologies of identification on individuals' relationships with their bodies: the end of the freedom of control over their own bodies.

Say no to a biometric ID card targeting the entire French population!

The INES project (for "identité électronique sécurisée" – "secure electronic identity") is the offshoot of a study launched in 2001 by the Ministry of the Interior to examine the possibility of a single process for the issue of all IDs, and the creation of a smart card containing biometric data (this project was called "Titre fondateur" – "founding document") (Lacouette-Fougère 2011). The initial idea explored through INES consisted in a paid-for, compulsory smart card featuring the bearer's photograph and fingerprints connected to several networked databases. This was debated online from February 2005, via a semi-governmental outlet called FDI (Internet forum on rights), as requested by the then Minister of the Interior, Dominique de Villepin, with several public meetings being organized in major cities. Based on the conclusions of FDI's final report (published June 17, 2005), which did mention significant resistance to INES, the new Minister of the

Interior, Nicolas Sarkozy, decided on June 20, 2005 to suspend its implementation and postpone the parliamentary debate on the subject.

While INES has been criticized by many actors, what mainly thwarted this biometric ID project was the resolutely activist stance of the "Collectif pour le retrait du projet INES" (Collective for the Withdrawal of the INES Project), which brought together five "community and union organizations working, together or separately, for respect for human rights, individual and civil liberties, democracy and the Rule of Law": the aforementioned LDH, SM, IRIS, as well as the Syndicat des avocats de France (SAF – lawyers' union) and the Association française des juristes démocrates (AFJD – French Association of Democrat Jurists). In an effort to raise awareness of the dangers of INES, this collective launched a website offering lots of information about the Ministry of Interior's high-tech individual identification project, as well as on other government initiatives, both in France and in Europe, aiming to integrate biometric elements into various identity and travel documents.[24] Following a press conference given in May 2005 at LDH headquarters, the collective also petitioned against the project. This petition, called "Inepte, Nocif, Effrayant, Scélérat" (Inept, Noxious, Frightening, Treacherous) obtained more than 8,000 individual and 77 organizational signatures.

The members of this collective, however, did not stop at setting up a website and presenting a petition, but further publicized the reasons for their hostility by directly tackling the authorities. Monique Hérold (a former president of LDH) and Alain Weber (from the Liberty and IT committee of LDH) were heard by the senatorial task force on the new generation of IDs and document forgery,[25] while Michel Tubiana (LDH), Côme Jacqmin (SM), and Meryem Marzouki (IRIS) went and voiced their criticism with the CNIL.[26] Furthermore, in July 2005, the collective sent a letter to Jean-Michel Charpin, the director of INSEE (the national statistics institute) to tell him how dangerous they thought it was to consider drawing upon the national registry used to identify physical persons (RNIPP – Répertoire national d'identification des personnes physiques) in order to certify the personal identification details that would be used to deliver biometric ID cards.[27] This letter was a follow-up on a pamphlet drafted a month earlier by a number of unions – including the INSEE inter-union confederation, and national unions such as CGT, CFDT, CGT-FO, SUD and CFTC – to raise awareness of the potential surveillance that such a procedure could generate, turning INSEE into "a police auxiliary, at the expense of its independence and ethics."

The collective justified its opposition to the INES project by observing that the online debate orchestrated by the FDI was at best a red herring – a democratic lure intended to legitimate biometric identification policies that had, in fact, already been defined by the government. It also stigmatized the weakness of the arguments put forward by the authorities to justify the implementation of ever more constraining biometric identification procedures: cost of identity fraud, requirements of the struggle against terrorism, etc. However, the most stigmatized aspect of the government's action was its attack on liberties. Indeed, recriminations expressed by the collective hinged mainly on the idea of a colonization of the individual's life experience by authorities who, often invoking deliberately fantasized threats (crime, immigration, terror, etc.), develop ever more intrusive modes of intervention to increase "filing," thus tightening the social control network. Besides, this excessive policing (*"flicage,"* as the French familiarly refer to it) of everyday life (which is perceived as deeply upsetting both individual liberties and privacy) is considered as all the more frightening given today's available technology, the specificity of the identifiers that can now be mobilized (and which, more than ever before, tend to freeze everybody's identity) and the increasingly international dimension of biometric identification schemes (Prüm Treaty, VIS and SIS II) (Broeders 2007). While these fears certainly have a lot to do with the establishment of centralized, potentially interconnected biometric mega-databases by the authorities at national and supranational level, they are also – in fact, mostly – induced by another issue: the advent of a logic of traceability and profiling of individuals that may significantly increase the arbitrary prerogatives of control enjoyed by law enforcement authorities, while at the same time radically challenging the very concept of 'anonymous' public space, not to mention certain rights considered as fundamental – such as the right to oblivion or the presumption of innocence. Thus, what is ultimately being condemned here is the implementation of a surveillance society pure and simple; a type of society in which everybody's slightest move is being spied upon and which, because it allows governments to considerably tighten their grip on the population as a whole, makes democracies dangerously akin to the worst totalitarian regimes.[28]

Following the successful mobilization against the INES project, two major actors in the collective (IRIS and the LDH) also endeavored to tackle the biometric passport issue by challenging the legality of the founding decree promulgated by the Ministry of Interior on April 30, 2008[29] and taking the case to the Conseil d'État (appeal of 4 July 4, 2008[30]). Beyond the aforementioned criticism, two other points have been made in what is the highest French administrative jurisdiction: first, the decree and the CNIL's recommendation had not been published simultaneously, and second, the measures it establishes (which include collecting the fingerprints of all passport applicants, and the creation of a central biometric database called TES – "Titres Électroniques Sécurisés"–"Secure electronic documents") conflict with national and supranational legislation on personal data protection. This initiative was not in vain, since following a three-year procedure, the Conseil d'État, on 26 October 2011, partially canceled section 5 of this decree, which allowed for eight fingerprints of passport holders to be stored in TES. The magistrates have considered that storing such a high number of fingerprints in this database seemed inadequate considering the official purpose of the whole scheme, i.e. simply to make the issue of this document more secure. They also stressed that such an initiative was not in line with the recommendations formulated in Council Regulation (EC) No 2252/2004 of December, 13 2004 on standards for security features and biometrics in passports and travel documents, which only provided for storing two fingerprints of the bearer in a database, as well as on the passport's smart chip. The Ministry of Interior was clearly rebuked here in terms of its intention to transform this database, whose initial purpose was to meet the needs of administrative authentication, into a policing tool that could be used for criminal identification purposes. What is more, the Ministry was placed in the extremely awkward situation of having to physically delete almost 38 million fingerprint records that had been illegally collected since the advent of the first biometric passport, on October 31, 2008.

Finally, it should be mentioned that the LDH, the SAV and the SM were among the first to inform the public – via a common December 2011 press release[31] – about the dangers of an "identity protection" bill of law presented to the Senate on July 27, 2010. The bill, which ultimately passed final reading at the Assemblée nationale on March 6, 2012, established a new biometric smart ID which will feature various data on the bearer, including two fingerprints. These data were to be stored in the TES centralized database, which would thus become – in the words of UMP senator François Pillet, who introduced the law – a "database of honest people." While this initiative – supported by UMP members of Parliament and Minister of Interior Claude Guéant – has been mostly noted for the bitter partisan political confrontations it has sparked in legislative houses, the LDH also played a significant whistleblowing role, by actively contributing to alerting the media.[32] Indeed, most of the point made by the LDH found their way into the text submitted to the Conseil Constitutionnel by more than 200 socialist, communist, and ecologist MPs in order to invalidate this bill. As a result, the Conseil did in fact, in a March 22, 2012 decision,[33] expurgate the most controversial data-protection-related items in the bill. Emphasizing the fact that the singular nature and scope of the collected biometric data, as well as the many potential uses of such data for policing purposes (judicial as well as administrative), appear to be not only disproportionate with regards to the official goals that are being offered as a justification (i.e. secure issue of ID and travel documents, and to eradicate document forgery), but also infringe on people's privacy (as defined in article 2 of the 1789 Declaration of the Rights of Man and of the Citizen), this institution repealed article 5, which established a centralized biometric database of the population, as well as article 10, which determined how the personal data stored in this file could be used by national police and gendarmerie forces.

Opposition to biometric controls at school

Biometrics first appeared in French public (i.e. 'state') schools in the early 2000s, and subsequently spread quite widely, the number of schools currently using such technologies to control student access to the school itself and other facilities, such as canteens in particular, being estimated at about 500 (Craipeau et al.2004; Guchet 2010: 161–176). It was mostly the members of the Collective against Biometrics who initially blew the whistle on the dangers of this deployment (which in some cases was carried out without even requesting approval from the CNIL). Indeed, on November 17, 2005, in Gif-sur-Yvette (Essonne, in the Paris-Ile-de-France region), about 20 militants entered a high school to raise awareness about the installation of two biometric access control devices. After improvising a sketch on the theme of "concentration camps and technologies of control," they proceeded to destroy the biometric systems that has been installed on the premises, and finally distributed brochures explaining their action.

Three of them were arrested during this operation. On February 17, 2006, the tribunal correctionnel d'Évry (the local criminal court in Évry) gave these students of philosophy and ethnology the Sorbonne, then aged 22 to 26, a three-month suspended prison sentence, and they also had to pay a €500 fine, plus €9,000 in damages. From the point of view of the collective, this sentence provided an opportunity to bring the issues of biometrics at school to the fore, both among the students' parents community and the Education Nationale staff.[34] It also triggered significant support for their cause: events, meetings, and even benefit concerts have been organized in Paris. Major actors in the struggle against biometric IDs have openly and officially stated their solidarity – the SM and the LDH are two examples, with their press releases of December 15 and 22, 2005, respectively.[35] Similarly, several high-profile "personalities" have resolutely backed these antibiometrics activists in their struggle. An example is the editorial published in *Le Monde* (December 5, 2005) by the philosopher Giorgio Agamben, entitled "No to biometrics":

> The young students who destroyed biometric terminals in the canteen of the Gif-sur-Yvette high school on 17 November have demonstrated much greater concern for individual liberties and democracy than those who had accepted this without a murmur. I hereby state my solidarity with the French students, and publicly declare that I shall refuse to abide by any biometric control whatsoever, even if this means relinquishing my passport and any other ID.

Finally, at the trial in Évry, teachers and child psychiatrists testified in favor of the defendants. In a similar move, this antibiometrics collective has been nominated for the Voltaire Prize for Vigilance, awarded to individuals who "get involved in exemplary fashion to inform the public on the excesses of automated processing and technology as a weapon.") at the 2005 *"Big Brother Awards France"* ceremony sponsored by Privacy International.

Despite their undeniable antisecuritarian dimension, the arguments put forward by the members of this collective are in fact much more typical of an anti-industrial movement inspired by Luddism. Biometric devices are first and foremost seen as "machines" ("cold monsters" is a recurrent set phrase) spreading everywhere, whose propagation must be stopped by "breaking" them, as the advent of the "machine-world" is bringing about a disastrous robotization of social relationships: machines are turning individuals into mere products, allowing "herd-like" discipline as well as the implementation of unacceptable sorting practice.[36] Célia Izoard, one of the defendants, does indeed claim that her struggle against biometrics is in fact part of a "wider attitude towards the sacralization of technology." As a militant, she has for instance translated into French Kirkpatrick Sale's *Rebels Against the Future: The Luddites and Their War on the Industrial Revolution: Lessons for the Computer Age* (Sale 2006), and published, in collaboration with other members of Pièces et main d'Œuvre,[37]

La Tyrannie technologique (Paris, L'Échappée, 2007). In Grenoble, two other groups of activists (Pièces et Main d'Œuvre – literally "Parts and labor" – and Oblomoff)[38] also share this perspective and expose the dangers of powerful technology, the negative effects of nanotechnologies in particular.

In the wake of the destruction perpetrated by the members of the Collective against Biometrics, other protesters took over the cause. For instance, in April 2008, several collectives against registration, CCTV, juvenile custody, etc., launched a national antibiometrics campaign ("Dépassons les bornes"), focusing on the need to actively protest and oppose the rise of biometrics in schools. As mentioned in their mission statement:

> Our basic objective is to generate disturbances in biometrized schools, and ideally to kick biometrics out; and to massively distribute flyers in schools where biometric devices have not yet been deployed, so as to discourage any such project. Practical evidence shows that both can work. We have noticed that it is fairly easy to enter the premises and distribute our flyers in faculty pigeonholes, or even to openly meet head teachers and supply them with posters. You will always find support among teachers or students. In various cities, it is possible to contact students, teacher unions (FEN, FSU, CGT éduc, CNT, SNES, SNUIPP, Sud éduc…) as well as parents' associations (FCPE …) to set up an information meeting. This has proved quite efficient so far, with the advantage that the struggle ends up in the hands of people who are most directly involved.[39]

These protesters mostly focused on the idea that the growing presence of biometrics at school tended to significantly alter the role of the institution. While the "Republican" school is meant to be a place of fulfillment for students, who may be introduced to creativity, critical thinking, and community values, biometric systems impose other, pernicious logics: those of "conditioning," control and punishment. Such is the discourse that has been pushed towards the general public and elected officials by the Collectif pour la défense des libertés (in Rouen)[40] or the Collective Non à l'éducation biométrique in the Hérault department,[41] which prompted a strong mobilization from students' parents in the junior high schools of Clermont-l'Hérault and Poussan (and earned the collective the 2009 Voltaire Prize). Besides, this collective has been actively involved in publicly a reprimanding an initiative from the Gixel (a trade organization defending the interests of the electronic and digital industries in France) which, in a *Livre bleu* (blue paper)presented to the government in July 2004, suggested no less than a strategy aiming to induce students to accept biometrics in their early years.[42]

In this perspective, biometrics also came under fire, albeit at slightly different angle, in terms of the potential damage it may inflict on the public school system: because it makes it possible to process students automatically, and is used as an argument to cut jobs in schools, teaching and maintenance, for instance. Ultimately, such a trend can only, albeit gradually, dehumanize the school system,[43] which ends up being managed exclusively by cold devices that prevent any emotional involvement ("renouncing a world that is being shaped between humans, by humans"[44]), deprive children of their surnames, and can only lead to the automation of constraining, repressive measures.

While some schools have renounced trying to implement biometric controls for their student population – especially because of the significant costs involved by the chosen technology[45] – the mobilization of school biometrics protesters have also brought about significant developments. In March 2006, the president of the Ile-de-France region (Jean-Paul Huchon) has pledged to

> communicate his disapproval of biometric systems to headteachers; not to fund the deployment of such systems either in high schools or vocational schools, and have the *Conseil régional* (the *département*-level elected assembly) hold a discussion among citizens, experts, and the various associations, on what is clearly a social issue.[46]."

In June 2007, elected representatives of the Provence-Alpes-Côte-d'Azur (PACA) region took a more radical step when they simply declared a moratorium on the deployment of biometric systems in high schools.[47] They were followed by the Conseil Général of the Hérault department, which refused to fund such biometric devices in schools.[48] Similarly, after one parents' association went to court to prevent the deployment of a biometric terminal at Lédignan high school (Casteau 2008), the Gard department's assembly decided, in December 2009, against use of hand scanners in their junior high schools. Simultaneously, the many protests and controversies had made the CNIL extra-cautious: not only did the Commission distribute to all secondary-level headteachers a "Liberties and IT guide" as a reminder of "the rules that have to be respected when creating databases or surveillance systems such as the biometric devices installed in school canteens, or CCTV," but it also rejected the deployment of fingerprint- or finger-vein-based scanning biometric control systems in schools, on the grounds that such systems infringed on the principles that had led to the agreement on the use of hand scanners for student identification purposes.[49]

Refusing DNA sampling

Obviously, many of the aforementioned opponents to biometrics[50] also strongly reject DNA sampling, an issue that allows them to stress the potential drift towards eugenics of genetic filing[51] and, more specifically, to develop a critique hinging on breaching the privacy of the body. Indeed, this sampling, generally performed by placing a cotton swab in individuals' mouths, is described as particularly detrimental to the right of intangibility of the human body. This idea is perfectly illustrated in a pamphlet that has been posted on many protest websites, featuring a DNA molecule captioned "My DNA belongs to me" which, as pointed out by Marie Bérard, is reminiscent of "'My body belongs to me', a popular feminist slogan of the 1960s and 1970s.[52]" Sampling is also presented as a capture, a seizure, an appropriation, a violation of the deepest nature, performed on individuals thereby entirely deprived of their individuality: their biological reality alone is taken into account, regardless of what they might think, say, or do, "with utter disregard for whatever social interactions they may experience" (Bérard 2008). Here, there is frequent reference to philosopher Giorgio Agamben's "biopolitical tattoo" concept, particularly the following section from a 2004 *Le Monde* article, a favorite of antibiometrics websites:

> What is at stake here is no less than the new, normal biopolitical relationship between the citizens and the State. This relationship no longer involves the free and active participation of the public sphere, but pertains to the registration and filing of the most private and incommunicable element of subjectivity: I am referring to the biological life of bodies.
>
> (Agamben 2004)

Hostility to DNA filing in France, however, is by no means restricted to such a theoretical denunciation. From about 2000 onwards, a movement started to take shape which advocated a practical mode of opposition: refusing to yield to genetic sampling procedures. This movement grew as a result of various initiatives taken by players from diverse horizons: union leaders recommending voluntary destruction of GM crops[53] or defending the unemployed,[54] prisoners,[55] etc. It then gradually became institutionalized, especially with the creation, in October 2006, of the Collective Refus ADN, which plays an important role via its website (http://refusadn.free.fr)[56] By shedding light on tangible cases of police DNA sampling being refused by certain individuals throughout France, the website does feed a discourse that mainly focuses on depicting a government which is using its more and more systematic genotyping policy as a pressure tool against so-called "deviant" populations: night-time gardeners, underprivileged youths, anti-ad activists, union leaders, etc., ... who are being stripped down to their very genes by the State[57]." Such a policy is perceived as a prelude to all-encompassing DNA filing of the population.[58] However, beyond sharing protest and useful information with anyone refusing DNA sampling (refreshers on legal texts, a short legal guide to custody, etc.), the website of the Refus ADN Collective also acts as a practical mobilization tool – petitioning for the repeal of FNAEG, distributing an activist poster ("Crachez ici c'est pour nos fichiers!" – "Spit in it, that's for our files!"), launching a national campaign to encourage people to demand that their records be deleted from FNAEG ... and most importantly calling for demonstrations outside courthouses where individuals are being sued for refusing to yield to DNA sampling, thereby putting some pressure on the judicial system.

These mobilizations have one major objective: that of making the government's genotyping policy ineffective by bringing about mass refusals. "A 10% refusal rate (2,000 people per month) would be enough to saturate the courts.[59]." As highlighted by Sylvaine Tuncer, the idea, more precisely, is to disrupt a scheme by attacking its faults:

Blocking the police station by provoking an unforeseen situation for which no *ad hoc* procedure exists, increasing the workload of officers by multiplying procedures, provoking an unusual gathering at the courthouse, and finally widening the scope of the individual case to turn the trial itself into a political critique.

(Tuncer 2009: 33)

While this strategy did not quite succeed in freezing the targeted system altogether, it certainly has had nontrivial repercussions. First of all, it did publicize a cause that was eventually widely discussed in the national media[60] and supported by several Green MPs, such as Noël Mamère (MP and Mayor of Bègles (Gironde)) and Marie-Christine Blandin (Senator of the *Nord* département). It seems that it also contributed to increasing individual instances of DNA sampling refusal.[61] Finally, the arguments developed by opponents to DNA filing convinced many a magistrate, who discharged quite a few defendants, often on the grounds that the court considered itself unable to appreciate whether the DNA sampling decision was justified or not, or because FNAEG registration of individuals who were merely "suspected" (and not "convicted") of a crime seemed excessive. In a July 9, 2008 ministerial circular (Crim-PJ n° 08-28. H5) sent to public prosecutors at appeal courts, the Minister of Justice himself stated his concern, admitting that "pursuing a penal policy consisting in systematically sampling anyone involved in a crime or misdemeanor could only fuel criticism of the [FNAEG] database and spark even more cases of sampling refusal, which in turn may prove difficult to bring to court because of an insubstantial legal basis." More recently, indeed, a further step has been taken by Justice when the Senlis criminal court recognized the "serious and relevant" nature of four applications for a priority preliminary ruling on the issue of constitutionality introduced by Xavier Renou[62] as part of his defense in his trial for refusing DNA sampling. However, on 19 June 2012, the Court of Appeal refused to transmit those applications to the Conseil Constitutionnel, which therefore shall not have to rule on whether the police is respecting the Constitution in its uses of the FNAEG.

Concluding remarks

This quick overview of the opponents to biometrics in France enables us to highlight several points of convergence in the modes of resistance that have been mobilized. First of all, the discussion hinges mostly on the attack on liberties, privacy and personal data introduced by ever more intrusive, wide-ranging, and systematic government-led database building practices – although some players do try to frame the issue in terms of more specific topics such as defending the education system, fighting political repression of dissenting social movements, or the threats introduced by the supremacy of technology in our modern societies, etc. We have then seen that the role of the Internet is a particularly decisive one in shaping the refusal front. The web makes it possible to massively and easily disseminate not only information about governmental biometric projects and actions, but also ready-to-use briefings against biometric identification devices. It also creates the possibility of federating, in a very short time, a multitude of players regrouped in national or local "committees" and "collectives." Moreover, the Internet makes it easy to quickly distribute petitions and "public calls to signatures," whose success guarantees significant media coverage and raises awareness on biometrics issues among elected officials, thereby offering better leverage on the authorities' actions. Finally, the courtroom has become an important resource in mobilization strategies. Appeals and lawsuits flourish, with various jurisdictions, challenging the lawfulness of biometric devices, while trials provide the opponents, eager to publicize their cause, with opportunities to turn courtrooms into political arenas.

However, although hidden behind this apparent consistency, there are significant divisions among biometrics protesters. While some opponents (such as the Brigade activiste des clowns, or Big Brother Awards France) rely on humor to stigmatize the dangers of the advent of a surveillance society, others view this niche as particularly counterproductive. Here is what Pièces et main d'Œuvre (2008, 117) wrote:

> For seven years now, in France and about fifteen other countries, Privacy International has been handing out the Big Brother Awards, modeled after the much-plagiarized Hollywood Oscars. Beyond the truly derisive aspects of such a derision-based critique, it has the drawback of trivializing the totalitarian ogre, which is ridiculed as a comedy bogeyman whose constant and multiple grindings become just as many jokes.[63]

These and other activists (Oblomoff members for instance), would rather resort to more radical modes of protest (such as refusing to submit to any government-led census process[64]) and do not hesitate to initiate spectacular actions in order to make their demands the focus of attention and question the authorities, as in February 2006, for instance, when they disrupted an exhibition entitled "Biometrics: the body as identity," at the *Cité des Sciences et de l'Industrie* in La Villette.[65]

Similarly, whereas some activists (Imaginons un Réseau Solidaire, in particular) do not rule out the idea of a dialogue with the CNIL (yet do criticize it) and consider their actions as a means to help improve the enforcement of the 1978 Informatique et liberté Act on freedom and data protection, a more virulent circle refuses to concede to this institution, which to them is nothing but a mere group of experts busy "elaborating a code of ethics for robots, pure and simple[66]," and whose independence and role are totally illusory. Worse still, in their view, the current all-out development of biometric devices in France is proof of the deep collusion that exists between this Commission, the state (characterized by an increasing propensity to filing) and *high-tech* industrials (who fully benefit from the economic opportunities created by the new security markets opened by the liberty-killing, free-market options chosen by politicians). Considering the CNIL more as "an agency for the development of policing control than an agency for the control of policing development,[67]" activists from "Oblomoff," "Pièces et main d'Œuvre," the "Mouvement pour l'abolition de la carte d'identité," or "Halte aux puces!" occupied its premises, on December 14, 2007, symbolically proclaiming the death of this institution with a banner that read: "1978–2007, la CNIL est dissoute" ("1978–2007, the CNIL is now dissolved").

Notes

1 Government-allocated IDs should thus fall under the "official acts of nomination" ("actes officiels de nomination") category, thus constituting what Pierre Bourdieu considered to be one of the most conspicuous instances of the State monopoly on symbolic violence. To Bourdieu, IDs are tools used by governments to force their own outlook onto the people. Their use of such tools "puts an end to argument about the way of naming by assigning an identity […] which, under the appearance of simply saying what is, tends additionally and tacitly to say what ought to be" (Bourdieu 2000: 187).
2 For a precise analysis of several historical instances of "individual refusal," see in particular the special issue of *Politix* about "Impostures," vol. 19, no. 74, April 2006.
3 For several recent examples in the Anglo-Saxon world, see in particular the *Surveillance & Society* (vol. 6, no. 3, 2009) issue on "Surveillance and Resistance."
4 FNAEG (National Automated Genetic Repository). Initially, the June 17, 1998 Act merely intended this database to be used for identifying sex offenders. Then, on November 15, 2001, another piece of legislation regulating daily security extended its scope to the "most serious damages done to people and goods" (atteintes aux personnes et aux biens les plus graves). Subsequently, the domestic security Act passed on March 18, 2003 decreed that virtually any offence might justify DNA sampling and that such sampling should be allowed on individuals who could be reasonably suspected of having committed any offence or crime. As of 2002, 2,635 individuals were registered in this database … a figure that has soared to more than 2 million today.
5 FAED (National Automated Fingerprint Repository). The creation of this database was decreed on April 8, 1987. In 1994, it became the first ever fully operational national biometric repository, accessible to both the police and the gendarmerie. Recorded and stored in it are, in particular, the fingerprints of any individual involved in a criminal procedure. The FAED's growth never stopped: 1.8 million individuals were filed in 200 vs. almost 4 million today.
6 http://www.iris.sgdg.org/. This organization was created in October 1997 and is concerned with "the political and social aspects of the Internet." One of its objectives is to "foster the defense and enlargement of individual rights to the free use of electronic networks." IRIS is a member of several French and international collectives and organizations, including EDRi (European Digital Rights), GILC (Global Internet Liberty Campaign), IFC (Informatique, Fichiers, Citoyenneté) and R@S (Réseau associatif et syndical).
7 http://www.piecesetmaindoeuvre.com/
8 http://www.millebabords.org/spip.php?article8694
9 http://souriez.info/
10 http://brigadeclowns.wordpress.com/
11 http://1984.over-blog.com/
12 http://refusadn.free.fr/spip.php?rubrique8
13 http://bigbrotherawards.eu.org/
14 http://www.syndicat-magistrature.org/-Surveillance-et-fichage-.html
15 http://rebellyon.info/Panoptique-ouverture-d-un-site-d.html
16 http://www.ldh-france.org/-Biometrie-

17 This section was translated from French into English by Thierry Balzacq.
18 Groups can act in different ways: taking out street signs, attacking genetically modified food (GMO) sites, etc. On GMO, for instance, see Tuncer (2009).
19 According to Christophe Traini (2011 : 11), "a sensitizing dispositif is the set of material platforms, a integrated set of objects, the staging that militants activate in order to provoke the affective reactions which prepare those who are persuaded to support or defend the cause".
20 Even though it failed to materialize, the "national campaign against biometric," entitled Let's go beyond borders," that was planned for Spring 2008, has been a moment of important creative activity. Some of the iconographic outputs are still available on the World Wide Web.
21 These brigades follow in the footsteps of the British CIRCA (Clandestine Insurgent Rebel Clown Army).
22 In French, the word "freedom" (*liberté*) allows a specific play on words that sounds like a sheep noise ("Libêêêêêêrté").
23 Following Henry David Thoreau's thought, disobedience and resistance are considered necessary for the opponents of biometry because the democratic state is seen as acting against its own founding principles.
24 http://www.ines.sgdg.org/
25 http://www.senat.fr/rap/r04-439/r04-4399.html#toc362
26 http://www.cnil.fr/fileadmin/documents/approfondir/dossier/CNI-biometrie/CRAUDITIONMARZOUKI.pdf
27 "Souriez, vous êtes filmés!" offers a letter template to be used by concerned citizens to inform the mayor of their place of residence of their own hostility to the INES project: http://souriez.info/breve.php3?id_breve=101.
28 This idea can be found in several online texts written by biometrics protesters, especially in a widely distributed piece entitled "Des moutons et des hommes" ("Of sheep and men"), by sheep farmer Nicolas Bonanni: "Are we willing to sacrifice all our liberties to live in 'security'? In that case, we should stop using the word 'democracy', recognize the totalitarian nature of these standardization tendencies, and ask ourselves what kind of 'security' are we gaining."
29 http://www.legifrance.gouv.fr/affichTexte.do?cidTexte=JORFTEXT000018743961
30 http://www.ines.sgdg.org/spip.php?article110
31 The press release states in particular the following: "This decision, which has no sensible justification, is in line with the overall citizen surveillance policy carried out by right-wing administrations which, in less than a decade, have passed no less than 42 bills on security and doubled the number of policing databases," http://www.syndicat-magistrature.org/Cartes-d-identite-biometriques.html
32 Especially through Jean-Claude Vitran (chair of the LDH Liberties and IT/communications Committee). See his critical stance in many press, online, and TV/radio pieces (*Le Nouvel Observateur*, *L'Est-Républicain*, Rue89, France 2, LCI, Radio Nova, Le Mouv, etc.).
33 http://www.conseil-constitutionnel.fr/decision/2012/2012-652-dc/decision-n-2012-652-dc-du-22-mars-2012.105165.html
34 On the reactions from the FSU, the Essone Sud Éducation teachers unions, and the Fédération des conseils de parents d'élèves, see in particular Christophe Guillemin, "Levée de boucliers contre la biométrie dans les lycées" (20 February 2006) : www.zdnet.fr/actualites/informatique/0,39040745,39313020,00.htm
35 The SM has considered that "the use of such techniques in school canteens epitomizes a general attempt at trivializing them, which is part of a wider securitarian ideology that has been growing over the last few years." Meanwhile, the LDH has specified that "the use – however experimental – and development of this technology in schools is part of the deployment of a permanent individual surveillance and controllin society, which is not compatible with human rights."

60   *Pierre Piazza*

36   After the biometric scanners were destroyed, pamphlets were left at the Gif-sur-Yvette high-school that read: "In our grandparents' time, science and technology were supposed to bring an end to poverty and inequalities. Today, the cherished progress of older generations reeks of prison and death. (…) Let's ask ourselves what biometrics and its chips have to offer. And let us not allow these damn sorting machines, which discriminate between the affluent and those who are sent to seek their food on the pavement, to be started again (…) And let's not hesitate to sabotage more!"

37   Pièces et Main d'œuvre (PMO) was founded in 2002. PMO claims to be heir to "a radical, minority, marginal, sporadic but ultimately enduring critique that has been around for about 39 years in Grenoble, embodied in bands, counter-information newspapers, pirate radios, flyers, pamphlets and posters. "Radical" here means "reaching to the root of all evils." Its members have created a "makeshift" website, featuring texts meant to foster a critical mindset in Grenoble, however they refuse to let their identities be known. To them, Grenoble is a "benchmark city for security" where a number of companies (including Thales, Blue Eye Video, Arjo Wiggins, etc.) create and experiment cutting-edge technological devices serving policing and industrial interests.

38   See in particular the online document entitled "Le futur triomphe mais nous n'avons plus d'avenir" ('The future triumphs but there is no tomorrow)': http://bellaciao.org/fr/IMG/pdf/Plateforme.pdf

39   http://www.planetenonviolence.org/Campagne-Nationale-Anti-Biometrie-Et-L-Intimite-Bordelle-_a1511.html

40   "Collective for the defense of liberties," which includes in particular Alternative libertaire, ATTAC, DAL, les Verts, etc. See "Contre la biométrie à l'école" ("Against biometrics at school"), a letter sent to various officials to raise awareness on this issue: http://www.millebabords.org/spip.php?article7424

41   "No to biometric education," chaired by Gilles Sainati, a magistrate and former vice-president of the Syndicat de la Magistrature.

42   An excerpt: "In our democratic societies, security is quite often considered as infringing on individual liberties. Hence, acceptance must be gained in the population for the proposed technologies, including biometrics, CCTV, and controls. Several methods will have to be developed by both public authorities and industrials to gain acceptance for biometrics. A special effort will have to be made in terms of user-friendliness, which will involve individual recognition and attractive functionalities:
     Kindergarten education: children use this technology to access and leave the premises, to have lunch, and the parents or their representatives shall have to provide proof of identification to fetch the children (…)."

43   Inspired by the British movement Circa (Clandestine Insurgent Rebel Clown Army), the Paris Brigade activiste des clowns (BAC) was founded in April 2005. Demonstrations are always nonviolent and performed in groups, based on humor and derision. On May 26, 2006, in Paris, the brigade visited Maurice Ravel High School (20th district) to denounce this "dehumanization": after singing a "biometric Marseillaise," its members mimicked the deployment of a biometric machine that turned humans into sheep.

44   This is the title of one of the chapters of *L'argumentaire à destination de toutes les personnes désireuses de s'opposer aux applications biométriques* ("Arguments to be used when willing to protest biometric applications"), which Samizdat, Indymedia, or Souriez, vous êtes filmés! have posted on their websites in the wake of the destruction of the Gif-sur-Yvette high school biometric scanners.

45   For instance at the Joliot-Curie high school, in Carqueiranne, which in 2002 had been the first to implement a biometric canteen management system: see Sylvain Mouhot, "Biométrie : pourquoi le collège Carqueiranne renonce," *Var Matin*, May 13, 2009.

46   Quoted in the article "Au collège de Lédignan, on dépasse les bornes tous les midis au réfectoire," *Numero Lambda*, June, 8 2010: http://numerolambda.wordpress.com/2010/06/08/college-ledignan-depasse-les-bornes/

47 See the document written by the president of the PACA region (Michel Vauzelle), June 21, 2007 http://www.archivehost.com/files/1056991/9ab27044b9c5af4deadb86 2e9c661cd246fb4b22/moratoire_paca_biometrie.pdf

48 See Christophe Casteau, "Le département lâche l'affaire," *Hérault du jour*, September, 5 2008.

49 For, as indicated by the CNIL: "This is moderately-identifying biometry: out of a large population, several individuals may present the same hand print. Therefore, while this technology makes it possible to identify people in a 100-strong student body, it would not be possible to identify the same person with any degree of certainty at the scale of a country; this is time-dependent biometry: hands grow, children's hands in particular. Even with adults, hand geometry may evolve (illness, pregnancy, weight gain or loss, etc.)."

50 On May 13, 2009, Oblomoff for instance held a public debate on "Genetics and liberties" during the "Festival des résistances et alternatives à Paris."

51 Opponents to biometrics consider that such eugenics drifts should still be taken very seriously, given certain statements from eminent politicians who consider that the "innate" takes precedence over the "acquired" (Nicolas Sarkozy for instance is quoted in *Philosophie Magazine*, no 8, April 2007 as saying: "As far as I am concerned, I would tend to think that people are born pedophiles; and as a matter of fact, our inability to cure this pathology is problematic indeed.").

52 Marie Bérard, « Le(s) mouvement(s) antibiométrie: mobilisation et modes d'action, » Master 1 dissertation in Political Science, Université Paris 1 Panthéon Sorbonne, 2008, p. 25.

53 For instance Benjamin Deceuninck, a farmer-unionist from *Travailleurs de la Terre et de l'Environnement* (STTE) in the Cévennes massif.

54 For instance Charles Hoareau, in charge of the Chômeurs-CGT committee in Marseilles.

55 In October 2003, about 20 inmates refused to be subjected to government-led DNA sampling in four prisons: Bordeaux-Gradignan (Gironde), Loos-lès-Lille (Nord), Muret (Haute-Garonne) and Neuvic (Dordogne). On Corsican political prisoners, see Jean-Guy Talamoni's contribution, "L'ADN d'Antigone: regards sur la 'jurisprudence Corse' relative aux prélèvements génétiques," at the "Libertés individuelles sous tension: vers une société de surveillance ?" colloquium, Corte University, October 14, 2011.

56 Benjamin Deceuninck is the creator of this collective which, through its website, aims to "build a network" of individuals who refuse DNA sampling "in order to resist, everywhere and together, genetics filing."

57 From a pamphlet entitled "Fichage ADN. La traçabilité comme outil de gestion politique," and distributed by Collectif refus ADN. This idea was picked up and developed in many online texts written by opponents to DNA filing, for instance the article entitled "Refuser le fichage ADN: pourquoi? Comment ?" (signed JSF and posted online on June 3, 2007 at newsoftomorrow.org) which reads: "While capitalism is imposing the domination of profits everywhere and produces the social and environmental disasters everybody knows about, the State is becoming ever more coercive, intrusive and ubiquitous. In such a context, it is no surprise that DNA filing is now targeting political activists: GM crops volunteer reapers who reject the dominance of multinationals on the rural world; anti-advertisement activists who reject the ongoing capitalistic bust advertising and the colonization of our fantasies; unionists who demonstrate against the destruction of labor laws or outsourcing; anti-CPE demonstrators who protested an unfair piece of legislation. It is no surprise either, however, that genetic filing does not apply to financial crime, 'white-collar' crime, misuse of company or public assets and other financial misappropriations. By penalizing political protest actions, DNA filing contributes to disseminating some rampant fear. Fear of opposing the law, fear of disobeying, of revolting, fear of fighting an unfair social order."

58   A symptomatic example of this is the case of two juvenile shoplifters, aged 8 and 11, whose DNA the gendarmerie wanted to sample after they had stolen cheap toys in a supermarket in northern France, in May 2007 (see "Des voleurs de joujoux évitent de peu le fichage ADN," *Libération*, 8 May 2007). Quite revealing also is the discourse of some politicians, such as MP Jean-Christophe Lagarde, who in January 2003 had told the Assemblée nationale that his political group (UDF, center) had considered presenting an amendment broadening the scope of the FNAEG to include the entire population.

59   From a leaflet entitled "Compilation d'informations et de soutien contre le fichage ADN" and distributed by Refus ADN.

60   Examples include: "La tentation du fichage génétique de masse" (*Le Monde*, September 25, 2006) ; "Les rebelles de l'ADN" (*Nouvel Observateur*, April 26, 2007) ; "Prélèvement de salive: le front du refus s'organise" (*Figaro*, May 16, 2007).

61   Despite the lack of accurate data on this phenomenon since 2006, the many trials for refusing DNA sampling reported both at http://refusadn.free.fr and in the press seem to point towards an increase in the figures given by the Ministry of Justice for 2003–2005: 63 individuals sentenced in 2003, 212 in 2004, and 353 in 2005.

62   Founder of the Collective "Les désobéissants" (http://www.desobeir.net/), who had refused to be subjected to DNA sampling after having 'decorated' (i.e. sprayed) Hubert Védrine (former General secretary of the Elysée Palace under François Mitterrand) with red food coloring to denounce the role played by France in the genocide in Rwanda.

63   Pièces et main d'Œuvre, *Terreur et obsession. Enquête sur la police des populations à l'ère technologique*, Paris, L'Échappée, 2008, p. 117.

64   http://www.piecesetmaindoeuvre.com/IMG/pdf/contre_le_recensement.pdf

65   The exhibition was decried as "one of the visible sides of the vested interests that link industrial groups to public authorities," in view of the fact that it was funded by Sagem morpho and was receiving technical support from the CNIL.

66   *Dissolution de la CNIL. Le temps des marchands de sable est passé*, co-authored and distributed by Oblomoff, Pièces et main d'Œuvre, Mouvement pour l'abolition de la carte d'identité, Haltes aux puces!, etc.

67   November 2007 pamphlet by the Mouvement pour l'abolition de la carte d'identité entitled "Pour l'abolition de la carte d'identité."

5 Poking holes and spreading cracks in the wall

Resistance to national security policies under Bush

Florent Blanc

Introduction

'America is at war'. This declaration is at the core, at the very heart of American political discourse on national security policy from the day the planes hit, on 11 September. It became the central legitimating argument after 14 September and the months to follow. This sentence will not be discussed, it will barely (have to) be argued during the post-attack period. More than ten years later, it is only weakly questioned, with the exception of scholars and jurists maybe.

The idea of being at war against terrorism, as contested as it has been, remains yet to be interrogated and debated by elected officials or within political circles, even with the change in presidency that took place in 2008 and its initial intentions. This formulation calls upon a particular vision of the world and conditions the one who accepts it to not question the measures that derive from it. 'America at war' is officially sanctioned in the political discourses calling for and announcing the adoption of the Authorization for Use of Military Force (AUMF)[1] on 14 September, before being printed on the front page of countless newspapers across the country.

America was at war through the adoption of a single and simply worded legislative measure, no longer than a single page, allowing the Executive

> to use all necessary and appropriate force against those nations, organizations, or persons he determines planned, authorized, committed, or aided the terrorist attacks that occurred on September 11, 2001, or harboured such organizations or persons, in order to prevent any future acts of international terrorism against the United States by such nations, organizations or persons'.[2]

Since then, many have reflected on whether or not this piece of legislation was to be considered a formal declaration of war in the sense intended by the War Powers Resolution of 1973.[3] More have bent thought about the legality of a declaration of war against an enemy that is not a state.

But the point to be made lies somewhere else. The interest is not simply in the legality of the measure itself but in the use of the AUMF, a measure of exception in itself, to provide legitimacy to a complete arsenal or repertoire of exceptional powers. Placed at the core of the discourse on national security, the AUMF enables the Executive to make decisions on its own as to the use of the Armed forces to fight terrorism. As such, the AUMF is invoked as a legitimating argument in different key decisions regarding national security after 9/11: the decision to send troops in Iraq, the National Security Agency unwarranted wiretap scandal or the Executive Order that sent Navy Seals commando to eliminate Bin Laden.[4] Founding pillar of the efforts deployed by the Bush administration to legitimize a seizure of power in the name of national security, the AUMF is the first matriochka doll, the justification for the measures of exception to follow.[5] It is the centre of the layers of exception that will have to be peeled off by those who claim that security never justified the deprivation of rights and democratic controls.

Despite the attempts of the Congressional commissions in charge of examining the legality of the security measures proposed, in the autumn of 2001, the Bush administration's discourses provided ground for a wide acceptance of the legitimacy to resort to exceptional powers to defend the nation, the state, the way of life, against the threat posed by terrorist groups. A few short weeks after the AUMF was voted with minimal, although crucial, modifications from the proposed text, Congress adopted the Patriot Act that profoundly expanded the scope of the Executive's powers regarding national security at home. In the following weeks, while the legitimating discourses were still alive and powerfully implanted in the political atmosphere, the Office of Legal Counsel (OLC), which advises the White House on the legality of proposed measures,[6] began drafting memoranda regarding the creation of an alternative legality enabling the Bush administration to deprive the individuals captured in the course of the war on terror of any legal protection and remove the camp(s) where they were to be detained from the map of the legal realm.[7]

To protect these measures from critical examination and to forbid any discussion of their merits, a blanket of arguments and practices aiming at deterring political opposition and dissent emerges in the autumn of 2001. It is insidious, of course, but contributes to spreading around the idea that opposing the government will send FBI agents to one's door, get one fired from his/her job for not being sufficiently patriotic[8] or simply alienate voters[9] and clients alike.[10] From the autumn of 2001 onwards, opposing the government's course of action regarding national security is depicted as failing to protect the American people and helping out the terrorists through a short syllogism, denounced by George W. Bush and his administration.[11] This simple argument will be used to fend off political opponents in Congress and reduce them to near-silence, but also attorneys who decide to take on the cases of Guantanamo detainees, of any organization and country challenging the national security policies and tactics abroad.

In the autumn of 2001, political opponents, citizens and civic-minded organizations were faced with the construction of a tightly-knitted wall of political arguments protecting the elaboration of an alternative legality regarding the treatment of prisoners as well as a complete overhaul of the guarantees on civil liberties. Despite what securitization theories and works on desecuritization have said before, what was at stake in the autumn of 2001 was not a strategy aiming at depoliticizing the issue of national security but rather the methodical construction of a series of legitimizing building blocks that enable the Executive to seize power and lower the possibility of checks and balances. The issue of national security against the threat of terrorism is still very much political, as the subject of choices made within certain circles where options are weighed and argued, but it was no longer the object of publicized debates.

In the light of this assessment, it seemed both relevant and useful to analyse the mechanisms and counter-strategies deployed by various actors opposing the Bush administration's policies in a context of national security crisis. For lack, at this point of a more suitable word, the term 'opposition' will be used to depict the action of constantly questioning the Administration's choices and policies and, as we will show, force it to re-integrate the fora of debate to expose its legitimating arguments.

Choosing to take some distance from the more theoretical contributions on the subject, we offer a sociological reading of the post-9/11 period in order to illustrate the resistance mechanisms at play. Rather than discussing the literature on exception and securitization, we chose to focus more closely on the notion of resistance through the mobilization of historical and sociological approaches that enable the understanding the origins of the values and *habitus* of political opponents in a time of political crisis.

If we know, since the discussions of Buzan and Waever's critical work (Buzan and Waever, 1996), that took place within the field, that securitization does not result from a mere *speech act*, we have to postulate that resistance to a securitizing move has to be a long and durable effort to deconstruct the discourses about the crisis of security. Resistance, as such, can only be perceived as a strategic effort to circumvent and eventually limit the possibilities for the groups in power to claim a legitimate exception to the rule of law. Resistance, it is our argument, in this case, is the act of reframing, once again, the practice of power through the imposition of the rule of law.

Through the analysis of the discourses and practices of resistance, this chapter shows how the legal tactics employed by opponents can be seen as a vector enabling them to penetrate the field of security professionals (Bigo, summer 2005) and thereby interacting directly with the field of power.

This contribution focuses on two national security policies – that is the US Patriot Act of 2001 and the indefinite detention policies and interrogation tactics used at Guantanamo. It will analyse the producers of resistance discourses as well as sources of legal arguments challenging the Administration's legal arsenal. We chose to concentrate on two groups, distinguished by their goals, functions, and the sociology of their members as well as their modes of relationship to the centres of power. The American Library Association, as the epicentre for the mobilization of American library patrons around the protection of intellectual freedom, and the coalition of lawyers organized by the Center for Constitutional Rights, both played the role of resistance networks' cores whose repertoires of contention will be analysed here.

Resisting like a lighthouse in the fog: revealing the hidden transcript of security

Without giving in to the most basic Manichaeism, one is bound to realize that, adopting a bourdieusian field-based analysis, the stakes of discursive opposition revolve around the imposition of a given argument or vision that, in turn, gives ground and legitimizes a claim of legitimacy for certain political options and subsequent measures. Once a (temporary) domination is established within a specific field it begins a continuous effort to maintain the truth claim and therefore preserve the legitimating hold on the definition of the threat and the ways to respond to it.

The metaphor contained within the subtitle above enables us to introduce the idea that resistance, in this particular context, results from the capacity of a certain set of actors who, given their professional socialization, managed to see through the fog. This mist, created by the White House's legal counsels played on a rhetoric of national unity that tends to hide the government's intentions, actions and full policies to prevent opponents from seeing the full picture but also painting them as endangering the security of their fellow citizens. It is easier, in the confines of a deep fog to create an alternative legality protected from the democratic requirement for transparency.

Adopting a logic borrowed from James C. Scott's vision of domination and power relationships (Scott, 1990), we perceive the post-September 11 context as a battleground were the tenants of power imposed a *public transcript* of national security, composed of the official discourses on the necessity of favouring security over liberty, us over 'them', and claiming the need for the temporary suspension of the rule of law to combat terrorist groups. But, parallel to this *official transcript*, a *hidden* one is written by dominated groups, or, in this context, the groups, individuals and organizations whose claims cannot be heard or are rejected.

In the days following the attacks – collective memory has forgotten – voices could be heard calling the Administration for restraint and carefulness. Reminding readers of excessive security reactions from the past, most often the attitudes towards German-Americans and Americans of Japanese ancestry, these voices, not unlike the Paris train conductor quoted by Bourdieu,[12] encouraged citizens and decision-makers to weigh the options and continue to think as a society despite the fear and the emotions. The voices heard then belonged to politicians, lawyers, members of civil liberties defence groups and librarians. Their sociology drew the profile of a certain configuration of social capitals that gave weight to their arguments. Rather than attempting to catalogue 'those who spoke', we found it more pertinent to focus our attention on the two main groups mentioned before: the American Library Association (ALA) and the coalition of attorneys and legal experts gathered by the Center for Constitutional Rights (CCR).

While the Administration and its proxies, as utterers of the dominant discourse about security, wrote the *public transcript*, this contribution is attached to the description of the mechanisms that enabled these groups to compose a *hidden transcript*. In a Scottian view, the *hidden transcript* as a discourse about the reality drawn from the perceptions and experiences of those whose capitals, in the post-2001 context, cannot penetrate the social field from where the dominant discourse emerges. Despite their expertise or the cause they defend, their speech is contested by those who compete for the possibility of writing the official discourse about the threat and its solutions. This explains why it is through the use of techniques and strategies that will create the occasion to confront their visions in a public forum that the actors of a resistance discourse patiently challenged the boundaries guarding the field of security professionals. This is exactly where librarians and attorneys focused their efforts to poke holes in the legitimating wall and spread cracks through the construction of an alternative legal reality.

Conversin' with the elders:[13] resistance is learnt

To fully grasp the particular sociology of the actors mobilized against the Administration's national security plans in the autumn of 2001, and understand how they saw through the fog the denials of liberties that were to come, it is necessary to suspend, for a moment, our examination, and devote our attention to the history of specific historical resistance movements in America.[14]

While Giorgio Agamben mentions, through a reference borrowed from Carl Friedrich, the idea that 'only the determination of the people' can guarantee that emergency powers will be used solely for the sake of protecting the Constitution (Agamben, 2005, 8), the real issue consists in figuring out what shape 'the people' take. Since most observers noted the inexistence of a popular movement opposing the Bush administration's national security policy, one needs to ponder about the process through which the practice of resisting the Administration, in this particular context, was left to lawyers and professionals, acting in the name of the defence of freedom and civil liberties.

Safe from retracing the comprehensive history of social relations in the United States, the focalization on episodes of national security crisis, can help uncover when episodes of specific learning and repertoire transmission have taken place.[15] This process answers to the necessity to avoid the repression unleashed by the government and its proxies while learning to speak a common language in order to enter a debate of ideas. The historical evolution, in the US, consisted in a continued trend, since the end of the Second World War that saw social movement organizations strip off their radical stripes and adopt a more balanced and controlled approach to social claims. By rejecting radicalism, social movement organizations, progressively became professionals and experts in their field and as such entered the circles close to power through their participation in the congressional auditions and expert contributions.

The works of sociologists such as Michael Rogin (Rogin, 1967, 1988), Gary T. Marx (Marx, 1988, Gilham and Marx, 2000) or Clark McPhail (McPhail *et al.*, 1998) served as the basis for retracing the history of the relationship between contesters and majority groups as well as understanding the evolution and transformation of the techniques they mobilized. The history of social struggles and behind it the struggle to maintain the structure of political power cannot be separated from the history of social control measures and surveillance techniques. From the dark days of the 1920s Red Squads to the surveillance of Iraq war opponents since 2002 (Donner, 1990), national security measures have been challenged in courts, thus creating an entire body of legal cases compiling the lessons learnt. As such, the American jurisprudence regarding the scope of the First Amendment was created through a series of decisions involving the policing of dissenters,[16] during the 1950s and 1960s. Then, a corpus of Supreme Court decisions, gathered in a doctrine, denounced, under a judicial format, the actions of the government intended to deter citizens and groups to exercise their rights to political opinion (Chertok and Marcus, 1970, 71–88). Closer to us in time, the *Handschu* decision of 1983[17] as well as the news of the reformation of police units in charge of compiling files about citizens and groups protesting against the Administration's security policies[18] came to remind Americans of the repressive tactics used in the past. If these practices had been curtailed by the Levi Guidelines of 1976 (Berman, 2011), the attacks of September 11 had reopened a window of opportunity to unleash some of the most outrageous police tactics. These techniques that aimed at deterring the expression of minority groups' claims challenging governmental policies laid the foundations for quick learning. The evolution of the repertoires resulted from a pressure to express a dissenting opinion despite the knowledge of assured repression and the necessity to finance the social movement organizations necessary to coordinate collective action tactics. Under this dual influence, most social movement organizations chose, during the 1960s to hire professionals (McCarthy and Zald, 1977).

McCarthy and Zald were the first to identify this trend. In their 1977 paper, the pair explained how hiring a few well-qualified professionals served the goals of the movement better than an army of volunteers whose time was limited by other activities. Professionalization enabled social movement organizations to adapt their positions and discourse and learn to speak the language of foundations and trusts capable of financing reformist but non-radical movements.

But professionalization did something else: recruiting managers, and specialists meant that, given the proper resources, social movements were able to attract personnel speaking the same language and function according to the same social codes as the ones populating the corridors of K street's and government's offices. Bonnie Honig explains that given the degree of technicality ingrained in political decisions, the actors challenging these policies have to be from the same cloth as the ones writing them (Honig, 2005). The technicality Bonnie Honig speaks about is a certain set of skills (government practice and constitutional law), social codes (networking skills, education) that condition how a discourse is heard, perceived and accepted among decision-making circles.

This idea of technicality and specialized agents means that little by little, social movement organizations aiming at reforming policy began recruiting professionals from the very field where decisions are made. Given our topic at heart here, it explains why civil liberties organizations hire lobbyists or key personnel directly from government agencies involved in law making or security. As such, the characteristics of the topic or domain contested impose that we analyse the personnel that are mobilized to conceive the opposing arguments, namely hear the campaign and legal claims to dismantle the matriochka-like legitimating construction around the Patriot Act and the policies and practices of indefinite detention and interrogation.

Librarians in times of crisis: the social construction of a duty to protect intellectual freedom

The mobilization of professional bodies, such as the American Library Association, is an answer to the evolution of the repertoires of contention (Tarrow and Tilly, 2006) understood within the specific context of national security crises throughout modern history. The positions it adopted, but also the social evolution of its members and leaders, have enabled the organization to grow and learn how to act when others did not have the tools and memory of resistance practices to see through the discursive clouds used by government agencies to mask the true goals of national security policies.

A long story

In the US, librarians' interests are defended by a professional organization – the American Library Association – founded in 1876. Unlike others, the history of the organization has accelerated during national security crises. Each of them, since its creation, compelled the organization as a social body but also its leaders to react to a crisis and adopt a position which in turn led the members to reflect on the role of the ALA in American society and on the position to adopt vis-à-vis the government. Progressively, throughout these steps, the organization learnt about itself and developed a perception about the position to adopt in times of crisis based on the construction of core values and ethics.

Conceived originally as a way to federate the efforts of private citizens opening their own libraries to a chosen public with the idea of helping spread knowledge, the ALA only began to think critically about its role towards the government during the First World War. Asked by the White House to provide entertainment for the troops by collecting magazines, the ALA is part of the effort to support the soldiers and promote a patriotic attitude among the American population. But the ALA goes further when libraries respond to pressure to clean their shelves of books written by German authors. At the end of the conflict, many within the organization reflected on the instrumentalization of libraries as part of the propaganda machine. A thought emerged on the necessity for libraries to adopt a position on intellectual freedom.

During the 1920s, the witch hunt launched by Hoover and Palmer against leftist movements and east European immigrants in general caught the ALA unprepared yet again. The shelves, once again, were considered an ideological battlefield. Libraries cleared out books by authors, even American ones, deemed to have socialist leanings. At the time, individual librarians decided to save some of these books by hiding them from the crowds.

Within the ALA, during the 1930s, some dared to ask publicly how the organization could stand against auto de fés while accepting to censor its acquisition policy in the name of patriotism. How can one promote intellectual freedom and justify that certain books be banned? The conservative and patriotic wings of the ALA, eager to show the usefulness of libraries in the general war efforts pushed back the adoption and implementation of new ethics standards. Libraries will work closely with the nascent intelligence community and prolong ideological wars.

Every crisis episode is thus the occasion for ALA members and committees to ponder about the degree of participation in the war effort or the implication of the search against an invisible internal enemy. Crisis after crisis, the attitude adopted evolved incrementally as a political consciousness emerged about the values the organization decided to promote and defend.

Begun in the early 1930s as a reaction to the 1920s Red Scare and the rise of the fascist movements in Europe, the ALA's reflections on its values, took shape with the adoption in 1939 of its first *Code of Ethics*[19] and the *Library Bill of Rights*.[20] Eventually, during the Cold War, the ALA began a very interesting reflection on the conservation of records with the adoption of the *Policy on Confidentiality of Library Records* (1971).[21] At the height of the Cold War, the FBI program approached certain librarians to ask them to report 'suspicious individuals' browsing the aisles where materials about chemicals, explosives and nuclear techniques were displayed.

Every crisis demonstrated the supreme importance of knowledge and collection of information for the government as well as the population. The volumes preserved by librarians and more importantly the records kept by them of who consulted, borrowed and even browsed them, quickly became information of strategic value for security forces. After reaffirming at the end of the Second World War its commitment to refuse censorship in its acquisition policies and taking a position on the confidentiality of library records, the ALA, to prevent the possibility of the instrumentalization of its files in a way that could deter patrons from borrowing and reading freely, decided to advise librarians to destroy their records on a regular basis.

When professional ethics became stronger than security discourses

In the days that followed the September 11 attacks, librarians, once again, found themselves in the middle of a debate about the role and attitude to adopt. The reason was that the FBI rapidly discovered that some of the hijackers, while living in Florida, had used public library computers to send emails and receive instructions. But, when FBI agents asked for a copy of the library records regarding computer usage, they were met with a refusal to comply unless they presented a warrant signed by a judge, as the law provides. Once leaked to the press, the information became a public scandal in which libraries were accused of being non-cooperative at best, and often called worst. The ALA went public and sent all of its members a memorandum reminding librarians that cooperation with security forces was possible granted all legal requirements be met.

Once again, the position of the ALA is an official statement that serves as a guideline, not an order. It means that libraries, public or private, make their own choices. A debate emerges regarding the position to adopt, the degree of cooperation to foster and the part in surveillance willing to be played. And once again, as shown by the Florida scandal, library records appear as a key stake in national security debates.

Indeed, on 26 October 2001, the adoption of the USA Patriot Act, in its section 215, allows security agents to access any records, library or otherwise, granted they show a National Security Letter. The NSL is different legally from a warrant. It is accompanied by a gagging-order which prevents the employee discussing the letter to discuss the content of the sought after files, including the user being the object of the search but also any legal counsel,.[22]

Strengthened by more than a century of evolution and ethical construction, the ALA is going to resist. The position it adopts is one of simple, efficient and morally strong resistance. From October 2001, the organization reminded its members of the necessity to destroy any unnecessary file regarding book circulations. The advice is simple: once returned, a book record has to be expunged from a user's file. Computer usage records, which require the library to match a computer with a time and date and the user's identity, also have to be destroyed after a given period of time.[23] In addition to this privacy-protection toolkit from the ALA, individual actions of resistance have to be considered. Certain libraries across the nation, in partnership with the American Civil Liberties Union (ACLU), decided, in the autumn of 2001, to warn their users against the potential use of the Patriot Act's section 215 by FBI agents to access their records without approval from a judge. The poster displayed throughout the library asked users to petition their elected officials to express their opinion.[24]

In various cities, librarians organized public protests during which activists borrowed and returned books chosen from a FBI watch list on Islamist movements, terrorism and explosives. The goal was to illustrate and raise awareness about the necessity of defending intellectual freedom. Through symbolic acts of resistance to the enforcement of the Patriot Act, librarians wanted to contribute to a public debate about national security measures. And since the most controversial sections of the Patriot Act are attached to a sunset clause, meaning that they will have to be re-authorized by Congress after a five year period, the actions of librarians clearly indicated their intention to have elected officials reconsider their position in preparation for this vote to come. By criticizing publicly the Patriot Act and raising the media's attention about their actions, the ALA took the lead in federating the efforts of civil liberties and intellectual freedom defence groups. As such, they poked a first hole in the national security discourse dike and contributed to the creation of future cracks in the efforts of the government to legitimize its exceptional powers.

These symbolic actions were backed, in the autumn of 2001, by a lobbying campaign design to inform lawmakers and elected officials in general of the Patriot Act's impact on library user' intellectual freedom. To support these claims, the ALA, in the spring of 2002, began to collect information about the number of national security letters received by librarians across the nation. The results were analysed in a study paid for by the ALA (Goodman, 2005) that revealed how little the section 215 was used to obtain library records. For the ALA, the measure was useless and needed to be repealed when the Patriot Act was re-examined by Congress in the summer of 2006.[25]

And here is the trick. Section 215 was never intended for the Department of Justice and FBI agents to gain access to book records in particular. It is aimed to provide easier access to any records, public or private, in general. Given how databases keep tracks of an individual's actions on a constant basis, one can postulate that, in the fight against terrorists, financial and communication records were certainly higher on the list of priorities than those kept by librarians. Indeed, if we go back to the Florida scandal, the files sought by FBI agents did not concern the books borrowed but instead the records of the sites consulted while using the computers available in the public library.

But here, it is critical to seize the importance of the history and evolution of the ALA. The organization has had more than a century to develop ethical standards and build a position towards the government in times of crisis. As such, it is equipped with a strong structure to defend certain values that constitute the core of its social function. On the other hand, the bulk of the information, gathered and kept by private companies, that is of interest for security services belongs to firms whose relationship with the government is crucial, banks, Internet Service Providers, airlines and others. None of these is built around core values related to freedom and rights. If each of these industries certainly has professional ethics, none revolves around the protection of civil liberties and privacy the way the ALA does. In this light, the ALA's resistance movement is the only one to raise the public's attention of the danger of allowing easier access to the personal data kept by organizations and companies. Indeed, in the following years, numerous scandals revealed that private firms, without protesting, opened up their data banks to the government, releasing identities, addresses, telephone and credit card numbers to the FBI and other security agencies.[26] The ALA was the only organization set up to oppose an alternative discourse.

Habeas corpus, no matter what: the Center for Constitutional Rights (CCR)

> I seem to thrive on losing (…) Over the years, we [the Center for Constitutional Rights' legal teams] were spectacularly unsuccessful in court with a few exceptions; we lost every case we litigated. (…) [But our efforts] were successful if they inspire others to struggle, to resist injustice together, and to eschew the easier, more 'successful' path.
>
> (Jules Lobel, vice-president du Center Constitutional Rights (CCR))

A key participant in the main legal battles fought by the CCR during the 1980s against the government, Lobel describes the act of resistance in a somewhat romantic way, explaining that despite losing in court, the ideas he and the CCR defended were often vindicated a few years later (Lobel, 2003). It is precisely this type of fight that the handful of attorneys gathered around the CCR in late autumn 2001 will wage on the government regarding the treatment of the individuals detained in Guantanamo B.

Created in 1966 to support and coordinate the lawyers defending civil rights movement activists on trial in the South, the CCR quickly became a centre for legal expertise designed to assist social movement working towards social progress. The lawyers working there mobilize their social capitals in the court system to defend and promote social change. During the 1970s and 1980s, they opposed the American government's decision to invade Grenada[27] and the imposition of economic sanctions against the left-wing Nicaraguan government.[28] The CCR's history and the sociology of the attorneys who joined its efforts in the autumn of 2001 are important elements in understanding how a professionalized resistance movement managed to poke holes in the government's national security logic.

The interviews we carried out with various lawyers between 2002 and 2010, as well as the analysis of the books some of them wrote, helped reveal this history. And it started with a bang. Indeed, the building where the CCR is renting out office space is located just a few blocks away from what is now Ground Zero. On September 11 2001, the windows were blown away when the WTC towers collapsed. Like any New Yorker, the CCR's personnel felt the attacks on a personal and emotion level, with fear and a certain element of anger and resentment. When a first call came in from a counsel representing Kuwaiti nationals captured by American troops, asking for assistance in obtaining their release, the reaction among the legal team was mixed. There were ethical points to take into account but they had to be weighed with the emotions felt.

A decision was made then to ask for advice from lawyers close to the organization in order to adopt a strategy. A conference call was made. The callers were CCR's legal team, a death-row specialist from Minnesota as well as the attorney from Washington DC who had taken on the case of Kuwaitis detained by the US as part of the 'war on terror'. At the time this conversation took place, no decision had been made by the government regarding the treatment of prisoners and no knowledge of such a case had surfaced among the legal community in the US. As far as the lawyers on the phone knew, the usual legal framework was applied which meant that the first step to take was to file a habeas corpus petition in front of a competent judge. Presented with such a request, the government has to demonstrate the need for an individual to remain in custody.

But on 13 November 2001, the White House announced that President George W. Bush has signed a Military Order[29] granting the Executive power the final authority in determining an individual to be an enemy combatant whose case can only be processed through a military commission while the individual remains in the custody of the Department of Defense.

The issue, for the CCR attorneys, was to see through the fog and determine a course of action to obtain a judge's decision as to the justification of the detention of the initial Kuwaiti nationals. The framework mobilized by the group revolved around the notion that, in times of conflict, the third Geneva Convention on the treatment of prisoners of war,[30] embedded with the US Army Field Manual,[31] stipulates that the status of the individuals captured on the battlefield has to be determined by a competent tribunal. It also stipulates that basic legal protections apply to every individual.

But, on the Afghan battlefield, in the autumn of 2001, no such judicial determination was being made. The number of captured individuals grew rapidly. Before the White House announced, in December 2001, that a camp would be created on the US Navy Base of Guantanamo Bay, Cuba, the CCR sent out a call for action to its network of lawyers in order to constitute a pool of attorneys willing to defend these detainees.

Only a handful were to respond at first. Among the initial respondents, a similar profile emerged: all had defended progressist causes and most had an activist background. But many also shared a similar characteristic which is to have defended clients on death row. During an interview, one of them explained why this was noteworthy. Indeed, clients being put on death row or facing death penalty have in common to be accused of a crime that the public deems so horrible as to mandate an execution. The legal battle is an uphill one in which the defence has to convince a popular jury, a judge as well as public opinion that the client is innocent or that the crime does not amount to such a sentence. The lawyers who choose to take on such cases have learnt how to work against all odds. They know that the fight is not to be won in the public arena but through the intricate knowledge of the legal system where the rights of any individuals are to be defended.

This particular socialization enabled the lawyers who decided to join forces with the CCR to see through the fog rapidly. And the fog was thick since Secretary of Defense Donald Rumsfeld announced that Camp Delta and then Camp X-Ray, at Guantanamo, would house detainees he characterized as 'the worst of the worst' in 2002.

During our interviews with these lawyers, most of them had a similar answer to the question why they had decided to get involved: 'who else could have done it?' And they were right. Only a seasoned attorneys, knowing their way in and out of the legal maze of government would be able to poke holes in the pseudo-legal walls built by the Office of Legal Counsel experts with whom they shared their education and against whom they had already fought similar battles regarding national security issues.[32]

Fight exception with the law, fight silence with the pen

It could seem easy to summarize ten years of legal battle as the process through which attorneys tried to force the government to simply implement its legal obligations based on national, military and international law regarding the treatment of prisoners. It could seem easy but it was not. It was a Sisyphean task they carried because they knew, since the beginning that they were right and that the government was abusing its power. A Chicago-based lawyer, who single-handedly was representing about a dozen of Yemeni detainees, said to us: 'since the beginning, we knew we were right. We knew deep in our hearts that the law did not authorize President Bush to treat human beings that way. We knew we were right, but we had to find a court and a judge in front of whom to be heard'.[33]

The strategy used is rather straightforward: find a test case on a particular point of the pseudo-legal construction legitimating Guantanamo and proceed. In a way much like the matriochka-style legal construction deployed by the government in the autumn of 2001, the deconstruction was to proceed the same way. Taking away the legitimating blocks piece by piece, shows their unconstitutionality until the holes in the wall become cracks that spread through the wall and let it crumble. That way, each legal battle, each case presented in front of a judge, acted as the occasion to deconstruct the system built around Guantanamo and the idea that military justice is the legitimate way to proceed.

The initial battle was initiated by the International Committee of the Red Cross (ICRC). The point, in the autumn of 2001, was to obtain from the government and the Department of Defense, the right to gain access to the first prisoners sent to Cuba. From the turn of the twentieth century and the codification of the laws of war, the ICRC had negotiated a right to inspect detention facilities and provide relief to prisoners. In exchange for this right, the ICRC agreed to remain neutral and to not use its reports publicly. As part of its humanitarian mission, ICRC personnel could provide detainees with postcard-style forms which the prisoners then used to send basic information about their situation to their families. The cards were checked by military authorities to prevent the transmission of security-relevant information. After a few rounds of negotiations, the ICRC was granted access to the detention camps in Guantanamo Bay and the first ICRC-letters were sent to the families of the detainees. Informed of the situation of their kin, some families were able to retain counsel and petition the American government for their release.

As such, this first contact, permitted by international treaties and conventions, allowed a first hole in the wall. Through this hole, the first mental pictures of the reality arrived at the persons standing outside of the camp. The first names were made public and the first legal mobilization on their behalf was made possible.

In fact, to maintain the fog around its national security-related activities and intentions, the Bush administration had refused to let anything filter out of the base. The list of names of the detainees would only be made public after a long legal battle involving a Freedom of Information Act petition filled in by press organizations and civil liberties groups in a combined effort to force the government to be transparent.[34] Little by little, the camp would be pierced with tiny holes and then larger openings revealing the intentions and goals of a government who knew, from the first memoranda released on the issue by the Office of Legal Counsel that their legitimating wall would crack eventually.

Shortly after the first prisoners arrived by military plane to Guantanamo, the CCR filed two habeas corpus petitions, one on behalf of Shafiq Rasul, Asif Iqbal and David Hicks,[35] and another one regarding the fate of Mamdouh Habib.[36] All of them had been captured in Afghanistan, so the CCR attorneys filed a motion in court in Washington, DC. The motion required the government to justify the reasons of their detention, to provide them with a legal representation and to have the right to a fair trial in before a regular court of justice. As planned by the OLC memoranda written in the autumn of 2001, the Washington DC district court excused itself arguing that it did not have jurisdiction over Guantanamo. In front of the Appellate Court for the District of Columbia, the CCR attorneys were told that no American court of justice has jurisdiction over the Guantanamo Bay, Cuba US Navy base. The Bush administration seemed to have won. But in September 2003, the CCR petitioned the US Supreme Court which decided to take on the case that would become *Rasul v. Bush*. In April 2004, the Supreme Court decision stated that despite what the Administration claimed, foreign-born detainees placed in detention under the authority of the Department of Defense at Guantanamo did indeed have a right to challenge their detention. The Court also declared that the Guantanamo detainees had a right to a legal counsel. It took the next twelve months for this decision to become effective on the ground. The Executive imposed that any civilian lawyer or interpreter setting foot on Guantanamo had to obtain security clearance.

From the moment of this initial Supreme Court decision, the White House and Department of Defense set up a legal strategy to avoid the full implementation of the decision. Rather than granting the detainees the right to challenge their detention before of a civilian court, the Administration decided to create an *ad hoc* legal system: the Combatant Status Review Tribunals (CSRT).[37] Their mission was to assert the guilt of the individual and to justify the prolonged detention of the detainees. Represented by military lawyers, indicted by military prosecutors and sentenced by military judges, the detainees were required to play along despite an obvious lack of legal protection.

Less than two months after they were set up, the CSRTs became the object of a court injunction requiring their suspension.[38] A year later, in *Hamdan v. Rumsfeld*,[39] the US Supreme Court stated that the President did not have the necessary authority to create a judicial system. This power only belonged to Congress. With this decision, the Supreme Court actually stated that despite the 14 September AUMF, the President could not decide every matter regarding the fight against national security even if the conduct of operations was under his purview as commander in chief. The decision also confirmed that the Geneva Conventions applied to any detainee and prisoner and that renaming them 'enemy combatant' did not change a thing when considering the minimal legal protections anyone enjoys. It was a serious blow to the matriochka construction and to the all-legitimating argument of national security.

In reaction, President Bush and the Republican camp managed to pass the Military Commission Act (MCA)[40] that granted the President the necessary authority to legitimize the use of military tribunals to indict Guantanamo detainees. The *ad hoc* military justice, itself an exceptional justice system, proceeded with the examination of the detainees' files. New rules were adopted which that time, prevented the detainees from receiving the assistance of anyone, during the trial, who would have any technical knowledge of the law. Outside of the walls, CCR lawyers became more numerous every day. They had one single goal: to argue a habeas corpus petition in front of a civilian court to make their case.

In December 2008, Lakhdar Boumedienne's case, wasconsolidated to argue a single issue, is decided by the Supreme Court.[41] His lawyers challenged the constitutionality of the Military Commission Act of 2006 and asked the Supreme Court justices to decide on one of the pillars of the Bush administration's national security policies: the possibility for the Executive to suspend the implementation of the right of habeas corpus in any given context. This legal point is key to a democratic state based on the separation of the three branches of government. The Court declared, in its decision, that the MCA of 2006 did not provide for the full exercise of the right of habeas corpus and therefore represented an illegal suspension of the law.

More than seven years after the first prisoners arrived in Guantanamo, and after seven years of legal battles, the Supreme Court justices declared that American law courts were competent on this issue and that they had jurisdiction to hear the case of Guantanamo detainees. The justices stated what they had not dared to write down in 2004, which is that foreign citizens detained by the US Department of Defense benefit from the full implementation of the Geneva Conventions. Therefore, a central building block of the Administration' national security architecture, the constructed category of 'enemy combatant', was voided of any legal meaning.

Paying attention to the evolution of the political context is crucial here since this decision came after Barack Obama's election as the next US President. While the Supreme Court is fully independent from the changes in the White House, it is not totally insensitive to the evolutions perceived among the general population. Indeed, since *Hamdan v. Rumsfeld* (2006), the Guantanamo lawyers had sensed a change in public opinion on this issue.

Reacting to this, they had changed their tactics. Outside of the prison walls and behind the doors of the courtrooms, lawyers had begun investing the public square. Many of them grabbed their pens to write columns and blogs about the situation in Guantanamo. Informing the public had become an important part of creating popular support against the abuse of government powers. With their pens, they poked additional holes to show the world the reality behind the fences and the bright orange jumpsuits. Slowly, the detainees became, in the eye of the public, human beings with rights (Falkoff, 2007; Ratner and Ray, 2004).

The revelation of the abuses committed by military personnel at Abu Ghraib contributed to shock the public. The Torture scandal spread from Abu Ghraib to Guantanamo and other detention facilities. Shortly after, the 'extraordinary rendition programs' which involved the secret transfer of high value prisoners between black sites and interrogation centres in less-than-democratic nations became a hot topic between the US and the European Union.

Progressively, the images of abuse being committed in the name of national security piled up and restricted the ability of the Bush administration to claim that its national security policies remained legitimate.

Court case after court case, decision after decision, the lawyers who had accepted representing, *pro bono*, the individuals placed behind bars in Guantanamo restricted the symbolic space the Administration could claim to do as it pleased. They demonstrated that the discursive arguments and legal constructions constructed by the Administration to support the creation of an interrogation camp at Guantanamo did not hold up in court. While convincing American opinion was a goal to reach, the real outcome, since the beginning, was to establish, in the minds of the nine Supreme Court justices that, even in times of national security crises, the Executive branch is bound to respect the law.

Every trial acted as the occasion for the CCR lawyers to present their legal arguments to the discourses of the Administration' counsels. The courtrooms became the arena where security professionals had to respond to the proponents of a challenging *transcript* on security. While the Administration and its proxies had managed to silence dissenters in the public and political arena, they no longer could in courts. Working patiently through the legal maze, the members of the informal Guantanamo Bar Association compelled the administration's advocates to recognize that international law sometimes supersedes American law (Slaughter, 2003; Kersch, 2006) and that the Latin maxim – *inter arma silent leges* – no longer applied. It actually never did.

Resistance and desecuritization

In a context of national security crisis, the government gives in to an impulsion it legitimizes through the argument of emergency. This impulsion is to silence any dissenting voice in the name of expediency, the fight against an existential threat and the absence of an alternative choice. In kind, opponents to the government's incentive have an initial reaction of resistance: speaking out and trying to restore public speech.

Speaking out publicly sets the terms of the issue, lays down the positions and anchors the mobilization efforts from members and strategic supporters. By speaking out, writing, informing, the actors of the resistance movement build protection mechanisms against the imposition and implantation of a dominating discourse deep within the collective memory. Every act of resistance is an element of critical thinking, an alternative around which to build a reflection. Describing their action as a 'light in the fog', one of the first lawyers to join forces with the CCR[42] explained that critical thinking skills were the articulations of any resistance movement. And as such, given the complexity of governmental action and regulations, it takes professional actors to be able to shine a light onto the actions the government would prefer to keep in darkness.

In the two cases we analysed in this chapter, the resistance strategy mobilized by both librarians and attorneys consisted in revealing and exposing the abuses of power committed by the Executive branch, documenting them and challenging them in court or in the public arena. But overall, in both cases, the resistance deployed aimed at changing the practices and changing the laws that enabled them. While lawyers challenged the constitutionality of the Bush administration's legal decision and legislative measures, librarians took the lead in raising awareness about the need to change some of the most outrageous sections of the Patriot Act when the law came under review in Congress in 2006. To prepare the examination of the law, the ALA petitioned the court to challenge the constitutionality of the National Security Letters,[43] thus raising the issue on the public agenda and calling elected officials to take a strong position. Playing on sympathy among the population, librarians gained the attention of the public and a strong group of representatives and senators. During the debates in commissions, the ALA's arguments were mentioned numerous times regarding the necessary protection of users' privacy and intellectual freedom.[44] In response, the Department of Justice' counsels and representatives were forced to argue about the necessity of these exceptional powers for law enforcement agencies. To sustain their demand for the extension of these powers of exception, the Department of Justice officials had to explain why, if these powers were not used to obtain library records, Congress had to extend them for an additional five years. In the end, after nine months of discussion, Congress revised the sixteen provisions of the Patriot Act but introduced new control mechanisms thus withdrawing the quasi-unchecked power of the Executive branch.[45]

The history of the resistance to the post-September 11 national security measure cannot be told fully through the sole analysis of two movements – there are many more, but the techniques used by lawyers and librarians show how resisting securitization means the re-politicization of the issue, the re-judiciarization of the measures of exception and then the desecuritization of the problem.

Four years after the Boumedienne decision and while Barack Obama was re-elected President in November 2012, the issue of the conduct of national security policy remains a grey area for democrats and progressives in America. A year after his inauguration and the promise to close down the detention camp in Guantanamo, Barack Obama had seriously disappointed those who had fought the policies of the Bush administration and who had believed in the capacity of the former Harvard law school professor to restore America's standing among the great democratic nations. Four years later, America's national security policy has changed but new exceptions have been accepted and remain mostly undiscussed. While Guantanamo is not yet closed and the Patriot Act has become part of the toolkit used daily, the war against terrorism is part of a common discourse that no one challenges. The issue of secrecy, which Obama's 2008 campaign had made a point of lifting, remains a strongly enforced tactic preventing the critical examination of the American government's security policies.[46]

Those who resisted, as Lobel wrote, might not have won directly but succeeded in implanting the memory of a mobilization when the time was not right, when the context was hard and when dissenting was difficult. Those who opposed the government in a time of national crisis made sure that the trust granted to elected official is not an excuse for actions going beyond the law no matter what legitimating architecture they manage to wrap the abuses of power in.

But those who participated in this fight left a lasting example to be emulated. During one of our last interviews, one of the lawyers who contributed to the

Boumedienne victory, who had become an eminent law school professor, had us listen to a message recorded on his office's answering machine. The death threats and insults were real but he was smiling. Resisting, it seemed then, meant to be able to preserve one's sense of humour while awaiting the students who were queuing the door to learn from someone who had stood up for a certain idea of freedom and democracy.

Notes

1 'To authorize the use of United States Armed Forces against those responsible for the recent attacks launched against the United States', Senate Joint Resolution, Public Law 107–40, October 18, 2001. Note from the author: this legislation was voted on 14 September but signed into law on 18 September.

2 AUMF, September 18, 2001, sec 2 (a).

3 War Powers Resolution of 1973 (50 U.S.C. 1541–1548).

4 The AUMF is evoked to legitimize the President's authority, as Commander in Chief, to place in indefinite detention any person he determines to be an enemy combatant (see the arguments used by the government's lawyers in the Supreme Court case *Hamdi v. Rumsfeld* (2004) and *Padilla v. Rumsfeld* (2004). The AUMF is also used to provide legitimacy to the decision to intervene in Iraq (see the text of the House Joint Resolution to Authorize the Use of the United States Armed Force Against Iraq H.J.Res. 114 of 2002). The introductory paragraphs, in all of these decisions, constitute a list of the legal arguments, designed to provide legitimacy. Among those, the AUMF sits at the core: http://www.gpo.gov/fdsys/pkg/BILLS-107hjres114enr/pdf/BILLS-107hjres114enr.pdf.

The same legislative measure provides a semblance of legitimacy to the NSA's unwarranted electronic communications' interception program. In of its *white papers,* the Justice Department calls upon the AUMF as moment when Congress granted the President the necessary authority that led to him authorizing the warrantless interception program (see 'Legal Authorities Supporting the Activities of the National Security Agency Described by the President', US Department of Justice, January 19 2006).

At last, Harold Koh, former Yale Law School dean and then-White House Legal Counsel, mentioned the September 14 2011 AUMF as the ground for the authority and legitimacy of President Obama's decision to send Navy Seal commandos to eliminate Bin Laden deep within Pakistani territory on 1 Ma 2011. His argument can be found on: http://opiniojuris.org/2011/05/19/the-lawfulness-of-the-us-operation-against-osama-bin-laden/

5 Uniting and Strengthening America by Providing Appropriate Tools Required to Intercept and Obstruct Terrorism (US Patriot Act) Act of 2001, Public Law 107-56, 107th Congress.

6 The Office of Legal Counsel is part of the Department of Justice. Its mission is to assist the Secretary of Justice and provide legal recommendations to the Executive branch. It is composed of members nominated by the White House. Its recommendations do not have legal force.

7 See especially the most important memoranda: Patrick Philbin, *Memorandum for Alberto Gonzales, Counsel to the President: Legality of the Use of Military Commission to Try Terrorists*; John Yoo, *Memorandum to Jim Haynes II: Application of Treaties and Laws to Al Qaeda and Taliban Detainees*, January 9 2002. The memorandum initiating the Administration's reflection on the use of 'extended interrogation techniques': Jay Bybee (OLC) for Jim Haynes II (DoD), January 26 2002, *Potential Legal Constraints Applicable to Interrogations of Persons Captured by US Armed Forces in Afghanistan.*

8 An example of such an attitude was the campaign launched by ACTA in the autumn of 2001 to shame university professors who had dared to discuss with their students the 11 September events and the rationales of the hijackers.

9 Florent Blanc, 'Unanimism in Congress', research paper, Sciences Po Paris, 2003 (unpublished).

10 Editorial: 'Unveiled Threats', *Washington Post*, January 12, 2007.

11 We are referring here to George W. Bush' speech 'if you're not with us you're with the terrorists'.

12 Pierre Bourdieu and Loic J. D. Wacquant, *Réponses: Pour Une Anthropologie Réflexive* (Paris: Seuil, 1992).

13 The title refers to a tribute album from jazzman James Carter (published by Atlantic Records, 1996). It calls upon the idea that jazz is a series of creations, reinterpretations, adaptations, much like what Tarrow and Tilly described in the notion of repertoire of contention.

14 This part of the chapter addresses, in too short a way, the timeframe debate within *securitization* studies. Without a proper understanding of the 'lessons learned' from past securitization moments in American history, the analysis of the resistance patterns to the post-9/11 era would fail.

15 The evolution of repertoires of contention happens on a continuous basis but it seemed that previous crises have enabled resisters to learn at an accelerated rate.

16 The following landmark cases deserve the reader's attention: *Yates v. United States* (1957) and *Brandeburg v. Ohio* (1969) regarding freedom of expression; *Brown v. Louisiana* (1966) and *Adderley v. Florida* (1966) for the codification of the right of assembly; and finally, regarding the right of association: *NAACP v. Alabama* (1958).

17 In *Handshu v. Special Services Division*, New York's Second District Court put an end to the activities of the NYPD's Special Division. This unit had previously been tasked with compiling information about the individuals participating in First Amendment protected activities.

18 TALON and CATIC are two databases created under the authority of the Department of Defense and California's Attorney General's Office. Both compile information about threats to public order and function under the assumption that public demonstrations can be used to cover up acts of terrorism.

19 At the core of the ethical construction of this organization, the Code of Ethics was revised and amended in 1981, 1995 and 2008.

20 Revised in 1944, 1948, 1961, 1967, 1980 and 1996.

21 Revised in 1975 and 1986.

22 A gagging order legally prohibits anyone subject to it from divulging certain information. Attached to section 215 of the Patriot Act, the gagging order, as part of the NSL, prohibits the persons contacted by law enforcement agents to mention the agents' request to the patron(s) identified in the document or the library's legal counsel. For more information refer to 'Section 505 – Miscellaneous National Security Authorities', in US Patriot Act, P.L. 107-56, October 26, 2001.

23 Read ALA's 'Privacy Toolkit: Guidelines for Developing a Library Privacy Policy'. In this document, the organization reasserts that libraries' mission not to keep unnecessary personal information. To avoid being put in a position to release such data, the ALA suggests that 'every library takes the proper measures to destroy any personal data or convert them in such a way as to render them anonymous' (cf. 4. Data integrity and security). The document is available at: http://www.ala.org/offices/oif/iftoolkits/toolkitsprivacy/guidelinesfordevelopingalibraryprivacypolicy/guidelinesprivacypolicy).

24 See in particular the 'campaign for reader privacy', launched in 2004. It aims at informing readers to get some information about the Patriot Act and petition their elected officials in Congress to reform the Patriot Act in order to protect library records from government intrusion. See http://www.readerprivacy.org/.

25 Supported by the ALA, a group of representatives and senators led by Russ Feingold introduced the Freedom to Read Protection Act, in 2003. They were responding to the ALA's Campaign for Reader Privacy, the slogan of which was "Is someone reading over your shoulder?"

26 See Jet Blue scandal in 2002–03.

27 See *Conyers v. Reagan* (1983), a case in which the CCR team challenged the constitutionality of President Reagan's decision to invade militarily the Island of Grenada. The case rested on CCR's argument according to which this decision did not respect the limit of the War Powers Resolution of 1974.

28 See *Veterans Peace Convoy v. Schultz* (1988). In this case, the judge sided with the CCR and declared anti-constitutional the measures adopted by the American Government to prevent or restrict humanitarian donations to Nicaragua.

29 See Military Order of November 13, 2001: Detention, Treatment and Trial of Certain Non-Citizens in the War against Terrorism, Washington: White House.

30 Refer to article 5 of the Third Geneva Convention, 1949.

31 The *US Army Field Manual on Interrogation*, also known as FM 34-52, provides the framework within which military interrogators operate when interrogating prisoners. The methods it described prior to its most recent revision integrated the requirements of the Geneva Conventions. Dick Cheney, when he signed the document authorizing fourteen additional interrogation techniques in August 2002 triggered an update of the manual: *FM 2-22.3 Human Intelligence Collector Operations.*

32 Honig B., *op. cit.*; Joel Handler, *Social Movements and the Legal System* (New York: Academic Press, 1978); David Luban, 'Lawfare and Legal Ethics in Guantanamo,' *Stanford Law Review* 60, no. 6 (2008); Geoffrey Stone, *Perilous Times: Free Speech in Wartime from the Seditious Act to the War on Terror* (New York: W.W. Norton, 2004).

33 Interview, Chicago, 2007.

34 The list of the prisoners' names was finally released in 2006 when the government was ordered by a judge to comply with a FOIA request filed by the *Washington Post*, Reuters and the *New York Times*.

35 The habeas corpus petitions filed on behalf of these men were regrouped in a single case *Rasul v. Bush*.

36 This case *Habib v. Bush* was finally examined by the Supreme Court in 2004 as well.

37 The CSRTs were established by the following decision, Deputy Secretary of Defense, *Memorandum for the Secretary of the Navy: Order Establishing Combatant Status Review Tribunals*, Washington, DC, July 7, 2004.

38 See District Court of Columbia, *Hamdan v. Rumsfeld* (2004). In this decision, the judge explained that according to the Geneva Conventions, a prisoner had to be considered as a prisoner of war until a competent tribunal determines otherwise. This decision was reversed by the District of Columbia Appellate Court before it reached the Supreme Court in 2006.

39 See *Hamdan v. Rumsfeld*, 548 U.S. 557 (2006).

40 Military Commission Act of 2006, Pub. L. No. 109–366, 120 Stat. 2600.

41 See *Boumediene v. Bush*, 553 U.S. 723 (2008).

42 This quote is excerpted from a personal interview, Chicago 2007.

43 See *Library Connection v. Gonzales* (2005). This case was brought before the court by the ACLU and the ALA. In 2004, the IT manager at Library Connection in Connecticut received a NSL requiring him to provide the law enforcement agents with a list of websites consulted from a specific computer between 4 and 4:45pm on 15 February 2006. The case rests on the notion that the gag order prevented the IT manager and librarian to speak freely at a moment when the ALA was lobbying Congress to reform the Patriot Act, which was coming up for re-authorization. Therefore, the imposition of a gagging order to the NSL constituted, according to the case, a restriction on the person's First Amendment rights. In September 2005, the judge stated that the gag

order constituted an unconstitutional restriction and would only be lifted officially in February 2006, i.e. three weeks after the Patriot Act was finally reauthorized by Congress.

44 For further details, refer to the debates that took place between 5 and 10 April 5 in the Senate Committee on the Judiciary.

45 See US Patriot Improvement and Reauthorization Act of 2005. It was voted by the Senate on 14 December 2005 and signed by the President on 9 March 2006.

46 Regarding the issue of the growing use of drones to implement a 'targeted killing' strategy, the ACLU and the CCR revived earlier tactics by launching a full FOIA campaign requesting information from the government about such program and following up with a test-case – *Al Aulaqi v. Panetta* – filed with the court of the District of Columbia.

Part II
Desecuritization

Editor's introduction

I

At the semantic level, though not at the political, desecuritization is the opposite of securitization. This is obviously not to say that there exists a unique understanding of desecuritization. Indeed, the meaning of the concept of "desecuritization" remains fragile. According to Wæver (1995: 74), for instance, desecuritzation is a way of "transcending a security problem … away from (security terms)". In *Security*, Buzan, Wæver and de Wilde argue that desecuritization refers to the restoration of routine procedures of politics. Specifically, it is "the shifting of issues out of emergency mode and into the normal bargaining process of the political sphere" (Buzan, Wæver and de Wilde, 1998: 74).

There is more, however. One of the points that is most interesting about desecuritization is that it provides the language for thinking about situations that are neither insecurity nor security (Hansen 2012). As Wæver (1995: 74) argues,

> to talk of a situation as characterized by security means that a threat is articulated but that sufficient counter-measures are felt available – in contrast to insecurity with a threat of insufficient defense. If the situation is taken out of the realm of security conceptualization, the situation might inelegantly be described as one of "a-security".

For Huysmans (1998a), de-securitization is the "unmaking" of the institutionalized threatening representation of public problems. Finally, Aradau (2004) holds that desecuritization is about the questioning of a naturalized "regime of truth" just as much, if not more, as it is about the desirability of a specific kind of politics. Yet, despite controversies over what desecuritization betokens, there is a widespread conviction that it brings politics back in and that it opens up the political game to a broader variety of actors (Hansen, 2012).

II

In relation to the societal security sector, a growing body of contemporary research on de-securitization focuses on the conditions of possibility of de-securitization and on how practicable is a de-securitizing project. This concern is important, primarily because it challenges the normative imperative of desecuritization. In particular, Roe (2004) has argued that de-securitization may be "logically impossible" in some cases, when an issue is intrinsically imbued with a certain degree of "security-ness"; in other words, this issue would disappear as such should a process of de-securitization take place. He illustrates his claim with the case of ethnic minority groups. Those are characterized by a specific collective identity. If one were to cease to use the language of security in relation to this specific identity, then it would not be maintained and the specific group as a distinct minority group would disappear.

Matti Jutila puts this view upside down. He detects a determinist impulse in Roe's account of societal security. By contrast, he argues, there is always a mercurial aspect in relations between groups that evades easy closure of alternative options. As he says, "desecuritization … is always logically possible, though in some cases it might be practically impossible" (Jutila, 2006: 167). Both Roe and Jutila claim that multiculturalism is a context conducive to the structuring of interactions between human collectives. But they do not accord it the same net effects. Roe (2004: 290) considers, for instance, that multiculturalism can only shift discourses and practices of insecurity to discourses and practices of security. From this perspective, a full desecuritization (a-security) is impossible. Jutila claims, by contrast, that desecuritization is logically possible. Suffice it to "shift from nationalizing, monocultural practices to multicultural policies" (Jutila, 2006: 180). In other words, identities, are not essentially threatening; it is through particular speech acts and practices that they are loaded and lead to conflicts among human collectives. Hence, to desecuritize is to regenerate identities in narratives that reallocate power relations between actors and provide an updated content to who they are. It is perhaps in this sense that Huysmans (1998a: 570) argues that de-securitization can have a major impact on the constitution of political communities. In his view, securitization is also about "how a community defines its just and good way of life".

> Desecuritization unmakes politics which identify the community on the basis of the expectations of hostility. Instead of simply removing policy questions from the security sector and plugging them into another sector, desecuritization turns into a political strategy which challenges the fundaments of the political realist (that is, Schmittian) constitution of the political community head on.
> (Huysmans, 1998a: 576)

III

What to do of this variety of meanings? Perhaps, a common deceptively simple idea: desecuritization is a grammar that underwrites the enactment of practices clear of the security-defence rationale (McDonald 2012). This Part identifies three distinctive lines of enquiry in the desecuritization scholarship. (i) the first focuses on the meaning of desecuritization (Chapter 6); (ii) the second emphasizes the desirability and/or feasibility of desecuritization (Chapter 7); (iii) the third examines the different ways in which desecuritization occurs and, correlatively, which method (if any) is the most effective approach to desecuritization? (Chapter 8). In many ways, however, there is no strict division of labour among the chapters brought together here. For instance, Aradau goes from a discussion of the emancipation–desecuritization relations to a deeper engagement with what she considers to be their common if unarticulated common plane: the question of universality. She develops an original typology of universality in order to sustain the argument that contesting security "inhabits paradoxes", wherein subjects navigate exclusion and appropriate universality. Chapter 7 focuses on one case, the liberalization of arms trade in the EU, in order to substantiate the view that desecuritization is no necessarily morally superior to securitization. It briefly reviews the literature in desecuritization, with the explicit aim to design an inclusive typology of desecuritization techniques, which it uses to analyse the case study chosen. Rita Floyd puts forward the challenging argument that desecuritization, as securitization, can be morally weighted. The chapter unpacks the meaning of politicization, securitization, and desecuritization and, then, normatively situates each in relation to the other. Criteria for just desecuritization and their potential objections are examined and discussed.

What occurs from all three chapters is a shared understanding of desecuritization as running along lines which are not entirely foreign to practices of emancipation. But none of the chapters subscribes to the view that security *is* emancipation. Rather, Chapter 7, for instance, considers emancipation as a sub-category of desecuritization. The idea is not that any form of emancipation could be subsumed under the general family of descecuritization. Instead, it means that in the security domain, when a security policy is deemed illegitimate, for example, if contestation takes the physiognomy of emancipation, it is necessarily a type of attempt to desecuritize the question and treat it by other means. In fact, to be precise, emancipation can happen in a wealth of sectors, while desecuritization is restricted to the security sector, including its practices and policies. In absolute terms, then, emancipation is broader than desecuritization; but in the strict security vernacular, it is narrower than desecuritization. Chapter 6 takes a more radical approach to the relationship between desecuritization and emancipation, in the sense that it displaces the discussion onto the terrain of universality and particularism, wherein a (critical) concern with the latter is not incompatible with a project that centers on the former. Thus, a primary object of critical security is to "inhabit paradoxes" (Aradau, this volume). In light of this, a decisive if uncommon aim of critical security studies is there to help us navigate the complicated, the difficult to understand and the ambiguous, which characterizes security practices.

6 Security as universality?

The Roma contesting security in Europe

Claudia Aradau

Introduction

Critical security studies have been divided over a seemingly unanswerable question: can security be for everybody? On the one hand, the answer assumed an insurmountable logic of security as war and exclusion, be it only because this logic has gained historical and practical dominance and it is continually entrenched through practices of governance; on the other, the possibility of multiple, plural, nuanced forms of security that encompass the desires and needs of many of the marginalized people of the world. Human security has perhaps made this rift most clear. In one perspective, human security is nothing more than a regime of power/knowledge which is implicated with the Realpolitik dominance of the international sphere (Grayson 2008). It effaces the global processes of ordering and the promotion of a liberal regime of governance under the mantra of 'global civil society' (Shepherd 2007). As a 'universalist tool of global governance' (Hudson 2005, 159), human security masks multiple and overlapping identities and promotes the hegemonic illusion of the disembodied male subject. Yet, human security has also been promoted as a shift away from the dominance of state security, a way of reopening the debate about what security is and whether it can be mobilized differently. Cautionary notes about human security abound, even in these more positive engagements. Being tied in with global institutions, rendered subservient to the state or working to channel state security in a different form, human security was itself broadened, reconfigured or supplemented by particular narratives and stories about security. It is difficult not to argue that human security reproduces particular hegemonic relations, forms of dominance, exclusion and liberal governance. At the same time, despite the theoretical and empirical qualms, it is difficult not to acknowledge that human security has opened a field of contestation about who counts as a subject of security. We are back to the initial impasse.

In this chapter, I propose to shed light on this apparently insurmountable impasse by taking a different theoretical vantage point. Rather than proposing a solution to this rift in critical security studies, I propose to ask the question differently, in order to make visible new political stakes. I suggest that the problem that critical security studies faces is that of the relation between security and universality.[1] By engaging with the problem of universality, I will also try to redefine this rift as a site of commonality rather than a line of separation. Security and universality have not been analysed in conjunction, despite universality having been one of the main assumptions for critical security studies. The proposed universality of security is seen as a hegemonic move, a ruse of liberal reason or as destructive of the particular needs of people around the world. Therefore, universality has often been opposed in favour of analyses that are 'context-specific; that recognize and interrogate the role of different security discourses and their effects in different settings; and that come to terms with sedimented meanings and logics without endorsing these as timeless and inevitable' (Browning and McDonald 2011, 15). Paul Roe enjoins a move to 'reclaim it [security/securitization] as a site for such contestations over the possibilities for inclusion/exclusion' (2012, 261). The distrust of the universal is also apparent in Lene Hansen's claim that 'there is no universalism that securitization theory can invoke in defence of desecuritization, which means that instances of rearticulation must be justified on substantial grounds' (Hansen 2012, 535). At the same time, universality is also defended in critical attempts to reconfigure security. 'When cultural values and norms oppress', argues Booth, 'universal human rights offer people some protection' (2007, 389). Both castigated and defended, universality has nonetheless remained under-explored in the debates about security.

Analysing security in relation to the claims to universality that it implies means that the critical positions can be interrogated anew. Rather than two irreconcilable positions, the critiques and endorsements of security are more entwined than the respective proponents have acknowledged so far. They are indicative, I argue, of the paradoxes of universality in modernity. In revisiting some of the debates around the concept of universality, I explore the implications of 'politics out of security' (Aradau, 2008) as 'inhabiting paradoxes'. This chapter argues that universality is key to our understanding of the limits of security as well as political action to unmake security. Understanding universality as paradoxical shows that security can be contested in a double move of *both* acceptance *and* refusal of security.

The chapter is set out in three stages. It starts by exploring how universality is implicitly or explicitly used in critical security studies. In a second step, it turns to conceptualizations of universality that allow us to understand the paradoxes of political claims and actions that imply invocations of universality. Finally, it unpacks the implications of this understanding of universality by analysing the ways in which the Roma in Europe today have contested security. The argument focuses in particular on the French situation and the dismantling of camps and deportations from 2010 through to today (at the time of writing, under the socialist Presidency of François Hollande in France).

Critical security studies and the problem of universality

Critical security studies have been split over the meaning of 'critical' and what the implications of critique are for security scholars. Should security scholars focus on developing theoretical tools and unpacking processes of securitization (Balzacq

2011a)? Should they focus on desecuritization instead (Aradau 2004)? Should we forget about security and stop using its language or grammar (Aradau 2008, Neocleous 2008)? Or should we aim for emancipation through security (Booth 2007)? These questions emerge out of various assumptions about what security is and does. They are political and ethical questions (Browning and McDonald 2011). At the same time, all these questions also make assumptions about the universality of security. Fleshing out these assumptions and various perspectives on universality allows me to shift the debate on a common terrain. I suggest that there are three main implicit or explicit understandings of universality in critical security studies: universality as hegemonic, universality as comprehensive and universality as an empty signifier.

In one perspective, security is seen as reproducing the logic of 'political realism' (Huysmans 1998a, Williams 2003), security as the other of democracy (Aradau 2004, Behnke 1999), security as exclusionary (Aradau 2008), security as a fetish (Neocleous 2008). Security discourses depend upon and sustain particular representations of the world, and they divide it between inside and outside (see e.g. Campbell 1992, Hansen 2006, Walker 1993). The inside becomes the realm of politics, while the outside is kept at bay in its equivalence with difference, alterity, and heterogeneity. As the principle of formation of the modern political subject (Dillon 1996), security presupposes trust and identity between members of a community, while it relegates indeterminacy, fear, and anarchy to an imaginary locus. This 'logic of security' has led to widespread suspicion of both speaking and writing security.[2]

Even as the logic of security is historically shifting, particularly with the deployment of new practices, the implicit connection with universality continues to undergird the debate. For instance, with the advent of the biopolitical state, security practices are also imbricated in the minute and everyday practices of ordering the life of populations (Foucault 1991, 2007). The state not only assigns membership in the political community and ensures the survival of the community, but is also in charge of the well-being of individuals (or of categories of the population). On the one hand, security is entwined with the development of the state in heterogeneous ways that go beyond the territorial and geopolitical dominant understanding of security. It functions in ways that complexify and disturb the state's taken-for-granted 'right to kill' and the legitimacy of rule. It becomes defined around the welfare of populations (with its underside – the elimination or containment of those who impede or disturb its welfare) and risky conduct. Rather than working simply through juridical prohibitions and drawing boundaries of life and death, power is deployed in much more insidious ways by disciplining subjects and governing the life of populations. On the other hand, Foucault's later concept of 'governmentality' relates security to institutions and forms of knowledge that are mobilized in the governing of societies and populations. Under liberal governance, governing security is directly related to the promotion and protection of the mobility and circulation of populations, goods, and services rather than the protection of territories (Dillon and Reid 2001, Dillon and Lobo-Guerrero 2008, Duffield 2007).

As part of this process of governing populations and securing order, boundaries are drawn, creating categories of individuals who are to be protected at the expense of the exclusion and elimination of others. The focus on historical practice and the concrete phenomenon of security does not efface the problem of universality. After all, security is defined in relation to a universal of 'humanity' to which different abnormals are opposed. Universality is always historically embodied in a particularity. As racial boundaries delimit and divide the life of the species between life worth living and life which is to be curtailed (Foucault 2004), security practices are exposed as inherently *insecuring*, dividing categories of populations and preparing some for elimination, disciplining or therapy. In Dillon's (2005, 41) words, the 'continuous biopolitical assaying of life proceeds through the epistemically driven and continuously changing interrogation of the worth and eligibility of the living across a terrain of value that is constantly changing'. If security is built upon the construction of the human as a universal to be protected and preserved, the 'normal order' of the political community is simultaneously a movement of exclusion, of classification and separation of the abnormal. The logic of security is rearticulated historically through different forms of boundary-drawing, exclusions and embodiments of universality.

Critical engagements with universality have pointed out its particularities of history and context to reveal the Eurocentric and orientalizing underpinnings of claims to universality.[3] The critique of security understood as a *dispositif* that takes hold of life, manages its abnormalities and attempts to prevent 'dangerous irruptions' (Castel 1991) in the future partakes of the hegemony of liberal universality. It undergirds imaginations of commonality and safety and of the universal value of life, while drawing lines, authorizing distinctions and legitimating inequalities. In these approaches, security is essentially an 'order of fear' (Dillon 1996, 16) constitutive of modern subjectivity. Security is rendered as the hegemonic project of normative liberals, unreconstructed modernists or imperialist neoconservatives (e.g. Chandler and Hynek 2011).

From this perspective, calls for the universalization of security such as individual or human security are met with suspicion, as another instantiation of liberal hegemony. This critique can be seen as a version of the Hegelian-Marxist tradition of thinking universality, in which universality and hegemony become equivalent (Balibar 2006). Universality is only made possible through the silencing and subordination of other voices and ideas. To return to the example of human security this chapter has started, with, human security is ultimately 'inhuman' (Neocleous 2011). I had also previously argued that security stands for a 'barred universality' inasmuch as security cannot sustain political practices of everybody being an equal partaker of security: 'closure and the creation of spaces of abjection are intrinsic to its practices. Security cannot remain open; it needs to draw boundaries between those who are to be secure and those who are endangering this security' (Aradau 2008, 162). Security is constitutive of boundaries and violence, whether those are materialized through more visible or more insidious practices.

This suspicion of universality means that many authors often revert to the terrain of particularity. Interestingly, the analyses of the 'logic of security' are often rendered in similar terms, as the imposition of universality (see e.g. Nunes 2012 and in this volume). The rejection of universality entails attention to particular voices, needs or silences, bearing in mind that '[u]niversals are effective within particular historical conjunctures that give them content and force' (Tsing 2005, 9). The language of security analysis is shifted on the terrain of particularity. At the same time, however, many critical security scholars have argued against the particular, locally-bound and temporally-defined exclusions that security practices enact. While security is intimately entwined with the project of modernity, its hegemonic universality is also open to contestation. Thus, many critical and feminist security scholars have attempted to reclaim, reconceptualize, civilize and redeploy security either in ways that reconstruct its universal appeal or in ways that make its universality more attuned to multiplicity and difference (Hudson 2005, Hoogensen and Stuvoy 2006, Tickner 1992, Wibben 2011b). Annick Wibben has argued that 'theorizing on the basis of everyday experience of gendered (and classed, raced, sexualized, etc.) subjects, inevitably provides for different kinds of security narratives than those traditionally told in the discipline of IR' (2011a).

In some of these debates, the reference to universality often disappears or universality appears to be rejected. Yet, as critical authors have long pointed out, the emphasis on particularity does not dispense with the question of universality. Universality needs to be particularized to take shape. Even when particularity is privileged, as universality is associated with totalizing totalitarianism or ahistorical imposition, the argument cannot remain simply in the realm of particularity. Rather, the argument seems to partake of an idea of what Judith Butler has seen as comprehensive universality, a supposedly 'more concrete and internally diverse "universality," a more synthetic and inclusive notion of the universal' (Butler 1994, 156). Particularism by itself does not contain the justification of why particular groups need to be included within the purview of universality. Why women's security rather than the security of racists? At the same time, universality as comprehensive form does not fully tackle the power relations that continue to persist between particular groups as universality is expanded.

Other critical security scholars see the universality of security as a terrain of struggle or what could be called in Ernesto Laclau's terms an 'empty signifier'.[4] The exclusions and violence that state security entails are indicative of a universal that can be challenged. For example, the 'indivisibility of security and human rights' can challenge the state-led implementation of human rights regime, the exclusion of political violence and structural inequalities (Dunne and Wheeler 2004, 9). Unlike the view of hegemonic universality or comprehensive universality, universality as empty signifier acknowledges both the particular embodiment of universality and the struggle that challenges this embodiment. In Laclau's terms, 'universalism as a horizon is expanded at the same time as its necessary attachment to any particular content is broken' (Laclau 1992, 90). Universality remains an empty signifier because there is no necessary connection to a particular embodiment. Any embodiment is the result of a process of hegemonization, which is less entrenched than Marxist critics assumed.

If states promise security to their citizens, yet fail to deliver or, moreover, create insecurity for their own citizens, particularizing the universality of security differently challenges the dominance of the state-based concept; hence the critical security studies' promise of expanding security to individuals as persons and individuals as citizens, trying to counter all forms of threat that those could encounter (Krause and Williams 1997). In this view, human security could be one of the attempts to hegemonize the empty signifier of security. Feminist security studies similarly argue for a definition of security in 'multidimensional and multilevel terms – as the diminution of all forms of violence' (Tickner 1997, 624).[5] The concept of security could in principle be re-appropriated for the benefit of those who are insecure, shifted from the state to individuals. This re-appropriation is possible only by virtue of the imaginary of security as a universal desire, a human possibility which is undermined by state practices as well as by other forms of domination and economic exploitation. It requires 'the growth of a cosmopolitan moral awareness such that we come to empathize with and respond to the sacrifices made by those fighting for basic rights in repressive regimes' (Dunne and Wheeler 2004, 19). At the same time, it requires an understanding and formulation of common humanity. In this approach, human security could be desirable, even a necessary claim in a world marked by continual violence. What differentiates some of these positions from those that reject security is the assumption of universality as either comprehensive or empty signifier and therefore a terrain to be occupied by other subjects through more or less struggle and contestation. Other readings of 'hegemonic universality' see it as inevitably carrying the traces of the dominant particularities and therefore being eminently inhospitable to any marginalized subjects who come to occupy the position of the modern subject to be protected.

So has this discussion of universality brought us back to an insurmountable rift, this time not between desecuritization and emancipation, but between three forms of universality? First, it seems to me that making visible the role of universality allows us to avoid easy accusations of liberal universality. Second, bringing universality under the purview of critical security debates allows us to avoid the unbridgeable gap that otherwise appears to plague critical security studies. For instance, in their introduction to *Critical Approaches to Human Security,* David Chandler and Nik Hynek (2011, 2–4) distinguish between approaches that analyse human security as a 'challenge to power' or as the 'reproduction to power'. Ultimately, there is no common ground between these two perspectives. It is also not clear how such opposed views can be sustained. It seems to me more productive to understand their disagreement as intrinsic to the paradoxes of universality.

What is missing in these approaches is an understanding of how paradoxes are tackled politically. This is the idea of 'inhabiting paradoxes' to which I will return in the next section. Stefan Jonsson has recently succinctly captured the stakes of this politicization of universality:

If there is today a global canon of universalism, it consists of documentary traces of past struggles in which oppression was resisted in the name of universal values. Like all canons, that of universalism is selective, and easily turned into a new instrument of oppression. Inevitably, every coding of universality is a particular representation. Universality, once represented, transforms itself into some more or less doctrinaire version of universalism, of which there exist a great number of varieties.

(Jonsson 2010, 118)

Jonsson opposes universality to universalism to delineate a dialectical position in which universality is neither immune to capture by power nor a mouldable tool of emancipation. I suggest taking these dilemmas seriously as indicative of the paradoxes of universality.

Paradoxes of universality

The approaches discussed in the previous section consider security largely either as a practice deployed in a device of power/knowledge (or that is deployed in the service of capital and to discipline the 'dangerous classes') or as a potentially transformative force in the international realm. The latter position sees security as a potentially comprehensive universality or as an empty signifier. Either a particular is a limited and only partial stand-in for the universal to the exclusion of other particulars or different particulars struggle over the empty terrain of universality. Critical security scholars would ultimately agree with Judith Butler's critique that the 'universalization of the particular seeks to elevate a specific content to a global condition, making an empire of its local meaning' (2000, 31). This means both that processes of universalization are needed to challenge particular hegemonic constructions and that they need to be continuously subjected to criticism 'to identify the "universalistic" roots of certain forms of oppression and subjection, or at least the roots of their legitimation' (Balibar 2012, 210). If universality is an inescapable element of political debates, engagements with universality presuppose a critique of both its conditions of possibility and its instantiation. A critique of security is implicitly a critique of the hegemony of universality. A critique of security is also a critique of particular regimes of power/knowledge in the name of universal claims.

Feminism has probably offered one of the most cogent critiques of the universality of security, either by taking issue with the abstract individual whose already given traits have been used to exclude women from the realm of humanity and/or citizenship or by concentrating on contestation and local struggles. When marginalized subjects have recourse to universal claims to challenge a security regime, it is important not to just focus on particular subjects but on how the relation between the particular and the universal is politicized in relation to security. Here, one's ally is the very tradition of feminist historiography and theory. Feminist engagements with the universal did not always amount to a wholesale rejection of universality as some of the security debates might indicate.

The feminist historian Joan W. Scott's work has explored the paradoxical relation that struggles for women's rights had with the universal. Drawing on an archive of eighteenth and nineteenth century feminist struggles in France, Scott shows that feminism and universality have been interdependent. Interdependence does not mean symbiosis but irreconcilable paradox:

> Feminist arguments were marked by the paradox of "sexual difference." When exclusion was legitimated by reference to the different functions and biologies of women and men, "sexual difference" was established not only as a natural fact, but as an ontological basis for social and political differentiation. "Women" came into being as political outsiders through the discourse of sexual difference. Feminism was a protest against women's political exclusion; its goal was to eliminate "sexual difference" in politics, but always on behalf of "women" (who were discursively produced through "sexual difference"). To the extent that it acted for "women," feminism produced the "sexual difference" it sought to eliminate. This paradox—the need both to accept *and* refuse "sexual difference" as a condition of inclusion in the universal—was the constitutive condition of feminism as a political movement throughout its long history.
>
> (Scott 1995, 6–7)

Scott's statement is particularly interesting for my purpose, as it raises the possibility of a different political engagement with universality. Women have to both accept a particular instantiation of universality in a historical conjuncture and reject it in order to resist domination, oppression and exclusion. She points out that women had both to refuse sexual difference and accept it to produce the voice of 'women'. If we analyse the production of the human within global regimes of security governance, Scott's insights might be helpful to understand political action against security. The acceptance of security means that we need to take seriously political struggles that take place on the terrain of security. Often, these struggles *both* accept *and* refuse security.

Refusing security means rendering explicit its hegemonic universality and the exclusions it leads to by taking seriously the struggles to move away from security. It is here, perhaps, one of the most difficult challenges for critical security studies. So far, we (and I count myself among the 'we') have either accepted or refused security. Critical security studies have shed light on security practices in the modality of 'either ... or ...': either national or human security; either state or pluralist political community; either security or politics. If one starts with the problem of universality, then 'politics out of security' might need to be rethought in the modality of 'both ... and ...'.

Etienne Balibar has similarly rendered the problem of 'ambiguous universality' as that of intensive or extensive universality (Balibar 1995). Extensive universality can be understood in similar terms to the comprehensive universality discussed here. Intensive universality makes visible the violence inherent to processes of universalization. Like hegemonic universality, intensive universality is embodied in particular subjects and institutes exclusion. At the same time, intensive universality makes possible resistance to these intrinsic exclusions. What makes these struggles different from a process of hegemonization of an empty signifier? For Balibar, this possibility resides in the traces of previous struggles. This does not mean that it is possible to differentiate between a true or false universality (Balibar 2007). In the terms of this chapter, it is not possible to draw the line between 'positive' and 'negative' security (Roe 2012). Rather, the problem of intensive universality draws attention to the struggles over the form and content of the universal. To make sense of how the relationship between universality and particularity can be thought of slightly differently, the final section analyses the struggles of Roma people against existing security regimes in France.

The Roma in Europe: securitizing dirt

France Defends Roma Expulsion Policy

(Davies 2010)

EU Says Monitoring France over Wave of Roma Expulsions

(Reuters 2012)

Italian Cities Plan to Shut Roma Camps

(Povoledo 2010)

New UNICEF Report Condemns German Policy of Deporting Roma Children
(Knight 2010)

Ireland Deports Roma after Stand-Off Over Roundabout

(Soares 2007)

This selection of titles could go on, as Roma deportations have made continual headlines after the end of the Cold War in Europe. However, since 2008, particularly given Italy's attempts to deport Romanian Roma, deportations raised simultaneous questions of human rights and security. As EU citizens, the Romanian Roma had the right to freedom of movement as any other citizens. These rights do not come without limitations – freedom of movement is allowed for a maximum of three months. Afterwards, citizens are expected to either be self-sufficient or find a job. However, in the case of Romania and Bulgaria, transitional arrangements mean that citizens from these two countries will not have access to many of the EU labour markets (France, Italy, Germany and the UK among others) until 2014. I want to approach this problem of deportations from the perspective of universality and security to understand how the Roma resist security by inhabiting the paradoxes of universality. The Roma reject a particular instantiation of security in the current historical conjuncture – the security of French, Italian or European citizens – at the expense of an internal exclusion – the constitution of the Roma as a 'dangerous' group. Visible in public spaces but also 'readily available for deportation' (Nacu 2012, 5) given their makeshift and marginalized settlements, the Roma have increasingly become the main referent of security discourses.

The securitization of the Roma in the European space does not rely on an explicit discourse of friend versus enemy. Rather, a whole series of connections are drawn between the Roma and a series of more or less minor 'illegalisms' such as theft, welfare fraud and cultural difference such as cleanliness and dirt. Rather than the more discussed accusation of criminality, I want to focus on the particular discourse of dirt and insalubrity that instantiates security in relation to a supposed universality of 'cleanliness'. In response to criticisms of the dismantling of camps in France, officials have argued that 'that conditions in the camps were "unsanitary" and that "tensions" with the local population had become "untenable"' (Human Rights Watch 2012). Similar arguments about both the security of the Roma and the security of political communities surfaces time and again in all the justifications of deportations, be those more or less voluntary. The security discourse about the Roma in Europe is a discourse of cleanliness. As Mary Douglas (2003) has shown, discourses of cleanliness and dirt and intrinsically connected with order and disorder, and the ordering of society.

What is interesting about the more recent French public discourse on camps and insalubrity is that it subtly shifts the discourse of emergency and security threat that had been formulated about the Roma by both the left and the right in Europe a few years before. Nando Sigona's remarks about the securitization of the Roma in Italy could be easily translated to the pre-2012 French context:

> The growing emphasis in the media and political debate on crime and security produced a discursive shift in the public discourse on the Roma and created the condition for the subsequent use of Prime Ministerial 'emergency' decrees to govern the presence of the Romani communities.
>
> (Sigona 2011, 602)

However, the 2012 election of the socialist François Hollande brought a humanitarian turn to this security discourse that created a continuum of insecurity-Roma-criminality-emergency. Manuel Valls, the Minister of Interior, repeatedly invoked the problem of insalubrity in the camps. The Roma, he argued, lived in inacceptable conditions (Cornevin 2013). Therefore, settlements were to be demolished and the Roma evicted. On the one hand, the reasons given were those of the protection of the Roma, their health and well-being. On the other hand, Valls admitted that the settlements 'are often located in the midst of working-class neighbourhoods and are a challenge to local community life' (Willsher 2012).

Against this smooth alignment of different security discourses, activists have made apparent in the case of France – as previously in Italy – the effects of the dismantling of camps for the lives of the Roma. Without any alternative accommodation, being tracked down by the police, under surveillance and under the threat of deportation, the camp inhabitants are either forced in even less secure and more insalubrious places or are forced to roam villages and towns for days on end (see Aradau *et al.* 2013). The dismantling of camps is also equivalent to the dismantlement of the forms of community and security that the Roma have created. Camps, Sigona reminds us, 'become a refuge, a place to find protection, where alliances and social networks may help to overcome the Roma deficiency in relation to citizenship and social entitlements' (Sigona 2005, 11).

Rather than a universal characteristic of humanity, cleanliness and salubrity are rendered as historically produced discourses, which depend on power relations and a whole series of exclusions. Insalubrity is produced through marginalization and exclusion from access to public services. In this first move, the hegemony of cleanliness in a purportedly universalistic discourse of security is resisted. Yet, a second interesting move takes place, in which universality is rendered as a terrain of conflict and struggle which makes apparent exclusion, while rearticulating salubrity and insalubrity away from discourses of security.

A 'cleaning day': inhabiting paradoxes of security

In trying to challenge the securitization discourse and its attendant practice of expulsion and repression, the Roma inhabit the paradoxes of universality. They both invoke cleanliness and by extension the security imaginary and reject its particular historical instantiations. To develop this argument, I draw on a documentary film, *Moulin Galant, La question rom,* shot by Mathieu Pheng in one of the Roma settlements in France (Pheng 2012). The documentary traces the struggles of the Roma, the relations with support associations and local authorities, and the mobilization to contest security.

The film opens with one of the representatives of a solidarity association (Association de Solidarité en Essonne) coming to the camp to explain to the inhabitants the 'rights' that they have according to European law. The explanations are given through a simultaneous movement of authorizing – 'the law is the law' – and of distancing – 'I don't like it, but there is nothing I can do'. A similar movement of authorizing and distancing is notable in the reaction of the local officials, who both claim concern for the Roma and the impossibility to respond to that concern given legal, political and economic constraints. Thus, one local mayor argues that the small villages ('communes') cannot take on the 'whole misery of the world' (Pheng 2012). They are too small to be left to deal with all these problems that the opening of borders has brought up. Interestingly, security practices emerge through withdrawal rather than through a sovereign institution of urgency and emergency. This situation is painfully captured in a blog written by a seven-year old Roma child, Marcel: 'The police say they follow orders; the prefect, Mr Carenco says he follows orders. Nobody is responsible, everybody follows orders. But who gives the orders? Who can give such a barbaric order to chase people day and night?' (Alain 2012). It is perhaps in this context of dispersion of responsibility that the accusations of a return to fascism ring true. Yet, for the purposes of this chapter, I want to focus on three moments in the film: one briefly renders a demonstration by the Roma and the solidarity association; the second is an encounter between the Roma, associations and local authorities to discuss insalubrity in the camps; the third is a 'cleaning day' in the settlement that brings together the Roma and friends of the Roma.

The demonstration takes place in a festive atmosphere. The Roma dance, talk about their problems and carry banners. The banners show different slogans such as 'No to expulsion' or 'We want to work'. The demonstrators chant 'No to expulsion'. One of the participants explains to an invisible spectator: 'we are human like you ... we cannot live like animals, like pigs [he shows the mud on his shoes] ... we have families'. The security discourse is replicated and simultaneously inverted. Insalubrious conditions are rendered as a condition for change that rejects expulsion and claims the right to work. The inversion is possible through the first claim to the universality of humanity: 'we are human like you'. The implication of 'we are human like you' is that the Roma should not be tracked down, chased, put under continuous surveillance. The problem of well-being, cleanliness and health which underpins the official security discourse is mobilized, while the repression it makes possible is rejected. The claim to universality to challenge the repression of security practices becomes evident in a second shot where the marchers chant the slogan of the French revolution 'Liberté, egalité, fraternité' (liberty, equality, fraternity). Taken together, the two moments of the demonstration show that there can be no humanity without the universal claim to be a political participant in the life of the community. If being human is reduced to health and cleanliness, then it buttresses a security discourse and its repressive practices. Here, health and cleanliness are invoked only to be displaced by the universality of the political subject, the citizen who gives herself the right to partake in politics or the 'right to have rights'.[6]

The second moment also problematizes the insalubrious conditions of the camps in discussions between the Roma, solidarity associations and local authorities. Officials do not deny the need to provide better conditions in the settlements. However, they link the provision of running water and toilets with the existence of a project of integration. Is there a project of integration, they ask, so that we can justify bringing running water and portable loos to the camps? Yet, as a representative of solidarity associations had pointed out earlier, local authorities had refused to remove rubbish from the illegal settlements and subsequently argued that insalubrity made these zones unliveable. The Roma 'problem' is framed around the materialities of daily life: running water, electricity, toilets, mud. In their absence, sending children to school becomes equivalent to a heroic exploit. Mothers carry their children on their backs so that children's shoes do not get muddy. Otherwise, their schoolmates laugh at them and the children do not want to go back. Families venture out on the road despite the risk of encounters with the police to fetch water daily. The security discourse of cleanliness reveals itself again as oppression. Anca Pusca has aptly observed that the Roma 'problem' in the EU is rendered as a 'space problem' (2010, 1), whereby the Roma are pushed to the margins of society, cordoned off and precariously tolerated in temporary settlements that point to a future elsewhere. Yet, resistance to marginalization does not translate only in architectural practices of building palaces, which have attracted the attention of authorities. The Roma resist marginalization by reclaiming the materiality of space and reformulating the imaginary of cleanliness in relation to being human.

The third moment depicted in the film challenges the security discourse through a form of collective action that recreates, I would suggest, cleanliness and dirt as political acts. Forms of practical solidarity are put in place, where the Roma and the association representatives decide on a strategy for managing the rubbish problem. The 'cleaning day' is prepared in advance in the camp and by the associations. The Roma mobilize all the inhabitants in the settlement to take part in the cleaning day. So do the solidarity associations. In a day, the Roma together with friends clean the camp and gather 2,500 garbage bins which they lay out by the road to be emptied. The rubbish is 'cleanly' lined up in rubbish bins. The 'cleaning day' thus turns the problem of security on its head. It does not reject the discourse of cleanliness and insalubrity, despite the dangers that this discourse has for politics in the settlements. It turns the security discourse on its head, by claiming particular conditions of existence and 'being human', and making visible a universal subject who can organize and be part of a political community. This is, however, not the liberal modern subject who is integrated in a predefined community. It is a collective subject who mobilizes in solidarity against a particular instantiation of the universality of security discourses.

Cleanliness is intrinsic to discourses of security, their orientalizing and hegemonizing logic. Yet, salubrity can also be part of the very possibility of political participation and visibility. The Roma render visible the internal exclusions of a hegemonic security discourse by refuting and reverting its logic. The insalubrity of the camps is produced by the practices of local authorities, lack of access to water and sewage, and refusal by public services to collect rubbish from the camps. In so doing, this paradoxical mobilization of the 'dirt problem' also brings back the question of responsibility inasmuch as the local authorities are now shown not to fulfil their duties towards the community. Why, one might rightly wonder, do they still refuse to dispose of the rubbish? The challenge does not pass unheeded by the local authorities, as the representatives of the solidarity association are called before the court as the 'cleaning day' is deemed to be against the law. Another demonstration follows this announcement. The Roma chant: 'Solidarity is not an offense. We are not criminals'. Ultimately, in these paradoxical movements between acceptance and refusal, between framing and reframing of universal claims to humanity, a different politics can be forged.

Conclusion

This chapter has rearticulated the problem of security in critical security studies by shifting the question to one of universality. Seemingly insurmountable differences in critical security studies are rearticulated to show the commonality of implicit or explicit assumptions about universality. 'Can security be for everybody?' This is a deceptively simple question, which has not so far received a satisfactory answer. Questions of desecuritization, emancipation and politics hover around this question.

Reformulating the problem of universality as a paradox has allowed me to think of political acts as 'inhabiting paradoxes'. Therefore, the contestation of security can be understood as a politics of 'both … and', both an acceptance and refusal of security discourse and practice. Critical security studies so far have privileged a model of universality that left little room for paradox. I started by unpacking three such forms of universality: universality as hegemonic, universality as comprehensive and universality as empty signifier. Assumptions of hegemonic universality are attentive to the power relations that undergird the security device and the reproduction of the liberal subject and its exclusions. Comprehensive universality moves rather quickly to an idea of an all-inclusive universality. Universality as empty signifier reintroduces the relations of power characteristic of hegemonic universality. In so doing, it is seen as as continuously transformed through historical struggles. Yet, universality is never empty as it bears traces of both hegemonic discourses and past struggles. Therefore, it is more productive to think of universality as a paradox and of the contestation of security as 'inhabiting paradoxes'.

To illustrate a politics of 'inhabiting paradoxes', the chapter turned to the so-called Roma 'problem' in the EU. It has drawn attention to the securitization of the Roma, not primarily through the creation of an inimical figure, but through more insidious production of cleanliness as a characteristic of humanity. Relegated to spaces of abnormality and abjection, the Roma are rendered insalubrious and by extension infra- or sub-human. Making these practices visible is, however, not sufficient for the contestation of security. How can the Roma lead their lives under these conditions? The rejection of security discourses of cleanliness is only a temporary move. It is a rejection that challenges its particular historical instantiation rather than simply drawing on a salubrity/insalubrity binary. Drawing on a documentary that traces the mobilization of the Roma in one of the camps in France, I have argued that the Roma make visible both the conditions of production of insalubrity and the need for some form of salubrity for their living conditions. In so doing, the contestation of security is a double movement: of simultaneous acceptance and rejection.

Post scriptum

The contestation opened by the double movement of 'inhabiting paradoxes' does not depend on the success or failure of political action. Rather, it is the act of inscribing and politicizing humanity that creates politics out of security. On 28 March 2013, the settlements at Moulin Galant were evacuated by the French authorities (Agence France Presse 2013).

Notes

1 Veronique Pin-Fat has shown that realist, cosmopolitan and communitarian approaches in IR are also committed (or 'seduced' in her language) by the notion of universality (2009). Unlike Pin-Fat, I do not think universality can be eschewed or

that it is a matter of 'seduction'. Universality is intrinsic to political action. Hence, the de-linking of security and universality has obscured politics.

2 See Nunes in this volume for a critique of the logic of security. In my view, the 'logic of security' can be more productively understood as a historically dominant and entrenched practice.

3 See Stefan Jonsson's (2010) article, which traces some of these arguments.

4 For Laclau, an empty signifier lacks a signified and it cancels all difference by creating 'equivalential chains' (1996, 39). See also the chapter by Juha Vuori in this book on security as 'master signifier'. Vuori does not discuss, however, the 'empty' element or the particularity of a Laclau-inspired analysis of master signifiers.

5 With usual insightfulness, Carol Cohn offers a slightly different reflection on 'feminist security studies', arguing that we need to 'think hard about what we really mean by security, or whether "security" is even an adequate rubric for our concerns' (2011, 584–5).

6 See Aradau *et al.* (2013) for an analysis of the 'right to have rights' in relation to Roma politics in Italy.

7 The political limits of desecuritization

Security, arms trade, and the EU's economic targets

Thierry Balzacq, Sara Depauw and Sarah Léonard

Introduction

This chapter argues that desecuritization, defined broadly as moving issues "out of the threat-defense sequence into the ordinary public sphere" (Buzan *et al.*, 1998: 29), can produce security predicaments. In fact, although there is little agreement in the literature over how desecuritization can be achieved or even what it means, most scholars concur that desecuritization *ought* to be sought on the grounds that it would normatively be better than securitization. This stance can be traced back to Wæver, who has emphasized his preference for desecuritization over securitization *ceteris paribus*, while also acknowledging that the latter may have some advantages:

> In some democratic perspective, "desecuritization" is probably the *ideal*, since it restores the possibility of exposing the issue to the normal haggling and questioning of politicization, but if one is actually concerned about something, securitization is an attractive tool that one might end up using – as a political actor.
> (Wæver, 2000: 251; emphasis added; see also Wæver, 1999: 335)

Unfortunately, the qualifier "probably" has been lost, so much so that it has become something of a "doxa"[1] to assume that for the Copenhagen School desecuritization is normatively superior to securitization. Thus, despite differences in what desecuritization betokens, there seems to be a widespread conviction that it should be sought. Various arguments have been put forward to support this claim. First of all, some argue that desecuritization is more effective than securitization. In an earlier work, Wæver himself (1995: 57) suggested that "desecuritizing politics (…), I suspect, would be more effective than securitizing problems." Several scholars have also privileged desecuritization because, so the argument goes, securitization leads to secretive and undemocratic decision processes to deal with them. Grayson (2003: 340) argues, for instance, that desecuritization is to be preferred to securitization as he notes that

> [the] temptation to securitize issues, thereby establishing (…) crystal-clear policy directives for ourselves, must be avoided. Although human security

agendas may broaden the range of issues under the rubric of security, this should be done to prioritize them within the bounds of normal politics while leaving policy open for discussion and constant scrutiny.

Recently, however, some scholars began to highlight that desecuritization is not necessarily without its problems. For example, MacKenzie (2009) suggests that the desecuritization of female soldiers in post-conflict Sierra Leone has been problematic. The reintegration of female soldiers has been seen as a "return to normal" and has thereby been neglected as an important dimension of the transition process, whereas demobilized male soldiers have been securitized. As a result, those have received considerably more attention in peace-building efforts and programs, while female soldiers have been relatively neglected. To some extent, this is not surprising, although this has not been outlined to date, as it mirrors the argument in the securitization literature that one of the advantages of securitizing an issue is that it gives it prominence and moves it upwards on the political agenda (Elbe, 2006). Conversely, desecuritizing an issue has the effect of downplaying its importance or urgency, which may also have negative effects in certain situations.

In this chapter, using the EU's policy in the liberalization of arms trade, we attempt to demonstrate that desecuritization can produce heightened security problems. The argument unfolds as follows. In the first part we examine the dominant cleavages among techniques of desecuritization addressed in the literature. In the second part, we explicitly examine the feasibility of desecuritization as such. Our discussion of this feasibility resonates well with the existing literature (cf. Roe, 2004; Jutila, 2006; Hansen, 2012); what is less traditional is probably our claim that desecuritization can create more security problems, than is often assumed. We show in practice how and why this happens.

Models of desecuritization: cleavages and convergences

Three distinctive sets of questions can be discerned in desecuritization scholarship: the first relates to "what" is desecuritization; the second focuses on "why" desecuritize; the third is concerned with "how" to desecuritize. The concept of desecuritization in critical approaches to security means different things to different scholars. For Wæver (1995, 2000) it refers to the restoration of routine procedures of politics. For Huysmans (1998a) desecuritization is the "unmaking" of the institutionalized threatening representation of public problems. Finally, Claudia Aradau (2004) holds that desecuritization is about the questioning of a naturalized "regime of truth" just as much, if not more, as it is about the desirability of a specific kind of politics.

While an important starting point for the study of desecuritization, however, definitions by themselves explain relatively little, as regards the conditions of possibility, and the techniques for desecuritization. One can emphasize, either symbolically or metaphorically, one set of questions at the expense of the other. Yet in doing this, one inevitably reduces desecuritization either to its justification or, in contrast, to the strategies which make it possible. Each results in significant obstacles to tracing practices of desecuritization. In general, however, when actors attempt to desecuritize, they often have reasons to do so and they do so in ways of their choosing. In brief, there is a fundamental co-dependency between the "why" and "how" questions. For instance, in an attempt to justify his "preference" for desecuritization, Wæver (1995: 57) laments: "We do not find much work aimed at desecuritizing politics which, I suspect, would be more *effective* than securitizing problems."[2] In fact, he surmises, "in some democratic perspective, 'desecuritization' is probably the ideal, since it restores the possibility of exposing the issue to the normal haggling and questioning of politicisation" (Wæver, 2000: 251). Thus, desecuritization is primarily a strategic device which strips issues of their security-ness and sets them back into the political realm. Against this view, Huysmans (1998a) denounces Wæver for studying desecuritization in "instrumental," "utilitarian" terms, while it is primarily a transformative practice. This is so, he insists, because Wæver reduces desecuritization to a matter of management, i.e., a strategic alternative of "relocating" problems from the security sector to the political sector. Although he concedes that Wæver's view is an important analytical advance, Huysmans disapprovingly notes that it falls short of granting desecuritization the full normative status it deserves in critical approaches to security. In this context, the main purpose of Huysmans's work is to redress this shortcoming. In short, his view integrates, but transcends Wæver's in that it calls for a radical enactment of politics.

A pioneer in the study of desecuritization, Jef Huysmans builds on – if not against – Carl Schmitt to establish the pervasiveness of the political significance of security and the normative mantle of desecuritization. For Huysmans, three strategies dominate desecuritization, the confusion of which can be a source of ambiguities: the *objectivist* model favored by realists, the *constructivist* technique of genealogists, and the *deconstructivist* strategy that he advocates. The objectivist model of desecuritization was long regarded as the orthodoxy. It confines desecuritization to counter-arguments aimed at disabling a securitizing discourse: "the objectivists will try to convince people of the fact that the migrant is not really a security problem. The strategy comes down to teaching the natives that migrant is not dangerous" (Huysmans, 1998a: 65). This usage of desecuritization reflects a realist division between objectivist and subjectivist views of security, as it aims at substantiating the argument, based on evidence, that something is not "really" a threat, but rather the sheer product of a subjective perception (Roe, 2004: 286). The problem with this objectivist position is that it can easily be countered by the argument that "it runs the risk of strengthening what it seeks to weaken: the securitized migrant and the xenophobic and racist reaction to him/her" (Huysmans, 1998a: 66). Thus, one could more accurately refer to this as "counter-securitization" in Aradau's (2004: 399) terminology. The second, constructivist strategy refers to understanding how issues become part of a "security drama." In this respect, desecuritization is grounded upon a heuristic imperative: grasping the internal mechanisms of the social construction of threats.

The third and final strategy turns the arrow of desecuritization in a different direction, emphasizing the restructuring of the world, through a sustained recounting of the story. Following this path to desecuritization means, to simplify a bit, assuming that the world can be "handled" differently.[3] Huysmans (1998a:67) puts it thus: "This strategy builds on the principle that to tell a story is to handle the world." In other words, he adds, the deconstructivist agent is "a story-teller who supposes that, by telling a story in a particular way, he/she contributes to the production and reproduction of the social world; telling a story is considered as an action inside the world which helps to structure it." Thus, desecuritization is meant to produce a distinct "signification of social relations," in the sense that it debases the current "register of meaning" of specific "security formations" (Huysmans, 1998b: 228).

The merit of Huysmans's approach to desecuritization depends to a great extent on how he articulates theoretical sophistication with actual, empirical concerns. The salience of desecuritization will be higher, Huysmans (1998a:588) argues, if a "political aesthetic of everydayness, which literally "absorb(s) security problems in a more general political narrative," could be effectively pursued. From that perspective, desecuritization does not stem from an objectivist strategy, but from creative political narratives that characterize "the public, political sphere in terms of the complexity and plurality of daily human practices" (ibid.). In other words, students of desecuritization need to observe and examine all those routine encounters that make up the intricacies of political communities.

The "aesthetic of everydayness" is not without problem, however. It pertains essentially to the dual, but incompatible functions (securitizing and desecuritizing) of the politics of everydayness. Leading the charge, Aradau (2004: 400) contends that desecuritization should not succumb to the misleading appeal of everyday life because, so the argument goes, "everyday life is also necessarily linked with the reproduction of hegemonic life." What is questioned, in other words, is the ambivalent feature of everydayness, which at once de-securitizes and legitimates securitization. Is not "securitization ... only successful when it finds supports in everyday life, when even the facts which at first sight seem to contradict it start working in its favor" (ibid.)? On this account, however, the "politics of aesthetic of everydayness" paradoxically serves the logic of particularization that it is supposed to dissolve. In short, the politics of everyday life may pursue important goals, says Aradau, but its intrinsic tensions, and vulnerabilities to prevailing securitizing hegemonic representations undermine its desecuritizing stamina.

Another important criticism leveled by Aradau targets the attempt to collapse emancipation with security (Booth, Wyn Jones). For her, this obliterates the discriminatory practices that the logic of security entails. Aradau's solution combines Jacques Rancière and Etienne Balibar's verdict against non-democratic politics of securitization. The claim is that a different treatment of emancipation is necessary for desecuritization, as democratic politics, to obtain. One virtue of this view, according to Aradau, is that it removes emancipation from security and links it to democratic politics. On this account, "emancipation activates a different logic based on universal address and recognition ... It disrupts the exclusionary logic of security and, at the same time, furnishes a principle upon which a new relationality with the other can be conceived" (Aradau, 2004: 401). This falls naturally within the transformative way of desecuritizing, because it institutes a new intersubjective relation embedded in democratic politics, not security, values (e.g., equality, fairness, transparency, etc.). Thus, desecuritization seeks to transform the register of meanings which previously organized the interactions among people. The objective, ultimately, is to contextualize subjects of security and set up a new "regime of truth." By countering the merely analytical character of desecuritization-as management, Aradau opens a whole new domain of enquiry traditionally overlooked. How, in practice, can security be unmade?

This is where Lene Hansen (2012) provides an original voice to the issue. In distinguishing four strategies of desecuritization – stabilization, silencing, rearticulation and replacement – Hansen builds on the extant empirical data to establish the varieties of political-normative spaces wherein desecuritization operates. To start with, *stabilization* is a "slow move out of an explicit security discourse" (Hansen, 2012: 539). It is expected that, thanks to interaction, the image of the phenomenon will evolve and eventually change. The second form of desecuritization, *rearticulation,* comes closest to Huysmans' "unmaking" or "deconstructivist" strategy, as it designates a process whereby an issue might be cast in new terms. *Replacement*, on the other hand, involves, as the name indicates, the substitution of one issue by another. Morozov (2004) supplies intriguing evidence to back this argument. He demonstrates that Russian desecuritization of the Baltic states was possible because the discursive structure of the war on terror eclipsed the menace of the Baltic states as "false," anti-Russian Europe (Morozov, 2004: 318). A similar view can be found in Andreas Behnke's (2006) discussion of Aradau's attempt to overcome the exclusionary impetus of security. He argues that "states ... continuously securitize issues and actors ... At some point, certain "threats" might no longer exercise our minds and imaginations sufficiently and be replaced by more powerful and stirring imageries" (Behnke, 2006: 65). Basically, the replacement thus consists of two simultaneous processes: some issues are desecuritized while others immediately "climb up the scale of securitization" (Aras and Polat, 2008: 502). In this light, it is probably difficult to fully desecuritize an issue, when speech is used. In fact, to Behnke (2006: 65), an issue becomes a non-security problem through the absence of discourse about its status. Put otherwise, "we need to see (or hear) nothing to suggest that an issue has been desecuritized" (Aras and Polat, 2008: 498–99). Finally, *silencing*, the fourth and final strategy of desecuritization, refers to explicit moves to avoid using the language of security. It should be noted, however, that there are two uses of silencing in securitization theory. On the one hand, silencing is a strategy that aims to "pre-empt or forestall securitization" (Wæver, 2000: 254). In this light, silencing prevents issues from being converted into, and treated as security problems. On the other hand, silencing is an *ex post* strategy which strives to take problems out of the security domain.

Scholars tend to disagree over whether securitization is feasible and under what conditions. However, they seem to converge around the view that there

Table 7.1 Two ways of de-securitizing

Management way of desecuritizing	Transformative way of desecuritizing
1. Constructivist	1. Deconstructivist
2. Analytical	2. Political
3. Instrumental	3. Normative
4. Objective: relocating the issue into a different functional sector or bestow it with another functional status	4. Objective: changing the nature of the issue itself
5. Argumentative processing of different images of the issue	5. Practice-oriented processing embedded in a new 'regime of truth'
6. Re-interpreting security	6. Unmaking security
7. Principle: regulating registers of meaning	7. Principle: dissolving registers of meaning
8. Logic: Outside-in	8. Logic: Inside-out

are many forms of desecuritization, which they claim differ on various points, including their rationale, objective, relation to politics, underlying drivers and logic. In the literature, the number of types of desecuritization varies from two to four. Obviously, it is not the number that matters, but the extent to which each conveys something important about desecuritization. Our suggestion is that the insights gleaned from the existing scholarship enables us to sort out two ideal-typical categories of desecuritization, management and transformative, as Table 7.1 shows. If placed on a matrix, the two categories will be on the x-axis while the categories developed by Hansen would be on the y-axis. This enables us to reconcile the ideal-types developed by Hansen, on the one hand, and the different types proposed by Huysmans and Aradau, on the other hand.

In our model, then, stabilization and replacement are primarily managerial strategies for desecuritization, while silence is essentially a transformative technique. Finally, rearticulation can be both managerial and transformative. Although they are interactive, management and transformative approaches to desecuritization present different features. A form of problem-solving, in the Frankfurt School's vocabulary, the management way of desecuritizing is fundamentally meant to relocate the security issue into a functional different sector. Empirical data suggests that it is the most used scheme of desecuritization; but it is also the one that raises more feasibility problems. Because of its conceit that prevailing security issues can be dissolved, the second, transformative way of desecuritizing is an attempt to overcome the exclusionary logic of security by unmaking hegemonic registers of meaning.

This figure is not meant to establish an absolute distinction between the two broad strategies of desecuritization; nor is it pretending that "out there" we have pure forms of any of the two strategies at play. Here, we only suggest that, in some cases, it is possible to identify activities which take more or less the shape of one of the two types. The section focuses on the operation and consequences of desecuritization-as-management. It highlights the conditions under which this form of desecuritization can lead to security problems. We do this by examining the EU's attempt to desecuritize arms trade within the borders of the EU.

The European Union and the balance of securitization/ desecuritization

This section illustrates the theoretical argument laid out above that, under certain circumstances, desecuritization can provoke serious security problems. To this purpose, we discuss a major policy development in the European Union, namely, the liberalization of the arms trade in order to strengthen the EU defence market.

Arms trade policy

The arms trade internationally gained salience from the end of the Cold War. Due to the increase of intra-state conflicts, the concern about the spread of small arms and light weapons (SALW) has developed rapidly since the mid-1990s. In the aftermath of the attacks of 11 September 2001, the focus shifted to proliferation of arms and the risk of possession of weapons of mass destruction (WMD) by non-state actors. The international community identified controls of trade in conventional weapons and dual-use items[4] as one of the key aspects in the fight against terrorism. Export control is seen as a preventive instrument that can help to reduce the risk on armed conflicts, the proliferation of WMD, and terrorist access to WMD-related material (Flemish Peace Institute, 2007).

Also the European Union (EU) put arms export controls at the top of its security agenda. In the European Security Strategy, proliferation of WMD is identified as "potentially the greatest threat to our security"… "the most frightening scenario is one in which terrorist groups acquire weapons of mass destruction. In this event, a small group would be able to inflict damage on a scale previously possible only for states and armies" (European Council, 2003). In its report on the implementation of the European Security Strategy, the European Council states that the risk for proliferation of WMD by both states and terrorists has even increased in those five years (European Council, 2005). Borrowing from Buzan *et al*, the European Security Strategy illustrates very well how proliferation of the arms trade is being securitized and presented as an "existential threat" (Buzan *et al.*, 1998: 23–24).

However, apart from its security purpose, arms export controls also form part of trade policy. Export control policies set the conditions under which trade in arms is allowed. Both on the national and the European level, arms trade policy is institutionally situated at the crossroads of trade and foreign policy.

The ongoing swing towards liberalization of the defense market leads to the question whether the initial security objectives are being undermined. The chapter highlights the delicate balance between security ambitions and economic aspirations in a policy area where both economic and security interests are at stake, and where one may jeopardize the other. Will the EU counterbalance recent initiatives for the liberalization of its defense market with a stringent European arms export control regime that prevents illicit arms trade? In other words, is the European arms trade policy an illustration of the EU as a security actor or does it reveal how the EU as an economic player outweighs the EU as a security actor?

European policy on arms export controls cannot be isolated from its broader armament policy and current developments on the defense market. The first part of this section outlines the context of European arms export controls, which is necessary to understand further developments. The following parts describe the development of a European arms export control regime for dual-use and military goods and illuminates the scattered institutional setting of arms export controls. Finally, the European defense package is being discussed. This document contains two proposals for directives that have far reaching consequences for the harmonization of European defense markets and the liberalization of arms trade.

Development of a European arms export control regime

Regulating arms export controls is about deciding what goods should be subject to restrictions in respect of which destinations and under which conditions (Davis, 2001: 82). Export control policies are mainly regulated and implemented on the national level (except in a case like Belgium where the competence has been delegated to the federated entities).

Before looking into the European export control regime, it is important to mention the distinction that is being made between trade in military equipment and trade in dual-use items. Both are subject to export controls and both types of export controls have the same objective: the prevention of destabilizing exports that might contribute to armed conflict elsewhere or threaten peace and security on the European continent. Military equipment are goods (including components of these goods) that are specifically designed for military purposes such as small arms and light weapons, battle tanks, artillery systems, military aircraft, and others. Not only equipment is being controlled, also the technology necessary for the development, the use or the maintenance of military goods is placed under control. Dual-use goods on the other hand, are not specifically designed for military use. These are products that are primarily intended for civil applications but might also be used for military purposes. Dual-use products are generally perceived as less sensitive. However, they may constitute a vital part of military equipment, including weapons of mass destruction. Electronics, navigation systems, nuclear reactors, compressors, certain types of vacuum pumps, natural occurring viruses and chemical products sold in industrial quantities are typical dual-use goods that are intended for civil purposes, but might be employed in military applications and are therefore to be controlled. The EU has adopted both a common list of military goods and of dual-use items that are placed under control on the EU level.

Control on trade in military equipment

The first steps towards a common European policy on the arms trade were taken at the European Council meetings of Luxembourg and Lisbon in 1991 and

1992, in the aftermath of the second Gulf War. This war was a painful example of inadequate national control policies. The denial of exports to Iraq by some states for reasons of international security achieved very little, given the export practices of other Western states such as the UK, Germany, France and Italy and other major arms suppliers in the former Soviet Union and China. Therefore, in 1991, the enthusiasm among likeminded Western states for tighter export controls increased (Ian Davis, 2001: 90).

In response to this war, the European Council adopted a "Declaration on non-proliferation and arms exports" in which it expressed its concern about the uncontrolled spread of weapons and military technologies. The heads of state and government listed eight common criteria, derived from a comparison of national policies on arms exports, and expressed their hope that "in the perspective of Political Union, on the basis of criteria of this nature a common approach will be made possible, leading to a harmonization of national policies" (European Council, 1991). This document served as a starting point for a more comprehensive EU Code of conduct on arms exports which was elaborated by COARM, the Council Working Party on Conventional Armaments, and adopted by the Council of Ministers on 8 June 1998.

The European code of conduct on arms exports (CoC) was the most far reaching cooperation between states on export controls of conventional weapons. The code encompassed eight criteria, which served as guidelines for the evaluation of applications for export licenses, and twelve operative provisions which specified how to implement the code. The code of conduct took form as a Council Declaration under the Common Foreign and Security Policy (CFSP) – it contained political commitments but was not legally binding (Bromley, 2008). In December 2008, ten years after its adoption, the Council reviewed the code of conduct and adopted the text as a common position, which is a legally binding instrument still under the second pillar.

The criteria, as they are written down in the common position, are rather general in nature. Taking into account the human rights record of the country of final destination, the preservation of regional peace and security, compliance with international commitments such as arms embargoes, the risk that the proposed export might be used for internal repression or the technological and economic capacity of the recipient country to "absorb" the imported weapons are some examples of criteria against which the legitimacy of arms exports should be judged.[5] Member states are required to assess exports of military goods that are adopted on the European list of military material against these European standards. The criteria were meant to lead to closer alignment of member states' arms export control policies (Davis, 2001). The decision whether or not to issue a license remains however a political judgment in the hands of national governments. There are several examples of export applications on which European governments came to different conclusions. One famous case is the decision of the Belgian government to export machine guns to Nepal in 2002, a country in civil war at the time, while three months before, a similar export of machine guns to Nepal was denied by the German government based on the risk of internal repression (criterion 2) and for fuelling existing tensions and armed conflict (criterion 3). The Belgian government on the other hand, justified its decision by emphasizing the Nepalese government's legitimate right to maintain domestic order (Holm, 2006).

The operative provisions on the other hand, have more tangible outcomes. With the aim of preventing unequal competition within the European defense markets, a consultation mechanism between member states has been installed to avoid "undercuts." Undercuts are deliveries by one member state after the deliverance of essentially the same goods was denied by another member state, as shown in the Nepal case. Undercuts illustrate the discrepancy in interpretation of the criteria among governments. National governments are also required to circulate annual reports on their defense exports and on national implementation of the CoC. Since 1999, at the insistence of NGOs, the European Parliament and the Finnish Presidency, a consolidated version of these national reports has been publicly available (Bauer and Bromley, 2004). Ever since, the quality of the European report has improved and the transparency of arms exports by European member states increased due to this European impetus. Another outcome of the operative provisions in the CoC is the publication of the European list of military goods which serves as a basis of products to be controlled in all member states. The operative provisions constituted the primary means to enforce the code. The transparency that was created by the annual report and by the notification procedure increased the pressure on member states to implement the criteria in a faithful manner (Holm, 2006: 215).

Control on trade in military goods forms part of the CFSP. Governments have been reluctant to transfer competence on exports of military equipment to the European level, and thus to transfer the export control policy on these goods to the former first pillar. It even took years before the Council agreed to transform the code of conduct to a legally binding common position. Especially France has been unwilling to upgrade the status of the document and linked the adoption of a common position to the controversial lifting of the EU arms embargo against China. In view of the liberalization of the internal market for trade in military equipment, it was no longer tenable to obstruct the adoption of a common position on arms exports. During the French Presidency in the second half of 2008, France radically shifted its position and used its role as EU president as a window of opportunity to put the adoption of the common position on the agenda.

Control on trade in dual-use goods

Parallel to the search for common grounds for a harmonization of arms export controls with regard to conventional weapons, discussions on a common policy for exports of dual-use goods started in the Commission. With a view to the completion of the internal market and considering that controls on trade in dual-use items within the EU could only be eliminated if all member states established effective controls based on common standards for exports to non-EU countries, the Commission submitted a proposal for a Council Regulation in August 1992.

On the basis of this proposal, the Council established on 19 December 1994 an arms export regime for dual-use goods consisting of a Council Regulation (first pillar) on the one hand that outlined how the regime would work and Council Decision (second pillar) on the other that contained the more strategic decisions of lists of controlled goods and countries of destinations (see infra) (Schmitt, 2001). The regime entered into force in 1995. In July 2000, both the regulation and the decision were replaced by one regulation (1334/2000) reforming the regime for the control of dual-use exports. Export controls on dual-use items are now fully part of community legislation under the first pillar. Dual-use items circulate freely within the internal market, except for a list of sensitive items (e.g., products to be used for nuclear technology) for which stricter controls apply. For exports of dual-use products adopted on the list of controlled goods to destinations outside the EU, a license is required. The regulation stipulates which type of products, for export to lists of destinations should be subjected to particular types of licenses. The regulation however did not create an EU licensing authority. Member states remain therefore the implementing bodies that assess the technical and political aspects of export licenses for dual-use goods (Remacle and Martinelli, 2004: 115).

Scattered institutional setting

Arms export policy falls simultaneously within the fields of competition and foreign and security policy, with different degrees of integration. It is both an intrinsic part of commercial policy, which lies within the exclusive competence of the European Union, and at the same time belongs to the intergovernmental Common Foreign and Security Policy (CFSP) of the EU. Moreover, the European policy on arms trade in both its commercial policy and CFSP leaves much discretion to the member states.

From the beginning, the blurred character of export control on dual-use items has caused vagueness on whether it forms part of the EU's exclusive competences or not. Indeed, the original dual-use regime was based on two different legal instruments: Regulation 3381/94, based on Article 133 and thus falling within the Common Commercial Policy, laid down the basic principles for export controls and administrative cooperation between member states. Those elements that were of a strategic nature however, were considered to fall under national jurisdiction of the member states and remained in the former second pillar (CFSP). Lists of dual-use items and destinations were drawn up under Joint Action CFSP/94/942 (European Commission, 2004). As such, the ability of the member states to define their security interests remained intact. ECJ case law has put an end to this ambiguity. The existing Regulation 1334/2000 was adopted following two decisions of the European Court of Justice in 1995 which affirmed the exclusive competences of the European Community in the area of external trade in dual-use items (European Commission 2006a). The dual-use Regulation 1334/2000 is based on Article 133 of the EC Treaty[6] and now entirely belongs to the Common Commercial Policy (Anthony 2001: 627–628).

The second contested aspect is the exclusion of trade in military goods from the functioning of the internal market. Article 296 of the EC Treaty (currently Art. 346 TFEU) allowed member states to invoke their security interests to exempt armaments from the internal market. Art. 296 b:

> any Member State may take such measures as it considers necessary for the protection of the essential interests of its security which are connected with the production of or trade in arms, munitions and war material; such measures shall not adversely affect the conditions of competition in the common market regarding products which are not intended for specifically military purposes.

According to the EU member states' interpretation of Article 296, matters related to the production and trade in armaments have therefore been excluded from EC law and remained under their national jurisdiction.

However, the Commission challenged this broad interpretation of Article 296 by member states and issued a communication on the application of Article 296 in which it states that

> uncertainty persists regarding the scope of Article 296 TEC, which allows member states to derogate from Internal Market rules when their essential security interests are at stake. Since the dividing line between defense acquisitions which concern essential security interests and those which do not is vague, it is not always clear which rules should apply [...]. In consequence, the application of Article 296 TEC remains problematic.
>
> (European Commission, 2006b)

In an attempt to create greater openness in European defense markets, the Commission adhered to a strict interpretation of Art. 296. Based on case law, the Commission stated that

> Article 296 TEC does not introduce an automatic exemption in the field of defense [...]. The objective justifying the exemption is only the protection of a member state's *essential security interests*. Other interests, in particular industrial and economic interests, although connected with the production of and trade in arms, munitions and war material, cannot justify by themselves an exemption on the basis of Article 296 (1)(b) [...]. Article 296 TEC is only applicable in clearly defined cases. It is the member states' prerogative to define their essential security interests and their duty to protect them. However, as guardian of the Treaty, the Commission may verify whether the conditions for exempting procurement contracts on the basis of Article 296 are fulfilled.
>
> (European Commission, 2006b)

This interpretation challenged member state practice so far, which excluded all trade and procurement in military equipment from the rules of the internal market.

The Commission made a case to move arms trade out of the protected security area of member states to the regular common trade policy of the EU, at least partially. A process of desecuritization of arms trade was established.

In December 2007, backed by legal arguments and heavily supported by the defense industry, the Commission launched two proposals for directives that transfer intra-EU trade in military equipment and defense procurement from the second to the first pillar. As such, EC law would cover trade in military equipment, subjecting the European defense market to a common legal framework. These two guidelines and an accompanying communication are known as the European defense package. Both directives were adopted by the European Parliament and the Council by mid-2009.[7]

Liberalization of European defense markets

The European defense package consists of two proposals for directives that lift regulation on arms exports and defense procurement[8] from the national to the European level. Regarding arms export controls, the directive aims at liberalizing trade in military goods within the EU. Intra-EU trade in defense-related products is not exempted from licensing, but the licensing system is to be simplified, which will significantly ease the administrative burden both on the government and the defense industry. This means that national control over weapon transfers within the European Union will become less stringent. In summary, the Commission proposed to replace the current system of individual licenses, whereby an individual license is required for each transaction, by a system of general[9] and global licenses[10] allowing one license to cover several transactions. The export of military goods to countries outside the European Union is not covered by this directive: such exports will continue to be regulated by national legislation with an individual license requirement. The liberalization of arms trade within the EU is thus not accompanied by common rules for exports to non-EU countries as is the case for trade in dual-use items.

In principle, the Commission could have gone further and propose to make intra-EU trade in military equipment free, similar to trade in dual-use. The Commission stated however that free trade in military goods is politically not feasible: "with a common foreign policy still at an infant stage and uneven levels of trust concerning the watertightness of certain external borders, promoting a licence-free zone would clearly go beyond what is politically achievable in the present context" (European Commission, 2007b: 24). Indeed, despite the European common position on arms export, the decision on whether or not to export military goods to destinations such as Israel, Saudi Arabia or Chad differs considerably among member states. Each government weighs political considerations against economic opportunities and finds its own compromise.

The Commission, the European Parliament and the Council agreed on a compromise text for both directives on defense procurement and intra-EU trade of military equipment. In accordance with the co-decision procedure, the proposals were adopted in the Spring of 2009 (May and July). As soon as the directive on intra-EU trade will be fully implemented,[11] defense companies will no longer be required to apply for individual licenses for transfers of military equipment to other member states. They will be able to make use of global and general licenses for intra-community trade, that cover several transfers within the EU. The directive will bring about a liberalization and simplification of the licensing system, and will reduce administrative costs for both the industry and the national governments. The licensing authorities of member states remain competent to set criteria and issue legislation to control export of military equipment to non-EU countries. While arms will circulate more freely within the EU, trade with third states remains untouched.

Control on end-use

The most crucial consequence of the directive concerns the control on end-use and on the final destination of military goods. Before the adoption of the directive, national licensing authorities examined for each license application the political situation in the countries of destination to which the military goods will be sent, as well as their end-use. An exporter should specify on the license application form both the country of the buyer and the country of final destination. The country of the buyer or the initial country of destination is the first country to which the goods are being sent. Often, the first destination of the goods is a defense company in another country, where they will be assembled into bigger weapon systems. Obviously, the defense company is not the final end-user of the goods, so if known, also the client of the finalized product in which the goods will be integrated is being taken into account. An example will make clear why all these actors are important to be taken up in the licensing process. In Belgium, the Flemish government decided not to export military equipment to Israel's military forces because of risks, among others, for regional stability and human rights violations. However, because of economic benefits, the government does approve exports of military goods to the defense industry in Israel, as long as they will be re-exported to a final destination outside Israel (usually the United States). Both the first and the final destination are thus taken into account and influence the government's final decision.

However, with the directive on intra-EU trade in military equipment, member states will lose substantial control on transfers of defense equipment to other EU member states, which might be re-exported from there to a final destination outside the Community. Already today, there is no common practice among member states to what extent the responsibility for exports to third countries is being transferred to other member states. Cases where one member state exports military goods to a defense company in another member state where the goods will be integrated in military products destined for a final user in a third country, have given rise to heated political debates. In Belgium for example, the Flemish government approved a license for export of military goods via the UK with end-use in Saudi Arabia, which was previously denied because of the political situation in Saudi Arabia. A new minister argued in this case that the responsibility for export to Saudi Arabia is being transferred to the UK (because of trust among member states), and decided no longer to take the final destination of the goods into account. Yet, not all member states are so confident about the export control policy of other member states. Countries such as the Netherlands or Sweden declare that the final end-use and final destination of the goods are taken up in the Dutch/Swedish licensing assessment, regardless of the status of the first country of destination. These countries will have difficulties to uphold this practice in a liberalized European defense market.[12]

A watertight European export control system where common standards and a common application of these standards are guaranteed when military goods are exported outside the European Union, would offer a valuable alternative to the national control of member states today. However, so far, no such system has been put in place.

Desecuritization of the arms trade

The question rises how the Commission succeeded in convincing member states to transfer sovereignty over intra-EU arms trade to the European level?

First, market imperatives called for a common European regulatory framework in order to guarantee equal competition for defense companies in European defense markets. An internationally organized defense industry with holdings and production sites based in several countries is strongly hindered by a fragmented legal framework that poses national export restrictions to trade. The globalized defense market gave rise to growing calls from industry for more coordination of arms export policies in order to facilitate cross-border cooperation (Bromley, 2008: 5). Lower trade barriers for intra-EU trade in military goods were deemed necessary in order to remain competitive in relation to other defense markets, in particular the US.

Second, a harmonized export control regime improves security of supply of European defense products for member states (European Commission, 2007a: 2). Since many, especially smaller member states have lost a sustainable autonomous national defense industry, their dependence on other states for supplies of defense-related equipment increased. The development of a European defense market creates trust among member states and compensates for the loss of national autonomy.

Finally, the Commission convinced the European Parliament and the member states that the liberalization of the arms trade does not entail a security risk. Since export of defense material to European member states hardly ever poses a risk for security and stability within Europe, these exports were almost never refused (15 refusals in 2003,[13] no single refusals since 2004). Since the risk for peace and security of intra-community trade is low, economic barriers to protect peace and security can be lowered as well, according to the Commission. Moreover, the Commission explicitly links the liberalization of intra-EU arms trade to the European Security and Defense Policy by emphasizing the need to build up a European defense market and a European defense capacity for the implementation of CSDP (European Commission, 2007b: 30). Indirectly, the liberalization of the arms trade contributes to the maintenance of peace and stability because of its utility for the development of CSDP. The discourse of the European Commission appeared successful. Whereas trade in military equipment used to be excluded from the internal market because of essential security interests, intra-EU trade in military goods is now no longer perceived as a security issue and forms part of the common trade policy of the European Union. If desecuritization means that "issues are moved out of the threat-defense sequence into the ordinary public sphere" (Wæver, 1989: 29), the transfer of intra-EU trade from CFSP to the Common Commercial Policy is a clear example of desecuritization.

Whereas desecuritization is commonly perceived as a positive evolution since it puts aside the defeatism of labelling social, economic, environmental and other problems as "threats," desecuritization in the field of arms trade is less favorable. Desecuritization of the arms trade might lead to a situation where economic imperatives prevail over security considerations, and where the security ambitions of the European Union and its image as a normative power will be seriously undermined.

In lieu of conclusion

While acknowledging the need to develop a European defense market, the current initiatives of the Commission risk to outbalance the crucial equilibrium between economic considerations and security concerns in the field of the arms trade. Steered by economic imperatives, a process of desecuritization set in, in a field that used to be, and is supposed to be, critical to the security policy of member states and of the EU as a whole. While the European Union promotes the adoption of international standards for arms trade in third countries and on international fora, it fails to set up a European export regime for arms trade where these European standards are applied in a uniform and consistent way.

When arms trade within the EU is transferred to the Common Commercial Policy, without transferring the competence on arms exports to countries outside the EU accordingly, illicit arms traders might benefit from the absence of a European legal framework and search for the weakest link in the export control policy of EU member states. If internal borders for the arms trade are being broken down, external borders should be strengthened by establishing a truly common policy on arms exports. The adoption of the common position under CFSP is a step in the right direction. However, having the status of a intergovernmental instrument, there are hardly any means to enforce a faithful implementation of these common standards. The text of the common position on arms exports remains too vague to ensure a shared interpretation of the criteria and a closer alignment of member states' arms export policies. Moreover, the sovereignty of member states is preserved and there is no European body that ensures a shared assessment of sensitive arms deals.

Even for trade in dual-use items, where both internal and external trade have been transferred to the exclusive competences of the EU, there is no common export policy. Today, the regime constitutes little more than a common framework for licensing procedures. There is no European licensing authority, no shared interpretation of common standards, nor a joint assessment of the political situation of the countries of destination. De facto, only a truly Common Foreign and Security Policy can shape the necessary conditions for a common export policy. The European Commission, however, is reluctant to take up a role in this regard.

If no closer alignment of member states' export policy will be reached, the loss of national control on arms trade will lead to a relaxed arms trade control policy where responsibility is being transferred and accountability is unsure. The liberalization of the internal defense market should be balanced by common security guarantees to prevent European defense products from destabilizing other regions in the world. The EU should not only be concerned with a flourishing European defense industry, but also with the question where these European defense goods are destined for. The liberalization of the European defense market might not pose a direct security risk to peace and security within the EU borders, but it raises the risk for peace and security outside the EU.

Notes

1   In Pierre Bourdieu's (1991: 68) words, the "doxa" is "all that is accepted as obvious, in particular the classifying schemes which determine what deserves attention and what does not."
2   Emphasis added.
3   Did Wæver (2000: 284) not argue that desecuritization is "situational, oriented to the *handling* of specifics"? Emphasis added.
4   Conventional weapons refer to military equipment (excluding WMD) whereas dual-use items are products that can be used both for civilian use and for military use, including in WMD (cf. infra).
5   In summary, the criteria include (1): respect for international commitments of the member states, (2) respect for human rights in the country of final destination, (3) internal situation in the country of final destination, (4) preservation of regional stability and peace, (5) the national security of the member states, (6) behavior of the buyer towards the international community, in particular its attitude towards terrorism, (7) the risk that the equipment will be diverted or re-exported, (8) compatibility of the arms exports with the technical and economic capacity of the recipient country.
6   Art. 133 EC Treaty describes the competences of the Commission and the Council in the area of the European common commercial policy.
7   Directive 2009/43/EC of the European Parliament and of the Council of 6 May 2009 simplifying terms and conditions of transfers of defense-related products within the Community, Official Journal of the European Union, 10 June 2009, pp. 1–36. Directive 2009/81/EC of the European Parliament and of the Council of 13 July 2009 on the coordination of procedures for the award of certain works contracts, supply contracts and service contracts by contracting authorities or entities in the field of defense and security, Official Journal of the European Union, 20 August 2009, pp. 76–136.
8   By introducing the directive on procedures for government procurement in the field of security and defense, the Commission aims to create a tailor-made legal framework to facilitate the harmonization of defense procurement. Currently, most member states do not handle defense contracts according to the general Treaty provisions and EC

legislation relating to procurement, but apply specific national procedures adapted to the special nature of defense deals. As a result, procedures vary widely among the member states. This lack of uniformity is an important obstacle to a unified defense market and goes against Treaty principles, especially the principles of transparency, non-discrimination and equal treatment. With a view to more open competition, the Commission issued common standards for defense procurement in order to streamline national policies in this regard. In this chapter, we will however not go further into the subject (Flemish Peace Institute, 2008).

9 A general license is a license issued by a member state which states that a specific product, or a list of products can be transferred to other member states by all companies on the member state's territory. For the transfer of these products, exporters are not required to apply for an individual or global license.

10 A global license is a license that allows a specific company to transfer a list of products to a list of countries of destinations. Contrary to general licenses, an exporter still needs to submit an application for a global license.

11 Directive 2009/43/EC should be in force (by national law) after 30 June 2012. It takes time however to implement the new licensing system in practice, e.g., because all defense companies making use of the new general licenses are required to get certified. The actual implementation proved to be more cumbersome than expected and the degree to which the new licensing system is already in use differs among member states.

12 Although a provision has been adopted in the proposal for a directive to accommodate this problem by offering the opportunity for member states to attach export restrictions (for exports to third countries) to issued licenses, it is unlikely that member states will use these export limitations but in exceptional circumstances.

13 These refusals concerned exports destined for the three Baltic States at a time when these were not EU members. The licenses were refused with reference to criterion 7 of the EU code of conduct, the risk of diversion and re-export.

8   Just and unjust desecuritization

Rita Floyd[1]

Introduction

The ethics of security is an intrinsic component of non-traditional/critical security theory with scholars routinely reflecting on the meaning and value of 'security as a state of being' (Herington, 2012: 11). The ethics of securitization, whereby security is understood as 'a set of social or political practices' (ibid.) is less developed, largely perhaps because the majority of securitization scholars seem convinced by the logic that desecuritization is – as the Copenhagen School (CS) of security studies would have it – 'the optimal long-range option' (Buzan *et al.*, 1998: 29).

In part inspired by problems inherent to desecuritization as a normative strategy, including the fact that it works only when objective existential threats (OETs) are ignored;[2] that desecuritization has more varied outcomes than the CS suggests; but also by the idea that being secure and thus security are actually positive things, some scholars have set out to theorize positive security/securitization (Roe 2012, 2008a; Hoogensen, 2012; Nunes, 2012; McDonald, this volume). While I too initially argued in terms of positive securitization (Floyd, 2007), more recently – inspired by the just war tradition – I have suggested that we ought to think in terms of just securitization and identify criteria that determine the *just resort* to securitization and *justice during* securitization (Floyd, 2011). My tentative list of criteria proposed in that same article, has since evolved into an extended version of a theory of just securitization, which I shall henceforth refer to as Just Securitization Theory (JST).

JST differentiates between morally permissible and prohibited securitizations only, in other words it is concerned with what securitizing actors are permitted to do, not with what they are morally required to do. For the purposes of JST, securitization is defined as the move from normal politics to exceptional security practice. My criteria determining just securitization are as follows:[3]

Just resort to securitization

1   There must be an objective existential threat to a referent object, which is to say a danger that – with a sufficiently high probability – threatens the survival of either a political or social order, an ecosystem, a non-human species, or a group of human beings.

2   Referent objects are entitled to defend themselves or are eligible for defensive assistance if they are morally justifiable. Referent objects are morally justifiable if they meet human needs, defined here as necessary components of human well-being. *Political and social orders* need to satisfy a minimum level of basic human needs. *Ecosystems* and *non-human species*, in turn, need to make a contribution to the human needs of a large group of people. *Human beings* are justifiable referent objects by virtue of being intrinsically valuable; all other referent objects therefore have instrumental value derived from the need of human beings. Note, however, only sufficiently large groups of human beings warrant protection by securitization, while morally wicked groups of people, even if sufficiently large, render themselves liable to being secured against.

Together criteria 1 and 2 make up the *just cause* for just securitization. Although vital the just cause alone does not determine just resort to securitization, instead it also includes also

3   The right intention for securitization is the just cause. The securitizing actor must be sincere in his or her intentions to protect the referent object they themselves identified and declared.
4   The good gained from securitization must be judged greater than the harm securitization is expected to entail or ultimately entails; and the only relevant good for proportionality is the good contained in the just cause.
5   Securitization should not lead to more insecurity than it aims to solve, and from the options available the one that causes, or is expected to cause, the least insecurity should be chosen.

Justice during securitization

6   The response must be appropriate and should aim to address the objective existential threat that occasions securitization only.
7   The response must cause, or risk, the least amount of harm possible and at the same time do less harm than there would be if securitization were abandoned.
8   Offenders and suspects detained as part of securitization must be treated humanely at all times.

These criteria highlight that what can be known and theorized in JST is significantly removed from the CS's securitization theory, while JST also operates with a different understanding of securitization (see below). Moreover, unlike the CS I openly advocate an objective moral standpoint; specifically I hold that human well-being is the highest moral value and as such determines whether something is worth defending. Human well-being can be located by measuring the relative satisfaction of two basic human needs – autonomy and physical health – which apply to all humans everywhere and are distinct from culturally specific goals (Doyal and Gough, 1991; Mulgan, 2001: 173; Floyd, 2011: 434).

JST is aimed simultaneously at scholars and practitioners of security. Thus the aim behind JST is to devise a theory that enables scholars to morally evaluate securitizations both before and after they have occurred,[4] and one that can guide the actions of security practitioners in relevant situations. In short, JST is a normative not an analytical theory. Of course, the possibility of abuse of such a theory is real, yet what Mark Evans has remarked of just war tradition also holds in this context: 'the propensity for misuse cannot itself be a reason for rejecting it' (Evans, 2005: 7).

More than most Ole Wæver has always been acutely aware of the possibility of abuse. The fact that the concept of societal security is easily abused by extremist groups to further their own ends is one of several realizations that have spurred his commitment to desecuritization (Floyd, 2010: 27). Despite the latter, securitization theory is not a normative theory but first and foremost an analytical theory (Taureck, 2006). Thus, the CS does not aim to bring about desecuritization; they merely anticipate that scholars can, by pointing to the negative outcomes of securitization 'help (in a truly Machiavellian sense) practitioners to pursue more enlightened policies' (Wæver, 1999: 337). So in the end, the CS would not be averse to having what I explicitly want – the prince's ear. While what the CS and I would have to say would be quite different, it is important to realize that the message of JST is not that securitization is good. JST is merely informed by the idea that sometimes even the use of extraordinary emergency measures is at least morally permissible because some values are worthwhile defending. The goal of JST then is, to paraphrase the just war theorist Brian Orend (2006: 31) to restrain both the incidence and destructiveness of securitization.[5] As such JST stands comfortably alongside the other strategies of contesting, or perhaps better, containing security featured in this volume.

Intellectually the idea that a set of criteria determines the morality of securitization is close to just war tradition where a set of criteria determines the morality of war (e.g. Walzer, 1977; Orend, 2006; McMahan, 2009). Lately just war traditions's often century-old criteria determining both *jus ad bellum* (just resort to war) and *jus in bello* (just conduct in war) are increasingly considered incomplete without a corresponding set of criteria that determine what should ideally follow war's ending. Many just war theorists now suggest criteria for *jus post bellum* (just peace), which may include criteria on rights vindication, compensation and rehabilitation, discrimination and punishment (Hayden, 2005: 169). I suggest in this chapter that JST remains incomplete without a set of criteria determining how securitization should ideally be terminated.

Empirical evidence suggests that securitization can change over time (Vuori, 2008). This can take different forms, for instance, the threat-narrative can alter, the security response can change as securitization proceeds, and/or the referent object of security can change. Change in securitization is perhaps most acute when securitization has become institutionalized, which is to say when the justification for securitization is no longer articulated and therefore no longer subject to public scrutiny. These changes to securitization over time pose a particular challenge to the concept of *just securitization*, as at once just securitization *can* easily become unjust as a result of change. In cases where the threat-narrative alters over time, for instance, securitization risks losing its once just cause. The ideal resolve of (just) securitization is just desecuritization. For that, however, we need to know what just desecuritization looks like. I propose that there are three criteria that determine the justice of desecuritization. They are as follows.

Justice after securitization

1   Timing: desecuritization of just securitization must occur when objective existential threats have been neutralized, whereas desecuritization of unjust securitization must occur immediately.
2   Action: security language and security practice should be terminated in full and with immediate effect.
3   Long-term aim: desecuritizing actors should avoid renewed and/or reactional securitization by building a stable desecuritized state of affairs.

Desecuritization is just when the three criteria are fulfilled at the same time with the caveat that desecuritization of just securitization can occur and might still be just, prior to the neutralization of the OET. Thus not even the existence of OETs *necessitates* recourse to securitization; it merely permits it. If securitizing actors find a way to address any given OET without continuing with securitization then that desecuritization might still be just. Colin McInnes and Simon Rushton, for example, argue that the UN is gradually desecuritizing HIV/AIDS 'because [...] securitization is not the only way of getting attention [the realization is rather that] 'developmentization' may work too' (2011: 16). Part of the point of criterion 1 of just desecuritization is to specify the final point in time when desecuritization of just securitization must occur; once this point is surpassed even a just securitization becomes unjust, because securitization cannot be just in the absence of a just cause. This observation reveals a crucial difference about the prescriptions or imperatives informing just securitization and just desecuritization respectively. While both are part of my wider JST (in the same way as just peace is part of many just war theories), just securitization is about what securitizing actors are permitted to do, while just desecuritization is about what desecuritizing actors are required to do. This shift from moral permissibility to what is morally required, is a function of the fact that while securitization is rarely morally required,[6] desecuritization is morally required in the absence of a just cause for securitization, because no securitization is morally permissible in the absence of a just cause.

This chapter is structured as follows. I begin by examining the meaning of the key terms securitization and desecuritization. I propose that desecuritization is best understood as an action or a sum of actions as opposed to a state of affairs. In short that it is a process not an outcome. By drawing parallels to just war tradition I then discuss why just desecuritization can be achieved independently of the nature of the preceding securitization. After briefly considering who can desecuritize, I go on to develop my criteria that determine just desecuritization.

The criteria are illustrated using empirical examples wherever possible. I then consider and refute three possible objections against what is proposed here. My conclusion highlights three insights gained into desecuritization that are relevant for securitization studies more generally.

What is securitization?

Given that desecuritization cannot exist independently of securitization (Roe, 2004: 284ff.; Aradau, 2004: 405ff; Hansen, 2012: 5–7), it is necessary to explain the meaning of securitization in the specific way this term is used in JST. From the point of view of social constructivism, there are very good reasons to hold that the meaning of securitization lies not in a particular course of conduct (notably on whether actors adopt extra-ordinary measures as part of their response to a threat), or on the involvement of particular actors (e.g. traditional practitioners of security such as the military or the police), but in its usage (Ciută, 2009). Or to be more explicit, we can say that the meaning of securitization depends on whether securitizing actors consider what they are doing in response to a securitizing move – which is performative only insofar as securitizing actors utter either a *warning* to an aggressor or offer a *promise* for protection to a threatened referent object, but by itself is no more than a the statement of intent[7] – as securitization (Floyd, 2010: 53). However, because practitioners (including but also beyond traditional practitioners of security) will disagree on what they mean by securitization, we are left with a very wide definition of securitization, i.e. securitization is ultimately what actors make of it. A wide definition of securitization is advantageous for security studies, as it allows security scholars to capture widely different dynamics, while securitization theory can then be used to explain lots of different things and occurrences in world politics. A wide definition is, however, a problem for a moral theory of security as is JST because in order to say when something is morally justifiable we need to know what that something is, and for that it has to be more concrete then simply 'what actors make of it.'

While securitization takes many forms, it is also the case, however, that not all of them throw up moral questions in the same way. For one thing not all securitizations have the same degree of impact on the world and people around them. The CS has long been aware of this which is why they are interested only in securitizations that involve the breaking of rules (Buzan *et al.*, 1998: 26), or in other words in securitizing moves that result in exceptional security practice. JST too is concerned only with securitization in its exceptional form. All this begs the tricky question what is the exception? As far as states are concerned many security scholars – including the CS – follow the Schmittian logic of executive unilateralism (see Neal, 2009; Williams, 2003). JST rejects this understanding of exception; instead it takes inspiration from the work of legal scholars who in the context of the war on terror have done much research into the nature of emergency politics. Among other things they contest the notion of the executive being above the law in emergency politics and argue instead that 'in order to overrule common law in a period of emergency, Parliament must pass new laws explicitly stating what the government can do. In this way, the rule of law is preserved, rather than suspended' (Sarat, 2010: 7; see also Feldman, 2010; Dyzenhaus, 2010). Consequently, we might say that – as far as states are concerned– the exception refers not to the suspension of law altogether, but rather to the situation when new laws are passed, and/or (new) emergency powers are granted that seek to govern the emergency, all of which are deemed permissible, including by an independent judiciary only in the context of the threat.

So far so good, as the CS has shown, however, sufficiently organized and powerful societal groupings united by a strong enough 'we – feeling' (Wæver *et al.*, 1993) also can revert to a course of conduct that can only be described as securitization. Unlike in the context of states where we have a reasonably clear idea of what counts as the procedure of normal politics, and consequently what counts as exceptional security practice, outside of concrete empirical examples, it is hard to say what counts as exception as far as non-state actors are concerned. In the end 'the exception' here might just be whatever most reasonable persons would agree constitutes exceptional measures mostly in terms of the amount of harm, risked/caused or intended and/or the level of violence employed. While this definition might be a bit sketchy, what matters is that securitization is not solely the domain of states, because non-state actors too can do things as part of defence most people involved in that securitization would otherwise not tolerate, but consider permissible in the context of the threat.

What is desecuritization?

Desecuritization is normally understood as the reverse of securitization, in Jef Huysmans' (1998c) words it is 'the unmaking of securitization'. According to the CS, desecuritization leads to politicization defined broadly as the state of affairs whereby 'an issue is part of public policy' (Wæver, 2003: 10). To put this differently, in this context politicization refers to an *outcome*; whereas elsewhere in the CS's framework it refers to a *process*, namely when it describes how non-politicized issues become matters of politics. If one accepts that only official political authority is decisive of whether something is politicized, it is possible to argue that desecuritization may *lead* to either the situation where the former security issue is depoliticized or to the situation where it continues to be part of official politics (Floyd 2010; Cui and Li, 2011). Depending on a whole host of issues either outcome may be deemed morally right or wrong. With reference to the environmental sector of security I have suggested elsewhere that environmental problems require political solutions and that therefore 'in almost all cases, desecuritisation as politicisation is morally right, whereas a desecuritisation as depoliticisation is morally wrong' (Floyd, 2010, 186).[8] While this may work for the environmental sector, problems with this approach become apparent as soon as we consider other sectors of security and other securitizing actors than states. In the first instance, in the absence of formal political authority it might be hard to say when something is not politicized, because everything that is not securitized can be said to be politicized. Second, even when we circumvent this problem and say, as I do here, that once desecuritized a former security issue is politicized if it remains on the political agenda of former securitizing actors or an equivalent agent (i.e. new leadership of an existing political group); whether or not this is preferable in any given situation is ultimately issue-dependent and quite possibly beyond the grasp of further theorization. In the societal sector, for instance, indefinite awareness of difference between ethnic groups formerly engaged in conflict (overt or otherwise) might be counterproductive and could lead to renewed tensions between parties. In the context of theorizing the role of forgiveness and reconciliation for a just peace, Andrew Rigby highlights this danger when he writes:

> Whatever new memories and interpretations of the past are created in the process of forgiveness, they are formed on the basis of the old. Under certain circumstances these deeper memories can resurface, resurrecting the old resentment, bitterness and the desire to avenge the past crimes and injustices suffered at the hands of the historical enemy.
>
> (2005:188)

In short in security sectors other than the environmental sector, continuous political attention to the former security issue may not be beneficial to keeping the peace.

Finally when desecuritization is defined exclusively in terms of its outcome, we cannot say anything meaningful about its ending. Sixty years after the end of WWII in Europe, for instance, are we still living with desecuritization right now or have we moved on? Given that desecuritization can lead to the situation where the former security issue is either politicized or depoliticized, at best we can know with certainty that desecuritization is not simply over when an issue has become depoliticized. Auspiciously, however, any attempt to evaluate the morality of desecuritization *exclusively* in terms of outcomes risks misunderstanding the meaning of desecuritization. Thus desecuritization is not an outcome or a state of affairs, but rather it is a sum of actions[9] which is to say a *process* (e.g. it involves the unmaking of security practice) that has a *desecuritized state of affairs* as its outcome. In the latter, a former security issue can be either politicized or depoliticized, and quite naturally for different issues one or the other may be better. As Figure 8.1 shows by means of either re-securitization or re-politicization a return to securitization is possible from both.

The ideal outcome of just desecuritization is a desecuritized state of affairs where actors objectively are, and subjectively feel secure to the extent that a return to the original securitization (for short: renewed securitization) and/or securitizations that seek to either counter, or are triggered by desecuritization (for short: reactionary securitization) are unlikely. This claim is of course quite different from Wæver's suggestion that desecuritization leads to a-security which he defines as 'a situation [...] simply not phrased in these terms, it is not a question

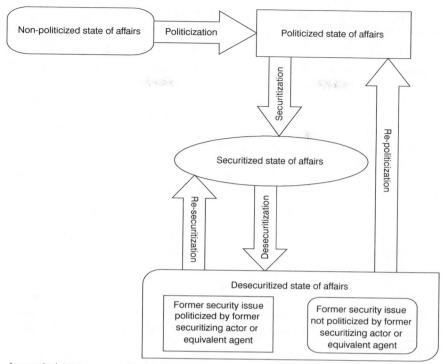

Arrows depict processes and textboxes outcomes

Figure 8.1 Progression and difference between processes and outcomes in relation to politicization, securitization and desecuritization

of being secure or not and there is not a perception of existential threats being present' (2003, 13). The idea that desecuritization can and should lead to basically human security is built on the assumption that there is a difference between the practice of security and the condition of being secure (Herington, 2012; Nunes this volume; Balzacq this volume). Securitization can lead to (human) security (for example, if real threats are neutralized) but it can also lead to insecurity (notably it can lead to the security dilemma). Especially if desecuritization is unjust it can, for instance, eventually lead to certain groups of society feeling disadvantaged, unforgiving and even insecure and securitizing moves on the part of these groups are likely.

Finally, thinking about desecuritization as a sum of actions also allows us to specify an end point of desecuritization. Thus using this definition, and instead of focusing on the outcome of desecuritization only, we can now know with certainty, for example, that desecuritization after WWII in Europe is long over, as here a desecuritized state of affairs has long been the norm.[10] To summarize, understood as a sum of actions, desecuritization becomes a short-time event that can be identified, studied and morally evaluated.

Does just desecuritization need to follow from just securitization?

If desecuritization is the unmaking of securitization, one issue that becomes relevant in our aim to morally evaluate desecuritization is whether the nature of the prior securitization influences the nature of desecuritization. Or in other words, can just desecuritization follow from an unjust securitization? A short excursion into the just war tradition is instructive here where the analogous question of whether a just peace can follow from an unjust war is contested. Some are adamant that only victors of just and lawful wars have the legitimacy to forge a just peace. Indeed, for Orend a just peace is an 'ethical exit strategy' for contesters of just wars only (Orend: 2002, 56). Extrapolating from Orend it could be argued just desecuritization can follow only from just securitization. Alex Bellamy has pointed out, however, that *not* separating 'just war' and 'just peace' produces 'counter-intuitive outcomes'. In the case of the Iraq war, for example, 'it would mean that the only just course of action would be immediate withdrawal of allied forces' (Bellamy, 2008: 622). When, in Walzer's terminology a 'just occupation', featuring rebuilding, investment and the training of police seems the better and more just alternative. This is not to suggest that a just peace can retrospectively justify an unjust war, but only that actors who have done wrong in the past can make amends and do the right thing subsequently. For this same practical reason we might then also want to consider the justice of desecuritization separately from the justice of securitization.

Who can desecuritize?

Some scholars, including in the present volume (see chapters by Blanc, Piazza and Vuori), suggest that desecuritization as resistance is an option open to a wide range of actors, not only to securitizing actors. Juha Vuori, for example, has argued that desecuritization can be thought of as resistance which is to say, 'as a counter-strategy or-move to securitization' (2011a: 191). An 'act of desecuritization' as resistance, for him, sees the relevant actors proclaim that 'we no longer accept (X is an existential threat to Y)' (Vuori, 2011a: 191). By way of illustration he provides the example of protestors in the failing GDR who through the slogan 'we are the people' no longer accepted that the West posed an existential threat to the people of the GDR, which in turn lead the ruling SED party to accept defeat (Vuori, 2011a, 207 FN16). However, Vuori also conceives of desecuritization as an 'active performative [...] as terminating the institutional facts of a securitized issue' (Vuori, 2011a: 191). And he stresses that although desecuritization moves can be articulated by anyone, 'the success of desecuritization may depend on actors with sufficient formal or other socio-political capital to perform or promote desecuritization' (Vuori, 2011b: 119). All this suggests that desecuritization is subject to similar power dynamics as is securitization. Accordingly, anyone can utter a 'desecuritizing move' – and, say, resist against any given securitization – but only some actors will have sufficient socio-political capital to, as Vuori puts it: 'terminate institutional facts' (Vuori, 2011a: 191). How this should ideally be done, is the subject of this chapter.

Three criteria for just desecuritization

1. Timing: desecuritization of just securitization must occur when objective existential threats have been neutralized, whereas desecuritization of unjust securitization must occur immediately

One important function of just desecuritization is to limit a just securitization from transforming into an unjust securitization. Securitization can only ever be justifiable if it is temporary, which is to say limited in time to the duration of the injustice that occasions it. Moreover, any securitization can *hope* to be just only if it addresses an objective existential threat (OET) to a morally valuable referent object of security. This follows that the natural, and simultaneously the final, point in time when just desecuritization of just securitization must begin is when the OET has been neutralized. It also follows that unjust securitization is to be terminated immediately in cases where there is no OET. While, for example, in cases where securitization is unjust because of the nature of the security response, the latter must at once be transformed into a just response, or else securitization must be abandoned and desecuritization must commence.

To understand this first criterion of just desecuritization it is important to remind ourselves that OETs are threats to the survival of actors, orders and other entities regardless of whether they are recognized as such. A standard way of assessing OETs rests with (a) examining an aggressor's intentions[11] (by comparing and contrasting what they say with their *immediate* actions[12]), followed by (b) capability assessment. Yet there are some situations which clearly are, or can be, objectively existentially threatening without someone actually 'doing the threatening'. Such intent-lacking threats[13] have come to the forefront in particular in the context of global environmental change and pandemics. JST cannot exclude securitizations of intent-lacking threats as unjust simply on the grounds that there is no aggressor intent on harming.[14] Here the possibility of harm needs to be gauged in other ways. The nature of threats originating in the environmental sector (which includes issues of health security) have the advantage that their presence can be determined by comparing research from the natural sciences with research from the social sciences (e.g. on state failure and infringement of basic human needs satisfaction). In the case of global climatic change, for example, research from within several natural sciences disciplines has conclusively suggested that climate change is man-made, already occurring and predictions on what is likely to happen in ecological terms if temperature increases by varying degrees have been provided. Together with research from the social sciences on livelihoods, vulnerability, the possibility of violent conflict and state failure it has been possible to generate a fairly clear picture of thresholds that when crossed will turn climate change into an OET to, for example, the state. A first attempt of this is offered by Joshua Busby who has identified conditions under which climate change poses a real threat to national security, including when 'it threatens the country's monopoly on the use of force, [or when it] leads to such catastrophic short-run loss of life or general well-being as to undermine the government's legitimacy' (Busby, 2008, 477). Similar thresholds would have to be developed for climate change as a threat to human security.

Moving on, we need to think about the point when such threats have been neutralized and about how we can know that this is so. Again things are a little easier where aggressors are at the source of such threats. Thus such threats are no longer real when a (former) aggressor no longer intends to do harm. To observe a change in intentions it will be necessary to examine whether an aggressor's language has changed and, because language alone is not conclusive of intent and can be changed for the purposes of deception, we need to examine also if his or her behaviour has changed. A good example is provided by the IRA during the lengthy Northern Irish peace process which did not only abandon threatening language, but also gradually as the peace process matured, disarmed.

Threats are also no longer real – here in a sense of not being credible – when an aggressor no longer has the capabilities to follow-through with a threat. For example, a terrorist organization that fails to recruit manpower because people no longer believe in its cause is likely to be unable to mount a credible threat.

In the case of an intent-lacking OET it is more difficult to establish when it has been neutralized. In the case of global environmental change, for example, there is no comparable point at which such threats suddenly are no longer threatening. Rather this is likely to be a gradual process. Although never securitized the case of the Ozone Hole demonstrates that once action is taken on an environmental issue it will take time for the damage to be reversed. This has implications for when to desecuritize. Thus if things improve as a result of security measures taken then such measures cannot simply be disbanded at the first sign of success (i.e. gradual shrinking of the Ozone Hole) but should continue until the threat is fully neutralized.

2. Action: security language and security practice should be terminated in full and with immediate effect

If desecuritization is the unmaking of securitization and if, in turn, securitization consists of speech act plus relevant security practice (exceptional action taken by the securitizing actor or someone instructed by the same) to that threat then desecuritization must consist of both the reverse of security language and security practice. Things are, however, not quite so straight forward. In the first instance, there is, as Lene Hansen has put it no 'desecurity speech act' (2012, 6) and more often than not former security concerns vanish quietly from political agendas. Ideally therefore when something is no longer a threat this should be publicly announced in the same way (most) securitizations are announced. Some analysts (e.g. Behnke, 2006: 65) would hold against this that desecuritization is 'logically impossible [as declaring something no longer a threat] would be invoking the language and logic of security' (Hansen, 2011: 6). While this objection might be a challenge to original securitization theory which believes in the securitizing force of language, it has no bearing on my framework where this logic is explicitly rejected, and security speech by securitizing actors amounts to no more than a warning and/or a promise (Floyd, 2010: 53–54).

There is good reason to believe that a public announcement of the onset of securitization is beneficial to the cause of just desecuritization, this much can be extrapolated from the work of mainstream constructivists who have found evidence that a hypocritical – which is to say an 'intentionally deceptive moral stance' (Lynch, 2008: 170) – public commitment to certain internationally accepted standards of behaviour (norms) can be turned to a force for good in world politics, specifically, into real commitment to the cause. This may happen in the following way:

> If –and only if– a public sphere exists which can make compelling demands upon states to redeem their rhetoric, normatively orientated critics can work to force great powers to live up to their strategically chosen rhetoric. Holding the powerful to their public commitments opens up possibilities for the weak to exercise power over the strong by shaming them with their own words.
> (Lynch, 2008: 175; see also Schimmelfennig, 2005: 157)

Extrapolating from this it seems to me that in democracies at least, the general public can hold desecuritizing actors to their commitment to desecuritization even if the relevant desecuritizing actor was insincere.[15] For that to happen, however, a public statement on desecuritization is required which is why a public announcement of the intention to desecuritize is considered important here.

A change of language or the end of the threat-defence narrative is of course only one part of any successful desecuritization; the other – and, given my definition of securitization, ultimately more important part – is the termination of security practice. In particular, just desecuritization requires the complete and immediate termination of all measures taken in response to a threat, which – it is vital to remember – actors are permitted to take only in the presence of a just cause. This is important, because as Andrew Neal has recently convincingly shown when the first emergency fades that legitimized exceptional security practice, desecuritization is not guaranteed, but rather 'emergencies become normalized' and are legislated for (Neal, 2012: 260).

The difficult question in this context is, however, whether there are any possible exceptions to requiring complete termination of security practice as part of just desecuritization. Thus, for example, what about cases where we as scholars think (backed by general consensus and even by common sense) that what is done in response to the securitizing move – i.e. the security practice – should, by and large, continue even beyond desecuritization? Or in other words, where we consider ourselves sure that the issue should be politicized once desecuritization is complete. This was perhaps first suggested by Paul Roe who in a 2004 article on securitization and desecuritization of minority rights argued that: 'To desecuritze minority rights, then, is to accept the previously unacceptable: to open up, through democratic federalism, the possibility of political autonomy, and secession; to make minority rights part of normal politics' (Roe, 2004: 291). I would argue, however, that there should be no exception to the rule of complete termination of security practice, and that, for example, the terms of minority rights would have to be renegotiated in the political realm, even if they end up taking a similar form.

3. Long-term aim: desecuritizing actors should avoid renewed and/or reactionary securitization by building a stable desecuritized state of affairs

The best possible outcome of desecuritization is a desecuritized state of affairs where diverse actors and groups are and feel secure to the extent that renewed and/or reactionary securitization is unlikely. This, however, cannot be achieved by simply rolling back security language and practice; instead restorative measures need to be put in place. In cases where securitization addressed intent-lacking threats, the chances for renewed and/or reactionary securitization are minimized by actors providing a detailed, public account of why there is no longer a threat, and also of why the security measures taken were necessary when the threat was acute. Compensation payments to those severely unintentionally harmed are also a possibility.

In desecuritizations of formerly securitized agent-intended OETs, the possibility of renewed and/or reactionary securitization is minimized by reintegrating formerly conflicting parties into society. It is important here to uphold the distinction between desecuritization as a process and its outcome: the desecuritized state of affairs. Accordingly I do not want to go as far as to suggest that a culture of forgiveness should be established as this would be tantamount to the issue being politicized once desecuritization is complete. Restorative measures should not blur the line between process and outcome of desecuritization; instead they are considered short-term measures that aim to facilitate reconciliation. How reconciliation is practised or implemented depends on the issue in question. Among restorative measures are compensation payments, while apologies by parties to the conflict to those unintentionally harmed also help (see Andrieu, 2009). The Northern Irish peace process serves once again as a good example with the IRA apologizing for the death of civilians to the families of the 650 civilians killed between 1969 and 1998.

It would appear that restorative measures are especially important in desecuritizations where the preceding securitization was unjust and where the desecuritizing actor is the same as the securitizing actor. This is so because the reasons for why the securitization was unjust generate different degrees of liability (see McMahan, 2009: 175). For instance a securitizing actor who falsely believed that there was a just cause and securitized with the good intention to achieve it, is comparatively less liable than an actor who did not have the right intention in securitizing, which is to say was not informed by the just cause (see McMahan, 2005: 5). While liability is likely to influence what precisely different types of desecuritizing actors will have to do as part of restorative measures, however, it remains to be seen whether this influences also *how much* they will have to do.[16] After all, all types of desecuritizing actors are obliged to do whatever is needed to maximize the chances of achieving a stable desecuritized state of affairs

Objections

In this section I will address three possible objections that could be raised against what is proposed here. This list is not meant to be exhaustive; it represents merely a selection of some of the most pressing objections. Objection 1 holds that there can be no universalizing criterion for when to desecuritize because desecuritization is a political choice. Objection 2 holds that the justice of securitization and desecuritization cannot be established outside of an open and inclusive political struggle. Objection 3 holds that a commitment to just desecuritization should form part of the criteria for just securitization.

Objection 1: there can be no universalizing criterion for when to desecuritize because desecuritization is a political choice

Securitization theory holds that both securitization and desecuritization are political choices that actors make irrespective of the existence of objective existential threats (OETs). Indeed the whole idea of securitization theory is that security is a self-referential practice, whereby issues become matters of security because they are addressed as such. And, if all threats are socially and politically constructed 'we cannot derive decisions on whether to (de)securitize from any objective status that threats might have' (Hansen, 2011: 11). JST which includes just desecuritization recognizes this logic but holds that we can and should differentiate between OETs and security threats. Not all security threats refer back to OETs and OETs become matters of security, and therefore 'security threats', only when a powerful actor frames and responds to them as such. In the context of OETs, it becomes possible to specify the latest point in time when just securitization should be abandoned (namely when the former have been neutralized) to have a hope of just desecuritization. While it also allows us to say that securitizations that lack a just reason (i.e. do not fulfil criterion 1 for just securitization) must be terminated immediately.

Objection 2: the justice of securitization and desecuritization cannot be established outside of an open and inclusive political struggle

A second possible objection against what is proposed here has been advanced by Wæver in the context of my 2011 'Security Dialogue' article where I first proposed the idea of just securitization. Thus Wæver rejects the idea that normative analysis can and should take the form, whereby what is valid, legitimate or just is universal and decided irrespective and outside of any given political situation

(Wæver, 2011: 473). Wæver's objection is longstanding and was influenced by his belief in Hannah Arendt's view 'that any position has to be judged by the effects it gains in interaction with others, and therefore "cannot" be good all on its own' (Floyd, 2010: 26). Notably, however, Wæver does not reject the idea that securitization can be more or less valuable, and he even argues that criteria for when securitization is valuable would have to be developed with recourse to 'discourse ethics' (Wæver, 2011: 473).

It is important to note that this is not the only time that discursive legitimation has been identified as relevant for securitization theory. Instead it is important also in the context that securitization is decided between the securitizing actor and a sanctioning audience, and never by an all-powerful securitizing actor (Williams, 2003: 523). Moreover, 'securitization is predominately received as a negative inasmuch as it is bad for democracy' (Roe, 2012: 260), while desecuritization is considered a positive development because it refers to politicization defined as openness, choice and collective decision-making (Wæver, 2003: 10–12), or in other words, to the political struggle. This begs a certain question. On what grounds is the political struggle valuable? Clearly its claim to value is logically based on another claim or set claims, for example, because it is fair, or because its outcomes are likely to be better and so on. My suspicion is that Wæver values democracy more for the former reason than the latter, but regardless of his precise reasons for valuing the political struggle, what matters is that it is valuable for non-discursive reasons.[17] For my purposes here this is relevant because if the political struggle can be valued on moral grounds, so can other practices.

Objection 3: a commitment to just desecuritization should form part of the criteria for just securitization

In the above I argued that desecuritization can be just irrespective of the justice of the preceding securitization. I have also argued that a just desecuritization cannot render an unjust securitization retrospectively just. What I have not yet addressed, is the related issue of whether an unjust desecuritization renders an otherwise just securitization unjust. This is an important issue, because by extrapolation, it could be objected that my account of just securitization is incomplete, and that a commitment to just desecuritization should form an additional criterion determining just securitization. In answering this question, it needs to be remembered, however, that the outcome of securitization is not a desecuritized state of affairs.[18] Instead securitization is a process with a distinct outcome, namely a securitized state of affairs; and we cannot judge the justice of one process (securitization) in terms of either (a) the justice of another process (desecuritization), or (b) the justice of the outcome of that other process (i.e. a desecuritized state of affairs). In other words, securitization and desecuritization are intimately related, but ultimately separate processes with distinct outcomes. And the justice of either should be evaluated separately from the other.

Conclusion

The underlying ideas informing the argument advanced in this chapter are that desecuritization is not necessarily a positive development and that it should be subject to a number of universally applicable rules concerning when and how to desecuritize and to what end. Overall, this chapter is part of a new moral security theory – Just Securitization Theory – that seeks to enable security scholars to morally evaluate securitizations both before and after they have occurred, and that aims to guide practitioners in relevant situations.

As part of the analysis, this chapter has revealed three new insights into desecuritization that are relevant for securitization studies more generally, irrespective of whether one accepts the specifics of JST. These are as follows: first, desecuritization is best thought of as a sum of actions and not an outcome (see Figure 8.1). This formulation means that desecuritization becomes a short-time event that can be identified, studied and morally evaluated.

Second, unlike Wæver has suggested, the desecuritized state of affairs following desecuritization is not 'a state of a-security'; instead the outcome of desecuritization is stable only if people enjoy levels of (human) security, sufficient enough to prevent them from opting for renewed and/or reactionary securitization.

Third, if desecuritization is to be just, it is likely to entail more than simply the reverse of securitization. Thus just desecuritization requires desecuritizing actors to work towards a stable desecuritized state of affairs and to achieve this they will have to go beyond simply undoing what was done and put restorative measures (compensation, apologies, resignation of perpetrators, etc.) in place. In short, the justice of desecuritization demands more than simply the unmaking of securitization.

Notes

1 I am very grateful to the many colleagues in different places who have engaged with different versions of this chapter. Specifically I would like to thank: Jonathan Floyd, Jonathan Herington, Juha Vuori, Lene Hansen, Adam Quinn, Jarrod Hayes, Nick Wheeler, Stuart Croft, João Nunes, Alex Homolar and many others who attended presentations of earlier versions of this paper at Warwick and Birmingham Universities as well as during a workshop at the Finnish Institute for International Affairs. I would also like to thank Thierry Balzacq, for his comments, patience and most of all for giving me this opportunity. This chapter is part of a longer book project with the provisional title *The Morality of Security: A Theory of Just Securitization*, which will hopefully clarify the many issues that remain underspecified in this piece due to the preclusion of space.

2 Because it aims to deprive securitizing actors of the ability to 'hide behind the claim that anything in itself constitutes a security issue' (Buzan *et al.*, 1998: 34).

3 These criteria remain a work in progress and are therefore subject to refinement.

4 That security studies needs to offer alongside explanatory theory also sound normative theory is evident from the fact that most (critical) scholars find it – for a variety of reasons, including responsibility for the potential effect of their own text – impossible to remain silent on the ethics of any given securitization. The otherwise analytically minded CS and their – all other things being equal – preference for desecuritization is a case in point.

5 The hope is that JST could bridge the gap between scholars and practitioners of security, which I – following the CS– consider functionally distinct. Thus JST does not recommend securitization. Instead it offers moral guidelines for practitioners should they decide to securitize. Moreover, if just securitization theory became a research project within security studies, with many people advancing their own criteria for just securitization and desecuritization, it might become known to practitioners and also the public and the latter could quite conceivably hold securitizing actors accountable for their actions in security politics. In short theories of just securitization have the potential to democratize security practice.

6 Instances are discussed in *The Morality of Security*.

7 I differentiate between mere utterers of securitizing moves, which could be anyone, and securitizing actors i.e. those agents whose relevant behavioural change constitutes securitization, or who are in a position of power over security professionals who execute security practice.

8 I am guilty here of the same crime as the CS insofar as I do not distinguish between outcome and procedure, to be clear, I mean outcomes in this instance.

9 I am extremely grateful to Jonathan Floyd for this formulation.

10 Signified by winning the Nobel Peace Prize in 2012.

11 On why intentions can be known see Floyd (2010: 43–44).

12 The observation that in order to locate intentions we need more than a simple statement of intent is central to criminal law. David Luban explains: 'Teenagers hanging out at a strip mall, passing a joint or drinking a six-pack, may while away the time with conversations that begin "Hey, why don't we rob the Seven-Eleven? ..." without ever seriously planning to do so. The basic US conspiracy statute requires not only a group plan but also at least one overt action taken in furtherance of the plan' (Luban, 2007: 192).

13 In *The Morality of Security* I differentiate in this category between agent-lacking and agent-caused threat, whereby the former refer to threats lacking human involvement (e.g. truly natural disasters) while the latter refer to threats caused by humans, but not intended by them (e.g. climate change).

14 This is a departure from my argument in Floyd (2011: 434) that I cannot elaborate on here but is explained in *The Morality of Security*

15 It is, for example, not unthinkable that following public pressure a national government declares a former terrorist group no longer a threat to security, but continues to survey individuals formerly associated with such groups in secret.

16 I discuss this at some length in *The Morality of Security*, Chapter 6.

17 This is why I use the language of morality in *Security and the Environment: Securitization Theory and US Environmental Security Policy* (2010) in the context of the CS's commitment to desecuritisation, even though the School does not use this language, and one School member has very much objected to this (de Wilde, 2012).

18 Unlike de Wilde I am also not convinced that desecuritization is the aim of security policies (de Wilde, 2008: 597). The aim of securitization (which could be described as implemented security policy) is rather – as Wæver has put it – to defend against a threat (Wæver, 2003).

Part III
Emancipation

Editor's introduction

I

In contrast to resistance, emancipation can be granted by a dominating power or by some established institutions. However, like resistance, emancipation can also be fought for by subjects who seek self-liberation from conditions that impair their autonomy of thought and action. Moreover, resistance is not always a progressive or revisionist move; in fact, to resist could also mean to strive for the status quo. On the other hand, emancipation generally involves a desire to escape from the current situation. It has a fundamentally proactive leaning.

Therefore it is misguided to assume, as Jürgen Habermas (1987) does, that emancipation is resistance by another name. Rather, by emphasizing its basic attributes, this Part aims to present emancipation as distinct, though not separate, from resistance. In many ways, there is an intimate relation between resistance and emancipation, in the specific sense that the former paves the way for the latter. According to Pieterse (1992: 13), "emancipation is not only about saying no, reacting, refusing, resisting, but also and primarily about social creativity, introducing new values and aims, new forms of cooperation and action." In other words, emancipation does not aim to preserve an existing or past policy; it works toward a new state of affairs.

II

Ken Booth (1991) was, to my knowledge, the first IR scholar to articulate explicitly emancipation and security. Emancipation, says Booth (2001: 110), "is the heart of critical theory of world security". The relation between emancipation and security is not one-directional, however. At root, there seems to be a co-constitution of security and emancipation. For Booth (1997:110), on the one hand, it is "emancipation … that leads to stable security." For Richard Wyn Jones (1999:126), on the other hand, "security … is an essential element in the struggle for emancipation." Claudia Aradau (2004) demurs. To think security in terms of emancipation is, she claims, to think security alternatively, not to question the ineluctable consequences of its functioning. The truth is that, so the argument goes, security and emancipation operate under incompatible logics: one exclusionary and the other inclusive. In other words, the politics of security and the politics of emancipation are of different extract, as security is often achieved at someone's expense.

Obviously, this presupposes that one accepts that security is always exclusive, and that, as a corollary, security policy's outcome are necessary zero sum games (McDonald 2012). Of course, when emancipatory activities start, one side of the interaction can feel threatened. Yet, if successful, does it necessary have to install a zero sum game between concerned agents? In fact, the literature in post-conflict reconstruction teaches us that when emancipation works, agents often find themselves in relative games. Some policy arrangements such as power sharing or affirmative action, despite their complexity and residual weaknesses, can be conducive to relative games among the participants. For instance, the fact that it is increasingly required in many Western democracies that women be integrated in public life, including parliamentary bodies, was probably seen by some males as a threatening move (and probably is still for some die hard conservative strands). But for the society, the result is, not only inclusiveness and better appreciation of what half of the population wants and aspires to, but also a more diverse spectrum of policy options and experiences.

III

This Part is organized around two chapters, each of which takes emancipation to its logical conclusion, focusing on its internal components and premises, and calling into question the various interpretations the emancipation-security nexus has been subjected to. Chapter 9 proposes to situate the relation between security and emancipation within the broader project of critical security studies. Put otherwise, rather than treating security in exclusively negative terms, João Nunes suggests that security be seen as embodying both a conservative and a transformative impetus. The chapter proposes to consider desecuritization as a groundwork for emancipation. Emphasizing activities aimed at contesting Australian border security, Chapter 10 explores the cosmopolitan ethical principle which undermines emancipatory security discourses. In other words, discourses of emancipation have their cosmopolitan articulations, which aim to shape security in rather progressive and integrative fashions.

9 Emancipation and the reality of security

A reconstructive agenda

João Nunes

Introduction: contestation and critique

The idea that security should be rendered problematic is one of the commitments of critical security studies (Krause and Williams 1997; Peoples and Vaughan-Williams 2010).[1] Since its inception, this body of literature has questioned commonsensical meanings of 'security' and 'threat'. Indeed, one of the assumptions of the critical literature is that the knowledge about security is the result of social and political processes. Securitization theory, one of the foremost critical approaches, took this insight further by arguing that the very reality of security should be placed under scrutiny (Wæver 1995). Securitization scholars refused to see security as an objective reality, arguing instead that 'security' should be approached as an intersubjective process between a securitizing actor and an audience that results in a specific modality for dealing with issues. This insight led many authors to investigate what the security modality does or entails, that is, the consequences of using a security perspective to frame and deal with issues. This proved to be a very popular line of enquiry; in some places, it has arguably become mainstream (Croft 2007, 508).[2] It signalled the shift from a concern with security towards an analysis of securitization moves. By differentiating security (as a condition of absence of threats) and securitization (the processes through which issues emerge as threats), securitization theory has impacted upon critical security studies in profound ways.

The nature of this impact was decisively conditioned by the refusal of securitization theory to see security as 'a good to be spread to ever more sectors' (Buzan *et al.*, 1998, 35). Instead, securitization was assumed to entail problematic consequences. For some, it meant framing an issue as a threat to the very existence of a referent, thus demanding exceptional measures to address it. Others focused on the 'routine' modality of securitization, showing that securitization often occurs as the outcome of a series of acts that do not necessarily require the explicit use of the language of threat (Bigo 2002; Huysmans 2000). In both cases, the outcome of securitization is overwhelmingly undesirable. It leads to the bypassing of normal democratic procedures, to unchecked policies and, sometimes, to violence. Securitization moves are thus seen to have pernicious consequences: they can be used to justify problematic measures, and they can also be self-defeating in their promotion of feelings of unease and danger about a particular issue.

The consequence of this view has been a normative preference for desecuritization. According to those subscribing to the premises of securitization theory, desecuritization means removing issues out of the security modality and bringing them back to the sphere of political deliberation. Although it has not been framed as absolute, the normative preference for desecuritization has remained largely unexplored; in fact, the criteria for the desirability of desecuritization are only now beginning to be studied (see Floyd, this volume).[3] In practical terms, this has meant that the default assumption that securitization is an undesirable thing has not been challenged to a great extent.

The shift of focus from security to securitization, and the overwhelming preference for desecuritization in detriment of securitization, are revealing of how the critique of security has evolved in recent years in a significant part of the security studies literature. However, they do not tell the whole story. This trajectory has interacted with the growth of a tendency to see security as having a negative logic. In other words, a profound distrust towards security has run parallel to the analysis of the undesirable effects of specific securitization processes. This distrust is present, for example, in the work of Michael Dillon (1996, 130), who identifies in Western thought a 'metaphysical politics of security' that makes 'politics a matter of command; membership of a political community a matter of obedience; love synonymous with a policing order; order a function of discipline; and identity a narcissistic paranoia'. Similarly, Didier Bigo (2008, 109) has argued that security is a political register that strives to make the world calculable, 'makes a fantasy of homogeneity and seeks the end of any resistances or struggles'. Mark Neocleous (2011) has even linked security to fascism.

These two tendencies have interacted in the critical security studies literature, in that the recognition of the problematic character of different instances of securitization is seen to confirm a wider malaise with the very idea of security. The continuum between the critique of securitization (in specific cases) to security (in itself) has been expressed by securitization theorist Ole Wæver: he begins by highlighting 'the inevitable effects of any securitization' in the form of a 'logic of necessity, the narrowing of choice, the empowerment of a smaller elite' (2011, 469), before arguing that '[t]he concept of *security* is Schmittian, because it defines security in terms of exception, emergency and a decision' (2011, 478, emphasis in the original). Even though they are not the same, securitization and security reinforce each other in this argument: by being fundamentally about exception and emergency, security provides a fertile ground in which securitizing moves with 'inevitable effects' can flourish.

One can thus identify in the critical security studies literature a tendency to see the nexus security-securitization as having a certain underlying logic, which is connected to exclusion, totalization and even violence. Claudia Aradau, for example, writes of an 'exclusionary logic of security' underpinning and legitimizing 'forms of domination' (2008, 72). Rens Van Munster assumes a 'logic of security', predicated upon a 'political organization on the exclusionary basis of fear' (2007, 239). Although there would probably be disagreement over the degree to which this logic is inescapable, it is symptomatic of an overwhelming pessimistic outlook that a great number of critical scholars are now making the case for moving away from security (Huysmans 2006; Bigo 2007; Aradau 2004). Security becomes something to be escaped (on the 'escapist' view of security, see McDonald, this volume). By assuming the form of a damning verdict on the supposed logic of the security-securitization nexus, the contestation of security becomes synonymous with the refusal of security.

As has been argued elsewhere (McDonald 2012; Nunes 2012), this trajectory is deeply problematic. It offers a deterministic view of security that overlooks the multiple ways in which the latter is understood and practised. Assuming from the start that security implies the narrowing of choice and the empowerment of an elite stops one from recognizing security claims that may seek to achieve the opposite: the acknowledgement of alternative possibilities in an already narrow debate and the contestation of elite power. In connection with this, this trajectory unnecessarily impairs the critical literature in its engagement with what should be its subject-matter: the situations of insecurity that are experienced by individuals and groups. These run the risk of being neglected if the desire to be more secure is identified with a compulsion towards 'totalization' and 'control'. Finally, this view forecloses the ability of critical security studies to play a role in a transformative politics seeking to redress insecurity. By escaping security, the critical field weakens its capacity to confront the exceptionalist connotations that security has acquired in certain policy circles. Instead, critical security studies ends up playing into this agenda by assuming that these connotations are somehow inevitable.

Whilst it is undeniable that securitization theory has been immensely beneficial to the theoretical development and the academic acceptance of critical security studies, it is also true that this approach has limitations. If left unchecked, these can be detrimental to the critique of security because of the impact that the nexus security-securitization is having upon the research agenda: as has been suggested above, this nexus unnecessarily restricts the analytical capacity of security studies and weakens its normative engagement with the world of insecurity. Interestingly, Wæver (2011) has recognized the pitfalls that are inherent in theory construction. Discussing the politics of theory design, which relates to the ways in which 'the structure and nature of a theory have systematic political implications', he argued that theory 'conditions analyses, because a theory is a construct that enables particular observations about cases' (Wæver 2011, 466).

This chapter starts with the observation that critical security studies – and the overall endeavour of contesting security – need to be more conscious of the trajectory described here. In particular, they need to be aware of its pitfalls, visible not so much in the kind of observations that this trajectory enables, but more precisely in the observations it forecloses. With a view of countering these pitfalls, the present chapter draws on the notion of 'security as emancipation' to offer a different perspective on how security may be contested.

Security as emancipation and the reality of security

Security as emancipation can be defined as the transformation of subjectivities, relations and structures that entail systematic inequality, disadvantage and vulnerability, thus resulting in individuals and groups suffering from different forms of harm.[4] Emancipatory transformation is enabled by the creation of spaces in people's lives in which they can make decisions and act beyond the basic necessities of survival. This understanding is inspired by, but goes beyond, the views put forward by Ken Booth (1991, 2007), Richard Wyn Jones (2005), Pinar Bilgin (2008) and Soumita Basu (2011).

It is important to clarify that this approach is different from contributions that have subscribed to an emancipatory commitment whilst keeping it separate from security (Aradau 2008; Peoples 2011; Wyn Jones 2012). The view advanced here is that the two terms cannot be separated without losing their meaning. Thus, on the one hand, security requires emancipation. For the world's most vulnerable, the achievement of lasting security necessitates the transformation of the structures and relations that are implicated in their insecurity. In other words, they need to emancipate themselves from the structural causes of their insecurity. They can only do so by having the possibility to think and act in ways that meaningfully impact upon their lives. In order for this emancipatory moment to be possible, they need to be able to deal with immediate threats; in other words, they must not have the totality of their energies devoted to the struggle for survival. Security from immediate threats to survival thus allows for emancipatory thought and action that, in turn, leads to lasting security. The security of people who do not need to worry constantly about their survival is also dependent on others enjoying a similar level of security – in other words, it also requires the transformation of the mechanisms that systematically promote the insecurity of some to the benefit of others.

This also means that emancipation only makes sense when coupled with security. Emancipation is the process of exercising a degree of freedom from the structures and relationships that curtail people's ability to determine the course of their lives. This freedom requires a measure of certainty, predictability and control over one's surroundings – or, at the very least, a situation in which one is not completely at the mercy of external circumstances.

This understanding of security as emancipation offers a perspective on the contestation of security that is markedly different from the 'escapist' view described above. This perspective is predicated upon the assumption that security is a condition whose meaning ultimately derives from a comprehensive engagement with reality – in particular, with actual insecurity as a 'life-determining condition' (Booth 2007, 101). With this engagement, security as emancipation sets out to recast the relationship between security theory and the reality of security. It does so 'not by rejecting *the idea of the real*' but by claiming access to an approach to reality that is 'more sophisticated' (Booth 2005, 10, emphasis in the original) – that is, one that is able to engage with the real conditions of existence and produce truer knowledge about the world.

In order to make sense of the 'condition' of insecurity, the writings of Booth and Wyn Jones have emphasized the experiences of insecurity of individuals and groups. This move is predicated upon the idea that individuals are the ultimate referent object of security. As Wyn Jones has (2005, 227) argued, 'the starting point for critical theory should not be some abstracted notion of emancipation and human potential but rather the corporeal, material existence and experiences of individual human beings'. The meaning of security stems from actual insecurities and the way they are experienced by individuals.

This emphasis on the 'bottom-up' experiences of insecurity is, in Booth's writings, combined with a more 'top-down' identification of actual dangers that determine the lives of individuals and groups. In this context, threats can 'range from direct bodily violence from other humans (war), through structural political and economic forms of oppression (slavery), into more existential threats to identity (cultural imperialism)' (Booth 1999, 49). The relation between the bottom-up and the top-down perspectives has not been elaborated in much detail by Booth or any other author writing in the security as emancipation approach. This point can be clarified further by exploring in more depth the question of the reality of security.

The reality of security is ultimately unknowable in an objective way. This is not the same as saying that it is not possible to strive for better accounts of this reality. Security may be said to have a subjective element, related to the experiences of insecurity of particular actors; an intersubjective element, pertaining to how these experiences are mediated and constituted; and a 'non-subjective' (Booth 2007, 105) element that relates to the structures that interact with these subjective and intersubjective processes, and which exist independently of the consciousness and interaction of *specific* subjects.[5] The intersubjective element is given great attention by approaches such as securitization theory, according to which security is not a concept that describes reality, but rather the constitution of reality through an interaction between a securitizing actor and an audience. According to this perspective, security can only be conceived as real within the remit of these interactions. Security becomes 'self-referential' (Huysmans 1998b, 232) because it is predominantly a signifier, a register of meaning that does things instead of describing things. Threats are made real by a securitizing move; they cannot be conceived beyond the meanings introduced by the latter. According to the intersubjective perspective, HIV/AIDS for example is a threat inasmuch as it is successfully framed as such by actors seeking to shape the political procedure for dealing with this issue, with the intention of getting more attention or resources.

The subjective element of security refers to insecurities as they are experienced – regardless of whether they result in successful securitizing moves or claims to insecurity. Subjective insecurities are, of course, always embedded in social relations, but they may or may not be accompanied by the intersubjective mediation of insecurity as 'threat'. In other words, subjectivities (including interests, feelings and emotions) are always social but subjective insecurity is not always accepted or recognized in the social sphere.

In addition to being embedded in social relations, subjective insecurities also relate in different ways with material and ideational structures entailing systematic vulnerability and/or harm. Although these structures are ultimately the result of human action, they exist regardless of whether they are recognized or not by the subjects involved. In this sense, we can term this element of security non-subjective, since it is not dependent for its existence on the mind and interaction of the specific actors involved (even though it is obviously dependent on human activity as a whole). Another part of this non-subjective element is the actual 'physical' content of the insecurity itself: a bullet or a disease may injure and kill regardless of what we think of them. Thus, HIV/AIDS can be experienced subjectively as a source of insecurity. This can happen in agreement with the non-subjective element in HIV/AIDS. For example, a person infected with the disease may fear for his/her ability to meaningfully shape the course of his/her life because of the effects of the virus in his/her body. Given the knowledge about how the virus is transmitted, a person living in a country with a high prevalence of the disease (in Swaziland, for example, with a 25.9 per cent adult prevalence in 2009) may legitimately worry about the possibility of becoming infected, particularly if this person is in a vulnerable social position. However, a person's fear of infection may disagree with the actual danger of becoming infected: a person may worry about the danger of becoming infected with HIV/AIDS by shaking hands or using public toilets. In this example, insecurity as a subjective experience agrees with certain instances of intersubjective mediation (panics about infections in public toilets) but it does not agree with the non-subjective element (how disease is actually transmitted).

Finally, there may be non-subjective elements of insecurity that go unnoticed and are not experienced as such: the international mechanisms and legislation that govern the supply and access to antiretroviral treatments and medical care; the social and religious taboos on the use of condoms; or the misogyny in society that reinforces a culture of sexual violence towards women are examples of underlying sources of insecurity that are not immediately apparent, and that can lead to people either becoming infected with HIV/AIDS or living extremely insecure lives when infected.

The tendency in the critical security studies literature has been to treat these three perspectives – intersubjective, subjective and non-subjective – as separate, or else to leave their cumulative effects unexplored. This argument has begun to show that it is possible to see them as interacting components of a complex reality. Subjective experiences of insecurity may correspond to non-subjective threats and may result in intersubjective processes. There may be non-subjective threats that do not elicit feelings of insecurity and do not lead to issues being securitized. There may be securitizing moves that do not correspond to non-subjective threats, but merely speak to people's anxieties – which in turn they help to heighten. In sum, there are different possible combinations of these three elements. Security as emancipation can draw on them to provide a novel approach to the contestation of security. It can do so, first, by considering the potential and limitations of each of the elements; and, second, by combining them into a more comprehensive and sophisticated take on the reality of security.

Dealing with the non-subjective layer of security raises a number of questions – for some, it may threaten to bring the analysis of security back to an objectivist standpoint. But claiming that security has a layer that is not dependent upon subjective representation or intersubjective mediation by specific actors is not the same as saying that security is independent of human activity (broadly conceived). Also, it does not mean that security is self-evident and can be known objectively (that is, neutrally or impartially). In fact, for all its attention towards non-subjective threats, security as emancipation has painstakingly affirmed that knowledge about security cannot be objective in the sense of being able to capture an underlying truth about it. Rather, knowledge is a social product and process, which derives from political interests, reflects existing opportunities and constraints, results from power struggles and is oriented towards political goals. Understandings of security are embedded in a social setting in which facts are established by a political negotiation. As Booth (2007, 246) has put it,

> [t]here is an 'out there' which can only be engaged through the theories 'in here,' but what is in our minds is only part of reality, never its whole. A critical theory of security is therefore empirical without being empiricist.

Because it is not possible to achieve a universal truth about security, the awareness of non-subjective threats needs to be supplemented with an engagement with experiences of insecurity. However, the subjective layer is not without its pitfalls. Whilst they may provide privileged windows into the condition of insecurity, experiences should not be seen as offering authentic or universally valid versions of it. In fact, the notion of experience has been the target of much scrutiny, particularly in the feminist literature where authors have debated the nature of the 'standpoint of women', that is, the distinctive point of view that supposedly gives feminist writing its authenticity.

Joan Scott, for example, has problematized the idea of a standpoint of women relying on experience. 'When experience is taken as the origin of knowledge', Scott (1992, 25) argues,

> the vision of the individual subject (the person who had the experience or the historian who recounts it) becomes the bedrock of evidence upon which explanation is built. Questions about the constructed nature of experience, about how subjects are constituted as different in the first place, about how one's vision is structured – about language (or discourse) and history – are left aside.

With experience taken as a given, feminist theory ends up falling once again into the trap of foundationalist thinking: '[t]he evidence of experience', as Scott (1992, 32–33) puts it, 'works as a foundation providing both a starting point and a conclusive kind of explanation, beyond which few questions need to or can be asked'. This precludes asking 'what counts as experience and who gets to make that determination' (Scott 1992, 33). In other words, it forecloses an examination of the political processes through which certain actors are given power to speak and certain authorized versions of reality are produced. Experience should thus be seen simultaneously as

> an interpretation *and* in need of interpretation. What counts as experience is neither self-evident nor straightforward; it is always contested, always therefore political. (Scott 1992, 37, emphasis in the original)

Scott's critique of experience thus allows one to understand the limitations of relying on subjective accounts of insecurity in an unexamined way. Simultaneously, it points to the need to consider the broader social and political setting in which subjective accounts of security emerge, as well as their political effects. In particular, Scott's argument brings the question of subjectivity to the fore. For Scott (1992, 28), the consequence of grounding knowledge upon a source that supposedly reflects reality is 'to constitute subjects as fixed and autonomous, and who are considered reliable sources of a knowledge that comes from access to the real by means of their experience'. Rather than instances of production and transmission of some kind of truth, the 'voicing' and 'listening' of experience should be seen as moments in which the subject who speaks and the subject who listens are constituted. Experience does not reflect or reveal a subject. Rather, it is an intrinsic part of the process through which the subject of experience – that is, the subject that experiences or to whom experience refers – is constituted.

By helping to crystallize a particular understanding of the subject, experience can also lead to the exclusion or de-legitimization of other forms that the subject might take. In addition to this, experience orders social relations by helping to define the relative positions of interlocutors: for example, a claim to insecurity may lead to the attribution of blame and/or to the allocation of responsibility for dealing with that particular understanding of insecurity. By mobilizing and helping to shape self-understandings and perceptions of the world, experience thus helps to define social roles and the content of social interactions.

It becomes clear that experience should not be seen in a vacuum. It needs to be understood as a social process of subject constitution and positioning. Understanding experience as process can benefit from being supplemented by an awareness of the intersubjective layer of reality. In fact, this discussion suggests that experience is a process with an important intersubjective component, inasmuch as it consists of a negotiation of meaning in the field of social interaction. At the same time, a full understanding of this process demands that one recognizes the underlying structures that condition the voicing and listening of experience, and which may or may not be immediately visible or intelligible. This brings us back to the non-subjective layer of reality.

In sum, these three elements of reality are imperfect when standing on their own, but conjoining them allows for a series of triangulations that help to address these limitations. Combining an awareness of underlying (non-subjective) structures, (subjective) experiences and (intersubjective) relations enables a comprehensive engagement with the reality of security. The next section of the argument shows how security and emancipation mobilizes this view of reality to offer a novel perspective into the contestation of security.

The reconstruction of security

On the basis of this understanding of reality, the security as emancipation approach understands critique as a thorough politicization of security. It sees security as a political phenomenon by focusing on different dimensions. The first pertains to how security is 'made' politically, that is, to the assumptions and processes that underlie the reproduction of certain ideas of security. Whilst security has non-subjective elements, they are always enveloped in political practice in the sense that they can only be made intelligible by using categories that are intrinsically political. To go back to the previous example, HIV/AIDS is a biological entity but we can only understand it by using lenses that are predicated on ideas – for example, ideas of danger, aversion, pity, solidarity, responsibility or guilt. The lenses we use to render threats intelligible – and which in turn help to frame our attitudes and responses towards them – are socially negotiated and sometimes fought over in the social field. In this sense, it is possible to speak of security as being 'made' politically.

The second dimension of the politicization of security relates to its political effects – in other words, to what security 'does'. To speak or think of an issue as being a matter of security is not merely to describe a reality, inasmuch as security also frames the way in which the issue is dealt with. Moreover, security is a broad register of meaning that contributes to ordering social relations.[6] Recognizing this work of political ordering that is performed by security significantly broadens our understanding of this phenomenon.

The next political dimension considered by security as emancipation pertains to the normative purposes underlying the study of security. Security as emancipation is not content with highlighting what security is; it also seeks to ascertain what security should be, that is, what it would mean to have more security in a particular situation. Focusing on the reality of security is always done with a purpose in mind, and for security as emancipation this purpose is, in a first moment, the normative evaluation of existing arrangements. Having shown that a particular meaning or practice of security is not natural or necessary, the question is then one of making a judgement as to the desirability of that meaning or practice. What is wrong with it? And should one seek to change it?

This ties in with the following dimension, which looks at the definition of strategies for changing arrangements that are deemed wrong and undesirable. Here, security as emancipation draws on the identification of existing transformative potentialities.[7] This potential may reside in the fault-lines, weaknesses or inconsistencies of the predominant state of affairs: for example, whether it fails to live up to its own commitments, or whether its core assumptions can be shown to be hollow or susceptible to subversion. The potential for change is also present in the form of alternative ideas and transformative actors. An approach to security should seek to garner existing alternative knowledge about an issue and collaborate with actors that are in a good position to bring about change.

The final dimension of the politicization of security follows on from the insight that security has an impact upon social relations and the political sphere. It provides a corollary of this idea by arguing that security can therefore be the entry point for broader transformative change. If security has such an important impact on politics, and if security is political in the sense of being made – and thus susceptible to being 'remade' – then an alternative understanding of security can help to transform the political in positive ways.

On the basis of this understanding of critique, the contestation of security provided by the security as emancipation approach has two core features. The first one is the retrieval of security. This approach brings the question of the reality of security back to the fore; it does so, however, not simply by rendering the reality of security problematic. Security as emancipation recognizes that the way we perceive, understand and convey reality is the result of social processes and political struggle. Nonetheless, it offers an approach to reality that goes beyond this, by showing that there is more to security (as a broad phenomenon) than the processes through which it is perceived, understood or conveyed.

Security goes beyond securitizing processes because, regardless of whether these processes are in place or not, there is insecurity in the experience of vulnerability and harm, as well as in the relations and structures that perpetuate it. The existence of insecurity means that it is possible to conceive security as the substantive state or condition of being able to deal with these relations and structures. This does not mean that one is envisaging an end-state of absolute security, but rather the possibility of people being less insecure. By bringing security back into the agenda, security as emancipation serves as a powerful counterbalance to the radical refusal of security advanced by some approaches. It shifts the focus back to the realities of insecurity and reaffirms a normative commitment to helping to alleviate it. The existence of insecurities means that security should not be seen merely as a representation to be rendered problematic. Rather, security is ultimately a good to be striven for. One should not try to escape it, but rather seek to promote it.

This discussion points to an overlapping second feature: security as emancipation contests 'security' by reclaiming its meaning, namely by offering a positive notion of it. The exclusionary ideas and forceful measures that have been attached to security do not capture its essence; rather, they are just undesirable appropriations and instrumentalizations of security to serve certain agendas at the expense of the interests of others. Some security scholars may have been too fast in identifying an overriding logic of security beyond these particular situations of cooptation. Security as emancipation holds that security is always specific and can only be understood by looking at how it is experienced and/or negotiated by actors in context – in other words, by engaging with its reality in a comprehensive way. Thus, whilst in some cases security claims may mask attempts of control on the part of powerful elites, in other cases they reveal lives faced with the harsh reality of survival. In the latter case, having more security is a good thing.

These two features – retrieving and reclaiming – configure the contestation of security offered by security as emancipation as a reconstructive project. In other words, security as emancipation contests security by showing that the particular meanings attached to it are not natural or necessary, and by putting forward alternative meanings that can contribute to changing the status quo. This focus on reconstructive critique is, however, very conscious of the lessons of the deconstruction of security. It concurs with approaches like securitization theory that it is important to look at the effects of security, and that it is possible that security is instrumentalized to have a pernicious political impact. However, security as emancipation believes that the work of critique is incomplete if we remain at the level of deconstruction. Rather, the objective is to draw on deconstruction to undertake an informed and cautious reconstructive move, aimed at changing predominant ideas and practices of security in an emancipatory way – that is, in a way that opens up space for people to make decisions and to act on matters pertaining to their own lives.

Conclusion

This chapter made three arguments. First, the idea of contesting security must be understood in light of the critical security literature and its trajectory. Here, the argument suggested that many authors increasingly see the contestation of security as the refusal of security – a development that can be considered problematic. On the basis of this diagnosis, the chapter advanced a second argument: the idea of security as emancipation offers an alternative pathway to the contestation of security by drawing on a comprehensive engagement with reality as comprising a non-subjective, a subjective and an intersubjective element. Finally, the chapter argued that this take on the critique/contestation of security configures a reconstructive moment based on the retrieval and the reclaiming of security as a positive thing.

The idea of security as emancipation has the potential to combine the deconstruction and the reconstruction of security in productive ways: by showing that there is nothing natural or necessary about the way security is understood and done; by suggesting that alternatives are latent in the specific claims and experiences of individuals and groups; by claiming that there are more or less emancipatory options in a given situation; and by seeking to engage and collaborate with transformative forces in society.

It is worth considering how this approach to contestation can relate to other strategies, namely desecuritization and resistance. In what concerns the former, it becomes immediately clear that there are diverging starting points to bear in mind. However, even though security as emancipation does not consider that securitization/desecuritization exhaust the meaning of security, an awareness of securitizing processes can be part of an emancipatory agenda. There is no fundamental incompatibility between pursuing an emancipatory purpose and seeking to identify the speech acts and the political and bureaucratic processes through which certain security understandings and practices are constituted, justified and legitimized. Put differently, there is nothing that prevents security as emancipation from incorporating securitization theory as a tool for understanding the ways in which security is used to frame particular issues, and with certain political outcomes as a result. This means that security as emancipation is also interested in how these effects (when seen as undesirable) can be ameliorated by drawing on strategies of desecuritization that bring issues back to the sphere of democratic deliberation, ethical reflection and participated politics. In this sense, desecuritization can be an important analytical and practical tool for the emancipatory purpose. In some cases, desecuritization, as the deconstruction of existing ideas and practices, may be an essential groundwork for envisaging alternatives.

Emancipation is also compatible with resistance. There are two ways in which the relationship between emancipation and resistance can be conceived. The first is resistance as subsidiary to emancipation. This is the view put forward by Booth (2007, 110–116), who has argued that resistance can be seen as localized, operational level of emancipation. This conceptualization sees resistance as part of the practical politics of opening up spaces in people's lives. In this view, emancipation effectively subsumes resistance. The agenda of emancipation includes but goes beyond resistance by claiming that particular instances of resistance need to be supplemented by a more encompassing effort of structural change.

Another view, arguably more productive, is to see resistance as a transformative strategy in its own right, consisting of an attitude of permanent questioning of ideas and practices of security that seeks to caution against their dangers and redress their undesirable effects. This definition echoes Foucault's idea of 'practices of freedom' and speaks to a Foucaultian notion of power as government (Foucault 2000 [1982]; Dean 1999; Gordon 1991). In this sense, the distinction between emancipation and resistance relates to the forms of power that one seeks to confront. Resistance is particularly suited to deal with the ways in which security appears as a form of government and constitution of subjects. It thus supplements emancipation as the transformation of structures and relations, which is arguably more suited to deal with other forms of power – namely those encompassing hierarchy, inequality and domination.

Notes

1 The author would like to thank Thierry Balzacq, Philippe Bourbeau and Rita Floyd for their comments on an earlier version of this chapter; and Mika Aaltola for hosting the workshop *Contesting Security*, Helsinki, 15–16 January 2013, in which the argument was presented.
2 In this respect, see also the quantitative survey in Gad and Petersen (2011, 316).
3 This work on the criteria of desecuritization follows in the wake of calls for a more nuanced approach to securitizing processes. See in this respect Floyd (2010) and Jutila (2006).
4 Subjectivities are constituted and performed in the realm of social life. Relations sediment into structures (material and ideational) and in turn contribute to reproducing

them. Structures, whilst being dependent on relations for their reproduction, also frame the meaning and content of subjectivities and relations. A mutually constitutive linkage is thus established between structures and the ways in which they are created, interpreted and performed in social practice.

5 It should be noted that Booth provides a different understanding of the meaning of non-subjective.

6 Michael Dillon (1996, 16) aptly described security as a 'principle of formation that does things'; however, *contra* Dillon, this does not mean that security cannot also be 'a noun that names something', in the sense of helping us make sense of a condition of security or insecurity.

7 The inspiration is the method of immanent critique. See, in this respect, Antonio (1981), Buchwalter (1991) and, of course, Horkheimer (1974 [1947], 182).

10 Contesting border security

Emancipation and asylum in the Australian context

Matt McDonald

Introduction

Contemporary accounts of the politics of security consistently point to the pernicious effects of securitization, or the inescapable ties between the preservation of states and the meaning of security in global politics. Those engaging directly with the question of the political function of security overwhelmingly view security not as an end to be furthered or desired, but as a political technology that consistently favours the interests of the powerful and enables both violence and exclusion. Indeed this view is to be found in a number of other offerings in this volume.

This account of security politics finds much support in contemporary international practice. From the language and practices of the 'war on terror' to brutal crackdowns on political dissent to states' treatment of refugees and asylum-seekers, we find a wealth of evidence to support this vision of security and the associated normative push to 'escape' security. At the heart of this 'escapist' position are two core and related claims, one analytical and one normative.

The first – analytical – claim is that security has a meaning and/or logic that is fixed and problematic. While drawing on various philosophical resources, the arguments advanced here are either that the association of security with the preservation of states and the state system has become hegemonic to the point of *constituting* security's meaning across time and space, or that the logic of security – tied to exceptionalism and the escape of normal politics – is such that securitization necessarily constrains political deliberation while enabling those in power to pursue their preferred course of action. The analytical claim here, then, is that there is something fixed about security: its meaning, its logic and consequences, or both.

The normative claim of this escapist position follows from the above. If the meaning and/or logic of security is viewed as fixed and inherently problematic, normative progress (however defined) can only be realized through resisting and ultimately escaping security. There is, for those who subscribe to this view, little to be gained through attempting to reformulate or rearticulate security, either through academic or practical debate.

This chapter, while acknowledging the dominance of such a conception of security in contemporary global politics, challenges these claims. Rather than the meaning and logic of security being fixed across time and space, I suggest that the meaning of security is fluid and permeable. This meaning is ultimately tied to the ways in which different political communities give content to their core values and the means of their protection or advancement, which of course differs across different communities and changes over time. Linked to this, the logic of security (the question of what security does) also shifts depending on the claims and commitments of the conception or discourse of security to come to prominence in those settings. In some instances, we may see clear illustration of the dynamics and dangers of securitization articulated by advocates of the Copenhagen School (Waever 1995; Floyd 2007). In others, we may see a different conception and logic of security, potentially oriented towards the rights and needs of others (Doty 1998/1999; McDonald 2012).

In short, I claim that what I call the 'escapist' approach to security rests on shaky analytical ground. While the normative impulse to reject statism, exclusion, exceptionalism and violence that informs these claims shares much with the emancipatory approach to security I endorse here, the associated push to reject or escape security is less an obvious response to the meaning and logic of security than it is a particular response to a specific security *discourse*. Worse, in rejecting security as a potential site of progress, such an approach risks endorsing a narrow security discourse as timeless and inevitable, paradoxically empowering those who benefit from its acceptance and institutionalization. In the process, articulated dangers associated with securitization or the spread of security agenda risk becoming something of a 'self-fulfilling prophesy'. If the promise of security is central to the legitimacy of the key institutions of world politics (from states to international organizations such as the United Nations), and if security is central to modern political life in general, then engaging with and attempting to reformulate security is a necessary scholarly enterprise. Indeed a range of actors in global politics make precisely this move in practice, articulating alternative conceptions of a society's values in need of being preserved or advanced, and the means through which this might be achieved (see McDonald 2012).

These claims are illustrated here through the examination of contestation over the treatment of asylum-seekers arriving by boat in Australia since 2001. This constitutes an ideal case study for the present analysis because the way in which liberal democratic states such as Australia have approached immigrants, asylum-seekers and refugees has been a core example for those concerned with the politics of security (e.g. Huysmans 2006; Bigo 2002). More directly, security concerns – in particular a concern with 'border security'– have been directly invoked to justify a highly restrictive approach to asylum-seekers in Australia, and the language of security employed by Australian political leaders has been the subject of a number of political analyses (e.g. McMaster 2002; McDonald 2011). Contestation of this depiction, however, has not been subjected to anything approaching the same degree of academic or political scrutiny.

This chapter therefore examines the ways in which marginal actors in the Australian context have engaged in public debate regarding asylum-seekers, and in particular have attempted to challenge the dominant discourse of (border) security regarding asylum-seekers. In the process I identify their attempts not simply to resist or 'escape' security, and in this instance the pernicious discourse of 'border security', but to articulate alternative understandings of security geared towards emancipatory ends.

The chapter proceeds in three stages. In the first I outline the 'escapist' position on the politics of security and contrast it with my own, noting my understanding of emancipation. The second section provides a brief overview of the dominant (border) security discourse regarding asylum in Australia before exploring attempts to challenge this discourse and articulate alternative conceptions of security in the process. The final section reflects on the conditions in which such a challenge might enjoy success, and reflects on what this analysis means for the way we understand the politics of security.

Escaping or reformulating security?

In international relations, security has long been associated with the territorial preservation of the nation-state from (usually) external military threat. In this image, states and military power is the stuff of security, memorably captured in Stephen Walt's (1991: 212) claim that the study of security was the study of 'the threat and use of force'.

Endorsement of this conception of security has come from a range of relatively (and surprisingly) disparate sources. Realist theorists of international relations, of course, have been happy to endorse such a conceptualization of security (e.g. Walt 1991; Lynn-Jones 1992), consistent as it is with their claims that states constitute the only consequential actors in global politics; that states are concerned ultimately with their survival as sovereign entities; and that force is an inevitable feature of a world defined by the absence of a higher power than states.

Endorsement of the conception of security noted above also comes, however, from a range of analysts concerned with conditions for normative progress in international relations. A number of these analysts ultimately validate the above account of security in contrasting such a discourse with (progressive) dynamics and practices in other settings. Accounts of the tension between security and liberty in the context of the 'war on terror', for example, consistently identified security as a negative property defined in terms of the concern with the sovereignty and territorial integrity of the state, contrasting it with the liberal concerns with individual freedom (e.g. Balzacq and Carrera 2006).

This also applies to a range of criticisms of state approaches to the issues of immigration and asylum, with critics contrasting the limited and state-based meaning of security with the cosmopolitan imperatives of concern for suffering outsiders such as refugees (e.g. Guild 2009; Hammerstad 2011). Finally, a range of critical scholars similarly suggest that such a conception of security is timeless or universal, including those who in other contexts endorse the idea that security is socially constructed: brought into being in different ways in different contexts. Most famously, Ole Wæver's analysis of the concept of security and imperative of desecuritization (1995) concluded that the latter was to be preferred because at the heart of security, 'we still find something to do with defence and the state'. In all of these accounts, the meaning of security is linked to the preservation of the territory and sovereignty of the state. And it is this (sedimented) meaning of security that should encourage us to escape security to locate possibilities for normative progress.

Suggestions that security is dangerous have – of late – been even more widespread among those concerned with the politics of security. Indeed as I have argued elsewhere (Browning and McDonald 2013), academic analyses of the politics of security – examining the question of what security *does* – have overwhelmingly identified the dangerous, exclusionary and exceptionalist logic at the heart of security (see also Roe 2012; Nunes 2012). This is prominent in Michael Dillon's (1996) account of the relationship between security and political legitimacy (see also Dillon and Reid 2009), and in Anthony Burke's (2001: 20) suggestion that security can be viewed 'as a political technology that enables, produces and constrains individuals within larger systems of power and institutional action'.

One prominent concern here has been with the notion of the exception, drawing on the work of Carl Schmitt, Walter Benjamin and more recently Georgio Agamben. The notion of the exception concerns the ways in which representations of existential threat or crises (for Schmitt, articulated by the sovereign) enable forms of extraordinary politics 'that would otherwise be stymied by normal liberal democratic checks and balances on coercive and authoritarian regimes' (Peoples and Vaughan-Williams 2010: 71). For these analysts, security is often seen as the archetypal moment of the exception, its invocation enabling the sovereign to suspend the 'normal rules of the game' and pursue extraordinary measures (see Agamben 2005; van Munster 2007).

Such analyses suggest an abiding suspicion of the logic of security, viewed as violent, exclusionary, limiting individual freedom and defining national community in narrow and exclusive terms (see Browning and McDonald 2013). Most starkly, Mark Neocleous (2008: 5) argues that:

> security has become the master narrative through which the state shapes our lives and imaginations ... producing and organizing subjects in a way that is always already predisposed towards the exercise of violence in defence of the established order.

This suspicion of security is of course also a prominent feature of the work of the so-called Copenhagen School. Here, Ole Wæver (1995) draws implicitly on Schmitt's notion of exceptionalism (see Williams 2003; Aradau 2004) to suggest that representations of existential threat can have significant performative effects (see also Wæver 2011). If an issue is securitized – represented as an existential threat by a consequential political actor (usually a state's leader) and accepted as such by a relevant audience (usually the domestic population) – it is ultimately elevated from the realm of 'normal politics' to the sphere of 'panic politics' (Buzan *et al.* 1998: 34).

Here, the way that issue is subsequently addressed is characterized by urgency, secrecy and the employment of extraordinary measures. In this context, Wæver (1995) and others advocate desecuritization as the ideal: the removal of issues from the exceptional realm of security and their return to the 'normal politics' of the (liberal democratic) realm (see Hansen 2012).

The above accounts of the meaning and logic of security capture something central to contemporary debates about and dynamics of security international relations. Security is certainly all too frequently invoked and justified in opposition to an open democratic sphere, an expansive notion of political community, or the rejection of violence, whether physical or structural. So what is wrong with these approaches, what do they ignore, and why are they limited in providing the basis for enabling progressive change? Here I identify four central limitations of these 'escapist' accounts of security.

First, while the above accounts tend towards representing a fixed and timeless meaning of security associated with the state and its defence, genealogies of security consistently point to the changing meaning of the concept over time. Analyses of the historical evolution of the concept of security (e.g. Rothschild 1995; Haftendorn 1991) suggest that the meaning of the concept has shifted, including on such fundamental questions as who security itself is primarily for and the extent to which the concept is imbued with positive or negative connotations. Most surprisingly, this is a theme of Ole Wæver's (2002) own conceptual history of security, even while suggesting in other work that there is something fixed about the content of security. In short, genealogies of security suggest that security has meant different things over time, and by extension its meaning could continue to shift. As Costas Constantinou (2000) has argued, it is possible to identify and further develop narratives of security 'that do not offer rhetorical legitimation to different regimes of power or justify the intervention of security experts and practitioners'.

Second, the meaning of security is different not only across time but also, crucially, across space. Simply, different political communities understand and approach security in different ways. This is something we intuitively know: while some states, for example, view any potential challenge to a narrowly-defined conception of sovereignty and identity as an existential threat, other states appear able to embrace a more expansive notion of political community that is deeply embedded in international society (see McDonald 2012). And as Roxanne Doty (1998/9) has argued, while states certainly conceive of issues such as immigration as security issues, it does not necessarily follow that such immigrants are presented as a threat to the nation-state. For Doty, different states (or the same states over time) embrace different security *discourses:* frameworks of meaning that define who and what values need securing and from what type of threats. Her analysis of immigration points to a core shift in American security discourse regarding Haitian immigrants: from one presenting such immigrants as a threat to the United States (Realism) to one presenting immigrants as those in need of protection (Human Security).

Understanding the meaning of security as something that – in substantive terms – changes across time and space is difficult to avoid if security is approached in terms of a political community's conception of its core values to be preserved or advanced (see Wolfers 1952). Such an understanding draws us towards examining how those values are defined; from what threats; and through what means it is seen as being best protected or furthered (see McDonald 2012). This account is suggestive of constructivist accounts of security and international relations, which attempt to explore the relationship between national identity, culture and values and the interests of political communities such as states. If we acknowledge that security is socially constructed (i.e. that it is brought into being through social interaction and processes of negotiation and contestation within political communities) then we should also acknowledge that different communities can and do understand security in different ways.

The third limitation of the approach noted follows directly from the above. Specifically, the practical effects of linking security with particular issues or policies – the implications of securitization – vary according to the different discourses of security that underpin the way particular issues are conceptualized and addressed by different political communities (see Roe 2012; Nunes 2012). Rather than a set logic of security 'kicking in' at the point at which the concept itself is invoked, in practice the implications of securitization depend on the discourse of security itself. As noted, this is a feature of Doty's analysis of changing approaches to immigration in the American context, and it is also a feature of my own book on contestation over environmental change. Here, I illustrate that the dangers of linking environmental change with security were only too prominent when security was understood as the preservation of a narrowly-defined conception of sovereignty, political community and the values of that community. In circumstances where a broader conception of a community's core values and its role in an international society were predominant, the linkage between security and environmental change was largely benign (McDonald 2012). In short, what matters politically is not the invocation of security in and of itself, but the discourse of security that underpins the way particular issues are conceptualized and addressed.

Finally, building on the analysis above and returning to the central claim of the chapter, escaping security only makes sense if this meaning and logic is taken as given. While the (albeit often implicit) ethical claim of the need to promote open dialogue, inclusive definitions of community and non-violent approaches (broadly defined) is entirely defensible, the means envisaged to achieve these ends – escaping security – does not necessarily follow from an analysis of the politics of security (see Browning and McDonald 2013; Nunes 2012). Indeed if security is seen as politically powerful and mobilizing then it is, as Antony Burke (2008) has argued, too important to be left to strategists. Rather we should acknowledge and explore the ways in which different political communities understand security, identify those actors articulating progressive security discourses, and explore the circumstances in which these more progressive understandings of security might come to prominence.

Ultimately, then, with these accounts we have a normative claim about the need to reject, contest, escape or dismantle security, one clearly oriented towards limiting the undemocratic, militarized or exclusionary politics of security. While sharing many of these normative concerns, I argue that the rejection of security as a site of progress or emancipation is built on shaky analytical ground. Specifically, this account makes sense to the extent that the meaning or logic of security is frozen across both time and space. If we acknowledge that the meaning of security has changed and can change further; that it is understood in different ways in different political communities; and that the practices to flow from particular security discourses is related to the structure and logic of the discourses themselves, then the rejection of security is less obvious as a strategy for enabling progressive change. More importantly, if security is central to the political legitimacy of key actors in global politics and is politically powerful or enabling, then 'giving up' on security could easily be construed as an abdication of moral responsibility (see Booth 2007). Rather than reject it, we are arguably compelled to attempt to reformulate such a powerful political concept and principle, in the process identifying those actors invoking progressive security discourses in concrete empirical contexts.

In the process, this chapter endorses Mark Neufeld's (2004: 111) argument that scholars of security should ask:

> How different conceptions of security – both traditional and expanded – find their way into public debates; how specific values are made socially concrete in this process; and how people both act and are acted upon in the process of history unfolding. The concern here is with identifying the political projects different notions of security may serve and, perhaps more importantly, the role of security discourses in policy-making, implementation and legitimation.

Security and emancipation

The above analysis strongly suggests the need to focus on possibilities for progress. Here, progress is defined in emancipatory terms, with emancipation understood (following Richard Ashley, 1981: 227), as 'freedom from unacknowledged constraints, relations of domination, conditions of distorted communication and understanding that deny humans the capacity to make their future through full will and consciousness'. Such an account clearly builds on Frankfurt School conceptions of emancipation, themselves drawing on Marx, and arguably encourages a focus on the circumstances and dynamics of communication whereby people/s are able to communicate their needs and interests to others.

A focus on communication as a key *means* for achieving emancipation clearly echoes the concerns of Frankfurt School theorists such as Habermas and Appel and, in international relations scholarship, Andrew Linklater (e.g. 1990; 1998). For these theorists, opening up space for dialogue creates the greatest opportunity for advancing a concern with overturning those structural constraints that prevent or limit human agency in different contexts. Paradoxically, such an account of conditions for progress could also fit relatively comfortably with the normative basis for arguments in favour of desecuritization (Browning and McDonald 2013; see also Nunes 2012). For proponents of desecuritization, it is the closing off of a form of liberal politics characterized by limits placed on normal political processes of deliberation that defines the logic of exceptionalism central to securitization (see Williams 2011a; Hansen 2011; Wæver 1995; Roe 2012). Indeed Claudia Aradau (2004) finds support for the desecuritization imperative in Laclau's conception of emancipation.

To reiterate an earlier point, however, admitting to common normative ground does not imply the same strategic response to 'security', especially if we understand the concept and its politics differently. Specifically, we should not give up on security despite the *possibility* of these illiberal dynamics because these dynamics are only a possibility (not an inevitability), and because the political category of security is too important to be left to state policy-makers and strategists (see Booth 2007). Instead, we would do well to identify and focus on immanent possibilities (those possibilities present in contemporary political orders and arrangements) for movement to a more progressive security discourse with alternative logics. Here, that entails examining the extent to which actors invoke an emancipatory security discourse: a discourse of security that is 'radically cosmopolitan; oriented to the concerns of the most vulnerable; concerned with overturning structures of oppression or exclusion; and the means envisaged to achieve these goals will not serve to deprive others of them' (McDonald 2012: 52). Such an approach entails a commitment to dialogue and deliberation with others, and as an orientation, entails what Peoples and Vaughan-Williams (2010: 26) describe as a commitment to an 'inclusionary and egalitarian' notion of identity and community.

Far from constituting a utopian vision of progress, I suggest that we can find examples of such a discourse being elaborated in a range of contexts, including by marginal actors contesting Australia's securitization of asylum-seekers. Before exploring such examples, however, it is worth providing some context to this political contestation through exploring dominant discourses of security regarding asylum in Australia, and the practices to which that discourse has been tied.

Australia and asylum-seekers

Since 2001, asylum-seekers in Australia have been represented as a threat to the security of Australia and Australians. In particular, asylum-seekers arriving by boat (often represented in short-hand as 'unauthorized arrivals' or 'boat-people') were seen as particular threats, challenging the values of Australians, the sovereignty of the country and the capacity of the Government to manage its borders. And as the 'war on terror' became the dominant security discourse in the Australian setting, asylum-seekers were represented as potential terrorists. The Government's (popular) position on asylum-seekers coalesced around the oft-repeated phrase 'we will decide who comes to this country, and the circumstances in which they come' (see Gelber and McDonald 2006).

For some (e.g. Burke 2008; Perera 2009; Hage 2003), the representation of asylum-seekers as a security threat is the latest reiteration of a dominant conception of security that has long governed Australian conceptions and practices of security. Burke (2008) locates the conservative Howard Government's approach to asylum-seekers in an enduring fear of (Asian) invasion that drove the push to Australian Federation and has underpinned geopolitical imaginaries and national identity discourses since.

The Howard Government's construction of asylum-seekers arriving by boat as a threat to Australian security reached its apogee with the 2001 blockade of the Norwegian cargo ship, the MV *Tampa*, which was carrying over 430 asylum-seekers that had been rescued from a sinking ship on its way to Australia. The Government deployed troops to blockade the vessel and engaged in a stand-off with the boat to prevent it reaching Australian shores. Following the incident, the Government also moved to excise Australian islands from the migration zone (under the Migration Amendment Act of 2001), developed offshore processing for asylum-seekers in poor Pacific Island states (the so-called Pacific solution) and moved to ensure that the media were unable to access asylum-seekers. These initiatives were strongly endorsed by the Australian public, with some polls showing support for the Government's stance as upwards of 70 per cent (see Dunn *et al.* 2007).

As I have argued elsewhere (McDonald 2011), this example seems to endorse the central claims of proponents of the securitization framework in both analytical and normative terms. Representations of threat by Government representatives were broadly endorsed in both Parliament and the broader public, and these seemed to allow emergency measures and exceptional practices (the deployment of troops, excision of migration zones). Further, the normative claims regarding the imperative of desecuritization seemed to be endorsed by the negative implications these practices had for asylum-seekers and genuinely open public debate about this issue. Asylum-seekers in need of protection were largely prevented from reaching Australian shores, while those who did were subject to mandatory detention that often involved long-term detention of asylum-seekers and associated mental health problems. The Government also developed a category of temporary protection visas (TPVs) that were granted to a range of asylum-seekers to stay for short periods, opening up the possibility that they may be sent back to their countries of origin if the political or security situations in those countries changed. This created serious uncertainty for these people in their attempts to rebuild their lives.

Evidence also emerged of misrepresentation of asylum-seekers' actions to fit within the Government's core narratives of security and the nature of the threat to Australian values posed by asylum-seekers. In late 2001, photographs of asylum-seekers surfaced that appeared to show asylum-seekers throwing children into the water to prompt rescue by Australian authorities, images later revealed to have been misrepresented (the boat in question had been sinking). At the time,

Government representatives argued that this indicated the depths asylum-seekers would stoop to in order to enter the country, with Prime Minister Howard arguing that these sort of people did not belong in Australia (see Marr and Wilkinson 2002). This supported the Government's argument that not only did asylum-seekers threaten the territorial integrity and sovereignty of the Australian state, they also threatened the values of Australia and Australians. The latter was also linked to claims in popular media outlets (particularly resonant in the context of the 'war on terror') that Islamic asylum-seekers would not integrate into Australian society and even seek the establishment of sharia law, for example. Finally, in a broader sense Australia's approach to asylum-seekers seemed to encourage a negative and exclusionary politics of identity to develop in the Australian context, with an associated assault on multiculturalism and manifesting itself in ugly race riots in Sydney's south in 2005 (see Perera 2009).

The securitization of asylum has arguably become institutionalized since 2001, such that the issue of asylum-seekers arriving by boat was largely viewed through the lens of 'border security' (rather than humanitarianism, for example). The 2007 federal election witnessed the election of a Labor Government led by Kevin Rudd, who promised a broader reform agenda in foreign policy and signalled a move away from the security focus of asylum policy. He promised to re-engage the UNHCR and an end to uniform mandatory detention and the Pacific solution, for example. By 2010, however, this approach was under serious political pressure with an upsurge in boat arrivals. The Government suspended processing of asylum claims from Sri Lanka and Afghanistan (in breach of the terms of the Refugee Convention), and after Kevin Rudd was deposed as Prime Minister by his own party (in favour of Julia Gillard), the Government retreated to the language of border security to demonstrate a commitment to protecting Australian sovereignty and identity. Within two and a half years of coming to power, the arrival of fewer than 5,000 asylum-seekers by boat in that time had precipitated a change of heart for the Labor Party, and saw the Government scrambling to claim that its position was effectively the same as that of the conservative opposition at the time of the 2010 election (see McDonald 2011). By 2013, the Labor Government had reinstated the fundamentals of the Pacific solution, once again embracing offshore processing and allowing asylum-seekers to remain in detention centres for several years (Manne 2013). And with the election of a conservative government in 2013, there has been a renewed effort to intercept and prevent asylum-seekers reaching Australia by boat using naval resources, in an operation known as Operation Sovereign Borders.

Despite all this, the claim I make here is that this example is not a simple story of the dangers of security and the imperative of locating possibilities for progress in a separate realm. Rather, this case illustrates the danger of a particular discourse of security defined in narrow, statist and exclusionary terms, positioned frequently in terms of a concern with border security and predicated on protecting a narrow vision of Australian community. We can imagine alternative security discourses, and perhaps more importantly can identify competing discourses of security in the Australian context. The following section illustrates the ways in which marginal actors articulated such alternatives, in the process holding out the possibility of an alternative (emancipatory) security discourse coming to define the relationship between security and asylum in the Australian context.

An emancipatory security discourse?

To reiterate an earlier claim, an emancipatory security discourse is one that is 'radically cosmopolitan; oriented to the concerns of the most vulnerable; concerned with overturning structures of oppression or exclusion; and the means envisaged to achieve these goals will not serve to deprive others of them' (McDonald 2012: 52). Such an approach entails a commitment to dialogue and deliberation and a commitment to an inclusive conception of community. The above discussion of Australia's approach to asylum-seekers illustrates that these commitments were far from underpinning the Government's approach, but these sentiments did find their way into the representations of a range of what we might call 'marginal' actors.

Before discussing the ways in which an emancipatory security discourse was represented by these marginal actors, it is important to note that 'security' was not directly invoked that regularly by these actors. Nor can 'security' feasibly be seen as the central means for mobilizing support for a more progressive approach to asylum. Yet it did feature (amid broader representations of rights, obligations and justice concerns), and an emancipatory security discourse was nonetheless evoked through representations of values in need of being protected, definitions of community, means of protecting them and threats to them.

While emphasizing Australia's international obligations and the associated rights of refugees, NGO groups and refugee peak body groups have advanced a particular conception of security in contesting the Australian Government's approach to asylum-seekers. In a submission to the 2008 Joint Standing Committee on Migration's Inquiry into Immigration Detention in Australia, the Human Rights and Equal Opportunity Commission (HREOC) argued that Australia's practice of mandatory detention of asylum-seekers breached the International Covenant on Civil and Political Rights. In particular, HREOC argued Australian practices breached article 9 (1), which stipulated that 'everyone has the right to liberty and security of person' (HREOC 2008). A peak body for refugee groups, the Refugee Council of Australia, also released a report in 2008 claiming that Australia should commit itself to 'human security', and move towards recognizing that refugees are ultimately the victims of insecurity or terrorism rather than agents of it (RCA 2008b: 8–9). Aside from invoking security to point to the need for a shift towards a more progressive approach oriented towards the most vulnerable, these interventions acknowledge the existence of distinctive security discourses at work (those oriented towards the state, and those oriented towards vulnerable populations).

Attempts to define Australian values in need of being preserved or advanced from the threat posed by asylum-seekers were both prominent and resonant in the Australian context (McKay *et al.* 2011). In this context, security and identity were tightly linked in suggesting that a (narrow conception of) Australian identity would be threatened by (different) others seeking to exploit the goodwill of Australians. Such representations (of a threat to core values) are important to acknowledge as security representations, defining who and what is in need of protection, and from what threats. In this context some marginal actors suggested that Australian values were threatened not by asylum-seekers, but by the measures Australia employed to prevent them coming ashore and processing them when they did. A submission by the group 'Australians for Just Refugee Programs' to a 2006 Senate Inquiry into Australia's Migration Amendment Act noted that the proposed law 'fails the Australian people. It offends Australian values and breaks international standards for human rights' (AJRP 2006). Such a representation suggested that the preservation of Australian values – a core component of a national conception of what is in need of being secured (see McDonald 2012: Chapter 1) – required a humane approach to asylum-seekers.

A diverse range of civil society groups – from church groups to medical associations and refugee groups themselves – argued that the practice of mandatory detention was 'barbaric', in the process suggesting the need to orient Australian practice towards a recognition of the rights and dignity of all persons (ABC 2011). Church groups even offered to take responsibility as 'agents' of security in this sense, offering to house asylum-seekers within the community while their claims for refugee status were processed (Wilson 2012). NGO groups such as Amnesty International called on Australia to recognize its membership in a broader global society, noting not only Australia's international obligations but also arguing that 'it should be remembered that asylum-seekers who come to Australia are human beings asking for our help' (in Akerman 2010). Representations of the humanity of asylum-seekers was also important in the context of the Government preventing media access to asylum-seekers themselves, a significant limitation given research consistently linking greater contact with asylum-seekers to more favourable attitudes towards them (Bleiker *et al.* 2013; McKay *et al.* 2011). Some critics also suggested that Australia's reputation as a 'good international citizen' was threatened, and with it the state's potential to be viewed as a constructive member of international society (see Devetak 2004). Then leader of the Australian Greens, Bob Brown, noted in Parliament in 2001 that 'this country has a reputation ... for being a country of a fair go and a country, therefore, that respects all human beings as deserving of a fair go. That reputation is now being tested' (in Every and Augustinos 2008: 575). Some members of the Labor Opposition also articulated similar views, suggesting in 2001 that Australia was 'a very multicultural society and we do live in harmony in this country. We should be an example to the world. But what kind of message are we sending?' (Hollis 2001: 30133). Here, Australian values and even its capacity to pursue its national interests through international fora were represented as that threatened by a restrictive approach to asylum.

Of course, asylum-seekers and refugees themselves have articulated an emancipatory security discourse, even while the process of mandatory detention and strict limits on access to asylum-seekers has severely limited the extent to which their voices could be heard. One detainee in a remote detention centre for almost two years – an Afghan Hazara named Hadi – noted that 'the day that I got here I was very happy that I'd come to a safe place with a humanitarian government' (in ABC 2011). This representation pointed both to the inconsistency of Australia's policies with Australians' self-image as a humanitarian people, while also reminding us of the failure of states to live up to their part of the social contract on which their security claims and political legitimacy rest. Indeed Hadi's experience with the Taleban in Afghanistan reminds us that states can be the cause of vulnerability for their own people. Widespread incidents of self-harm within detention centres, and the conclusion drawn by detainees that they had simply been imprisoned by the Australian Government (ABC 2011), evoked emancipatory imperatives concerned with the rights and needs of those populations and the need to have their voices heard.

Finally, minor political parties such as the Greens have, as noted, articulated an emancipatory security discourse regarding asylum-seekers. In a representative speech on asylum in 2010, Green Senator Hanson-Young (2010) noted the imperative of a system that oriented towards 'the needs of asylum-seekers in a practical, humane and long-term manner'. Senator Hanson-Young (2010: 1565) also noted that Australia's approach to asylum-seekers was inconsistent with that of 'a country that considers itself compassionate and a champion of the "fair go"'. This latter representation – of a restrictive approach and the 'demonization' of asylum-seekers as a threat to Australian values – is important to note given the tendency for harsh attitudes on asylum to orient around the threat asylum-seekers pose to Australian values (see McKay *et al.* 2011; Pickering 2011) and given the mobilizing potential of such identity narratives in advancing alternative security discourses. For the purposes of this chapter, such representations also illustrate the ways in which marginal actors can and do evoke emancipatory security discourses through articulating alternative conceptions of the boundaries of the community concerned, the values of that community in need of being preserved, and the means of protecting or advancing those values.

The case of Australia's approach to asylum-seekers represents a 'hard case' for those attempting to locate progress through (alternative discourses of) security. The dominant discourse of security regarding this issue was one oriented towards border security and the preservation of a narrowly-defined national community from the threats posed by asylum-seekers, and actors contesting such an approach frequently argued against a security framing of this issue. In this sense, the push to escape security makes normative sense, as does the broader association of security with illiberal practices. Yet even here, marginal actors can and do articulate alternative discourses of security. By pointing to the ways in which these marginal actors evoke an alternative (emancipatory) understanding of security, we recognize security as a site of contestation, and we recognize a multiplicity of ways in which security can be understood and approached.[1] The marginal emancipatory security discourse briefly mapped above constitutes what Jennifer Milliken (1999: 243) defines as 'subjugated knowledges'[2]: frameworks marginal to the conduct of debate or pursuit of policy but which can work 'to create conditions for resistance to a dominating discourse, and perhaps an exploration of how the dominating discourse excludes or silences its alternative'. While the association of security with a restrictive approach to asylum-seekers is clearly problematic, it ultimately does not represent the essence of security's meaning and logic. Rather, it represents the dominance of a particular security discourse over others that can be, and are, articulated in the political struggle over Australia's approach to asylum-seekers.

Conclusion

In this chapter I have argued that the 'escapist' position on security is based on broadly sound (if underspecified) normative commitments but ultimately rests on shaky analytical ground. It is only when we accept a particular meaning and logic of security as universal and timeless – in the process serving to further sediment a security discourse – that the normative imperative of escaping security makes sense. If, by contrast, we acknowledge security to be a social construction, the meaning of which changes over time and for different political communities, we open up the possibility for security meaning and doing something quite different from the dominant politics of security in contemporary global politics. Indeed I have argued that not only can we imagine alternative security discourses with varying logics, progressive security discourses are actually invoked by actors in concrete political contest. This suggests immanent possibilities for a progressive shift in the discourse of security that comes to dominate the way a particular community conceives of its values, the threat to those values and the means through which they might be best protected or advanced.

I have defined progress here in emancipatory terms, orienting around a conception of security that is built on an inclusive and egalitarian community, entails a commitment to dialogue and deliberation, is focused on the rights and needs of the most vulnerable and is concerned with the removal of structural impediments to peoples' capacity to exercise control over their own lives. Such a conception of security is, of course, not without its drawbacks or critics, including among those deeply sceptical of the benefits of linking security and progress (see McDonald 2012: Chapter 2). Yet as the case noted above illustrates, the central claims or tenets of this discourse were invoked by actors precisely contesting the problematic politics of a narrow, exclusive and militarist discourse of security in the Australian setting.

Perhaps the key question to emerge from this account is: to what extent can we imagine such a conception of security genuinely underpinning the way a political community such as Australia approaches asylum-seekers? Here there is certainly much cause for pessimism, not least given popular support for restrictive measures in Australian approaches to asylum-seekers arriving by boat even in the context of very few arrivals in either historical or comparative context. The 2010 federal election, for example, saw the major political parties scrambling to portray themselves as tougher on this issue, in a competition Senator Green described aptly as a 'race to the bottom' (Hanson-Young 2010). For both parties, its approach to asylum-seekers was to be underpinned by a concern with 'border security'.

The dominance of this discourse of security was enabled by the failure of Labor Government that replaced the architect of Australia's Pacific Solution – John Howard – to articulate a feasible alternative conception of Australian identity and values to which a more progressive approach to asylum might be tied. The Labor Party ultimately worked with a conception of national identity inherited from the previous government, manifested in the political assault on multiculturalism, the rejection of 'black armband' history pointing to the indigenous dispossession central to colonization, the celebration of participation in war as the founding of the Australian nation, and ultimately the celebration of a narrow conception of national identity.

Identity, like security, is constructed and permeable. 'Identity entrepeneurs' would do well here to emphasize nascent and progressive narratives of national identity linked to the realities of living in a multicultural society, the values of egalitarianism, and the ethics of compassion and care for suffering others. Such expressions of what it means to be Australian can be found in a range of accounts of Australian history and identity (see White 1981), but have not been strongly mobilized in support of a compassionate (or even reasoned) approach to asylum-seekers arriving by boat. Following constructivist insights into identity narratives (e.g. Barnett 1999) and even the work of Bourdieu on symbolic power (1991: Chapter 7), for example, invoking and attempting to embed such conceptions of Australian identity can provide a powerful basis for enabling and furthering progressive change. Such shifts will not be easy, but immanent possibilities certainly exist within the contemporary Australian context.

Notes

1 This contestation is particularly intense and complex in the case of immigration and minority groups , where strategies of desecuritization that might downplay distinctive values and identities of such groups can be complicated by those actors' determination to precisely emphasize their distinct values and 'societal identity'. On this point, see Roe (2004), and for a counter-point, Jutila (2006). I am grateful to Paul Rodgers and Thierry Balzacq on this point.

2 The concept of 'subjugated knowledges' was originally articulated by Foucault (1980: 82). I am grateful to Thierry Balzacq for drawing this to my attention.

Part IV
Resilience

Editor's introduction

I

Of the four strategies of contesting security, resilience raises a set of new and difficult to tackle questions for security scholars. In part, this is because resilience is a concept whose transfer to security studies is still in its infancy. Moreover, resilience evokes many experiences and meanings, which convey distinct types of concerns (Anthony, 1987; Cicchetti and Garmezy, 1993; Beardslee, 1989; Rutter, 2006; Rogers, 2012a).

That said, three understandings of resilience can be singled out. First, materials sciences, for instance, defines resilience as "the ability of a material to resume its original shape or position after being spent, stretched, or compressed" (Goldstein and Brooks, 2013: 8). It is in this sense that contemporary policies on the protection of critical infrastructures tend to emphasize the necessity for developing resilient systems in different sectors. The aim here is threefold: to reduce the vulnerability of these infrastructures; to improve their capacity to absorb attacks of various sorts, and recover easily if affected; and to design in-built resilient properties for new infrastructures, such as adaptive structures in earthquakes. Second, resilience is also used to characterize subjects' ability to "overcome significant adversity considered to impair normal development" (Goldstein and Brooks, 2013: 8). Third, resilience refers to policies which strive to protect the identity if not the physical integrity of the subject. In this context, it comes close to resistance: subjects can face hardship and nonetheless move on successfully (Bourbeau, 2013c). In fact, it is this special capacity of some to beat the odds that was featured in one of the very first articles published on the topic by the *Washington Post*, on 7 March 1976.

Thus, the journey from material sciences and clinical psychology to security studies has taken more than three decades. I guess what I want to suggest here is that in order to get the most out of the concepts of resilience students of security studies should delve deeper in the insights generated by previous attempts at understanding what resilience is, why and when does it obtain or not, and whether collective actors (not only individuals) can be resilient (cf. Lee, 2005; Hartling, 2008; Clauss-Ehlers and Levi, 2002).

II

One of the most intriguing elements is the extent to which resilience can be learned. If it can, then, what are the most important factors that are conducive to an effective construction of a resilient subject? In general, public policies that call for resilience often assume away non-learned features that might impact on a subject's resilience (age, hereditary health conditions, etc.). Instead, the emphasis is put upon the strategies that can be deployed in order to enable subjects to overcome adversity and allow the society to continue to operate without or with little disturbance.

Taken from the point of view of security policy's targets, the question becomes: how do subjects offset the undesirable consequences of security policies on their lives? How do they operate effectively and thrive despite the constraining pressure of negative forms of security policies? Obviously, many factors can be taken into account in order to provide an explanation. They range from religious beliefs to education, gender, personal history, family conditions, societal characteristics, etc. In other words, why some are resilient more than others is not an easy to answer sort of question. And the chapters falling within this section will not attempt to do so. But those interested in this type of topic will find a rich body of literature in clinical works on resilience (cf. Lindström, 2001; Masten, 1994; Luthar, 1993; Patterson, 2002).

Paradoxically, resilience combines status quo and change. A resilient subject does not remain inactive in face of adversity or merely react to risk hazards. In the first case, the subject is passive; in the second, the subject is resisting. Resilience is not a fatalistic attitude of an almost unavoidable threat. It is a proactive ability to absorb risk hazards and pursue life without becoming dysfunctional. In short, it is the "capacity to maintain adaptive functioning in spite of serious risk hazards" (Rutter, 1990: 209). This means, at the same time, that resilience involves various intrapsychic as well as social processes, which enable a subject to deal with obstacles (Walker and Salt, 2012: 14).

III

The contributions gathered in this Part stress the diffuse understanding of the concept of "resilience" and work towards clarifying its meanings, as well as social and political usages. In Chapter 11, Philippe Bourbeau distinguishes three types of resilience (resilience as maintenance, resilience as marginality and resilience as renewal), which he sees as having their own internal structure and rationale. However, the chapter insists that there is no normative hierarchy among the three forms of resilience as they can be present in various proportions in a given society, as regards a specific issue. The chapter offers a new reading of the management of migration in France and Canada, using this new understanding of resilience. In Chapter 12, Peter Rogers uses disaster management in order to substantiate his thesis that resilience can be a very effective tool for promoting fixity and neutralize creativity. Building on a very specific understanding of societal security, which he connects to a neoliberal ideology, Rogers argues that the management of resilience often resorts to the standardization of thought and practice, which lead to the impoverishment of creativity. The same empirically grounded reading of resilience permeates Chapter 13. Mika Aaltola discloses the ways in which resilience discourse operates at the global level. He does so by investigating the life cycle of pandemic scares (SARS, avian flu, swine flu) through the imaginaries of securitization/medicalization. One of the compelling results is that in the global health sector, resilience tends to be embodied in metaphors of immunity. However, as this immunity is acquired, or so the argument runs, discourses of resilience calls for a reform of global health systems in line with the new type of fast-spreading diseases. In this sense, the chapter is also an inquiry into the ways in which resilience might transform our understanding of global governance.

11 Resiliencism and security studies
Initiating a dialogue

Philippe Bourbeau

Introduction[1]

In recent years, a great deal has been written in the scholarly literature about the role of resilience in our social world. This scholarship has sparked vivid theoretical debates in psychology, criminology, social work, and political geography about the nature of resilience and how scholars should go about studying it. Indeed, psychologists have sought to uncover the internal and external resilient qualities that help people to bounce back and to adapt positively in the face of profound adversity – that is, adaptation that is substantially better than would have been expected given the circumstances. Several criminologists and social workers have proposed instead to 'de-individualize' resilience and to see it as a temporally and contextually informed process. Political geographers have employed resilience to analyse how co-evolving societies and natural/ecological systems can cope with, and develop from, disturbances. Understandably, environmental change and the environmental regime have been a central focus of attention for this literature.

Yet, political science, International Relations, and particularly security studies have been relatively absent from the vibrant discussion. To be sure, references to resilience have been made in terms of the erosion of sovereignty, social capital and the welfare state in the face of economic liberalization and globalization. Equally, a focus on urban resilience in the face of terrorism and counter insurgency has grown to become a dynamic field of research in the past decade. But while this scholarship has opened up a convincing space for understanding the role of resilience in the study of world politics there is very little coherence and consensus as to the nature and substance of resilience. The term is employed but rarely unpacked, let alone theoretically analysed.

It is therefore imperative to attempt to pull together the pieces and to suggest a theorization of resiliencism as applied to world politics, and particularly to the securitization process. Indeed, resiliencism could lead to new theoretical and empirical ways of understanding the contemporary security world and could help us to gain a better understanding of the securitization process – i.e. the process of integrating an issue into security frameworks that emphasize policing and defence. The gist of the set of arguments that I put forward in this chapter is that resiliencism sheds new and significant light on the securitization process as well as on the instruments, strategies, and practices of contesting the securitization process.

The first section of this chapter provides a brief introduction to how the concept of resilience has been defined and deployed within social sciences and beyond. While recognizing the importance of these contributions, I argue that they all share elements that are problematic in a study about the relationship between contestation and securitization: they eschew that resilience has a dark side and that resilience is always a matter of degree. The second section proposes a typology of resilience – resilience as maintenance, resilience as marginality, and resilience as renewal (in short, the MMR resilience). In an effort to establish a dialogue between ideas and evidence, I illustrate my arguments with the case of the securitization of migration in France and in Canada. This section also initiates a dialogue and offers suggestion as to what a resiliencist approach brings to securitization research. The concluding remarks summon up the set of arguments presented and seek to identify some of the main challenges for research on resilience in world politics.

The dark side of resilience

Resilience is a concept that cut across several disciplines. Psychology, ecology, criminology, engineering sciences, human resources studies, nursing, organizational studies, computer science, and social work have all either tackled, debunked, measured, employed, studied, tested, hypothesized or criticized resilience (Anaut 2005, Bruneau,*et al.* 2003, Luthans 2002, Ollier-Malaterre 2010). Resilience has been identified as one of the most important and challenging concepts in contemporary psychology (von Eye and Schuster 2000), in ecology (Brand and Jax 2007), and in human geography (Zimmerer 1994). As works on resilience have increased in recent years, so too have criticisms that resilience is imprecise or useless (Klein *et al.* 2003, Tisseron 2007). Needless to say, thus, resilience has attracted a significant amount of scholars' attention.

Psychologists, criminologists and social workers have been studying and theorizing resilience for a long time (Garmezy 1974, Rutter 1987). One of the main elements in this scholarship is the notion of 'bouncing back'. After all, the English word 'resilience' originated in the sixteenth and seventeenth centuries, deriving from the verb 'resile', which in turn was drawn from the Latin verb 'resilire', meaning to 'jump back, recoil'. Thus, the ability to recover from or adjust easily to misfortune, adversity, unease, conflict, failure, and/or change is central (Seery *et al.* 2010). A large strand of this scholarship aimed at uncovering the internal and external resilient qualities that help people to bounce back and to adapt positively in the face of profound adversity – that is, adaptation that is substantially better than would have been expected given the circumstances (Bonanno 2004, Donnon and Hammond 2007, Hauser 1999). Wanting to move away from a conception of resilience as a set of dispositional qualities or protective mechanisms of the individual, several criminologists and social workers have proposed instead to 'de-individualize' resilience and to see it as a process (Gilgun

2005, Norris, Stevens *et al.* 2008, Rumgay 2004, Seccombe 2002). As such, the definition of resilience was slightly modified to 'a dynamic process encompassing positive adaptation within the context of significant adversity' (Luthar *et al.* 2000: 543, see also Masten and Powell 2003). Resilience is therefore seen not as a set of predetermined qualities that an individual possesses (or not), but as a temporally and contextually informed process (Ronel and Elisha 2011, Schoon 2006, Ungar 2004, 2011).

The fields of political geography and environmental studies have also been dynamic in studying resilience, albeit from a different angle. A large strand of literature employs resilience to analyse how co-evolving societies and natural/ ecological systems can cope with, and develop from, disturbances. Stemming from the ecological sciences, this scholarship seeks to address persistence and change in ecosystems (Carpenter *et al.* 2001, Gunderson 2000, Holling 1996), socio-ecological systems (Berkes *et al.* 2003, Walker *et al.* 2006), and in terms of the impacts of natural hazards (Cutter 2008, Klein *et al.* 2003, Renaud *et al.* 2010, Zhou *et al.* 2010). Three main currents have emerged from this literature: engineering resilience, ecological resilience, and socio-ecological resilience. Engineering resilience is associated with the concept of equilibrium and is about studying the conditions specifying how far a system can be displaced from a fixed point of equilibrium and still return to that equilibrium once the disturbance has passed. Ecological resilience somewhat moves away from the idea of equilibrium and is defined as the capacity of a system to experience disturbance and still maintain its ongoing functions and controls (Holling 1973). Social-ecological resilience postulates that the focus of resilience is not only on being robust to disturbance but also on the opportunities that emerge, in terms of self-reorganization, recombination, and the emergence of new trajectories (Berkes and Folke 1998, Folke 2006, Walker and Meyers 2004).

Political science, and security studies in particular, is a late comer in this field of research. The concept started to make inroads in International Relations a decade ago when scholars connected resilience with global governance, highlighting resilience in the face of economic liberalization (Pfister and Suter 1987, Ross Schneider 2008), of globalization and labour market reforms (Yan Kong 2006), and of change in public service reforms (Clark 2002). References to resilience has been made in terms of erosion (or lack thereof) of sovereignty (Ansell and Weber 1999) and about NATO's future in a post-Cold war era (Barany and Rauchhaus 2011), while others have employed the concept to describe Indonesia's national security doctrine in the 1960s (Acharya 1998, Dewitt 1994, Emmers 2009). In the same lineage, resilience of authoritarian regimes to democratic pressures has been underscored (Byman and Lind 2010, Case 2004, Gilley 2003, Kamrava 1998, Nathan 2003, Slater 2003) and the resilience of nationalism in the face of regionalism has been studied (Dieckhoff and Jaffrelot 2004). Peter Hall (1999) has spoken about the resilience of social capital in Britain in light of the apparent erosion of social capital in the United States and Paul Pierson (1996) about the resilience of the welfare state (see also Lindbom and Rothstein 2006).

In spite of IR scholars relative neglect, the idea of resilience in the context of terrorism and of international intervention has gained popularity in recent years (Baruah 2009). America, for example, has been said to be resilient in its fight against terrorism and in mitigating natural disasters (Flynn 2008). Fuelled by the 2005 London bombings and the SARS outbreak, a focus on urban security and threat/risk management has grown to become a dynamic field of research (Coaffee and Murakami Wood 2006, Coaffee and Rogers 2008, Harrigan and Martin 2002, Rogers 2012a, Vale and Campanella 2005). Efforts to improve preparedness, especially at the community and local level, were intensified, and emergency management infrastructure became a top priority for several governments (Edwards 2009, Kahan *et al.* 2009, Rogers 2011b). Other scholars juxtaposing resilience with biopolitic/biosecurity have interpreted resilience as a strategy for reconciling liberty and security (Lentzos and Rose 2009, Lundborg and Vaughan-Williams 2011). From a quite different angle, David Chandler has recently proposed distinguishing between the resilience paradigm and the liberal internationalist paradigm to the study of international intervention; the former being about prevention, empowerment, and responsible agency. He defines resilience as 'the capacity to positively or successfully adapt to external problems or threats' (Chandler 2012: 217). Whereas Mark Duffield, in his study of the aid industry, understands resilience as a postmodernist technology that internalizes emergency within society and focuses upon the adaptation of the individual (Duffield 2012, see also O'Malley 2010).

The importance of these studies should not be underestimated, particularly in making steps towards introducing resilience into the IR literature (broadly defined). Yet, these studies do not seek to theorize resilience nor do they offer any discussion towards such a goal for they are simply asking different sets of questions.

In fact, these conceptualizations of resilience share three elements that are problematic for the transference of resilience thinking to the study of IR and particularly to securitization studies. First, they start with the premise that the disturbance (or the shock) is inherently negative and that resilience is about positive adaptation. There is indeed a large acceptance in this literature that resilience is good and thus must be promoted. This might simply be a disciplinary bias as resilience is often employed to describe the capacity to react to sexual abuse, terrorist attacks, or disturbances of global ecological systems. Being resilient in the face of such trauma is unequivocally a positive adaptation.

Notwithstanding, these definitions eschew that resilience has a dark side, especially in societal terms. Resilience is not always a desirable feature of social, political or economic life. Being resilient might in fact mean being an obstacle to positive change in some cases. I am not arguing that one should find a way to interpret terrorist attacks in large cities as positive policy. But I do argue that there might be good reasons for wanting to transform a social structure, a given situation, a regime, a norm, an economic system of exploitation, etc., and that being resilient to these changes could be considered as negative. Displaying an *a priori* normative bias seems rather limiting here as adaptability may be both positive and negative. Furthermore, as heated debates are currently unfolding in securitization research about whether the process of securitizing an issue is inherently normatively positive (as the chapters by Rita Floyd, Thierry Balzacq, Sara Depauw, and Sarah Leonard, and Claudia Aradau in the book illustrate nicely, see also Hansen 2012, McDonald 2011, Roe 2008b), it appears rather timely and important that our understanding of resilience remains normatively open and avoids this closure.

The second element that these models have in common is their tendency to understand resilience in a binary way. Resilience is usually seen as an all or nothing concept: either there is resilience or there is not. One direct consequence of this is that the notion of a scalar understanding of resilience is either under-theorized or entirely lacking in some cases. Just as there is a scale of securitization there is a scale of resilience (Bourbeau 2011, 2014). Another consequence of treating resilience in a binary way is that it eschews the question of types of resilience. This is problematic because it creates a disconnection – in theoretical and empirical terms – between the complexity of contemporary security policy and the analytical framework proposed to make sense of the different patterns of response that security policy brings.

A third limit of some of these models – especially the engineering and ecological resilience approaches – is their positivist inclinations and traditional linear conception of causality. These models have difficulties accommodating the plurality of meanings, the complexity of social worlds, the inter-subjectivity of knowledge and measurement, and multifaceted contexts. The applicability of ecosystem-derived dynamics to explain the social world composed of complex social structures and reflexive agents remains, thus far, unclear and unconvincing (Adger 2000).

Resiliencism: typology and promises

With the limits of these definitions in mind, I suggest an alternative conceptualization of resilience as the process of patterned adjustments adopted by a society or an individual in the face of endogenous or exogenous shocks. Resiliencism is then a conceptual framework for understanding how continuity and transformation take place under these circumstances (Bourbeau 2013c).

Inspired by Stephen Dovers and John Handmer's typology (1992, Handmer and Dovers 1996), I further propose to identify three types of resilience (see Table 11.1). I indeed distinguish between resilience as Maintenance, resilience as Marginality, and resilience as Renewal – in short the 'MMR' typology.

The first type – resilience as Maintenance – is characterized by adaptation in which resources and energy will be expended in maintaining the status quo. The importance and saliency (and 'threateness') of the problem will often be exaggerated in order to better justify the necessity to implement measures to uphold the status quo against changes provoked by the events. Re-affirmation of the value, benefit, and importance of the status quo will be made on several occasions. A society relying strongly on this type of resilience will deal with

Table 11.1 Resilience in securitization research: a typology

Types	Focus	Discourses and practices	Outcome	International migration
Resilience as maintenance	Quest for constancy and stability	Often aligned	Fixing national identity; resurgence and/or saliency of political usage of collective memory; reinforcement of existing agents' power relations	Arrival of boatload of refugees interpreted as a security issue for a society; potential threat to social cohesion if nothing is done
Resilience as marginality	Marginal adjustments	Often not aligned	Changes at the margins that do not fundamentally challenge a policy; responses within the boundaries of the norm or social structure	No wholescale rethinking of the immigration policy; dominant discourses highlight that current immigration policy can adapt successfully
Resilience as renewal	Efforts to remodel social structures	Often aligned	Remodelling of a given policy or social structures; pressure (and potentially shift) in agents' power relations; low mobilization of collective/social memory	Profound reform of immigration and citizenship policy; the arrival of boatloads of refugees seen as offering a window of opportunity for a new beginning

endogenous and exogenous shocks with rigidity and will underscore the potentially negative transformative consequences brought about by these events. Disturbances or shocks are not by definition problematic or negative; they will be socially constructed as being threatening and dangerous by dominant discourses. Although the possibility that a disconnection between security discourses and security practices exists, resilience as maintenance will often see an alignment of discourse and practices. Rhetoric and discursive powers will be deployed to portray the event as a significant threat and security practices will also be either implemented or strengthened as a response.

In the context of international migration, a society opting for resilience as maintenance will identify the movement of people (either through an emphasis on 'mass migration' or 'illegal migration') as an important security threat and as a threat to collective identity that should be fought. The arrival of boatloads of refugees on the country's shores will be interpreted as a security threat to the host society and its social cohesion. Agents' securitizing moves will reinforce the saliency of the threat and the need to further fix collective/national identity.

The case of how dominant narratives in France interpreted the so-called worldwide refugee crisis of the early 1990s and the chosen pattern of adaptation to this exogenous shock is a clear example of resilience as maintenance. Indeed, while the number of refugees worldwide was 9 million in 1984, it reached a peak of 18 million in 1992. The surge gave rise to all sorts of projections and scenarios such as the image of waves of refugees and the uncontrollable and unstoppable movement of people. And it gave securitizing agents the opportunity, if they were so inclined, to present international migration as a security threat requiring an urgent and strong response otherwise the breakdown of social cohesion beckoned and the very notion of a French nation was in peril. It turned out that there were numerous agents happy to use such a triggering set of events to pursue a securitization agenda.

As early as 1991, Socialist Minister of the Interior Philippe Marchand (January 1991 to April 1992) argued that uncontrolled migratory movement would be a threat to France's economy and security (Marchand 1991). His successor, Paul Quilès (April 1992 to March 1993) spoke of the security threat of irregular migration on a number of occasions, arguing that regaining control over immigration was a fundamental element in maintaining social cohesion in France and that irregular immigration had be fought accordingly. Sections of the media joined in, *Le Figaro*, one of the most important newspapers in France with a weekly circulation of 2 million copies, argued in 1990 that 'we must suspend immigration otherwise everything is possible: the country is on the verge of burning fiercely' (Giesbert 1990b: 1) and that immigration was 'de-structuralizing French society' (Giesbert 1990a: 1). Other editorialists openly wondered whether France had a future as a nation (Lambroschini 1992: 1) on the basis that 'the wave will never stop growing' (Marchetti 1993: 1).

In 1993, centre-right Prime Minister Édouard Balladur (March 1993 to May 1995) argued that the early 1990s was no ordinary time in the history of France. In fact, it was 'the most difficult period since the war' and that bridging the traditional left/right political division was essential to tackle the problem effectively (Balladur 1993b). He further argued that if measures were not implemented, then 'what is happening elsewhere would happen in France: principles to which we are profoundly attached [would be put] in serious peril'. 'France is an old nation', he continued, 'which intends to survive and remain the same' (Balladur 1993a: 4).

Echoes of resilience as maintenance also found expressions in Charles Pasqua's mandate as Minister of the Interior in the Balladur government. Pasqua pushed for a securitization of migration in an unprecedented way, arguing that international migration, particularly clandestine immigration, needed to be urgently and strongly combated otherwise France's national cohesion would be threatened and France's national identity would disappear. French people needed to remain strongly together, to foster the national community, and to understand that his bill reinforcing repressive measures to impede access to French territory and to limit the entry of several categories of migrants constituted the 'last chance to save France's integration model' (Pasqua 1993).

The second type – resilience as Marginality – is characterized by responses that bring changes at the margins but that do not challenge the basis of a policy (or a society). Resilience as marginality implies responding within the boundaries of the current policy, norm, and/or social structure. The nature and importance of the 'problem' will often be presented as being less salient than with the first type of resilience, but an effort to acknowledge the issue and to recognize that marginal adjustment is needed will be made. There is a danger that the minor changes implemented may delay the major changes that some may argue are required. There is also the possibility that the marginal adjustments made at one point in time (and thought of as being marginal at that time) become extremely important and influential at another point in time (and thus not seen as marginal anymore). This type of resilience will often see a disconnection between security discourses and security practices. In some cases, discursive powers will be almost absent and marginal changes in security practices will take place. In other cases, security practices will mostly remain the same but a shift in discourse and how the event is discursively represented will constitute the source of marginal yet important adjustments. As such, studies emphasizing the role of security practices might reveal different patterns of responses than a focus on speech and discourses – and vice versa.

In the particular context of international migration, a society opting for resilience as marginal change will emphasize the need for marginal adjustment given the considerable increase in the movement of people in the past two decades. But there will not be a whole scale rethinking of the immigration policy. Dominant discourses will highlight the need to keep adjustments within the boundaries of the existing immigration policy. 'New challenges' brought by the disturbances will be acknowledged but reassurance will be made that current immigration policy can adapt successfully and that an extensive revision of the policy is not required to deal with these challenges. Efforts to crystallize the collective identity of the host society will be present but less salient and powerful than with resilience as maintenance. Practices at the heart of the securitization of migration (e.g. detention policy) will be maintained and most likely further developed and expanded. However, no fundamental governmental reorganization will be pursued as a response to the disturbance.

The arrival of 599 Chinese refugees on Canada's western shores in four decrepit boats and one shipping container during the late summer of 1999 – the so-called 'Chinese summer of 1999' – is illustrative of resilience as marginality. This exogenous shock resulted in a groundswell of emotion across Canada and significant media coverage for a few months, and it prompted debate over state sovereignty, radicalization, citizenship, collective identity and failing immigration and refugee policies (Bourbeau 2011, 2013a, 2013b, Mountz 2010). While Prime Minister Jean Chrétien (November 1993 to December 2003) played down the arrival by emphasizing that more asylum applicants arrive in Toronto (Canada's largest city) every month than arrived by ship on Canada's west coast in summer 1999, two political agents, in particular, competed in the effort to inscribe meaning to the crisis and to define Canada's reaction to the exogenous shock: Lloyd Axworthy, Minister of Foreign Affairs (January 1996 to October 2000), and Elinor Caplan, Minister of Citizenship and Immigration (August 1999 to January 2002). Caplan's interpretation of the 'Chinese summer of 1999', and what it meant for the immigration and security policy of Canada, ultimately prevailed.

Instead of mounting a charge to the effect that immigration was bringing all sorts of security problems to Canada, Axworthy (1999: 3) cast the whole incident under the human security agenda. That is, that the arrival of the boats 'brought home to Canadians the ugly reality of another human security threat of global proportions – the smuggling and trafficking of human beings'. In fact, the 'Chinese summer of 1999' was a sordid illustration that

> millions of vulnerable people have been forced from their homes; been driven to borders which are open one minute and closed the next; forced into hiding; separated from their families; made to act as human shields; stripped of their identities; sexually abused; and callously killed.
>
> (Axworthy 2000)

Citizenship and Immigration Minister Elinor Caplan decided to interpret this exogenous shock differently. In one of her first speeches following the event, Caplan kept the traditional focus on the 'abusers' while adding something new: a security component through the issue of detention. 'We know that if an accelerated process is part of the solution, so is an enhanced detention policy' argued the Minister. 'We have already announced proposals to increase detention if a person is undocumented and uncooperative ... We will take every action necessary to deal with the abuse of immigration and refugee processes' continued Caplan (1999b: 4).

Caplan's key message was that there was no need for a large-scale rethinking of Canada's immigration policy, only adaptation at the margins of how Canada dealt with some aspects of the movement of people (Caplan 1999a, 1999b, 1999c, 2000, 2001). Detaining migrants in correctional facilities to counter the security threat of the arrival of boats loaded with refugees was the key adaptation to the Chinese summer. Citizenship and Immigration Canada had had a contingency plan for the arrival of refugee boats since the late 1980s, but changes were made to the plan to allow the systematic use of containment and detention in cases similar to the Chinese summer. Unsurprisingly, the use of detention of migrants in correctional facilities to manage refugee and migration flows saw an increase of more than 50 per cent between 1999 and 2003 (Bourbeau 2011).

The third type – resilience as Renewal – is characterized by responses that transform basic policy assumptions and, thus, potentially remodel social structures. Resilience as renewal implies introducing novel vectors of response that will (in an implicit or explicit way) fundamentally change existing policies and set new directions for governance in this field. Redefinitions, however, do not take place in a vacuum but draw on past experiences, collective memory and social history, as well as the windows of opportunity upon which agential powers decide to act (or not) (Bourbeau 2011). As with resilience as maintenance, the importance of the disturbance (or the shock) may often be exaggerated, but unlike the objectives of the first type of resilience, that seek to maintain the status quo, the goal here is to present the option of renewal as inescapable. The disturbance has such profound ramifications that substantial reorganization of the policy is strongly desired. Redefinition often involves important shifts in interpretation and meaning, in agents' power relations, as well as in institutional and organizational configurations. The particular social mechanisms by which redefinition and renewal are carried through are multiple and could include analytic deliberation, nesting strategies, institutional variety, etc. (Dietz *et al.* 2003).

This is not to argue that everything would be created anew after a disturbance, as if events and agency were unfolding in a social vacuum. Yet, resilience as renewal means that disturbances would play a triggering role in a sustained and systematic effort to change profoundly a given policy or how a society understands and interprets a particular set of issues.

In the context of securitized migration, a society opting for resilience as renewal will identify the disturbances created by international migration as a window of opportunity to reform their understanding of the movement of people, and eventually their relationship with diversity and alterity. Renewal could take the form of embarking on a profound remodelling of how migration is described and perceived. Citizenship and refugee determination policy programmes or national security policy might be entirely reformed, for example.

These types are not mutually exclusive and they can be found in the same society diachronically and synchronically. Furthermore, a society can adopt one type of resilience in one domain and another type of resilience in another domain. By definition, resilience as maintenance is no more normatively negative or positive than resilience as renewal; as such, there is no normative continuum that starts with maintenance and ends with renewal.

A resiliencist approach underscores that the sources of change may be endogenous or exogenous and that the outcome of change is not necessarily a return to a previous equilibrium; resilience is thereby grasped as an inherently dynamic and complex process. Resilience does not imply finality as the process can never be fully completed; the process is inherently dynamic and always in movement. As such, resilience is always a matter of degree; complete immunity towards disturbances and shocks does not exist. Resilience is also constantly in flux. It is not a fixed attribute or an unchangeable characteristic of a society or an individual. No society is always resilient and resilience does not express itself in a flat, stable, or variation-free way Resilience is also dependent on time; resilience can refer to how well a society is navigating through some past adversity such as 9/11 (retrospective), how successfully a society is navigating through some current adversity (concurrent), or the likelihood that a society will successfully navigate through disturbance in the future (prospective). Resilience takes context seriously, which render difficult – if not impossible – the development of a comprehensive theory of resilience but it does stimulate a richer dialogue between ideas and evidence (Bourbeau 2013c).

Understanding resilience as the process of patterned adjustments adopted by a society or an individual in the face of endogenous or exogenous shocks shed new light on securitization studies and on the contemporary security world. Without a doubt, resiliencism in security studies is still in its infancy and there is a need to develop research programs if it wants to establish itself as a dynamic and stimulating approach in securitization research. In what follows, I want to make few steps in that direction in suggesting ways of broadening and deepening resiliencist research agendas.

First, a resiliencist approach can improve research on the questions of change and endurance in the securitization process. Indeed, continuity and change are concepts that current models (or theories) of securitization have difficulty to theorize convincingly. On one hand, the CoS' model by focusing only on moments where exception is invoked misses the numerous ways in which security practices are reproduced across time. Unless we accept the proposition that we are living in a permanent state of exception and that exception-is-the-rule (see Prozorov 2005, Wood *et al.* 2003), the CoS' model has difficulty dealing with the idea that mechanisms of security are proliferating and generating a constant sense of insecurity, fear, and danger (Dillon 1996, Doucet and de Larrinaga 2010, Huysmans 2011, Neocleous 2008, Walker 2006, Weldes *et al.* 1999). On the other hand, what a sole focus on security practices has a hard time explaining are change and critical junctures as well as the impacts of these 'window of opportunities' on contemporary security affairs. Advocates of the 'practice turn' in security studies have not yet proposed guiding principles to make sense of key moments of change in the securitization process where actors step out of adopted boundaries and transcend the field of action in which they normally are engaged. By emphasizing the social mechanisms through which the securitization process is reproduced, the routinization of security practices approach downplays the factors that might tell us how the securitization process can be changed. In a friendly critique, Michael C. Williams argues that if security is defined away from an explicit logic of extremity then there is a danger that it will become difficult to distinguish any number of policy changes from ones that specifically relate to security. He further points out that

> while the language of emergency can appear an obstacle to more theoretically nuanced and empirically grounded understanding of concrete practices, it may at the same time provide an anchoring device through which 'security' dynamics can be discerned and distinguished from 'normal' change with the policy process.
>
> (Williams 2011b: 217)

Research on resilience has already started to make inroads into these questions. Rogers (2012a) has indeed shown that resilience allows for a revised understanding of changes in regulation of urban order and security. Employing the method of spatial history, he argues that urban security was (re)constituted through a process of struggle between social forces that sought renewal and social forces that opted for maintenance. Resiliencism offers thus one way of reconstituting change over time, space, and place in order to better understand the social and practice patterns that (re)constitute everyday life and bring 'security home' (Coaffee and Murakami Wood 2006, Coaffee and Rogers 2008, Rogers 2012a). In the field of international intervention, David Chandler has recently argued that it is because the discursive power of human security stems from its articulation with the resilience paradigm, which stresses in this field of research a programme of empowerment and capacity-building, that we can better grasp the shift in dominant security discourses 'away from the liberal internationalist framework and towards a growing emphasis on preventive intervention' (Chandler 2012: 216).

By underscoring the role of critical junctures and path-dependence in the securitization process, resilience studies would also supply one way (among others) to strengthen the ties between securitization research and the literature on self-reinforcing dynamics, enduring consequences of history and legacy, and the importance of imprints left by social norms and culture (Capoccia and Keleman 2007, Falleti and Lynch 2009, Hacker 2002, Mahoney 2000, Mahoney and Thelen 2010). At the moment, arguments about these elements are scattered and dispersed in the literature on securitization. A resiliencist approach would offer a unifying analytical category to better understand the nature and expressions of these elements in the securitization process.

In fact, resilience's focus on critical junctures (or endogenous/exogenous shocks) would nicely complement research on the role of context in the securitization process. One of leading sociological explanations of a context-informed securitization focuses on distant and proximate context, which highlights respectively the genre of interaction among participants and the macro-sociocultural inscriptions of securitizing practices (Balzacq 2011a). Yet, scholars attuned to this approach have so far found it rather difficult to anchor their theoretical arguments with extensive empirical research. Very few studies have sought to empirically demonstrate the importance of context in the securitization process (Bourbeau 2011, Curley and Wong 2008, Salter 2008). By providing analytical axioms (such as the MMR typology proposed) through which "context" can be further conceptually and empirically studied, resiliencism might fruitfully connect the fuzzy and elusive notion of context with contemporary social world.

Second, current research on the variation in securitization cries for a resiliencist approach. Scholars have recently argued that an important flaw of securitization research and particularly of the Copenhagen's school (CoS) is that it does not take into account scale of securitization. The only variation that the CoS recognizes, for example, is along the spectrum of non-politicization, politicization, securitization, and desecuritization. The CoS appears to be treating security as a binary notion: either an issue is securitized or it is not. As such the CoS has difficulty distinguishing whether an issue (whether compared across time within case or across cases) is strongly securitized or weakly securitized (Bourbeau 2011, 2013a, 2013b).

To be sure, there are methodological and empirical issues about the idea of a scalar understanding of securitization that this chapter cannot fully engage with. In the case of securitized migration, I have tackled the issue of variation at some length elsewhere where I have developed a set of indicators that includes institutional (I) and security practices (P) indicators. I have registered the most important Acts as well as provisions relating to the linkage between migration and security making sure to highlight their content along the migration-security nexus (I-1). I have explored whether immigration is listed as a security concern in policy statements that relate to security and foreign affairs, and I have codified the existence (or not) of a particular department in charge of border control and national security in which immigration is seen as a key element (I-2). I have then measured the saliency of the link between migration and security within these policy statements (I-3). In terms of security practices, indicators that relate to the migration-security nexus, I have looked at interdiction practices (P-1) and at the magnitude of the detention of immigrants both in absolute terms and in terms of the proportion of detained immigrants versus the immigration intake (P-2). On the basis of these indicators, I have demonstrated that both Canada and France score on all indicators of securitized migration *and* that significant variation exists between these two cases: the outcome for Canada, with low saliency and low detention rate, is a weak securitization, whereas the outcome for France, with high saliency and a high level of immigrant detainees, is a strong securitization.

Conceptualizing resilience as MMR types suggests moving away from understanding securitization as a binary notion. Indeed, it could provide guidance for the suggestion of hypotheses in order to gain deeper insights into the question of variation in degree of securitization within case across time and across cases. If we accept that the securitization process is first and foremost about the mutual constitution of security performances and social structures, surely then hypotheses put forward to make sense of the variation might have included societies' processes of adaptation? The central question about scale of securitization is neither whether a variation exists or not (clearly it does) nor whether the variation is objectively true or not. Rather, the question is how societies' processes of adjustment to shocks and to security performances, produced at a particular moment in time, differ from that of the same societies at a different time or from that of a different society.

For instance, in the particular context of securitized migration, findings suggest a correlation between on the one hand differences in scale of securitized migration between Canada and France (Bourbeau 2011) and on the other hand the MMR typology of resilience aforementioned. When dominant forces in a society manage to implement a resilience as Maintenance type (France) the outcome is a strong securitization of international migration, whereas if resilience as Marginality is the preferred option (Canada) the outcome is a weak securitization. Obviously, this correlation is so far nothing more than a correlation. Yet, it certainly represents a worth-pursuing research hypothesis in a relatively uncharted field of research.

Third, and in a related way, juxtaposing securitization research with research on resilience provides a leeway into the thorny issue of audiences in the securitization process. The place, role, and nature of audiences in the securitization process have captured a significant amount of attention of late in the literature.

Seminal contributions have proposed to conceptualized audiences as those who decided whether a securitization is successful (Buzan, Wæver *et al.* 1998), as providing moral and formal support (Balzacq 2005), as different settings in which securitization takes place (Salter 2008), or with insights from Kingdon's three streams model (Leonard and Kaunert 2011). These studies have considerably improved our understanding of the significance of audiences in the securitization process. Yet, a consensus remains in the literature that the question of audiences is left under-theorized and/or under-specified in most models (or approaches) to securitization and that the documented empirical analysis of 'audiences' remains murky at best.

Resilience could complement these studies. Since resilience is always a matter of degree, as societies can be more or less resilient both diachronically and synchronically, resiliencism seems well suited to further develop and understand some aspects of the question of audiences. Distinguishing between resilience as Maintenance, as Marginality, and as Renewal, resiliencism indeed offers an analytical framework that moves away from an understanding of the role of audiences as one of 'accepting' a given security speech act, that traces the impact of both security performances and audiences' adjustments on the development of a given policy response and on the contemporary social world, and that permits the study of how dominant ways of framing (and adapting to) issues emerge within a society. In other words, resilience broadens our understanding of the multi-directional relationship between agents' security performances, societies' processes of adaptation, and endogenous/exogenous shocks.

Conclusion

A number of researchers have recently questioned the theoretical approaches of the securitization process by emphasizing the role of contesting strategies in security studies, as the contributions to this book illustrate nicely. Still, studying social mechanisms of contesting securitization in IR remains an uphill debate with many questions being raised but few being resolved. This chapter has sought to deepen our understanding of the various meanings and practices that can be attached to resiliencism in different socio-cultural contexts. In doing so, I have (a) briefly traced the evolution of the definition of resilience; (b) proposed to distinguish between three types of resilience, and (c) offered suggestion as to what resilience brings to securitization research.

While resilience has been a central field of research in psychology, criminology, and ecology for the last decades, it is only recently that it has gained attraction in IR and in security studies. The fact that in the past few years the UK and Canada (to take only two examples) have launched huge governmental initiatives to help build local and national resilience is probably not a coincidence in this regard. Yet, and more to the point in the context of this chapter, the fact that students of security studies are still struggling with difficult questions associated with the process of securitization, such as the question of change and continuity in the securitization process and how societies/individuals navigate through, facilitate or limit the securitization process is no coincidence either to the emergence of resilience in security studies. In their search for a better understanding and convincing explanation to these questions, scholars have found it increasingly useful to expand the tool kit provided by key securitization models, theories, or schools – as illustrated by several contributions to this volume.

The question is then not so much why we need to develop (or invent) a new concept (this is obviously not the case) but rather to what extent this already existing and interdisciplinary concept is helpful for IR and security studies scholars. In other words, what is the added-value of importing resilience into security studies? Although the jury is still very much out on this question, this chapter took small steps in answering – in an affirmative way – that question. Indeed, I have argued that resiliencism holds a great deal of potential for renewing the wider security and governance research agenda. Multi-type resilience helps in understanding the constant and complex interplay between persistence and change, reproduction and transformation. A resiliencist approach provides one among several arenas for generating integrative and interdisciplinary collaboration on issues of change and stability, adaptation and design, hierarchy and self-organization in the study of contemporary security governance. All in all, resiliencism may hold the key for developing securitization research in dynamic directions as it may establish new areas of empirical investigation currently either ignored by mainstream security scholars or overlooked by critical security scholars.

Notwithstanding these potentials, resiliencism comes with thorny challenges that will most likely orient future research. One of the most important challenges is a methodological one. Undoubtedly, there is a lack of a methodological toolkit that could adequately capture the role of resilience in securitization research and in world politics. This is hardly surprising given the fact that a resilient approach to the study of securitization is still very much in its infancy. Yet, the question of whether mainstream social sciences methods are capable of incorporating all aspects of resilience might be the logical and conventional place to start. Research attuned to practices, genealogy, and deconstruction might offer more promises. Another avenue of promising cross-fertilisation might be a more thorough engagement with comparative scholars' expertise in research design. For example, importing David Laitin's (2002) provocative set of arguments about a tripartite methodology would perhaps provide resilience studies with tremendous depth and sophistication. A better understanding of the comparative similarities and differences would significantly foster research on when and how individuals or a society engage in the process of patterned adjustments in the face of endogenous or exogenous shocks. Still, another worth-pursuing research method would be process-tracing, which and particularly so with its recent refinements might allow scholars to broaden our understanding of the social mechanisms at play in resilience (Bennett and Checkel forthcoming, Collier 2011, George and Bennett 2005, Gerring 2007). In the thorny challenge of identifying order-in-complexity, the best we can hope at this stage of the research is the participation of a multiplicity of research methods in our quest to better understand resilience in world politics.

Note

1   I thank Routledge for its permission to reuse some material previously published in my article 'Resiliencism: Premises and Promises in Securitisation Research', *Resilience: International Policies, Practices and Discourses*, vol. 1, no. 1 (2013), 3–17. For useful comments on previous versions of this paper I would like to thank Thierry Balzacq, Barbara Delcourt, Valérie Rosoux, Christian Olson, David Chandler, Lene Hansen, Peter Rogers, Juha Vuori, Rita Floyd, Mika Aaltola, Florent Blanc, João Nunes, members of the Tocqueville Chair in Security Policies at the University of Namur, workshop participants at the University of Copenhagen, the Université Libre de Bruxelles, and the Université Catholique de Louvain.

12 Resilience as standard

Risks, hazards and threats

Peter Rogers

Introduction

This chapter offers a critical social science approach to contesting security. Links are clarified between the rearticulation of 'disaster resilience'[1] with that of societal security. It is not the purpose of this chapter to address the genealogy of societal security and resilience,[2] but to offer a different approach to their contestation. The focus here is narrower. I will use 'standards' to reappraise the links between security and resilience, using *professional quality standards* as an area within which these concepts are contested. Of particular importance to this contestation is the critique of resilience through the lens of neoliberalisation – particularly in international relations, sociology and political geography. If one accepts that 'neoliberalization [is] the reorganisation of societies through the widespread imposition of market relationships' (Graham, 2010) then the critical appraisal of resilience *and* security should be embedded in these relationships. This allows for the conceptual contestation to be grounded in practical issues of governance across all forms of risk, hazard and threat – not limited to 'realist' conceptions of military security or to the critique of the Copenhagen School narrative as discussed in other chapters of this volume.

I have argued elsewhere that resilience is best understood by identifying the characteristics and features of ways of thinking, doing and acting as they are rearticulated in cycles of neoliberalisation (Rogers, 2013a). An addition to this approach, offered here, is to begin identifying the institutional foundations of being resilient and trace them through policy-based 'speech-acts'. These acts inform the practical actions undertaken to improve security – be that individual, household or inter-state – and help map the overlap and interplay of diverse dangers from distinctly different sources that increasingly blur the boundaries of a broadened security concept in practice. Clear examples of this ongoing process are found in the standardisation of disaster management, risk management and societal security, discussed below. In 'societal security' standards we can trace the concrete issue of disasters (regardless of type) and map how this becomes 'principled' by the standardisation of practical actions taken by both experts and lay-persons. Interplay emerges when the standardised principles and practices for dealing with danger are legitimised through the discourse of 'resilience'.

Resilience becomes a speech-act used to legitimise the experimental regulatory reforms. Where the order thus imposed is rigid regulatory 'rigidity traps' – in operational practices, tactics, metrics and measurements – are created. These limit resilience creating maladaptation, described here as *negative trajectories*. Where the order thus imposed by such speech-acts creates an improved flexible capacity to mitigate crises across complex systemic interdependencies – in networks, systems and processes – the outcomes are here described as *positive trajectories*. However it is important to remain critical.

Where the metaphor (as speech-act) of *disaster* resilience seeds positive regulatory reforms the concept is utilised as an all-encompassing framework. Within this framework a range of standards and tools can be mobilised, without restricting contextual innovations. Such tools become means to an end rather than ends in and of themselves; they are not *measurable forms of* 'resilience' but rather *toolkits for building* 'resiliency'.[3] It is possible in this reading that targeted standards for best practice (e.g. in vulnerability analysis, risk management, command and control and so on) may be used guide the sharing of best practice. The governance of crises requires complex interdependent ways of thinking, doing and acting for actors in their individual or organisational context. The challenge is to strike a balance between the need for professional standards of best practice (across diverse local, regional, national and international contexts) when the policy convergence of regulatory reforms is contested. The lack of clarity in such processes may lead to arbitrary installation of limited and risk-averse regulatory standards – simpler to understand, measure and evaluate, but also replicating a linear, militarised governance model.

By genealogically mapping the re-emergence of resilience in professional quality standards we have the opportunity to contest security, opening new avenues for the critique of neoliberal governance. Where standards of measurement are most common in this area is in the operational duties of emergency services, volunteer groups, civil services and political actors, applied to notions of risk, hazard and threat within the emergence of disaster resilience as a profession. Risk may be seen as tendentially bound to a standardised 'risk management'; hazard is bound to environmental, socio-technical and industrial 'events' and threat is often bound to security, terrorism and militarised geo-political issues. However these distinctions are increasingly rendered permeable, not the least through the overlap of organisational roles and responsibilities and the growing calls for professionalisation of the flexible skills central to the broadened responsibilities of the emergency and security professionals. As resilience has been used to encapsulate all categories of danger within a single discourse the resilience speech-act is a powerful tool. It can be deployed as a lens through which to map the features and characteristics of successful practice of what is becoming a contested metaphor of societal security. Critical reflection, such as that undertaken below, also helps highlight the dangers of 'over' standardising the management of disasters, which undermines the societal security thus contested.

Resilience (RE)conceptualised: management, disasters, standards

It is a sad reality that when disasters strike, despite the best efforts to prepare, there will always be vulnerabilities, things that did not work as planned, resulting in new lessons to be learned and improvements to be made. New vulnerabilities are discovered after exposure to some form of negative, and often destructive, stimuli. Organisations[4] are able to learn from what worked and what went wrong before, during and after an event; but as the expansion of deregulated capital has become increasingly global, contradictions have also become increasingly apparent between 'capitalism' and 'democracy'. One such example is the structure of opportunity surrounding disasters; especially when the disaster is treated as a process allowing at once (a) pre-emptive mitigation and prevention through comprehensive approaches to planning, testing and preparing for disasters, but also (b) targeted investment that ensures the tactics and tools of response and recovery are as cost-efficient as possible, yet able to minimise human and economic losses. This wicked problem of reconciling pre-emption and reaction has seen the rise of a policy metaphor of 'resilience' to all forms of danger and new economic opportunities and challenges to be understood. The resilience metaphor incorporates a sense of learning from experience into a logic of adaptation, better understanding the transformative potential of all individuals, agencies, resources (etc.) that are a part and parcel of the disaster cycle (before, during and after the event). Perhaps the key challenge then has become how to evaluate, track and measure the outcomes of increased investment in disaster resilience and ensure that both the actors and the tools they use to deal with danger are rigorously assessed and fit for the task. Substantial financial investments must be evaluated to tender proof of success. This is even more so a concern during times of international financial austerity. Such tracking and evaluation is one the one hand the purview of governments, but the responsibility for developing and implementing the technical mechanisms and tools that underpin the cost-efficient reform of the regulatory regime are not only the task of government and civil service; they are also frequently undertaken by corporate, industrial, research and professional organisations. Such endeavours may include the development of metrics to assess or indicate compliance to quality standards as well as the coordinated professionalisation of niche employment areas (such as security professionals, humanitarian workers and emergency managers) as demand grows for skilled workers in these fields. The transfer of international expertise through these regulatory regime changes is as such less a feature of governance policy, as a political or ideological agenda, and more driven by the conflation of issues such as: public liability; policy evaluations; cost-benefit measurements; performance metrics; best practice and quality standards. An international industry has emerged stimulated by crises requiring better coordination of such actors. Professional networks, targeted government funding initiatives and the enhancement of professional training have all also contributed significantly to the shape and focus of how danger is to be dealt with.

Within the regulatory regime changes occurring in the management of disasters, the forms of danger have come to be treated not as specific events to be responded to and recovered from, but as a cycle of capabilities to be mobilised before, during and after the event. Through the disaster cycle as a process-driven approach risk can be pre-emptively assessed and managed, hazards and threats can be understood and mitigated, the adaptive capacities of 'resilient subjects' can be increased and the overall 'societal security' of a given social order can be enhanced. The regulatory reform thus shifts the focus of experts from rational and risk driven response and recovery models prevalent during the Cold War towards the dual rhetoric of risk and resilience. Under this articulation resilience incorporates all hazards – anthropogenic (be they military or civil), technological (industrial and infrastructure), or ecological (from the immediate impactful event to gradual climate change). The focus of working seeks to balance standardised risk-based toolkits with flexible multi-skilled actors engaged in quality-driven process improvements. In this context professional, national and international quality standards have come to supplement, and in some cases effectively replace legislation. Standards appear able to cross-jurisdictional and organisational boundaries with less difficulty and can be reviewed or amended more swiftly in ensuring the fulfilment of the statutory obligation of governments to protect in a complex and uncertain working environment. Important standards of note in discussing risk and resilience are the ISO31000 'Risk Management' and the ISO22300 'Societal Security' standards, though there are a range of related standards affecting niche market expertise across the broader field of security and emergency.

Regulatory regime reform: the role of international standards

International quality standards are a key component of the regulatory rule regimes underpinning neoliberal alignments of governance, but as yet they have not been adequately addressed by research. A push for standardisation of best-practice, professional accreditation of expertise and coordinated training for identifiable skills sets in security and emergency professionals is increasingly embedded in the regulatory regime change underpinning the globalisation of disaster resilience. Such a process is not new; it has been embedded in economic and public policy for many years – e.g. the expansion of labour and trade standards through the World Trade Organisation (WTO) / North American Free Trade Agreement (NAFTA). This process is central to the cycles of realignment through which neoliberal governance practices are perpetuated, rhizomatically reappearing within seemingly unrelated areas. For evidence of this 'flat' ontological rearticulation across fields of knowledge one need only look to the reappearance of the RAND Cold War rationalism in psychology (for example see Laing, 1967) and economic policy (for example see James, 1991) in the twentieth century; a process now also encompassing what has been called 'disaster capitalism' (Klein, 2008) and elsewhere the governance of 'disaster resilience' (Rogers, 2012b).

The management of disasters has been tied to different iterations of civil defence, civil protection and civil contingencies as well as ecological, human and economic variations on security (see Coaffee *et al.*, 2009; Rogers, 2012c) but an increasing interest in the regulatory regimes of risk is embedded in the rise of resilience. Critique of the negative implications of regulatory reform reflects the critique of risk – as a repackaged global-local realignment of neoliberal managerialism (Peck and Tickell, 1994; Peck *et al.*, 2010).[5] This has implications for the socio-economic securitisation of related disaster work, such as humanitarian aid.[6] The positive implications however suggest that within this regulatory reform lie the seeds of a disaggregated counter-neoliberalism driven by contextual variation of best practice at the local level (Rogers, 2013c). However the nature of standards needs to be further unpacked before either of these claims or trajectories of change can be understood in an applied context.

The international standards organisation (ISO) is one of the organisations central to the development, distribution and adoption of professional standards in a number of areas – though it must be acknowledged that national and industry specific bodies also operate in tandem and sometimes competition with this group. Standards tendential to disaster resilience include, but are not limited to; information security (ISO27000 series), risk management (ISO31000 series) and, at the time of writing, a suite of standards across operational elements of what has been branded as 'societal security' (ISO22300 series). This kind of international standard is distinct from operational principles and guidance that are developed by specific international governance agencies, for example the United Nations (UN). There are similarities however in the role such documents play in generating convergence in broader policy metaphors, as well as in the institutionalisation of specific operational benchmarks and practices. UN guidance documents have a connection to disaster resilience but less in terms of the specific operational practices of emergency and security professionals. This example of resilient thinking may be more commonly apparent in humanitarian aid and the management of displaced persons emerging from civil and military conflict or following natural disaster relief operations by non-governmental humanitarian organisations. The complexity of establishing standard requirements for practices of intervention is a complex issue. Such humanitarian guidance may rest on a policy continuum somewhere between military interventions to prevent or limit genocide and the responsibility to protect (R2P doctrine). In such cases the form and type of intervention different from ecological disasters, where threat to life is military or conflict-driven any marginal threat to human rights, even emerging from generalised civil disorder, may justify a 'violation' of the sovereign rights of a given nation-state (Pape, 2012). Humanitarian guidelines are often as such often voluntary general principles, as are some of the ISO standards. These differ again from regulatory regimes associated with trade or workplace rights which tend to more legislative forms of statutory obligation. Acceptance and implementation of these practices vary greatly across the context in which they may be applied, and thus variations by organisation, jurisdiction, and the type of crisis or event to which such issues appertain are common. The shift most relevant to understanding the implications of the regulatory rule regime of disaster resilience, as distinct from Cold War rationalist rhetoric, is in the focus of governance. The political rationale underpinning previous approaches to the governance of danger has privileged the understanding of risks. Risk assessment before disasters is used to help strategically target resources, enabling a swift response to and recovery from distinct events. So pervasive has this become that an industry of risk management has emerged, as has a critique of the role risk plays as a dominant influence on the wider governance of everyday life. In a civil defence model, this places the emphasis soundly on the actions of experts during and after the disaster occurs. As this has evolved however the pre-emptive nature of risk has been used to justify the logic of perpetual uncertainty, some social problems have become ongoing militarised crises (e.g. the war on drugs, the war on poverty) and military conflicts themselves have moved beyond the post-Westphalian conflicts of nation-states to the disaggregated cellular struggles, such as the 'war on terror', with potentially no recognisable end or victory.

The implications for governance of disasters and the logic of resilience are manifold. As risk has become incorporated into pre-emptive actions as well as responses to distinct events a number of key changes have emerged in understanding the roles and responsibilities of key stakeholders and experts. The actions available to experts are increasingly repackaged as individual and organisational capabilities. The mobilisation of these capabilities is now seen increasingly as the capacity of the components in an interdependent system to cope with stress, both external and internal in origin. The understanding of events themselves has been realigned from a treatment of the disaster as a distinct external hazard event to one that understands disasters as a manageable cycle of capabilities. These capabilities are embedded into the everyday actions of individuals and organisations, helping to reduce the danger by imagining and understanding potential risks, hazards and threats regardless of whether they occur or not. The policy rationale underpinning disaster resilience is thus one that moves beyond the specific capabilities of experts and widens the lens from response and recovery after the fact to a two-stage cycle of anticipation, assessment, prevention and preparation as *pre-emptive* and response and recovery as *reactive*. This notionally is seen as a cycle by which the recovery phase is joined up to new vulnerabilities identified by exposure to an event, and then reassessment of the capabilities and capacity of the system to cope, with training and planning to better mitigate and prepare for future occurrences. Disaster resilience thus operates as a perpetual cycle of learning, driven by the need to enhance and improve the tools and processes of crisis management.

Standards play a key role in this cycle as they provide recognisable and identifiable toolkits based in principle on the lessons learned from exposure to previous events, shared apolitically across jurisdictions and organisational boundaries where otherwise information sharing and knowledge exchange may be limited to those few individuals active during the disaster cycle for a specific event. Standards organisations like ISO are often recognised as politically neutral by many politically accountable organisations (such as local and state emergency services and civil government). This increases the potential for standards agencies to inform best practice where statutory obligations may vary in specific national jurisdictions, and to offer benchmarks for the development of variations by nation-state – through bodies like Standards Australia (SA). International/ national standards provide benchmarks and best practice but do not create a legal obligation to conform, nor do ISO regulate conformance in local, regional or national contexts. Regulatory processes are the province of governments and industry. The institutionalised standard offers a set of features and characteristics for improved 'ways of doing' in different organisations. As such standards provide measurable benchmarks for conformance that can be evaluated and scored against key performance indicators, a key feature of neoliberal governance in many contentious areas. Such practices have been used widely to regulate the performance of education (Apple, 2004) and public services (Clark, 2002) and increasingly recognisable in the governance reform within the neoliberalisation of disaster resilience. This contextually embeds these principles as features of organisational practice and workplace culture, but the extent of this as real change is specific to the organisation – in many cases appearing as 'old wine in new skins' to many experienced professionals entrenched in previous models or methods.

Both standards and guidelines may recommend or demand conformance, where voluntary adoption shows willing engagement; rejection of these standards may lead to exclusion from the growing profits to be made in the market-place of security, resilience and disaster capitalism. Potential economic benefits are not limited to tax breaks for utilities providers, cost-saving product development in partnership with government organisations (with a statutory obligation to conform not shared by the private sector) and rebuilding, repairing or upgrading critical infrastructure and disaster defences (e.g. pipelines, cables, flood barriers, border security etc.). All of these factors have the potential to affect change on a range of best practices in diverse agencies, of course:

> this increasingly occurs within a geo-regulatory context defined by systemic tendencies towards market-disciplinary institutional reform, the formation of transnational webs of market-oriented policy transfer, deepening patterns of crisis formation and accelerating cycles of crisis-driven policy experimentation.
>
> (Brenner *et al.*, 2011)

The Risk Management Standard (ISO31000:2009) is perhaps the best example of a market-driven need translated into an cross-sectoral industry standard then becoming common practice and thoroughly embedded in diverse organisational contexts. Components of the ISO31000 series are now commonly used in: the financial sector (from commercial to investment banking), utilities, food services, occupational health and safety, postal delivery, emergency management and more. The ongoing development of 'societal security' standards is now extending beyond the principles of risk management to offer minimum standards for emergency planning and disaster responses in a way not previously seen. These range from, but are not limited to: the creation of a common vocabulary, the requirements for preparedness and continuity management systems, video surveillance format for system interoperability, business continuity management systems, emergency management command and control, exercises and testing guidelines and the set-up of statutory public-private partnership arrangements (ISO, 2011). Such developments suggest that there is a formal regulatory regime of emergency and crisis management taking root at the international level under the parabulia of resilience; creating at once a common language, a common set of tools and a commonly shared set of best practices potentially at odds with the fluidity implicit in a more metaphorical resilience. It is unclear at this stage however to what extent these international standards are driving regulatory reforms or reacting to an identified need, if they have engaged the diversity of expertise at local levels in different contexts or if they may create top-down rigidity traps through over-standardisation and uncritical policy transfer or convergence. Brenner *et al.* (2010) have suggested that neoliberalisation is a process of change rather than a specific form of governance, and one that thrives on the differentiated incorporation of the alternatives into its own regulatory regime. In this reading the potential for change may be limited by the swift incorporation of resilience into the pre-existing ways of thinking, doing and acting. Whilst it contains the potential for a positive reformation of the regulatory regime this may not occur where resistance to the idealised policy metaphor is limited by organisational culture and established standards that do not reflect the adaptive nuance of resiliency. As such, it may become little more than the expected 'old wine in new skins' (O'Brien *et al.*, 2005). The relevance and applicability of standards and the role they play in the convergence of policy and practice across national, regional and local scales of expertise is yet to be fully understood and requires further investigation.

Reconciling resilience with policy convergence

As suggested in the introduction to this chapter this section will not seek to offer a comprehensive overview of the contested theories of policy convergence in international relations, however there are some useful synergies to be identified between these fields and the critical appraisal of regulatory regime reforms emerging from the discussions of neoliberalisation introduced above. To this end, some of the broad areas of contestation can be identified and aligned with this discourse to help shape the analysis of resilience as an exemplar of regulatory reforms that may offer positive and negative outcomes from convergence, coordination and transfer from policy rhetoric to implemented operational tactics *in situ*.

Perhaps the most common or influential critique of policy convergence is the 'race to the bottom' (RTB) thesis, itself perhaps a notional political-economic expansion of the rational choice game 'the prisoners dilemma' into the field of international relations. A simplified rendition of this theory perspective suggests that in order to maintain the interest of footloose capital investment then nation-states must engage in a form of regulatory competition with each other to create the most attractive and profitable market. The result is a 'race to the bottom' in the progressive reduction of citizen protections (such as workplace rights, trade unionism, etc.) in favour of the potential capital gains for non-state profit-making organisations. This can be seen reflected in the neoliberal economic strategies and social policies emerging from public choice, mass privatisation and deregulation of financial markets and many of the privatised industries over the last 50 years. Karl Polyani has been much cited in warning of the potential negative impacts of an unregulated race to the bottom:

> To allow the market mechanism to be the sole director of the fate of human beings and their natural environment, indeed, even of the amount and use of purchasing power, would result in the destruction of society ... nature would be reduced to its elements, neighbourhoods and landscapes defiled, rivers polluted, military safety jeopardised, the power to produce food and raw materials destroyed. Finally the market administration of purchasing power would periodically liquidate business enterprise, for shortages and surfeits of money would prove as disastrous to business as floods and droughts in primitive society.
>
> (Polyani, 1944: 57)

Such circumstances have been realised in the ruthless deregulation of Russia, following the collapse of the Soviet Block, and of Iraq, following the military intervention by the US-led coalition. Perhaps somewhat ironically it is the very frequency and scale of disaster events, such as floods and droughts, which are now key drivers of the regulatory regime reform underway through the rise of resilience thinking. The RTB doctrine also runs counter to the reflexive need to increase the security and performance of critical infrastructures, many of which are now privatised, embedded in the logic of resiliency. Where the globalisation of neoliberal capitalism is a financial dream (rather than a moral one) resiliency implies the inverse, requiring a greater corporate social responsibility. Critical infrastructures cannot be run into the ground for profit in an uncertain and insecure world, such the water pipelines in areas of the UK – which may cause cascade failure of transport networks, also threatening supply chains and the distribution of goods or even affect other utilities. Many of the regulatory reforms aligned with risk management and business continuity inculcated into the resilience remit have as such been mobilised and marketed as cost-saving measures rather than regulatory interventions when liaising with private sector partners.

Perhaps more aligned with experience of disaster resilience regulatory reform, and less extreme in its predictions, is the neoliberal institutionalism approach. This approach supposes that nation-states consciously coordinate policy through a relatively small coalition of actors. This renders monitoring easier but requires international organisations to coordinate the institutionalisation of ways of thinking and doing into ways of acting (such as enforcement strategies across jurisdictional contexts).[7] This approach also supposes that coordination operates better through regional organisations as opposed to global groups as the complexity of competing interests is reduced along with the number of actors. However: 'because of the possibility of multiple equilibria, neoliberal institutionalism is fuzzier about the location of convergent policies' (Drezner, 1997: 61). Professional associations without the legislative limitations of state-based organisations seem to offer a potential site for the coordination of multiple equilibria, guided by the clearer definition of organisational roles and responsibilities such coalitions provide.

Resilience does not fit neatly into political-economic models of international relations, as its prime emphasis is 'processual'. The alignment of multiple equilibria across scales of action is perhaps rendered less opaque by mobilising a neo-Foucauldian critique of neoliberalisation alongside these theories of policy convergence, one which further allows room for incorporation of the individual subject in potentially more critically productive ways (see for example O'Malley, 2011). A 'processual' critique conceives of a relationship between processes of neoliberalisation and the uneven regulatory development embedded in variegated scalar contexts as at once national, territorial and bipolar (Brenner *et al.*, 2010: 188). However the assumption of homogeneity within national regulatory regimes struggles to articulate the organisational variations of regulatory principles and practices embedded in specific professional skills sets and across sub-national organisational contexts. One cannot assume that the regulatory regimes will be the same in all locales, or states in Australia, for example. The sub-national legislative, organisational, jurisdictional diversity defines homogeneity, rather evoking the need for a reflexive pluralism when reaching out to implement resilience in regulatory reforms.

Professional networks form communicatory pathways which can be read as a combination of mimetic transfer – in the adoption of the policy rhetoric – which results in regulatory reform through compliance to industry specific, non-statutory operational standards. What has been here described as a neo-Foucauldian approach to the process of neoliberalisation thus frames 'convergence' as occurring through interspatial circulatory systems. Such systems do not create a homogenous or 'smooth' policy transfer process. Rather the result is contextually variegated cross-jurisdictional forms of 'borrowing, appropriation, learning, cross-referencing and coevolution' (ibid.: 189). Numerous trajectories for the extent of regulatory restructuring open up in different contexts. The context-specific forms of regulatory restructuring, the processual systems of inter-jurisdictional policy transfer and the resultant rule regime parameterizations form a complex variegated interplay, ongoing over time – e.g. as funding, government priorities, organisational coalitions shift over time. As this is not a static or linear process of change the outcomes of efforts to increase resiliency are uncertain. However through exposure to disaster events in recent years it has been proven that a lack of interoperability and over-specialisation leads to higher negative impacts. In the London bombings of 2005 a lack of interoperability in the communications systems hampered the response in clearing the train tunnels after the bombing. A lack of clarity in the roles and responsibilities of key agencies was one of many factors that stymied the response to Hurricane Katrina in the USA, also in 2005. In Australia a lack of flexible and high-speed communication and information reporting increased the vulnerability of many individuals and communities to a fast moving bushfire of unprecedented scale in 2009. In disaster riven Haiti in recent years, a lack of communication and coordination between responding agencies led to large-scale under occupation of emergency housing by local populations as the provision did not match local family living habits or socio-cultural needs during the recovery. In all these cases the vulnerabilities were identified as a result of exposure to disaster events despite comprehensive regulatory reform, preparatory and preventative measures in years preceding them; even in some cases for humanitarian aid agencies with a wide range of previous experience in disaster relief. Similar examples of vulnerabilities identified after exposure emerge around the world (from biological crises like SARS to earthquakes and tsunami). The negative impacts of unforeseeable or large-scale events might have been reduced by the high standard of the organisational resilience structures and operational practices; but it must be acknowledged that they can never be fully removed. As such the perpetual process improvement cycle embedded in the treatment of disasters is increasingly important. International standards provided from the top-down by international organisations provide a means by which to formalise the lessons learned from best practice, but at the same time where these are uncritically mapped across jurisdictional contexts they risk embedding an inflexibility to those diverse local, regional and national variations of expertise and organisational structure. Policy convergence thus requires an appreciation of the disaggregated nature of governance that encourages pluralism in multiple equilibria, and feedback from the bottom-up as well as leadership from the top-down. A homogenous mono-cultural model of governance, of resilience or of societal security is neither accurate nor useful. Resilience as a form of regulatory rule regime thus operates in a different way from classical neoliberal managerialism. The significance of quality standards for societal security is in the inculcation of standards beneath the political-economic positivism and legislative structuralism in everyday actions of individuals. Resilience operates at the level of beliefs, values and practices for those agents forced to make decisions in variegated organisational contexts. From a cynical appraisal of the existing trajectory of neoliberalisation one may suggest that the positive potential of resilience is often limited by the wider reliance on a structural critique that may miss the nuance of procedural analysis at the level of experience. There may be in the disarticulated forms of counter-neoliberalisation occurring at local levels through community driven resilience initiatives where opportunities emerge to create regulatory experiments that seed a deeper socialisation of market forces. Here also we can see these opportunities in climate change adaption strategies at the individual level, such as sustainable food collectives and household based renewable energy incentives that increase broader resiliency for individual, households and communities. Further examples can be found in the self-organisation of education and participation strategies in areas prone to flood and bushfire that have emerged following high-profile and large-scale events.

There are equally signs of the more negative trajectories of what has been called 'zombie neoliberalization' (Brenner *et al.*, 2010; 2011) – where the market continues to dominate regulatory experiments, policy transfer and broader parameters of governance. Examples might be the rearticulation of disaster insurance in high-risk areas and in some cases the refusal to re-insure properties that are built in high-risk areas after large- scale disaster events make the insurance package unprofitable for the corporations. However this is not to suggest that the market does find new opportunities in these events, such insurance packages that increase information of householders on their vulnerability and the mapping of their risks are also available, for example the 'Know Risk' iPhone application that allows real-time upload of information into a database for reassessment of the extent, type and form of insurance a household may require. As the information available on mapping of natural hazards and increases we are seeing increasingly innovative responses within both of these broader trajectories that require further study for comprehensive mapping of the potential changes they engender. Though positive trajectories are perhaps seeded in the implementation and experience of resilience at different levels these are still at high risk of absorption by the somewhat parasitic dynamics of regulatory reform that reify or reinvent the primacy of economic concerns, or seek to narrow the focus of security back towards the discourse of 'realism' and inter-state violence.

Convergence between resilience and societal security?

This chapter began by suggesting that identifying the characteristics and features of resilient ways of thinking, doing and working should be central to the rearticulation of neoliberalisation for an increased societal security. This rearticulation of neoliberalisation is ongoing and perpetual, of which the reform of regulatory rule regimes is a key component. Standards and professional associations are potentially two areas available for the development of empirical case studies of a processual approach to societal security in situ. Resilience appears to offer a different and more positive avenue than emphasis on work relations and trade that dominate much of the policy convergence discussion. In reconciling the political-economic interpretations of neoliberalisation with the institutionalisation of resilience in regulatory rule regimes one is required to both ask a new question and perhaps also make a suggestion. Is it possible that an orderly societal security can ever be fully assured through a standardised best practice of resilience? Perhaps not at first glance. One thing is certainly clear; the deeper critique of resilience and societal security is ongoing. A greater understanding of the implications for resilience as an influential aspect of regulatory regime reforms will also be helped by a greater understanding of those tasked with the management of crises. It is in this role that standards are an inlet into our understanding of societal security, as resilience generates new articulations of adaptation and transformation. These hold the potential for a more positive trajectory towards disarticulated counter-neoliberalisation yet untapped.

The implication is that the suite of tools incorporated into 'disaster resilience' can be used to trace the patterns of resilient thinking, doing and acting aimed at increasing societal security. This contestation of societal security is not framed as 'identity security' as in the security studies discourse (Buzan, 1991,

Buzan *et al.* 1998), but rather as the overlap of military, economic, environmental and political security in the *shared responsibility* of the public *and* government to *be prepared* for *any* potential disaster. One can trace this shift through the regulatory experiments that seek to institutionalised disaster resilience via professional standards[8] offering more depth to the critique of neoliberalisation, whilst also contesting the dominant discourse of societal security. Societal security standards merge the concept with disaster management, and legitimise the regulatory reforms through discourse of resilience, rather than national security. As such ecological concerns perhaps subsume military concerns in this changing landscape of risk, hazard and threat as the primary driver of change.

In terms of practice the positive and negative trajectories discussed throughout this chapter uncover an emerging need to balance the benefits of standardised processes by sharing *flexible* skillsets amongst security and emergency professionals, where this fails these standards create rigidity traps that increase vulnerability. This is particularly important when standards may underpin regulatory reforms across diverse geo-political, social, cultural and environmental contexts, not to mention the immanent institutional and organisational idiosyncrasies thus in play. If rigidity is built into regulatory regimes through prescriptive quality standards, this is likely to undermine local knowledge and expertise. Thus the positive adaptive capacity of resilience is aligned to the features and characteristics of particular networks of capability. These networks emerge when specific toolkits of expertise are implemented across international, national and local levels in forms contextually aligned to the capabilities of the protagonists in each case. A positive reading of resilience can be mobilised to enhance social order or and the negative can equally create greater levels of disruption and disorder depending on which features and characteristics are dominant in the alignment of individuals, institutions and organisations. This needfully must be read not at one level but across all levels as the scale and impact of disasters becomes more international. These considerations are evermore central to understanding the link between neoliberalisation, resilience, crisis and disaster. It is also a driver of the need to understand the transfer of the rhetorical metaphor to implementable operational practice on the frontlines.

The broad metaphor of resilience is now being modelled into practical strategies and tactics for the management of disasters, though this has been widened into a somewhat amorphous sense of societal coping capacity embodied in the capabilities of individuals, communities, corporations and governance agencies – broadly including both government organisations (civil and emergency services) and non-government organisations (e.g. volunteer groups, professional associations, international governance agencies). If bound by the metaphor resilience may be seen as something intangible or ephemeral. However, drawing on the interplay of research and policy articulations it is often now seen as a cycle of adaptive learning and a perpetual cycle of process improvement (Rogers, 2012c). It would be disingenuous to present resilience as a singular defined 'thing', it is not. In reality resilience is being embedded in governance as an institutional characteristic, as part of the 'rules of the game' and thus as a general principle.

This is increasingly showing signs of what might be called 'function creep' where the pervasive metaphor reappears in other agendas, such as anti-radicalisation, community cohesion, social inclusion, climate change, and even building regulations.[9] Resilience may eventually become a ubiquitous institutionalised characteristic of individual behaviour – being prepared for emergencies as commonplace in thinking as wearing a seatbelt. Certainly there are indications that a more dynamic interplay between individual citizens and the emergency and security professions could be used to combine individual agency and collective action in innovative forms of 'community resilience' (Rogers, 2013a). However, there is equal potential for resilience to become incorporated into the regulatory realignment of neoliberal global governance for efforts to mitigate the impacts and control the disorder caused by disasters, reifying the current increasingly global political-economic order.

As a contested concept resilience remains difficult to measure or standardise. There are different types of resilience, including but not limited to organisational resilience (of governance agencies or corporations), technological resilience (of critical infrastructures), community resilience (in the strength or capital in social networks, citizen demographics or specific geographical sites), and individual resilience (as the awareness and responsibility of individuals facing danger). These all require different approaches and potentially different tools for measuring the impact of investments and the gain in coping capacity from adopting new standards, even as they emerge. The positive potential may easily in such a contested landscape be stifled by the inertia of existing regulatory regimes or organisational cultures and working practices. Many professionals have questioned the usefulness of resilience, seeing this new metaphor as no more than rebadging existing practices with a new name – when in practice it is much more than that. Equally it is important to understand the role of professional associations and international standards as these are often non-governance agencies operating outside of the legislative remit of government itself. Where such organisations are affecting regulatory regime reforms, they do so in many ways 'via the back door' using un-credentialed expertise without formal governance regulation or oversight. It is important therefore to better understand the form and role of standards in the wider interplay of policy generation, transfer and convergence.

Conclusions

This debate does not offer a conclusive mapping of the contested relationships between societal security and resilience, but it does offer a clear warning. If the lessons of the past are not learned then 'zombie neoliberalisation' may absorb the positive trajectories opened by the broadening of societal security and the regulatory reform of resilience. The resultant maladaptive rigidity may lead to higher negative impacts from disaster events. The lessons learned from bushfires and floods in Australia, or biological disasters in the UK, from the war on terror around the world have shown that exposure to danger and to disaster are not simple, nor purely negative, despite the tragedy for many of those affected. Being exposed to disasters can increase societal security. Societal security when appended with socio-cultural identity can then include a broader sense of shared responsibility; through improved technical, human, organisational, and functional interoperability and the enhancement of shared situational awareness, but amongst all interested parties, not just specialists and 'experts'. This broadens the discussion beyond experts to incorporate the general public, who are most certainly 'interested parties' in being resilient to potential disasters. Such an approach can increase the reflexive awareness of vulnerability amongst all actors and may stimulate innovative regulatory experimentation; with potential for increased accountability amongst those who implement, or fail to implement the required identified mitigations to the systemic and infrastructural vulnerabilities exposed before, during and after such crises.

Meaningful change requires that engagement is collective. It also requires that standards that are implemented in diverse contexts must themselves be critically reviewed regularly. The treatment of disaster resilience through societal security standards is a professionalised attempt to focus the capabilities and capacities of stakeholders in this broadened conceptual framework – be they civil government, private sector or individuals in the community. Greater resiliency helps to generate adaptive attitudes and flexible systems of working for the future but such discussions and that offered here only begin to bridge the complexity of how these policies and practices are generated, implemented and transferred across organisations, jurisdictions and territories. Whilst disaster capitalism continues to replicate the self-legitimation of crisis and risk-averse governmentalities, then the seeds of counter-neoliberalisation remain at the local level, in community driven forms of action. This needs to be better joined up in both theory and practice if the counter-neoliberalisation potential is to become more tangible.

Notes

1 A good review of the broader definition in relation to disaster specifically can be found in Plodinec (2009).
2 For examples addressing 'resilience' Rogers (2012b, 2012c), Walker and Cooper (2011), for societal security see Buzan *et al.* (1998) and Saleh (2010).
3 As suggested by Masten and Powell resilience as a normative concept is extremely difficult to measure using the established quantitative techniques (2003: 4).
4 Conceived of here broadly through the North, Wallis and Weingast definition as coalitions of the like-minded individuals sharing a common purpose (2009), this can range from community to corporation to governance to trade unions. It is a widely cast net.
5 Often limited to geo-political economic approaches (Sparke, 2006).
6 Where security is a rising concern for those working in fragile or failing states (Hameiri, 2008), often states disadvantaged by global neoliberal economics.
7 A good example of this logic can be seen in Rodrik's discussion of trade and domestic social arrangements (1997). Here it is suggested that the tensions between the UK and many other EU countries were balanced through a high degree of social and economic homogeneity amongst the original member states, but did not preclude regulatory competition: 'The system of "competition among rules", just like harmonization,

implies eventual convergence – in this case through the competitive process of "good " rules driving out the "bad"' (ibid.: 40).

8 Others may be found in the treatment of rioting and the overlap of community resilience and crime control, others through risk management and industrial risks, others still through food security and supply chain management (see Rogers, 2012d).

9 For a useful definition and discussion of function creep in surveillance see Lyon (2001) and in the use of Information, Communication Technologies in social policy see Garret (2005). This notion can be mobilised here to articulate one form of the spread of resilience as a way of thinking into other fields of governance where it may be mobilised for different ends using a similar rhetoric.

13 Pandemics as staging grounds for resilient world order

SARS, avian flu, and the evolving forms of secure political solidarity

Mika Aaltola

Introduction

Modernity has experienced an expansion of the medicalized sphere of our existence (e.g. Latour 1988). At the same time, the language of security has spread to cover increasingly many modalities of the social realm. This phenomenon is prominent especially in the areas where political action can represent an issue as an existential threat that requires exceptional emergency measures (Buzan *et al.* 1998, 23–25). Stating that "we have entered a new era of deep microbial unease", Elbe (2011) adds that the emerging era of dis-ease has to do with "the growing tendency to articulate international health policy in the metaphors and vocabulary of security." These two tendencies meet in the case on pandemic emergencies, when pandemics are securitized and security is, to a degree, medicalized. The medicalizing moves overlap with securitizing attempts in the discourse of pandemic threats. The resulting overall medico-security paradigm tends to focus on catastrophic scenarios that have an applicability to bioterrorism and to overall preparedness and resilience. The recent confluences between these two tendencies have led to the emergence of the global health security discourse. The way in which the pandemic emergencies are presented to the public debate turns them into exceptionally heightened security matters to be managed through medical means (e.g. Elbe 2006, 125). Medical expertise is turned into a defensive force that can make the global eradication of distance and intimate interconnectedness safer through rendering the global system more resilient.

It may be suggested that, at the background of the global pandemic security, looms a more political mission to make global society more "resilient" to mutating and invisible microbial threats. This involves the reformation of the existing networks of political solidarity of the feverishly globalizing world whereby an increasing number of multi-national corporations as well as international and global actors have to be sewn into the "resilient" and "prepared" global fabric. From this perspective, the imageries of resilience are inherently political as they emphasize a "somatically safe" world based on new and reformed relationships between various domestic, international, and transnational actors. In many cases, different actors' global relevance is evaluated against the standards of their pandemic preparedness. Furthermore, reaching high preparedness means taking actions when there are no acute pandemic threats. In this sense, the medicalization has changed the way in which security practices are understood. Elbe (2011, 848) notes three tendencies: central insecurities are countered by medical and not only by military measures; medical experts have become more prominent in who-is-who of security; practices of security have started to include measures such as medical development, bio-surveillance, stockpiling of vaccines and other medicines, securing the sources of medicines in case of an outbreak, and preparing the societies for the pandemic emergency. The language of resilience has become increasingly prominent as a growing need is seen for governments to be proactive in deploying their medical countermeasures (Elbe 2011, 856).

First and foremost, the medico-security paradigm highlights the need for state- and society-level immunity against pandemic threats of naturally occurring diseases and bioterrorism. This immunity refers to reform of global and local system so that it would be prepared and resilience to pathogens. The term "resilience" has its origin in the ability of materials to bounce back and recoil after an impact. This shock-resistance may also refer to the ability to absorb sudden change (Carver 1998, 247). The language of resilience spread to social studies under scenarios of critical infrastructure management, mitigation of ecological change, and disaster preparedness (e.g. Lundborg and Vaughan-Williams 2011). The adaptive and shock-absorbing nature of the critical infrastructure – in normal, turbulent, and emergency situations – was seen as a way of being prepared in the face of a multitude of potential risks. This idea of core functions of a system means that a system can fulfill certain key tasks even though more unessential functions might be lost. Many things can go wrong. The perfect equilibrium might be lost and the system could still fulfill its basic purposes. In this sense, resilience differs from static and rigid resistance to change. It is a more dynamic characteristic that seeks different equilibriums in order to fulfill its key functions (Norris *et al.* 2008, 130). Despite its dynamic nature, resilience has retained a more passive characteristic and connotation. Namely, as the risks were seen to be increasingly complex, resilience was regarded as a capacity to function irrespective of foreseen and unforeseen scenarios ranging from cyber threats and pandemics to terrorism and war (e.g. Lundborg and Vaughan-Williams 2011). This chapter will study how the scenario of the resilient global system actualized itself in the case of three pandemic outbreaks. In these cases, the resilience is a background template that enabled and manifested itself in diverse speech acts which would not have been meaningful in the absence of the resilience paradigm. Even when the explicit language is about mutation, super-spreaders, flight connections, surveillance, and vaccinations, the background condition of resilience is being re-staged and re-articulated. The overview of the complex dynamics of resilience and resistance is based on two case studies: avian flu and SARS. The main interest is on detailing the modalities of resilience and preparedness discourses as they have been developed in the global health security texts, namely media and UN documents.

Case 1: avian flu's geo-imageries of resilience

Avian influenza is caused by viruses adapted to wild and domestic birds. In poultry, it may rapidly kill up to 90 percent of the flock. Most alarmingly, the causative agents can in rare cases spread to humans although no human-to-human transmission has ever been recorded. However, the mere possibility of mutation into a human form allowed for media, states, and international organizations to invest speculative and financial resources to warn and, on the other hand, to highlight preparedness for the disease's possible movement across the species and geopolitical boundaries. The diverse imageries of elastic and shock-absorbing advanced communities at local, national, and global levels offer insights into how contagious diseases still serve one of their historical modalities: They are still used to materially and/or imaginarily separate, contain, and limit. In the case of avian flu, prepared advanced societies were separated from the less prepared ones and from the "premodern" hotspots. The underlying containing and cordoning is qualitatively different now when security scenarios concentrate on the vanishing and porous nature of geographical, political, and cultural boundaries. It is also at this junction when the term resilience has become increasingly referred to in global health security.

The overall form of a pandemic scare is becoming globally shared and synchronized (Price-Smith 2009, 192–196). Here, the attention is on if and how the media speculation provided the means to build scenarios of national high preparedness and underlying communal healthiness. At the same time, avian flu provided opportunities for the narration of the dramatic dangers stemming from faraway places and their cultures. One possible hypothesis is that the scare was set in motion by the contemporaneous representational potentials inherent in the imaginaries of dangerous contact between distinct polito-cultural entities, e.g. West-East, US-China, and modern-premodern. By examining the media speculation from the vantage point of a major US media outlet, the *New York Times* (*NYT*), the idea is to discern the dominant uses of the pandemic scenario-building and to detect cross-cutting themes. The use of the *New York Times'* texts illustrates the contemporary US public cognitions concerning bundles of insecurities and possible sources of resilience.

I reviewed the *NYT's* articles on avian flu from 1983 to 2005 when the pandemic scare took over reporting. The idea is that these stories will shed light on how the disease developed into the cultural construct that it was during the peak of the avian flu scare in 2006 and 2007. The first avian flu-related news story was published on December 13, 1983. It was a short piece that briefly overviewed the containment and quarantine policies that were were said to stop the spread of the "deadly" disease of birds in Pennsylvania and New Jersey. The spread of avian flu to domestic and wild birds was actively followed during the winter of 1983–1884 mostly due to economic concerns. In a story published on February 26, 1984, the disease was claimed to have killed some 75 percent of the chickens and left the rest of the birds unprofitable. It was pointed out that the disease was considered so virulent that when it is noticed, all the birds in the flock have to be immediately culled and carefully buried to stop its spread.

This contrasts with the later avian flu narrative. No one seems worried about the disease crossing the species boundary to humans. Because there is no speculation concerning the human variant, there is no fear of consumer panic in the *NYT's* stories. The mutability scenarios had not yet emerged although it was starting to develop at the same time in connection with HIV/AIDS. The contemporary conceptual security-related conceptual bridges between food production and illnesses had not yet been formed. These conceptual connections started to develop only during the late 1980s. The first such discursive innovation was the worry over the mutability of the flu in birds. The first news story in the *NYT* that highlighted such mutability as a worrying aspect was published on February 23, 1986. In the story, there was a description of the new phase of the disease in the state of Connecticut. The story pointed out how the disease had markedly mutated into a more potent form that could kill about 10 percent of the flock in a single day. The story mentioned that this was in stark contrast with the earlier variant, which was not as intensively deadly. *avian flu was reframed as a disease that had mutated and might continue to do so in the future.* The last news concerning the disease for ten years was published on August 16, 1987. The story on that day overviewed the disease's mutability and its pattern of distribution on the East coast of the United States from 1983 to 1984, during which period, millions of birds had to be "destroyed."

The news stories changed dramatically in the 1990s as the *coming plague* genre took hold in the public domain with its fundamental notion of mutability and deep vulnerability, or lack of resilience, of the disease agents. The next *NYT* news story about avian flu is dated December 21, 1997. It is an interview with two specialists on the issue, Kennedy F. Shortridge, a microbiologist at the University of Hong Kong, and Dr. Daniel Lavanchy, the head of the World Health Organization's influenza program. This story managed to capture many new conceptual innovations and expansions. These innovations had been made in connection with HIV/AIDS, ebola, and BSE (Mad Cow Disease). It is worth reviewing it at length. The domestic focus had changed here into a global one. The headline emphasized that China was seen as the epicenter of the disease as it spread. The news story started with the following graphic statement: "A violent-yellow sign stenciled with interlocking black rings and a single word hangs over Kennedy F. Shortridge's laboratory. That word is 'Biohazard'." The hyperbole present in this story portrayed a very changed affective climate as compared to the earlier news stories. The ingredients and characteristics of the situational pandemic scenarios had changed. Among them was the idea of reforming the global community towards more prepared state and increasing its resilience.

The disease had been reframed as a biohazard, a word that echoed by then recent experiences with ebola in Zaire during the spring of 1995. Ebola was connected with the eating of badly cooked monkey meat. The ebola scare highlighted the vulnerability of the global community to fast spreading contagion via the international transportation infrastructure. The word, "pandemic," had also emerged into global awareness by the 1990s. It had started to be a marker of great anxiety and worry. Another important template for the changed understanding of avian flu was the experience with another animal-related food-borne scare, BSE or Mad Cow Disease in 1996. BSE changed the way in which animal-borne diseases were understood (e.g. Aaltola 1999). BSE caused economic disturbances and market reactions; it was mystified into a complex bundle fed by rumors, lack of information and by the detection of a novel disease agent, a prion; it was turned into a myriad of new and lasting administrative practices such as obligatory marking of the origin of bovine products. It embodied a tangible sense of anxiety over the dangers inherent in modern industrial food production. It was politicized and localized when many cautionary measures were directed against the UK. The continued *NYT* reframing of avian flu expanded the nature of alarm by trying out these new combinatorial possibilities of the coming plague discourse.

Thus, the way in which *NYT* framed avian flu was deeply entangled with the medico-security landscape of the late 1990s. Another new element in the stories was the foresight aspect of the containment drama. The scenarios of mutability allowed for speculative pandemic-related security scenarios. Although the disease had not yet become a significant threat, according to the story, it could turn into a lethal epidemic any time in the future. Because of this alarming prognostication, the "seeds" of a future pandemic needed to be handled carefully in biohazard facilities. The bio-containment facilities were in themselves further markers of danger in the pandemic discourse. The great concern felt over the handling of the disease in the story reinforced military metaphors. The bio-containment, protective gear, and disease-warrior tropes were widespread in the epochal works of popular culture. Pandemic movies such as *The Outbreak* brought to people's attention certain ways of talking about a pandemic disease. Many works in non--fiction further induced immense worry. These works also reinforced certain expectations, which were integrated into the account by *NYT*.

The news story's focus on China reiterated that there were some weak spots in the global preparedness and resilience to fight disease, and these spots on the globe could turn into disease hotspots. The use of the words, "a violent yellow sign," was polysemous enough to allow for the connection with the US discourse of the "yellow danger." Through this combinatorial performative, China was turned into a new danger because of the perceptions of its "teeming" cities, its different ideology and culture, and its veil of secrecy. All of this was implicated as being conducive for the emergence of pandemic threats. Moreover, it is significant that the story claimed that the disease jumped from animals to humans for the first time in China. The story assumes that China could provide the location for future inter-species jumps. The story explained its reasoning through a reference to the premodern agricultural practices in China. The combination of premodern and modern practices prevalent in rapidly growing China is seen as making it the ideal "incubator" for avian flu: "the emergence of a new influenza virus, while not necessarily this particular one, seemed inevitable, given both ancient agricultural practices in China and the current system of farming in Guangdong province, the source of much of Hong Kong's food." While China as a whole was seen as the main reservoir of the disease, southern China was described as the likely disease hub: "China is the principal reservoir for influenza," [Mr Shortridge] said, "and southern China is the influenza epicenter." China was admittedly a modern economic juggernaut; however, within China, dangerous premodern practices were noted. The story went on to explain how the mixing of modern and premodern practices – and humans with animals – in China was a cause for concern: "And because in most southern Chinese villages, ducks and chickens and pigs and people all live in very close contact, often with the animals next to or even in houses, influenza viruses moved into pigs and then to humans." The interview was very confident in its ability to locate avian flu in China, although many aspects of the disease remained mysterious. Through the act of localization, China itself was turned into a hostile element. It is possible to link this sense of enmity with the high political tensions between China and the West, which were present before-9/11, the late 1990s. This hostility resonated with much older orientalist images of China, which conceived it as a mysterious place and gave room for corresponding medico-security speculation.

The next stories were published in 2003; there were several news stories dealing with diseases in the context of SARS and, notably, in connection with the claims concerning the Iraqi WMDs (Aaltola 2012). These stories differed from the stories of 1997. They did not speculate as much as they refocused on the domestic context of avian flu. It seems that the domestic disease was not as interesting as the disease in China. For once, the US was not turned into a possible hub for a future pandemic. In this respect, the US was treated in a notably different manner from China. The non-speculative stories treated the disease as an ordinary animal disease. The central position was given to the economic repercussions, which included consumer reactions and large-scale culling. It can be suggested that the greater geographical, cultural and political distance enabled "wilder" interpretations and prognostications than a disease in an intimately close domestic context. A disease that caused a global pandemic was much easier to connect with a distant location such as China than with the US. It could be that the elliptic treatment of avian flu in the US was partially caused by the saturation of the collective psyche with the hyperbolic SARS stories. However, certain modalities remained the same. The SARS stories also focused much attention on China and Asia.

On January 27, 2004, the *NYT* published a news story on how the pattern of distribution was closely connected with migratory wild birds. This novel emphasis created further alarm and worry that went beyond farming and culling. Now wild birds became the target of the containment drama. The movement of the diseased birds around the world was tracked continuously. Cases were reported around Asia and increasingly close to the West. This conceptual development heightened the sense of scare exponentially. Inter-species boundaries overlapped with the spread of the disease across cultural, ethnic, and political boundaries.

Another notable feature of these news stories was the focus on efforts by public health authorities to defeat the potential pandemic. This overlaps with the themes of preparedness and resilience. At the beginning of 2004, the *NYT* focused on the efforts of the World Health Organization (WHO) and Centers for Disease Control and Prevention (CDC), together with the pharmaceutical industry, to develop new drugs and vaccines. For example, on February 5, 2004, the *NYT* reported on the progress of the development of a vaccine for avian flu. At the same time, the news story stated that the disease was not likely to spread in the US because the farms there were being monitored carefully and because important bans had been implemented. It seems that is was taken for granted that US was more resilient at this new junction of avian flu. However, the hype about avian flu died down early in the summer of 2004, although many stories warned that the nation should be prepared for a re-emergence of the disease. During the fall of 2004, the stories focused on preparing for a future outbreak. International measures and cooperation were reviewed in the context of vaccine development. On September 12, 2004, the *NYT* carried the following headline: "A War and a Mystery: Confronting Avian Flu." Attention was directed to the occasional bits of news on the various outbreaks of avian flu in Asia. During the following year, the *NYT* concentrated on worries over lagging efforts to fight the disease, as in the headline of September 9, 2005: "The Frontlines in the Battle against Avian Flu are Running Short of Money." At the same time, there was a lot of focus on medical advances against avian flu. On April 5, 2004, the newspaper reported on a new drug, Tamiflu: "Should We All be Stocking Tamiflu?" At this point, it seems that there were concrete policies that could be taken up to raise the national preparedness. The US government's efforts to stock Tamiflu and other medications were reported. At the same time, the reports pointed out the inequalities in the global public health efforts; some governments were seen as not doing enough, while others were regarded as too mismanaged and poor. These deficiencies in the global effort were seen as risking a failure in the fight against avian flu.

Case 2: SARS and the resilience of the global critical infrastructure

The spring of 2003 was tense with speculation and building up of worst-case scenarios. Much of this was based more on imagination than facts, as in the case of the hyped Iraqi chemical and biological WMDs. Some were more factual, as in the case of the severe acute respiratory syndrome (SARS), although even that was more of a scare than an actual killer disease. It may be claimed that these two imaginaries were partly intertwined and mutually supportive (Aaltola 2012). SARS arguably reflected the prevailing anxieties over the sustainability of the modern world order. With the US anthrax attacks still fresh in people's minds, there was much talk about bio-terror, which recycled the pandemic "coming plague" scenarios that had become so popular in the 1990s. Furthermore, the pandemic imagery developed in 1990s was notably built into the case made against Iraq when it was accused of developing military uses of epidemic diseases. In addition, the overall fears, worries and suspicions gave specific nuances to and strengthened insecurities over of air mobility. This global main artery was increasingly seen not only as a signifier of global connectedness, but also as a register of immense vulnerability. The different security scenarios became entangled in a way that defies the seeming conceptual distance between them and highlights how any temporal context produces nexuses and bundles of security. This case study overviews these momentary dynamics and the more lasting cross-cutting conceptual influences over the development of the resilience-practice.

The contagion dynamic is often used in making sense of how things get out of control and how events accelerate the associated political disorder (e.g. Koslowski and Kratochwil 1994, 215, 247). Broadly speaking, the term, "contagion," is often used in reference to the idea that political violence – as, for example, disturbances, external wars, or internal conflicts – in one region influences the possibility of violence in another region or state (e.g. Li and Thompson 1975, 63). On the other hand, disease metaphors are used to understand enemy images and to construct threats. Enemies and the perceived "evils" of the situation are often approached as if they were horrid diseases (Sontag 1988, 63; Tuan 1979, 87). Another important conceptual bridge between wars and diseases is the often-mentioned belief that wars are disease amplifiers. This often repeated reach of war has deep historical roots and has recently acquired additional strength in the context of the pandemic scares and biological weapons threats (Longrigg 1992, 27; Price-Smith 2009, 1–10). Based on these historically conditioned conceptual bridges, it may be suggested that the SARS scare was amplified and acted as an amplifier in the tense spring of 2003.[1]

The situation was partly conceived in terms of spiraling hostility; there was much fear of the contagion potential of the situation, and the metaphors of contagion and disease were used to construct threats. For example, Secretary of State Colin Powell gave a hyped-up speech to the United Nations Security Council on February 5, 2003. The aim of the speech was to convince and persuade: "My colleagues, every statement I make today is backed up by sources, solid sources. These are not assertions. What we are giving you are facts and conclusions based on solid intelligence." Powell concretizes the WMD threat, especially through their biological disease-related dimension, arguably to make the threat easier.

> Saddam Hussein has investigated dozens of biological agents causing diseases such as gas-gangrene, plague, typhus, tetanus, cholera, camelpox, and hemorrhagic fever. And he also has the wherewithal to develop smallpox.

The point was that Saddam, as an agent of evil inhumanity, had turned plagues into weapons:

> There can be no doubt that Saddam Hussein has biological weapons and the capability to rapidly produce more, many more. And he has the ability to dispense these lethal poisons and diseases in ways that can cause massive death and destruction.

Furthermore, the US documents on SARS often highlighted the close connection between naturally occurring and intentionally caused outbreaks of disease. It was perceived that the measures aimed against naturally occurring outbreaks offered ways to defend and gain resilience against intentional outbreaks.

Similarly, the preparedness over naturally occurring diseases was seen as a testing ground for developing resilience over possible biological warfare. The combined securitizing dynamics was often captured in the term, "health security." The documents conceive of new health threats stemming from (re)emerging diseases and biological warfare agents: "Given American leadership in the biomedical field and Singapore's advanced research facilities, President Bush and Prime Minister Goh agreed that the two countries should explore prospects for collaborative efforts [... and] to begin consultations on possible joint projects."[2] From the US perspective, the SARS-related outlook was part of a larger vision to the world. The presidential directive, "Biodefense for the 21st Century" is said to provide

> a comprehensive framework for our nation's biodefense. [It] builds on past accomplishments, specifies roles and responsibilities, and integrates the programs and efforts of various communities – national security, medical, public health, intelligence, diplomatic, agricultural and law enforcement – into a sustained and focused national effort against biological weapons threats.[3]

The integrated approach to meet the threat of terrorism and WMDs subsumed much of the work against naturally occurring diseases. The two scenarios began to overlap ever more tightly. The probable consequence was that the occurrence of a natural epidemic disease, SARS, heightened the security-related concerns over something according. The infamous speech by Powell started to become comprehensible.

However, the securitizing entanglements had much wider confluences. In popular imagery, the SARS scare of 2003 was often linked with the global age of connectedness and the increasingly tightly-knit fabric of interdependence. Health Canada (2003, 1) noted this association: "Old diseases usually spread slowly ... SARS, on the other hand, moved at the speed of a jet airplane. Within days of its arrival in Hong Kong, it had circled the globe." Crawford (2007, 29) uses the hyperbolic antagonistic term, "super-spreader," for a figure that, in global health language, is referred to as an "index case": "the virus spread round the globe, aided by super-spreaders (like the doctor at the Metropole Hotel in Hong Kong) and fast international air travel." Similarly, Noun and Chyba (2008, 20.8) state that "during the early stages of the SARS pandemic, a single patient, the 'super-spreader', infected every one of 50 health workers who treated him." This stock antagonistic figure appeared in the popular accounts of SARS. *The Sunday Telegraph*, for example, reported on March 23, 2003 the following dramatized scene:

> As he shuffled through the lobby of the Hotel Metropole, the elderly professor was feeling feverish and faint. At the lift, he steadied himself for a moment in the open doorway before his body convulsed in a series of wracking coughs that sprayed fine droplets of saliva onto the walls and the people waiting inside.

As a signifier of global vulnerability, a super-spreader is a term with a loaded cultural history that connects it with the figure of "Patient Zero" in the HIV and

AIDS narratives. During the late 1980s, there was much speculation about the original Patient Zero, Gaetan Dugas, who, through his work as an air steward, was able to fly all over the world and spread HIV to others. Varying numbers of HIV infections have been linked to him: "Dugas was a hub in the network of sexual contacts" (Mitchell 2009, 50). Crawford (2007, 20) uses another modern air mobility trope, "city hopping," to drive home the point about the avian flu-related dangers. Evidently, the figure of a super-spreader carries with it a multidimensional understanding of the failure of pandemic containment and the acute need to build resilience. The term, super-spreader, ceases to be a mere technical epidemiological term. It turns into a signifier that blends together into one figure multiple engrossing images and then projects them into the context of major metropolitan hotels and into the global aviopolis. As a construct, it enables the underlying invisible world of viruses to be made visible and culturally comprehensible. The mobility of these dangerous types reframe air mobility networks, which have been commonly articulated in a far more progressive light.

The vunerability introduced by SARS seems to be odds with the often repeated view that the air mobility system is shock-absorbing and resilient. Urry (2009, 34) makes the case that aero-mobility is based on "a dynamic and flexible systemic structure articulated horizontally across the globe." This dynamic and flexible framework is in accordance with the contours of the existing assemblages of hegemonic governance and provides a major expression of what is meant by global interdependence (Hardt and Negri 2000, 13–14; Aaltola 2005, 268; Agamben 1998, 123; Dillon and Reid 2000, 117). From this bridgehead, the air mobility flows have become an increasingly important register of security (e.g. Crang 2002, 571; Dodge and Kitchin 2004, 195). It is notable that the post-9/11 air mobility scenario includes a marked dystopian element (e.g., Knox *et al.* 2007, 267). The ebola scare in the mid-1990s had already given content to these distopian framings of the modern aviopolis.

Next, I will review a "comprehensive chronology of SARS-related events" as published in the World Health Organization (WHO) publication, *SARS – How a Global Epidemic was Stopped* (2006). I will examine how the chronology frames the vulnerability and resilience of international air travel in the context of SARS through various tropes and figures. The WHO report notes February 21, 2003 as the day on which SARS went international:

> Index case of the Metropole Hotel outbreak arrives from Guangdong; international spread of virus begins: Professor LJL, a 64-year-old physician from Guangzhou, arrives ... to attend a wedding. He developed flu-like symptoms on 15 February, having been infected in the hospital where he worked ... At least 16 other guests and one visitor are infected during his one-night stay in room 911 of the Metropole Hotel.

This item in the chronology states the profession, a professor and physician, of the index case. The chronology does not explicitly use the term, "super-spreader." Rather, it refers to "super-spreading events" and "index cases." The context is an international metropolitan hotel in Hong Kong. This is significant and the mentioning of the index case's profession is used to imply two things. First, the doctor was probably infected in Guangdong through his work. Second, it also brings the disease to a new level when, instead of an average local person, a person with an access to the global arteries catches and spreads a disease. The chronology accounts for one further place where this index case infected more people before dying:

> Professor LJL is admitted to the intensive care unit of the Kwong Wah Hospital for respiratory failure. Besides the hotel guests, three members of his family ... and one nurse at the hospital are infected. Professor LJL will die on 4 March.

The chronology can be interpreted to construct the doctor as a super-spreader and both hotels and hospitals as possible disease hubs. The next item in the chronology that indicates further international spread is dated February 26, 2003:

> Hanoi index case is hospitalized: Mr JC, a 48-year-old merchandise manager from New York, is admitted to the Hanoi-French Hospital. He arrived in Viet Nam on 23 February after travelling to China and Hong Kong ... The WHO office in Viet Nam will be notified of the case the next morning, and its advice sought.

Being an international businessman is clearly meant to be relevant for imagining how he might have been infected and gauging the potential for further spread. An infected disease-warrior is also a signifier of frequent international travel, a worrying sign as it is used in the chronology. The next item on the chronological list reports the spread of SARS to Singapore:

> Singapore index case is hospitalized: Ms EM is admitted to Tan Tock Seng Hospital with pneumonia. She has been unwell since returning from a shopping trip to Hong Kong on 25 February. The 22-year-old, who stayed in room 938 at the Metropole Hotel ... will pass on the virus to 22 close contacts.

This index case, infected by an index case, is identified, not through her profession, but through her consumption-related activity. She is a young tourist who has been on an international shopping trip. Being a tourist is regarded as a significant status for it implies possibilities of an international and, in his case and in the case of the New York businessman, intercontinental pattern of spread.

On March 3, 2003, the chronology mentions a first signifier of the global resilience system beginning to have an effect:

> Dr Urbani examines Hanoi index case: In Hanoi, WHO's communicable disease expert in Viet Nam, Dr Carlo Urbani, examines Mr JC, the American businessman who was admitted to the Hanoi-French Hospital on 26 February

with a severe form of pneumonia. Dr Urbani sends a report to WHO's Regional Office, emphasizes the need for strict infection controls, and arranges for Mr JC's serum and throat swabs to be sent to laboratories in Tokyo, Atlanta, and Hanoi.

The chronology makes an exception here in naming an eventual victim, Dr. Urbani. His diligent and alert actions are seen in an inherently positive light in the otherwise factual chronology. He is not identified as a potential spreader, but as a disease-warrior and germ hunter. Dr. Urbani is turned into the hardworking exemplary hero of the chronology. Because of this position, it may be argued that his probable role in passing on the disease is not considered worth mentioning. Dr. Urbani is turned into a model of how to act in a pandemic emergency. He is also used to embody the effectiveness and vigilance of the global organization he works for, WHO.

However, on March 5, 2003, the chronology recounts the intercontinental leap of SARS to Canada:

> Toronto index case dies: Ms KSC, 78 years old, dies in her Toronto, Ontario, home. The death certificate attributes her death to heart attack. In fact, she died from SARS acquired at the Metropole Hotel in Hong Kong. Before dying, she has passed the virus on to four members of her extended family, who will then spark the Toronto outbreak.

The chronology reports misdiagnosis and recounts its negative consequences. This is the antithesis of Dr. Urbani's work. The chronology also implies a failure in the containment and follow-up procedures since the index case's stay at the Hotel Metropole should have been suspected by then. This stands in contrast with the next item in the chronology:

> Mr JC, the Hanoi index case who has been medically evacuated, arrives at the Princess Margaret Hospital, where he will die on 13 March. The WHO Regional Office informs Hong Kong and Singapore officials about his transfer. Singapore is informed because the medical evacuation team is from Singapore. Because of strict infection controls, no health worker in the Princess Margaret Hospital is infected by Mr JC.

Although there were further alarming cases, this chronology details how WHO got its global machinery of resilience fully working. However, one should note that all this activity takes place a full month after the first accounts of the disease in Hong Kong and months after the first outbreak occurred in China.

SARS blended with the tense political processes of its day and acquired modalities that seemed to exemplify alarm over the "health" of the hub-and-spoke skeleton of globality. Disease-related dramas often picture things in a way that is culturally significant: What are the prominent ways of portraying authority and those who are exceptionally deviant? Who are the villains and who are the heroes?

These plays put the relevant actors in their respective, but interactive, positions and give them roles and backgrounds. The SARS play's "vigilant" national and international actors, such as the US Centers for Disease Control and Prevention (CDC) and WHO, got their share of authority and legitimacy, while those authorities – most prominently, the Chinese – that were somehow connected with the origin or further spread of the disease were portrayed as illegitimate. It can be argued that resilience was the prominent template for understanding what was meant by normatively sanctioned vigilance. The two pandemic scenarios offered different actors opportunities to demonstrate diligent adherence to the practices of containment and their high degree of expertise. Such rules ascertaining and according actions can be instrumental in conveying the health of the underlying political order and reassuring the public against the actual realization of the worst-case scenarios. At the end when the dust settled down, the SARS emergency allowed for displays of new containment oriented practices and representations of more resilient global travel and health systems. In several important ways, the pattern of "hub-and-spoke" and the figure of "frequent travel" became signifiers of a possible horrible failure in the resilience drama. They seemed to defy the usual notions of protective barriers and cordons sanitaires. The containment measures tailored to air traffic seemed inadequate. For example, the screening measures, although widely used and highly publicized, proved to be insufficient. WHO recommended that travelers be screened at airports for symptoms and signs of SARS, such as sneezing and fever: "In spite of intensive screening, no SARS cases were detected by the border-authorities (St. John *et al.* 2006, 6). There was a sense of helplessness as the severing of connections did not seem to be an attractive option since air transportation can be seen as the modus operandi of the global order. However, the pandemic scare led to the reduction of flights and, more importantly, to a decrease in individuals' desire to fly, if not trying to flee infected areas (Caballero 2005, 483). Although the checks and screening created a particular sentiment of suspicion and, perhaps, counter-intuitively, an air of security, at least, something "resilient" and "robust" was being performed.

Conclusion

Although thoroughly interconnected, the global fabric space is not evenly spread. It thickens near and gravitates towards the global hubs. This pattern contains the seeds for the overall re-imagination of the changing patterns of political solidarity. In a sense, the global air traffic embodies this uneven or lumpy pattern. At the same time, pandemic diseases – diseases affecting the whole of the "pandemos" – can embody and be used to narrate the different fears that this system might become conducive to regressive spiraling processes. While the global hub-and-spoke system is a signifier of globalization, pandemics register long-existing fears and worries that the rapid long-distance connections are dangerously dis-easing. To a large extent, especially SARS and to some extent avian flu came to be constructed as a disease of global networks. At the macro level, SARS was seen as having the capacity to force the closure of modern life's support systems and turn upside down the polities that have become reliant on them. In a way, it was interpreted to have come with an ominous message for political reform. This message was often read as one of creating more resilient and prepared global society. Thus, the discourse of pandemic security presents a way to secure the new hub-and-spoke patterns of interdependence. It is in this context that resilience becomes the scenario of security knowledge. It is related to the main arteries of the global order. It is different from the nation-state centered practices of "defense." However, it plays the same overall function of securing a political entity – in the case of the system of asymmetric interdependencies and global flows.

The resilient global order highlighted in SARS and avian flu spectacles seemed to demand the re-imagining of social organization, political authority and expert governance, and to hammer home the importance of resilience and preparedness as the key signifiers of future security. The official documents on pandemic diseases often highlighted the close connection between naturally occurring and intentionally caused outbreaks of disease. Moreover, it was perceived that the measures aimed against naturally occurring outbreaks offered a way to combat possible intentional outbreaks. The preparedness over naturally occurring diseases was seen as a testing ground for developing security in the case of biological warfare. This combined dynamics provided a powerful undercurrent to the term, "global health security." It follows from the emphasis on readiness, preparedness and resilience that there is a strategic interest involved in why societies readily turn into paranoid sites, "where even an unsubstantiated claim about a threat to public health is likely be taken seriously" (Loosemore 2006). The discourses of pandemics are likely to be used to create senses of security utterly unrelated to what pandemics as epidemiological phenomena are supposed to be. The stock pandemic scenario is not value neutral. It inevitably contains a particular vision of human solidarity, namely, of the particular utopian vision of prepared and resilient polities that could meet the challenge of the shape-shifting mutable enemy. This often used speculative vision promotes according to national and global governance structures as well as containment oriented, resilient, national communities.

Notes

1 The following exchange from a White House Press Briefing (May 19, 2003) illustrates the multiple uses of disease metaphors in the War against Terror:
Question: She [President Arroyo of Philippines] said, terrorism is like SARS, it's almost like SARS. Is it spreading because we still have yet to find the core, Osama bin Laden?
Answer: That's the nature of terrorism. It's the nature of hatred. Hatred doesn't exist only because of one person; hatred exists. In this case, it's the most virulent hatred because it's carried out in the form of murder – murder against Americans; murder against Westerners.
2 "Joint Statement between the United States of America and Singapore" on May 6, 2003.
3 "BioDefense Fact Sheet," April 28, 2004.

Conclusion
Towards an ontopolitics of security[1]

Lene Hansen

Introduction

Usually thirteen is said to be an unlucky number, but the richness of the thirteen chapters that come before this Conclusion has proven this axiom wrong. Organized into four sections each devoted to a particular concept – resistance, desecuritization, emancipation, and resilience – *Contesting Security* offers insightful theoretical and empirical explorations that trace the analytical strengths and weaknesses as well as normative implications of "security" and its associated concepts. Although each chapter is located within a specific conceptual section, most chapters weave comparisons and connections with other concepts into their analysis. As such what arise are focused conceptual engagements and a charting of the wider field of critical security studies.[2]

Looking to the field of Security Studies there is no shortage of works on "security," and the sub-field of critical security studies is a major supplier thereof. Articles on critical security theories are prominently featured in generalist International Relations (IR) journals like *International Studies Quarterly*, *European Journal of International Relations*, *International Theory*, and *Review of International Studies*. There are field journals such as *Security Dialogue* and *Critical Studies on Security*, and textbook introductions on what critical security studies is and how to do it facilitate easy – or at least easier – entry for the uninitiated (see for example Fierke 2007; Peoples and Vaughan-Williams 2010; Salter and Mutlu 2012). Given the crowded nature of the critical security studies market, it is worth pointing out what sets *Contesting Security* aside.

First, although there is a large and thriving scholarship within critical security studies on how "security" should be de- and re-constructed much of the conceptual debate concerns "hyphenations of security," that is the widening of security beyond the military to include for example cyber security, environmental security, and societal security, and the deepening of security beyond the state as the privileged referent object to include for instance human security, gender security, and global security (Krause and Williams 1996). These debates have been – and still are – important for establishing the implications of concepts other than "national security." Yet, while the widening-deepening debate is not solved or over, there is an extent to which it tends to repeat a set of entrenched positions.

Contesting Security's move to consider "security" through a series of "sub-concepts" provides a fresh perspective that promises to reconfigure the widening-deepening debate.

Second, while there is a considerable literature on "security," including work that explores the sub-concepts of desecuritization, resilience, emancipation and resistance, it is rare to find a volume that explores the relations between all four of these, their conflicting differences and alliances, and their relationships to "security" proper.

Third, *Contesting Security* is striking in terms of the internal dissidence allowed. What the title suggests is that each of the four concepts – or as Thierry Balzacq (Chapter 1: 8) calls them "modalities" – structuring the book provide a contestation of "security." The title makes in that sense a performative move: it constructs a unity among the four concepts holding that they all "contest." On first view what is contested seems pretty clear: it is a narrow, mainstream, state-centric, military-materiality based conception of security. Yet, as poststructuralists tell us, such seemingly straightforward constructions of identity and difference often unravel as one moves closer: there are considerable differences among "the contesters" when it comes to how "mainstream security" should be viewed, what should replace it, and even, on how the sub-concepts should be defined. Thus what brings the contributions to *Contesting Security* together is not agreement on a shared substantial revision of "security," but rather on the kind of critical engagement which is necessary. All chapters insist – some more explicitly than others – on what David Campbell (drawing on Derrida) has defined as an ontopological engagement with security, that is a critical discussion of the ontopological assumptions about who should be the subjects of security, how "security" is achieved, what the logic of security is and could be, and thus what "we" (as scholars, citizens, policy advisors) might do to increase it (Campbell 1998: 80; see also Buzan and Hansen 2009: 21–38). Because these questions are simultaneously ontological and political, I use the term *ontopolitical* to sum up the approach of *Contesting Security*.

This Conclusion will continue on the conceptual path creatively envisioned by Balzacq and his collaborators. It will also strive to be respectful of the internal dissidence of *Contesting Security* in that the Conclusion is not set up to adjudicate which of the four "contesting" concepts shows more promise nor will it enter into detailed discussions of how to define each of them authoritatively. The overall goal of the Conclusion is instead to explore the meta-approach suggested by *Contesting Security* by offering a set of reflections on what can be gained by approaching the ontopolitics of security through resistance, desecuritization, emancipation and resilience. The first section begins with a summary of how the four sub-concepts contest security, then follows an attempt to situate them on the terrain of critical security studies. The second section turns to the "master concern" for *Contesting Security*: the link between the four sub-concepts and the logic of security. Debates over which logic of security should be adopted by critical security studies cannot, I argue, be solved through reference to materiality and the world "out there" as security theories construct particular "worlds" as significant. The third section moves from the specific positions adopted by contributors to *Contesting Security* to what it implies to ask conceptual questions in Security Studies. I argue that as Critical security studies pursues non-positivist epistemologies, the social science criteria for understanding strength and weaknesses of conceptualizations of security are not whether the latter can be proven true or false, but conceptual clarity and consistency, applicability, and theoretical depth. The fourth and final section raises the question where the conceptually focused and ontopolitically attuned research program launched by *Contesting Security* might move. My suggestion is that there are at least two routes worthy of further pursuit: comparative case-studies and genealogical studies of contestation in Security Studies more broadly.

Contesting concepts and critical security studies

As noted above, what unite the four concepts featured in *Contesting Security*'s subtitle is that they all do something to "contest" "security," that is, they share a commitment to the significance of asking ontopolitical questions. What is a threat? Is progress possible? What does it mean to engage critically in logics and discourses of security? What is a politically and ethically desirable security policy? The chapters agree to ask these questions, while providing multiple accounts of what "contestation" as well as "security" are. The rich ontopolitical status of the four concepts is further indicated by the fact that none of them refers to an easily identifiable empirical phenomenon. Resistance, desecuritization, emancipation and resilience are not things "out there" like the environment, critical infrastructures or the stock market.

It is perhaps no wonder that *resistance* has been allocated the prominent spot as the first "contesting concept": in many cases, and everyday parlance, "resistance" and "contestation" are seen as largely synonymous. Because resistance risks evoking a dichotomous "good resisters'"-"bad governors'" world view, it is crucial that most contributors take issue with this conception. Balzacq's "editor's introduction" mobilizes Foucault's understanding of power as productive against this dichotomy and Juha Vuori's decision to include "contestation" at the elite level underlines that critique is not a prerogative of the "powerless." As Vuori (Chapter 3: 32) aptly puts it "One should thus not see the relationship between the state and civil society as a binary position, for neither the state nor civil society is monolithic." "Resistance", therefore, "is never in a position of complete exteriority in relation to power." That resistance is never exterior to power is underscored by the fact that it is a concept that points to action and agency. The empirical existence of resistant practices is brought out by Pierre Piazza's chapter on biometrics in France and Florent Blanc's on librarians' and lawyers' battles against national security policies under George W. Bush. Two lessons from Piazza's analysis are worth emphasizing. First, while resistance has influenced public policy at the level of broader objectives as well as specific identification schemes, there are important differences within the counter-biometric movement, for example on whether parody and humor are strategies to be adopted. Resistance is not, in short, a homogeneous block. Second, one should be wary, shows Piazza's case, of romanticizing resistance movements, as resistance is in part based on arguments "typical of an anti-industrial movement inspired by Luddism," hence a backward, rather than a forward looking critique (Chapter 4: 52).

As we move from resistance to *desecuritization*, the discussion changes from the identification of a rather broad phenomenon (resistance) to a set of quite specific debates on a particular concept (desecuritization) defined by Balzacq in his editor's introduction (p. 85) as "fragile." In Rita Floyd's view, securitization theory is an analytical, not a normative theory, a shortcoming her chapter seeks to remedy. Balzacq by contrast stresses that "despite controversies over what desecuritization betokens, there is a widespread conviction that it brings politics back in and that it opens up the political game to a broader variety of actors." The most explicit attempt to shore up the fragility of desecuritization comes in Balzacq, Sara Depauw, and Sarah Léonard's chapter. They suggest (Chapter 7: 109) that there are two forms of desecuritization: the "management way of desecuritizing" that relocates "the security issue into a functional different sector" and the "transformative way of desecuritizing" which is "an attempt to overcome the exclusionary logic of security by unmaking hegemonic registers of meaning." This distinction speaks effectively to longstanding debates in critical security studies whether desecuritization in Wæver's classical formulation is a managerial concept lacking in genuine political content (Huysmans 1998a; Aradau 2004), or whether it should be read as having an explicit normative and political status (Williams 2003; Hansen 2012). This discussion is intimately related to the question whether desecuritization defines a move from the securitized to the politicized, or whether desecuritization can have two outcomes: a shift to the politicized or to the non-politicized, that is, the technical or even silenced. Within securitization theory, the politicized and the non-politicized have different normative standing with the former being a site of contestation, the latter not. Balzacq *et al.*'s distinction between managerial and transformative desecuritization is thus a very promising one as it links desecuritization directly to the theme of contestation: it differentiates between depoliticization- managerialism on the one hand and politicization-contestation on the other.

Although the section on *emancipation* is the shortest with only two chapters, it is perhaps here that we find the most detailed discussions of how a concept contests. Given the wealth of definitions of emancipation in social and political thought, it is perhaps not too surprising. As Balzacq's editor's introduction lays out even within Critical Security Studies we find different views on the relationship between security and emancipation with Ken Booth seeing emancipation as leading to security, while Richard Wyn Jones positions security as essential for achieving emancipation. João Nunes's position in Chapter 9 (p. 144) is that security and emancipation must be seen together and his definition is worth quoting at length:

> Security as emancipation can be defined as the transformation of subjectivities, relations and structures that entail systematic inequality, disadvantage and vulnerability, thus resulting in individuals and groups suffering from different forms of harm. Emancipatory transformation is enabled by the creation of

spaces in people's lives in which they can make decisions and act beyond the basic necessities of survival.

Worth stressing here is that emancipation is connected with the transformation of structures but that it is not readily apparent who undertakes the "transformation" and "creation of spaces," in other words how agency comes in. Some passages suggest that it falls upon those who are disadvantaged to undertake their own emancipation as "they [the world's most vulnerable] need to emancipate themselves from the structural causes of their insecurity," yet there are other passages that evoke a wider sense of responsibility as "An approach to security should seek to garner existing alternative knowledge about an issue and collaborate with actors that are in a good position to bring about change" (Chapter 9: 144 and 150). Such "good positioned actors" assumingly would usually not be those most vulnerable and structurally impoverished. The structural inequalities stressed by Nunes (Chapter 9: 150) conjure an understanding of security that is probably not devoid of conflict. Yet, the logic of security that arises with Nunes' concept of emancipation is a decidedly different one from the one of threat, dangers, and radical emergency measures of securitization theory. "Security as emancipation," holds Nunes, "contests "security" by reclaiming its meaning, namely by offering a positive notion of it." This positive reading of security is shared by Matt McDonald (Chapter 10: 160) who following in the tradition of Habermas defines emancipation as implying a "focus on the circumstances and dynamics of communication whereby people/s are able to communicate their needs and interests to others." This focus on the desirability of dialogue creates a normative overlap with securitization theory's preference for desecuritization (that is, in Balzacq *et al.*'s terminology, "transformative desecuritization") (see also Williams 2003).

As the newcomer to critical security studies *resilience* is in some respects at a disadvantage when it comes to "contesting security." First, because whereas most students of critical security studies will be quite familiar with the concepts of securitization/desecuritization and emancipation, they are likely not to have a similar grasp of resilience. Second, because as Balzacq's editor's introduction and the chapters by Philippe Bourbeau and Peter Rogers show there is no established concept of resilience to draw in, either from the fields where resilience has a longer history of use or from policy discourse itself. The chapters in this section thus have more of a "concept clearing/cleaning" mission to undertake. Balzacq points out that resilience concerns the ability of both critical infrastructures, human societies and individual subjects to sustain vulnerabilities and shocks. Drawing on a critical reading of these distinctions in the existing literature, Bourbeau (Chapter 11: 177) advocates a definition of resilience as "the process of patterned adjustments adopted by a society or an individual in the face of endogenous or exogenous shocks." Focusing on the societal adjustments, Bourbeau further suggests a typology that captures degrees thereof ranging from resilience as maintenance over resilience as marginal adjustments to resilience as societal renewal. What is most noteworthy in terms of resilience's status as a concept contesting security is that it is seen as a more ambiguous "contesting" concepts by "its" contributors than is the case of the other three. Balzacq holds in Chapter 1 (p. 9) that "resilience does not aim to transform security, but the way it is dealt with or lived with" and thus it should "be investigated primarily in relation to resistance and emancipation ... depending on whether it aims to escape the fear of threat or absorb the shock provoked by a security problem." Bourbeau (Chapter 11: 174) puts it succinctly "resilience has a dark side" not unrelated to its possible use in governmental policy: it is not hard to see how a vision of "resilient societies" can be mobilized to encourage that shocks are simply "absorbed," rather than used as an incentive to ponder the structural adjustments that for example Nunes' conceptualization of emancipation requires. Or put differently, such visions of resilience obscure the fact that, as Mika Aaltola points out in Chapter 13 (p. 205), "the imageries of resilience are inherently political."

Situating the four sub-concepts on the wider terrain of (critical) Security Studies, it is clear that they come with different histories and allies. Resistance has a resonance with everyday language; the others do not. Resilience is adopted within selected policy discourses; the others are not. Desecuritization comes out of a very specific security theory, namely securitization, while resistance and emancipation are key concepts and concerns of a Marxist and post-Marxist (Frankfurt School) tradition much broader than Security Studies. In terms of the contemporary terrain of critical security studies, desecuritization is firmly located with the Copenhagen School; emancipation is a, if not the, core concept of Critical Security Studies. Both the Copenhagen School and Critical Security Studies were being established in the 1990s, and have generated a wealth of second- and third-generation scholarship following in the footsteps of Ole Wæver and Barry Buzan (Copenhagen School) and Ken Booth and Richard Wyn Jones (Critical Security Studies). Resistance by comparison does not have a school as such, but it appears as a thematic and critique linked to securitization and desecuritization as brought out in Vuori's chapter on resistance and contestation in China as well as in discussions of emancipation (see Nunes' careful conceptual engagement with emancipation, securitization and resistance in Chapter 9). The status of resilience in critical security studies is, as Bourbeau shows in Chapter 11 even more precarious: depending on how resilience is approached it might, as Bourbeau (Chapter 11: 173) suggests, facilitate "a better understanding of the securitization process" or it might link in with the literature on risk management as brought out by Peter Rogers in Chapter 12 and through that with the growing literature on risk in Security Studies. The latter is, holds Karen Lund Petersen (2012), a complex enterprise comprising critical risk studies (within critical security studies but using "risk" to challenge the focus on states and exceptional politics), global risk management (risk as having replaced security in the management of global threats) and political risk studies (assessments of direct, foreign investments). Thus where resilience fits within – or against – the more established positions on the terrain of critical security studies is still undecided as is, according to Bourbeau, the degree to which it can generate a research program that allows it to establish itself.

Logics of security revisited

This brief positioning of resistance, desecuritization, emancipation and resilience within critical security studies may give some indication of how contributors approach logics of security. The logic of security, it is worth stressing, is the master concern for *Contesting Security*: the four sub-concepts or modalities are invoked not simply because critical security scholars might benefit from hearing more about them, but because they allow for a discussion of what security is and how and why it might be changed.

At the center of *Contesting Security* stands the logic of security as laid out by securitization theory in its classic form, that is, the view that what distinguishes "security" is the logic of radical threats and dangers, the need for the adoption of emergency measures, and a move out of the "normal politics" logic of public deliberation and dialogue. Those adopting a critical security studies perspective advocate on the contrary that "security" need not comply with such an exclusionary position. Rather as McDonald (Chapter 10: 155) puts it, one should take the view that "the meaning of security is fluid and permeable" and thus open to cosmopolitan and inclusive discourses. Securitization theory – and other theories who adopt a similar view of the logic of security – is, argues McDonald (Chapter 10: 155, 160) "escapist" in that it implies a preference for avoiding the logic of security and hence "the rejection of security as a site of progress or emancipation." McDonald (Chapter 10: 158, 160) holds further that escapist views of security are built on "shaky analytical ground" in that they overlook how the concept of security has changed over time and that "different political communities understand and approach security in different ways." Underlining the normative implication of this position, Balzacq states in Chapter 1 (pp. 4–5) that "Understanding security in exclusively negative terms amounts to a cheap ethics, of sorts, as it puts critical security scholars on the rather defensive position of having to resist anything that looks like a security practice." Looking for defenders of securitization theory, the closest ally appears to be Vuori (Chapter 3: 29) who states that "security means different things to different societies," but also that this is a difference that stems from the fact that "the core fears of any group or nation are unique and relate to vulnerabilities and historical experiences." The empirical variation in "security" is thus not due to differences in terms of the "logic of security," but due to the fact that the logic of fear and vulnerability manifests itself differently across time and place.

As indicated in Figure 14.1, I suggest that there are two issues that are central to unpacking debates at the level of logics of security: the ability of a critical security theory to bring the "real world" into analytical and normative view and the philosophical and political theories that inform and legitimize the chosen conception of "security." My choice of the term "unpacking" here is meant to underscore that I do not think that the debate over the logic of security can be solved as it rests upon deeper philosophical and political commitments that are themselves "unsolvable." This however does not mean that critical security studies should stop having "logics of security" discussions or that the quality of

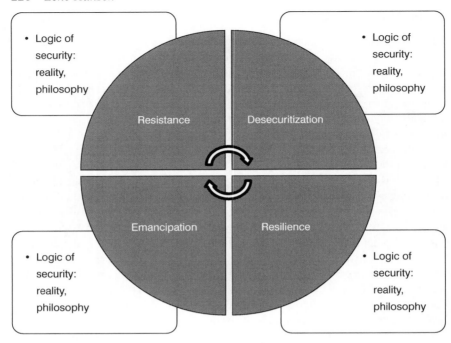

- Logic of
  security:
  reality,
  philosophy

- Logic of
  security:
  reality,
  philosophy

- Logic of
  security:
  reality,
  philosophy

- Logic of
  security:
  reality,
  philosophy

Resistance

Desecuritization

Emancipation

Resilience

Figure 14.1 The elements of an ontopolitics of security

such discussions cannot be improved. In fact, *Contesting Security* is an excellent indication that such improvements are possible.

So how do we unpack and improve logics of security discussions? First, we need to consider the status of "the real world" in arguments over logics of security. What makes these debates tricky to navigate is that debates over the concept of security are at the meta-theoretical level best conceived of as constructivist. That is, theories about security define particular concepts of security, which in turn provide a particular lens that allows materiality, power, interests, identities etc. to come into analytical view (Wendt 1999: 92–96). Concepts of security are thus based on a series of ontological assumptions about what constitutes the most important actors and subjects, what a threat is and how to identify it, and what "logics of security" can be found. More generally, this corresponds with an understanding of theories as providing us with particular representations of "reality," rather than reality itself (Dunne *et al.* 2013). As a consequence, no security scholar can claim victory for her or his conceptualization through reference to "the empirical world out there." One cannot say that security is "really" about the military as this is proven by events in Crimea in the Winter and Spring 2014, but nor can one say that security is "really" about famine because more people die of hunger than combat. What we can say – and critically discuss – is what subject, threats, logics and insecurities *appear* through particular lenses and concepts of security.

Put differently, logics of security do not exist out there. They are dynamics identified by security theorists. To return to McDonald's critique of securitization theory for assuming a universal logic of security on the grounds that there *is* empirical variation in the concept of security across time and place, this variation only appears due to McDonald's own conceptualization of security. The theorization of "security" in securitization theory is not based on the word "security" being invoked, but on the "modality" of security (that is the threat, danger, and emergency measures logic) being in place (Buzan *et al.* 1998: 27). As such, the theory is applicable as long as that modality can be found. If it cannot, then we would according to securitization theory simply be dealing with a case where security dynamics were not in place. But the loss of empirical materiality as the arbiter of debates over the concept and logic of security is not the end of the story as security theorists generally want their theories to matter. That is, if the world that comes into view through a critical security theory's conceptualization of security grows smaller and smaller there is likely to be a concern with how this theory's scope can be adjusted and expanded.

Second, as come out in several of the contributions but perhaps most strongly in Claudia Aradau's analysis of the significance of universality for security theory in Chapter 6, critical security theories draw – and reinforce – their views of the logic of security through references to wider bodies of political and social theory. Recognizing this dynamic is important because it shows that no critical security theory is immune to criticism: if securitization theory draws on Carl Schmitt, then it is vulnerable to critique of Carl Schmitt; if Critical Security Studies draws on Habermas, then it is vulnerable to critiques of Habermas. It also underlines that an important element in discussions of the ontopolitical implications of security theories is to unpack the larger philosophical principles and positions that conceptualizations of security rest upon. Such unpacking make it clear where security concepts come from and it may also facilitate the introduction of new possible lineages of security thinking. This is exactly what Aradau (Chapter 6: 90) does in her double reading, first of universality as a constituent of security and then by reading universality as paradoxical, she brings out how "security can be contested in a double move of *both* acceptance *and* refusal of security." Again, such critical engagements cannot show that, say, a Schmittian inspired approach is "wrong," but rather that it rests upon a particular set of assumptions about politics, identity, and authority that can be brought into question.

Approaching security through concepts: challenges and criteria

The research agenda set up by *Contesting Security* is effectively one that approaches "security" through concepts, more specifically through explorations of four sub-concepts thus effectively also adopting a conceptual comparative perspective. As this promises to become an agenda adopted by other scholars and students it seems useful to ponder more generally which social science criteria we should use when making such conceptual comparisons. Given the post-positivist epistemological and methodological approach of critical security studies – at least as conceived in *Contesting Security* – we cannot base our criteria on whether concepts are accurate representations of "reality" nor on whether they allow for the establishment of falsifiable hypotheses. This however does not mean that we cannot establish any criteria, nor that criteria are not already being used. In fact, I would argue that the four criteria laid out below are to a large extent already implicitly adopted by a significant portion of critical security studies scholarship.

The first criterion is conceptual clarity, that is whether concepts clearly define a phenomenon, a set of dynamics, the scope conditions under which they apply, and where relevant the difference from other definitions of the same concept. At first, it would seem obvious that theories built around unclear concepts are unlikely to succeed because security scholars and students would be at a loss in terms of how to apply them. Yet, when we look to how Security Studies has developed that is far from always the case, especially in the case of scholarship that does not rely on measuring concepts and quantifying variables in large-N studies. Take the concept of power and its associated concepts such as the balance of power, a hugely influential concept in Security Studies, IR and political thought in general. If power is defined as a state's military capabilities, the concept scores high in terms of clarity, although "military capabilities" create challenges as nuclear and conventional weapons for examples are to be aggregated (or not). Yet, even realists can be skeptical that "power" can be captured solely by material measures (Buzan and Wæver 2003: 30–39). Looking to IR more broadly, the concept of power has been consistently fought over as competing approaches are trying to make the concept "clear" (for an overview in IR, see Barnett and Duvall 2005).

One should note also that the clarity of key concepts is not the same as whether concepts produce straightforward conclusions. Securitization theory illustrates this difference. Contra McDonald's description of this theory as built on "shaky analytical ground," I would argue that this a theory that scores high on conceptual clarity: security is defined as a speech act followed by a set of clearly delineated concepts that identify the conditions under which securitization is successful (securitizing actors, existential threat to a referent object, the adoption of emergency measures, and the acceptance thereof by the relevant audience). Yet, while securitization theory provides us with a series of concepts from which we can identify and analyze securitizations, it does not establish objective, measurable criteria such as "when embassies are attacked it is a clear evidence of securitization," or, "because the military budget rose with 5 percent, we have a case of securitization." Because securitizations are situated within particular temporal and spatial contexts, and because the word "security" (spoken or written) is not the methodological basis upon which securitizations can be identified (Buzan *et al.* 1998: 27), it is impossible to establish universal standards of identification.

Finally, even concepts that appear clearly defined at first may seem less clear when held up to closer theoretical and empirical scrutiny. Theoretically rich concepts such as those that stand at the center of *Contesting Security* may thus be vulnerable to a "zooming in" on those concepts. To continue with the example of securitization theory, one might ask "well, what is a speech act really?," "how is the agency of the audience actually conceived?," and "what is the political role that emergency measures play?" The point here is not that we should abandon theories as such "zooming in" questions arise, or that the appropriate response is to erect a battery of specific conditions under which X, Y, and Z apply, but rather that we should be aware that the strength of theoretically rich concepts is the wider scope and discussions they allow, not that they produce an univocal, "objective," measurable outcome.

The second criterion takes us from the clarity of specific concepts to that of the conceptual consistency of a security theory as a wider theoretical whole. In short, are the different concepts defined such that they are ontologically and epistemologically compatible with one another? The inclusion of multiple epistemological perspectives – such as in Nunes' call for seeing security as being subjective, intersubjective and non-subjective – has the advantage of allowing a theory to capture more aspects of the world "out there." But this comes with the risk that such combinations are at epistemological odds with one another. Thus, for example, we would not know how to judge between subjective, intersubjective and non-subjective definitions of security if these line up in contradictory ways. Unfortunately, there is no universal rule that can be applied to this dilemma. Because security theories are not exclusively about securing analytical consistency – they are not mathematical systems – but equally guided by political and normative concerns, there might be situations where one might prefer a theory with less than perfect consistency because it brings important parts of the social world into analytical view. Perhaps what Security Studies scholarship can do is to be more explicit about the adoption of such conceptual inconsistencies and why they might be preferable over "cleaner," more consistent theories.

The third criterion is that of a concept's and a security theory's applicability. That is, what are the phenomena, events, and processes that a theory can be applied to? Security scholars seek to build theories that are applicable to the phenomena they deem important at the ontopolitical level, yet the more exact applicability of a theory and its concepts often only appears as a theory is taken on board and used by other scholars. Probably because scholars working in the tradition of critical security studies adopt non-positivist epistemologies and hence do not evaluate their theories through falsifiable hypothesis testing, they rarely present studies that demonstrate the inapplicability of theoretical approaches. If a theoretical and conceptual lens does not work, it seems more logical to simply move on and find one that does. Yet, just to show that such instances of theoretical inapplicability *do* occur, let me report that I once tried to apply securitization theory to editorial cartoons on the Muhammad Cartoon Crisis (Hansen 2010). However, after trying to force the theory and the empirics together I came to the conclusion that securitization theory was not really applicable to this body of texts and images: there were no explicit responses to any of the cartoons and they included very little text which in turn made it hard, if not impossible, to assess whether securitizations or desecuritizations had been made. As sociology of science has pointed out if critical questions are raised about a theory's applicability to central phenomena, it is often the case that a theory is adjusted such that it can now be applied (Kuhn

1962). The applicability criterion is thus itself a dynamic target with scholars debating when and where it is met.

If clarity, consistency, and applicability were the only things that mattered to how critical security studies selected its concepts decisions would be relatively easy. Yet, clarity and consistency are not the only criteria that go into selecting and theorizing concepts. Concepts with long and complex philosophical histories cannot be narrowed down to straightforward empirical measures without a loss of their theoretical richness. Conceptual inconsistency is therefore sometimes seen as desirable on the grounds that it allows a necessarily complicated and plural vision of the world. Thus a fourth, and more amorphous criterion is that of theoretical depth, that is, the complexity and political, analytical and normative nuance that a concept brings with it. Considerations of theoretical depth are important because they provide us with an understanding of why concepts that arguable are not scoring maximum points in terms of clarity, consistency or even applicability are still playing important roles in Security Studies. The example of power was mentioned above, and one could make the case that the concept of emancipation, a notoriously contested and complicated concept, has a similar make-up. Yet, as many of the contributions to *Contesting Security* have shown, critical security studies would be an impoverished field of study were there no "emancipation" to remind us of the need for taking structures, progress and community into account and for doing so in rich and complicated ways.

Furthering a contesting security research agenda

Let me bring this Conclusion to a close by briefly suggesting two avenues that further research on the concepts that contest security might venture onto. First, many of the chapters of *Contesting Security* are ripe with analysis of the relationships between the four sub-concepts. Differences are laid out, but so are commonalities and interfaces. Balzacq writes for example in his editor's introduction (p. 13) to resistance that "desecuritization may relate to resistance, but not as a sufficient condition: resistance to security policies can lead to other security policies; and not every form of desecuritization depends on resistance." Vuori (Chapter 3: 30) holds in that "desecuritization is viewed here as a means of contestation and resistance." For Nunes (Chapter 9: 152), "there is nothing that prevents security as emancipation from incorporating securitization theory as a tool for understanding the ways in which security is used to frame particular issues, and with certain political outcomes as a result." Bourbeau (Chapter 11: 173) links resilience and securitization theory suggesting that "resiliencism could lead to new theoretical and empirical ways of understanding the contemporary security world and could help us to gain a better understanding of the securitization process." And, these are just some of the conceptual interfaces, competitions and collaborations put forward.

One avenue for further research would be to continue these conceptual discussions at the level of theory and concepts themselves, and given the richness of – and divergence between – the contributions to *Contesting Security* this is both a necessary and promising undertaking. Yet having turned the last page of Chapter 13, I was left with a slightly different curiosity, namely how authors – and concepts – would approach and analyze a similar set of cases. This points in the direction of something so seemingly conventional as comparative case-studies. Not so much comparative case-studies set within particular sub-concepts – Vuori and Blanc for example do that well – but across the four sub-concepts. What would a study of China, immigration or biometric politics look like if approached by all four perspectives? Could there be an agreement on which material would form the basis for such a study? If so, how would epistemological and methodological differences translate into differences at the applied analytical level? My point here is not that we should strive for a coherent perspective that unites all four sub-concepts – something which is probably impossible in any case – or that we can design such studies to adjudicate which concepts and theories are better. My sense is simply that after the lengthy and thorough conceptual exegeses and debate that *Contesting Security* has generously provided, we might learn something new from seeing how concepts and theories produce different – or perhaps not so different – visions of the security world.

Second, I was struck by Balzacq's remark in his editor's introduction to resistance (p. 11) that "In fact, it was not until the so-called cultural turn of the 1980s that resistance became a consistent and dynamic field of study." It made me wonder if there is not a longer history of "resistance" – and "contestation" more broadly – in Security Studies worthy of genealogical discovery? Nunes' emphasis on structural injustice in Chapter 9 had for example echoes of Galtung's theory of structural violence (Galtung 1969), and McDonald mobilized no one less than Arnold Wolfers in his defense of an empirically and politically open conception of the logic of security (Wolfers 1952). This suggests that there might be ways to read "contestation" as a concern situated at the heart of Security Studies from its post-World War II genesis onwards. Uncovering this legacy would not only provide legitimacy and support for the research agenda envisioned by *Contesting Security*, it would draw our attention to the inherent contestedness of *all* writings on security and hence why defining security – or any of the concepts that surround it – once and for all is an impossible mission.

Notes

1 I wish to thank Thierry Balzacq and Simone Molin Friis for their insightful comments on an earlier draft of this chapter.
2 I use "critical security studies" to refer to the broader field of non-traditional Security Studies, and "Critical Security Studies" to refer to the so-called Welsh School whose prominent authors include Ken Booth and Richard Wyn Jones.

References

Aaltola, M. (1999) *Rhythm, Rule, and Exception in International Relations: The Case of the Mad Cow Disease*, Tampere: Tampere University Press.

Aaltola, M. (2005) "The international airport: the hub-and-spoke pedagogy of the American empire", *Global Networks*, 5(3): 261–278.

Aaltola, M. (2012) "Contagious insecurity: three inter-related security scenarios of 2003", *Contemporary Politics*, 2: 120–145.

ABC (2011) Asylum. *ABC Four Corners Program*, 3 November. Available at http://www.abc.net.au/4corners/stories/2011/10/20/3344543.htm.

About, I. and Denis, V. (2010) *Histoire de l'identification des personnes*, Paris: La Découverte.

Acharya, A. (1998) "Culture, security, multilateralism: the 'ASEAN way' and regional order", *Contemporary Security Policy*, 19(1): 55–84.

Adger, N. (2000) "Social and ecological resilience: are they related?", *Progress in Human Geography*, 24(3): 347–364.

Agamben, G. (1998) *Homo Sacer: Sovereign Power and Bare Life*, Stanford: Stanford University Press.

Agamben, G. (2004) "Non au tatouage biopolitique", *Le Monde*, 11 January.

Agamben, G. (2005) *State of Exception*, Chicago: University of Chicago Press.

AJRP (Australians for Just Refugee Programs) (2006) A test of MPs' values: submission to the Senate legal and constitution references committee inquiry into the provisions of the migration amendment (Designated Unauthorised Arrivals) Bill 2006. Available at http://www.ajustaustralia.com/resource.php?act=attache&id=183.

Akerman, P. (2010) "Refugee policy blamed for wreck", *The Australian*, 16 December.

Alain, P. (2012) *Enfants Roms: l'autre tweet de Valérie*, Mediapart.

Amoore, L. (2005) "Introduction: global resistance-global politics", in L. Amoore (ed.), *The Global Resistance Reader*, London: Routledge.

Anaut, M. (2005) "Le concept de résilience et ses applications cliniques", *Recherche en soins infirmiers*, 82: 4–10.

Andrieu, K. (2009) "'Sorry for the genocide': how public apologies can help promote national reconciliation", *Millennium – Journal of International Studies*, 38(1): 3–23.

Ansell, C. and Weber, S. (1999) "Organizing international politics: sovereignty and open systems", *International Political Science Review*, 20(1): 73–93.

Anthony, E. J. (1987) "Risk, vulnerability and resilience", in E. J. Anthony and B. Cohler (eds), *The vulnerable child*, New York: Guilford.

Anthony, I. (2001) "Multilateral weapon and technology export controls", in: SIPRI, *SIPRI Yearbook 2001: Armaments, Disarmament and International Security*, New York: Oxford University Press.

Antonio, R. J. (1981) "Immanent critique as the core of critical theory: its origins and developments in Hegel, Marx and contemporary thought". *British Journal of Sociology* 32(3): 330–345.

Apple, M. (2004) "Creating difference: neo-liberalism, neo-conservatism and the politics of educational reform", *Educational Policy*, 18(1): 12–44.

Aradau, C. (2004) "Security and the democratic scene: desecuritization and emancipation", *Journal of International Relations and Development*, 7(4): 388–413.

Aradau, C. (2008) *Rethinking Trafficking in Women. Politics out of Security*, Basingstoke: Palgrave Macmillan.

Aradau, C., Huysmans, J., Macioti, P. and Squire, V. (2013) "Mobility interrogating freedom of Movement? Roma acts of European citizenship" in E. F. Isin and M. Saward (eds), *Enacting European Citizenship*, Cambridge: Cambridge University Press.

Aras, B. and Polat, R. K. (2008) "From conflict to cooperation: desecuritization of Turkey's relations with Syria and Iran", *Security Dialogue*, 39(5):495–535.

Arendt, H. (1971) "Civil disobedience", in E. Rostow (ed.), *Is law dead?*, New York: Simon and Schuster.

Ashley, R. (1981) "Political realism and human interests", *International Studies Quarterly*, 25(2): 204–236.

Axworthy, L. (1999) *Notes for an Address by the Honourable Lloyd Axworthy, Minister of Foreign Affairs, to the Atlantic Diplomatic Forum*, Ottawa: Department of Foreign Affairs, November 5.

Axworthy, L. (2000) *Notes for an Address by the Honourable Lloyd Axworthy, Minister of Foreign Affairs, to the Middlebury College 200th Anniversary Symposium on International Affairs*, Ottawa: Department of Foreign Affairs, March 30.

Balibar, E. (1995) "Ambiguous universality", *Differences: A Journal of Feminist Cultural Studies*, 7(1): 48–74.

Balibar, E. (2006) "Sub Specie Universitatis", *Topoi*, 25: 3–16.

Balibar, E. (2007) *Debating with Badiou on Universalism*, Irvine, CA: University of California at Irvine.

Balibar, E. (2012) "Civic universalism and its internal exclusions: the issue of anthropological difference", *Boundary 2*, 39(1): 207–229.

Balladur, E. (1993a) *Déclaration de M. Édouard Balladur, Premier ministre, sur le bilan des réformes du gouvernement, aux journées parlementaires du RPR, La Rochelle*, Paris : Bureau du Premier Ministre.

Balladur, E. (1993b) *Déclaration de politique générale de M. Édouard Balladur, Premier ministre, à l'Assemblée nationale*, Paris, Bureau du Premier Ministre, 8 April, http://discours.vie-publique.fr/notices/933113800.html (accessed December 19, 2012).

Balzacq, T. (2005) "The three faces of securitization: political agency, audience and context", *European Journal of International Relations*, 11(2): 171–201.

Balzacq, T. (ed.) (2011a) *Securitization Theory. How Security Problems Emerge and Dissolve*, London: Routledge.

Balzacq, T. (2011b) "A theory of securitization: origins, core assumptions and wariants", in T. Balzacq (ed.), *Securitization Theory: How Security Problems Emerge and Dissolve*, London: Routledge.

Balzacq, T. and Carrera, S. (eds) (2006) *Security versus Freedom*, London: Ashgate.

Barany, Z. and Rauchhaus, R. (2011) "Explaining NATO's resilience: is international relations theory useful?", *Contemporary Security Policy*, 32(2): 286–307.

Barnett, M. (1999) "Culture, strategy and foreign policy change", *European Journal of International Relations*, 5(1): 5–36.

Barnett, M. and Duvall, R. (2005) "Power in international politics", *International Organization*, 59(1): 39–75.

Baruah, S. (2009) "Separatist militants and contentious politics in Assam, India: the limits of counterinsurgency", *Asian Survey*, 49(6): 951–974.

Basu, S. (2011) "Security as emancipation: A feminist perspective". In J. A. Tickner and L. Sjoberg (eds) *Feminism and International Relations: Conversations about the Past, Present and Future*. Abingdon: Routledge.

Bauer, S. and Bromley, M. (2004) "The european code of conduct on arms exports", *SIPRI Policy Paper* 8, Stockholm: SIPRI.

Bauman, Z. and Lyon, D. (2012) *Liquid Surveillance. A Conversation*, Cambridge: Polity Press.

Beardslee, W. R. (1989) "The role of self-understanding in resilient individuals", *The American Journal of Orthopsychiatry*, 59(2): 266–278.

Beck, U. (1992) *Risk Society*, London: Sage.

Becker, H. (1963) *Outsiders*, New York: Free Press.

Beetham, D. (1991) *The Legitimation of Power*, New York: Palgrave Macmillan.

Behnke, A. (1999) "Postmodernising security". Paper presented at the ECPR Joint Sessions of Workshops, Mannheim.

Behnke, A. (2006) "No way out: desecuritization, emancipation and the eternal return of the political", *Journal of International Relations and Development*, 9(1): 62–69.

Bell, D. J. (1973) *Resistance and Revolution*, Boston, MA: Houghton Mifflin.

Bellamy, A. (2008) "The responsibilities of victory: *Jus Post Bellum* and the Just War", *Review of International Studies*, 34: 601–625.

Bennett, A. and Checkel, J. (eds) (forthcoming) *Process Tracing in the Social Science: From Metaphor to Analytic Tool*, Cambridge: Cambridge University Press.

Bennett, C. and Haggerty, K. (2011) *Security Games: Surveillance and Control at Mega-Events*, London: Taylor and Francis.

Bérard, M. (2008) "Le(s) mouvement(s) antibiométrie : mobilisation et modes d'action", master's dissertation in political science, Université Paris 1 Panthéon Sorbonne.

Berkes, F., Colding, J. and Folke, C. (eds) (2003) *Navigating Social-ecological Systems: Building Resilience for complexity and change*, Cambridge: Cambridge University Press.

Berkes, F. and Folke, C. (eds) (1998) *Linking social and ecological systems: management and Practices and Social Mechanisms*, Cambridge: Cambridge University Press.

Berman, E. (2011) *Domestic Intelligence: New Powers, New Risks*, New York, Brennan Center for Justice, NYU Law School.

Bigo, D. (2002) "Security and immigration: toward a critique of the governmentality of unease", *Alternatives*, 27(1): 63–92.

Bigo, D. (2006) "Globalized (in)security: fhe field and the ban-opticon", in D. Bigo and A. Tsoukala (eds), *Illiberal practices of liberal regimes: The (In)security Games*, Paris: L'Harmattan.

Bilgin, P. (2008) "Critical theory". In P. D. Williams (ed.) *Security Studies: An Introduction*. London and New York: Routledge.

Binfield, K. (2004) *Writings of Luddites*, Baltimore, MD: Johns Hopkins University Press.

Blanc, F. (2012) "La resistance des hystériques: bibliothécaires et avocats dans les champ de la sécurité nationale americaine", *Culture et Conflicts*, 84: 81–102.

Bleiker, R. (2000) *Popular Dissent, Human Agency and Global Politics*, Cambridge: Cambridge University Press.

Bleiker, R., Campbell, D., Hutchison, E. and Nicholson, X. (2013) "The visual dehumanisation of refugees", *Australian Journal of Political Science*, 48(3) 398–416.

Blumer, H. (1957) "Collective behavior", in A. M. Lee. (ed.), *New Outline of the Principles of Sociology*, New York: Barnes and Noble.

Bromley, M. (2008) *The Impact on Domestic Policy of the EU Code of Conduct on Arms Exports, the Czech Republic, the Netherlands and Spain*, SIPRI Policy Paper no. 21.

Bonanno, G. (2004) "Loss, trauma, and human resilience. Have we underestimated the human capacity to thrive after extremely aversive events?", *American Psychologist*, 59(1): 20–28.

Booth, K. (1991) "Security and emancipation", *Review of International Studies*, 17(4): 313–326.

Booth, K. (1999) "Nuclearism, human rights and constructions of security (Part 2)". *The International Journal of Human Rights* 3(3): 44–61.

Booth, K. (2005) "Critical explorations". In K. Booth (ed) *Critical Security Studies and World Politics*. Boulder, CO and London: Lynne Rienner Publishers.

Booth, K. (2007) *Theory of World Security*, Cambridge: Cambridge University Press.

Bourbeau, P. (2011) *The Securitization of Migration. A Study of Movement and Order*, London: Routledge.

Bourbeau, P. (2013a) "Politisation et sécuritisation des migrations internationales: une relation à définir", *Critique Internationale*, 61(4): 125–146.

Bourbeau, P. (2013b) "Processus et acteurs d'une vision sécuritaire des migrations: le cas du Canada", *Revue Européenne des Migrations Internationales*, 29(4): 21–41.

Bourbeau, P. (2013c) "Resiliencism: premises and promises in securitization research", *Resilience: International Policies, Practices and Discourses*, 1(1): 4–17.

Bourbeau, P. (2014) "Moving forward together: logics of the securitization process", *Millennium: Journal of International Studies*, 43(1): 187–206.

Bourdeau, V., Jarrige, F. and Julien, V. (2006), *Les luddites. Bris de machine, économie politique et histoire*, Maisons-Alfort: Editions Ère.

Bourdieu, P. (1977) *Outline of a Theory of Practice*, Cambridge: Cambridge University Press.

Bourdieu, P. (1984) *Distinction*, London: Routledge.

Bourdieu, P. (1991) *Language and Symbolic Power*, ed. J. Thompson, transl. G. Raymond and M. Adamson, Cambridge: Polity.

Bourdieu, P. (2000) *Pascalian Meditations*, Stanford, CA: Stanford University Press.

Bourdieu, P. and Wacquant, L. (1992) *Réponses: pour une anthropologie réflexive*, Paris: Seuil.

Brand, F. S. and Jax, K. (2007) "Focusing the meaning(s) of resilience: resilience as a descriptive concept and a boundary object", *Ecology and Society*, 12(1): 23–38.

Brenner, N., Peck, J. and Theodore, N. (2010) "Variegated neoliberalization: geographies, modalities, pathways", *Global Networks*, 10(2): 182–222.

Brenner, N., Peck, J. and Theodore, N. (2011) "After neoliberalization?", *Globalizations*, 7(3): 327–334.

Brown, M. F. (1996) "On resisting resistance", *American Anthropologist*, 98(4): 729–749.

Browning, C. and McDonald, M. (2013) "The future of critical security studies: Ethics and the politics of security", *European Journal of International Relations*, 19(2): 235–255.

Bruneau, M. *et al.* (2003) "A framework to quantitatively assess and enhance the seismic resilience of communities", *Earthquake Spectra*, 19(4): 733–752.

Bubandt, N. (2005) "Vernacular security: the politics of feeling safe in global, national and local worlds", *Security Dialogue*, 36(3): 275–296.

Buchwalter, A. (1991) "Hegel, Marx, and the concept of immanent critique". *Journal of the History of Philosophy* 29(3): 253–279.

Burgess, P. J. (2010) *The Ethical Subject of Security*, London: Routledge.

Burke, A. (2001) *In Fear of Security,* Sydney: Pluto.

Burke, A. (2007) "What security makes possible: some thoughts on critical security studies", *Mimeo*, ANU Department of International Relations.

Burke, A. (2008) *Fear of Security: Australia's Invasion Anxiety*, Melbourne: Cambridge University Press.

Busby, J. (2008) "Who cares about the weather? Climate change and US national security", *Security Studies*, 17: 468–504.

Butler, J. (1994) "Contingent foundations: feminism and the question of 'postmodernism," in S. Seidman (ed.), *The Postmodern Turn: New Perspectives on Social Theory*, Cambridge: Cambridge University Press.

Butler, J. (2000) "Restaging the universal: hegemony and the limits of formalism", in J. Butler, E. Laclau and S. Žižek (eds), *Contingency, Hegemony, Universality: Contemporary Dialogues on the Left*, London: Verso.

Butler, J. (2006) *Precarious Life: The Powers of Mourning and Violence*, London: Verso.

Buzan, B. (1991) *People, States and Fear: An Agenda for International Security Studies in the Post-Cold War Era*, London: Harvester Wheatsheaf.

Buzan, B. and Hansen, L. (2009) *The Evolution of International Security Studies*, Cambridge: Cambridge University Press.

Buzan, B. and Richard, L. (2001) "Why international relations has failed as an intellectual project and what to do about it", *Millennium: Journal of International Studies*, 30(1): 19–39.

Buzan, B. and Wæver, O. (2003) *Regions and Powers: The Structure of International Security*, Cambridge: Cambridge University Press.

Buzan, B., Wæver, O and de Wilde, J. (1998) *Security: A New Framework for Analysis,* Boulder, CO: Lynne Rienner.

Byman, D. and Lind, J. (2010) "Pyongyang's survival strategy: tools of authoritarian control in North Korea", *International Security*, 35(1): 44–74.

Caballero, M. (2005) "SARS in Asia: crisis, vulnerabilities, and regional responses", *Asian Survey*, 45(3): 475–495.

Callahan, W. (2006) *Cultural Governance and Resistance in Pacific Asia*, London: Routledge.

Campbell, D. (1992) *Writing Security: United States Foreign Policy and the Politics of Identity*, Manchester: Manchester University Press.

Campbell, D. (1998) *National Deconstruction: Violence, Identity and Justice in Bosnia*, Minneapolis, MN: University of Minnesota Press.

Caplan, E. (1999a) *Notes for an Address by the Honourable Elinor Caplan, Minister of Citizenship and Immigration, to the Annual Meeting of the Canadian Council for Refugees*. Ottawa: Department of Citizenship and Immigration, December 3.

Caplan, E. (1999b) *Remarks by the Honourable Elinor Caplan, Minister of Citizenship and Immigration, to the Canadian Club*, Ottawa: Department of Citizenship and Immigration, September 9.

Caplan, E. (1999c) *Statement by the Honourable Elinor Caplan, Minister of Citizenship and Immigration, on Illegal Human Smuggling to Canada*, Ottawa: Department of Citizenship and Immigration, August 11.

Caplan, E. (2000) *Notes for an Address by the Honourable Elinor Caplan, Minister of Citizenship and Immigration, to the European Union Seminar on Illegal Migration*, Ottawa: Department of Citizenship and Immigration, July 20.

Caplan, E. (2001). *Notes for an Address by the Honourable Elinor Caplan, Minister of Citizenship and Immigration, to the Standing Committee on Citizenship and Immigration on Bill C-11 The Immigration and Refugee Protection Act*, Ottawa: Department of Citizenship and Immigration, March 1.

Capoccia, G. and Keleman, D. (2007) "The study of critical junctures: theory, narrative and counterfactuals in historical institutionalism", *World Politics*, 59: 341–369.

Carpenter, S. R., Walker, B., Anderies, J. M. and Abel, N. (2001) "From metaphor to measurement: resilience of what to what?", *Ecosystems*, 4: 765–781.

Carver, C. S. (1998). "Resilience and thriving: issues, models, and linkages," *Journal of Social Issues*, 54(2): 245–366

CASE collective (2006) "Critical approaches to security in Europe: a networked Manifesto", *Security Dialogue*, 37(4): 443–487.

Case, W. (2004) "New uncertainties for an old pseudo-democracy: the case of Malaysia", *Comparative Politics*, 37(1): 83–104.

Casteau, C. (2008) "Le département lâche l'affaire", *Hérault du jour*, 5 September.

Castel, R. (1991) "From dangerousness to risk", in G. Burchell, C. Gordon and P. Miles (eds), *The Foucault Effect: Studies in Governmentality*, Chicago, IL: University of Chicago Press.

Ceyhan, A. and Piazza, P. (eds.) (2011), *L'identification biométrique. Champs, acteurs, enjeux et controverses*, Paris: Editions de la MSH.

Chandler, D. (2012) "Resilience and human security: the post-interventionist paradigm", *Security Dialogue*, 43(3): 213–229.

Chandler, D. and Hynek, N. (2011) *Critical perspectives on Human Security: Rethinking Emancipation and Power in International Relations*, PRIO New Security Studies, Abingdon: Routledge.

Chertok, M. and Marcus, S. (1970) "Chilling political expression by use of police intelligence files: Anderson V. Sills", *Harvard Civil Rights & Civil Liberties Review*, (5)1: 71–88.

Cicchetti, D. and Garmezy, F. (1993) "Prospects and promises in the study of resilience", *Development and Psychopathology*, 5(4): 597–600.

Ciută, F. (2009) "Security and the problem of context: a hermeneutical critique of securitization theory", *Review of International Studies*, 35(2): 301–326.

Clark, D. (2002) "Neoliberalism and public service reform: Canada in comparative perspective", *Canadian Journal of Political Science*, 35(4): 771–793.

Claus-Ehlers, C. S. and Levi, L. L. (2002) "Violence and community, terms and conflict: an ecological approach to resilience", *Journal of Social Distress and the Homeless*, 11(4): 265–278.

Coaffee, J. and Murakami Wood, D. (2006) "Security is coming home: rethinking scale and constructing resilience in the global urban response to rerrorist risk", *International Relations*, 20(4): 503–517.

Coaffee, J., Murakami Wood, D. and Rogers, P. (2009) *The Everyday Resilience of the City: How Cities Respond to Terrorism and Disaster*, London: Palgrave Macmillan.

Coaffee, J. and Rogers, P. (2008) "Rebordering the city for new security challenges: from counter-terrorism to community resilience", *Space and Polity*, 12(1): 101–118.

Cohn, C. (2011) "'Feminist security studies': toward a reflexive practice", *Politics & Gender*, 7(4): 581–586.

Coicaud, J.-M. (2002) *Legitimacy and Politics: A Contribution to the Study of Political Right and Political Responsibility*, trans. by D. A. Curtis, Cambridge: Cambridge University Press.

Collier, D. (2011) "Understanding process tracing", *PS: Political Science and Politics*, 44(4): 823–830.

Constantinou, C. (2000) "Poetics of security", *Alternatives*, 25(3): 287–306.

Craipeau, S., Dubey, G., and Guchet, X. (2004) *La biométrie. Usages et représentations*. Rapport de recherche, projet BIOLAB. Évry: Institut National des Télécommunications.

Crang, M. (2002) "Between places: producing hubs flows and networks", *Environment and Planning A*, 34: 569–574.

Crawford, D. (2007) *Deadly Companion: How Microbes Shape Our History*, Oxford: Oxford University Press.

Crettiez, X. (2006) "Les cartes d'identité régionalistes", in X. Crettiez and P. Piazza (eds.), *Du papier à la biométrie. Identifier les individus*, Paris: Presses de Sciences Po.

Croft, S. (2007) "What future for security studies?" In P. D. Williams (ed.) *Security Studies: An Introduction*. London and New York: Routledge.

Cui, S and Li, J. (2011) "(De)securitizing frontier security in China: beyond the positive and negative debate", *Cooperation and Conflict*, 46: 144–165.

Curley, M. and Wong, S. (eds) (2008) *Security and Migration in Asia: The Dynamics of Securitisation*, London: Routledge.

Cutter, S. (2008) "A place-based model for understanding community resilience to natural disasters", *Global Environmental Change*, 18: 598–606.

Dahl, R. A. (1984) *Modern Political Analysis*, Englewood Cliffs: Prentice Hall.

Davis, I. (2001) *Regulation of European Arms and Dual-use Exports in a Transnational Defence Industrial Environment: The EU Code of Conduct on Arms Exports*, Luxembourg: European Communities, COST Action A10.

DeRose, K. (2009) *The Case for Contextualism: Knowledge, Skepticism and Context, Vol. 1*, Oxford: Oxford University Press.

Devetak, R. (2004) "In fear of refugees: the politics of border protection in Australia", *International Journal of Human Rights*, 8(1):101–109.

De Wilde, J. (2008) "Environmental security deconstructed', in H. G. Brauch, J. Grin, C. Mesjasz, P. Dunay, N. Chadha Behera, B. Chourou, U. Oswald Spring, P. H. Liotta, P. Kameri-Mbote (eds), *Globalisation and Environmental Challenges: Reconceptualising Security in the 21st Century*, Berlin,Heidelberg, New York: Springer-Verlag.

De Wilde, J. (2012) "Review of Rita Floyd, 2010, *Security and the Environment: Securitisation Theory and US Environmental Security Policy*", *Perspectives on Politics*, 10(1): 213–214.

Dean, M. (1999) *Governmentality: Power and Rule in Modern Society*. London: SAGE.

Denis, V. (2008) *Une histoire de l'identité: France, 1715–1815*. Seyssel: Champ Vallon.

Dewitt, D. (1994) "Common, comprehensive, and cooperative security", *The Pacific Review*, 7(1): 1–15.

Dieckhoff, A. and Jaffrelot, C. (2004) "La résilience du nationalism face aux régionalismes et à la mondialisation", *Critique Internationale*, 23(2): 128–139.

Dietz, T., Ostrom, E. and Stern, P. C. (2003) "The struggle to govern the commons", *Science*, 302(5652): 1907–1912.

Dillon, M. (1996) *The Politics of Security: Towards a Political Philosophy of Continental Thought*, London: Routledge.

Dillon, M. (2005) "Cared to Death. The biopoliticised time of your life", *Foucault Studies*, 2: 37–46.

Dillon, M. and Lobo-Guerrero, L. (2008) "Biopolitics of security in the 21st century: an introduction", *Review of International Studies*, 34(2): 265–292.

Dillon, M. and Reid, J. (2000) "Global governance liberal peace and complex emergency", *Alternatives*, 25(1): 117–143.

Dillon, M. and Reid, J. (2001) "Global liberal governance: biopolitics, security and War", *Millennium: Journal of International Studies*, 30(1): 41–66.

Dillon, M. and Reid, J. (2009) *The Liberal Way of War*, London: Routledge.

Dodge, M. and Kitchin, R. (2004) "Flying through code/space: the real virtuality of air travel", *Environment and Planning A*, 36(2): 195–211.

Donner, F. (1990) *Protectors of Privileges: Red Squads and Police Repression in Urban America*, Berkeley, CA: University of California Press.

Donnon, T. and Hammond, W. (2007) "Understanding the relationships between resiliency and bullying in adolescence", *Child and Adolescent Psychiatric Clinics of North America*, 16: 449–472.

Doty, R. (1998/9) "Immigration and the politics of security", *Security Studies*, 8(2–3): 71–93.

Doucet, M. and de Larrinaga, M. (eds) (2010) *Security and Global Governmentality: Globalization, Governance, and the State*, London: Routledge.

Douglas, M. (2003) *Purity and Danger: An Analysis of Concepts of Pollution and Taboo. Vol. 2*, New York: Routledge.

Dovers, S. and Handmer, J. (1992) "Uncertainty, sustainability and change", *Global Environmental Change*, 2(4): 262–276.

Doyal, L. and Gough, I. (1991) *A Theory of Human Needs*, Basingstoke: Palgrave Macmillan.

Drezner, D. (1997). "Allies, adversaries, and economic coercion: Russian foreign economic policy since 1991". *Security Studies*, 6(3), 65–111.

Dubey, G. (2008), "Nouvelles techniques d'identification, nouveaux pouvoirs. Le cas de la biométrie", *Cahiers internationaux de sociologie*, 125: 263–79.

Duffield, M. (2007) *Development, Security and Unending War. Governing the World of Peoples*, Cambridge: Polity Press.

Duffield, M. (2012) "Challenging environments: danger, resilience and the aid industry", *Security Dialogue*, 43(5): 475–492.

Dunn, K., Klocker, N. and Salabay, T. (2007) "Contemporary racism and Islamaphobia in Australia: racializing religion", *Ethnicities*, 7(4): 564–589.

Dunne, T., Hansen, L. and Wight, C. (2013) "The end of international relations theory?", *European Journal of International Relations*, 19(3): 405–425.

Dunne, T. and Wheeler, N. (2004) "'We the peoples': contending discourses of security in human rights theory and practice", *International Relations*, 18(1): 9–23.

Dupont, B. (2008) "Hacking the panopticon: distributed online surveillance and resistance", *Sociology of Crime, Law & Deviance*, 10: 259–280.

Dyzenhaus, D. (2010) "The 'organic law' of ex parte Milligan", in A. Sarat (ed). *Sovereignty, Emergency, Legality*, Cambridge: Cambridge University Press.

Earl, J. and Kimport, K. (2011) *Digitally Enabled Social Change*, Cambridge, MA: MIT Press.

Easton, D. (1965) *A Systems Analysis of Political Life*, New York: Wiley.

Economou, N. "2010) "Election maths underpins Gillard's asylum seeker policy", *Neo Kosmos News*, July 13.

Edwards, C. (2009) *Resilient Nation*. London: Demos.

Elbe, S. (2006) "Should HIV/AIDS be securitized? The ethical dilemmas of linking HIV/AIDS and security", *International Studies Quarterly*, 50(1): 119–144.

Elbe, S. (2011) "Pandemics on the radar screen: health security, infectious disease and the medicalisation of insecurity", *Political Studies*, 59: 848–866.

Emmers, R. (2009). "Comprehensive security and resilience in Southeast Asia: ASEANS' approach to terrorism", *The Pacific Review*, 22(2): 159–177.

Ericson, R. and Haggerty, K. (2007) *Policing the Risk Society.* Oxford: Oxford University Press.

Erikson, K. (1966) *Wayward Puritans*, Glencoe, IL: Free Press.

European Commission (2004) Commission staff working paper, *Report to the Parliament and the Council on the Implementation of Council Regulation (EC) 1334/2000 Setting up a Community Regime for the Control of Exports of Dual-use Items and Technology October 2000 to May 2004*, SEC(2004)1158, Brussels 17 September 2004.

European Commission (2006) *Interpretative Communication on the Application of Article 296 of the Treaty in the Field of Defence Procurement,* COM(2006)779 final, Brussels 7 December 2006.

European Commission (2006a) *Proposal for a Council Regulation setting up a Community regime for the control of exports of dual-use items and technology,* COM(2006)829 final, Brussels 18 December 2006.

European Commission (2007a), *Proposal for a directive of the European Parliament and the Council on simplifying terms and conditions of transfers of defence-related products within the Community*, COM (2007) 765 final, Brussels, 5 December 2007.

European Commission (2007b), *Impact assessment on a Commission proposal for a directive of the European Parliament and of the Council on simplifying terms and conditions of transfers of defence related products within the Community*, Brussels SEC(2007) 1593.

European Council (1991) European Council in Luxembourg (28–29 June 1991) Conclusions of the Presidency, DOC/91/2, date 29 June 1991.

European Council (2003) *A Secure Europe in a Better World – The European Security Strategy*, Brussels 12 December 2003.

Evans, M. (2005) 'Moral theory and the idea of a just war' in M. Evans (ed.), *Just War Theory: A Reappraisal,* Edinburgh: Edinburgh University Press, pp. 1–24.

Every, D. and Augoustinos, M. (2008) 'Constructions of Australia in pro- and anti-asylum seeker political discourse', *Nations and Nationalism*, 14(3): 562–580.

Falkoff, M. (2007) *Poems from Guantanamo: The Detainees Speak*, Iowa City, IA: University of Iowa Press.

Falleti, T. G. and Lynch, J. F. (2009) "Context and causal mechanisms in political analysis." *Comparative Political Studies*, 42(9): 1143–1166.

Feldman, L. C. (2010) "The banality of emergency: on the time and space of 'political necessity'", in A. Sarat (eds), *Sovereignty, Emergency, Legality* Cambridge: Cambridge University Press, pp.136–164

Ferree, M. M. (2005) 'Soft repression: ridicule, stigma, and silencing in gender-based movements', in C. and H. Johnston and C. Mueller (eds), *Repression and Mobilization*, Minneapolis, MN: University of Minnesota Press.

Fierke, K. M. (2007) *Critical Approaches to International Security*, Cambridge: Polity Press.

Flemish Peace Institute (2007) *Enhancing Cooperation to Strengthen Export Controls*, Brussels, advisory note. Available at via http://www.vlaamsvredesinstituut.eu/get_pdf.php?ID=226&lang=EN (accessed 20 March 2007).

Floyd, R. (2007) "Towards a consequentialist evaluation of security: Bringing together the Copenhagen School and the Welsh School of Security Studies", *Review of International Studies*, 33(2): 327–350

Floyd, R. (2010) *Security and the Environment: Securitization Theory and US Environmental Security Policy*, Cambridge: Cambridge University Press.

Floyd, R. (2011) "Can securitization theory be used in normative analysis? Towards a just securitization theory', *Security Dialogue*, 42(4–5): 427–439.

Flynn, S. E. (2008) "America the resilient: defying terrorism and mitigating natural disasters", *Foreign Affairs*, 87(2): 2–8.

Folke, C. (2006) "Resilience: the emergence of a perspective for social-ecological systems analyses", *Global Environmental Change*, 16: 253–267.

Foucault, M. (1976), *La volonté de savoir*, Paris: Gallimard (this is volume I of the book published under "The History of sexuality").

Foucault, M. (1977) *Discipline and Punish: The Birth of the Prison*, New York: Pantheon.

Foucault, M. (1979a) *Discipline and Punish: The Birth of the Prison*, trans. A. Sheridan, London: Penguin Books.

Foucault, M. (1979b) *The History of Sexuality. Vol. I, An Introduction*, Harmondsworth: Penguin.

Foucault, M. (1980) *Power/ Knowledge: Selected Interviews and Other Writings 1972–1977*, New York: Pantheon.

Foucault, M. (1991) "Governmentality", in Graham Burchell, Colin Gordon and Peter Miller (eds), *The Foucault Effect. Studies in Governmentality*. Chicago, IL: University of Chicago Press, pp. 87–104.

Foucault, M. (2000 [1982]). "The subject and power". In *Power: Essential Works of Foucault, 1954–1984*, edited by J. D. Faubion. London: Penguin.

Foucault, M. (2004) *Society Must Be Defended*, trans David Macey, London: Penguin Books.

Foucault, M. (2007) *Security, Territory, Population*. Basingstoke: Palgrave.

Gad, U. P., and Petersen, K. L. (2011) "Concepts of politics in securitization studies". *Security Dialogue* 42(4–5): 315–328.

Galtung, J. (1969) "Violence, peace and peace research", *Journal of Peace Research*, 6(3): 167–191.

Garmezy, N. (1974) "The study of competence in children at risk for severe psychopathology", in E. J. Anthony and C. Koupernik (eds), *The Child in his Family: Children at Psychiatric Risk: III*, New York: Wiley.

Gelber, K. and McDonald, M. (2006) "Ethics and exclusion: representations of sovereignty in Australia's approach to asylum-seekers", *Review of International Studies*, 32(2): 269–289.

George, A. and Bennett, A. (2005) *Case Studies and Theory Development in the Social Sciences*, Cambridge, MA: MIT Press.

Gerring, J. (2007) *Case Study Research: Principles and Practices*, Cambridge: Cambridge University Press.

Gibbons, A. and Iatrona, L. D. (2009) "Networks and resistance: investigating online advocacy networks as a modality for resisting state surveillance", *Surveillance and Society*, 6(3): 233–258.

Giesbert, F.-O. (1990a) "Éditorial", *Le Figaro* 29 mai.

Giesbert, F.-O. (1990b) "Éditorial", *Le Figaro* 2 avril.

Gilgun, J. (2005) "Evidence-based practice, descriptive research and the resilience-schema-gender-brain functioning assessment", *British Journal of Social Work*, 35(6): 843–862.

Gilham, P. and Marx, G. (2000) "Complexity and irony in policing and protesting", *Social Justice*, 27(2): 212–236.

Gilley, B. (2003) "The limits of authoritarian resilience", *Journal of Democracy*, 14(1): 18–26.

Gilley, B. (2007) *The Right to Rule: How States Win and Lose Legitimacy*, New York: Columbia University Press.

Gjørv, G. H. (2012), "Security by any other name: negative security, positive security, and multi-actor security approach", *Review of International Studies*, 38(4): 835–859.

Glynos, J. and Howarth, D. (2007) *Logics of Critical Explanation in Social and Political Theory*, London: Routledge.

Goffman, E. (1961) *Asylums: Essays in the Social Situation of Mental Patients and Other Inmates*, Garden City, NY: Anchor Books.

Goffman, E. (1991), *Les cadres de l'expérience*, Paris: Les Editions de Minuit.

Goldstein, S. and Brooks, R. (2013), "Why study resilience?", in S. Goldstein and R. B. Brooks (eds), *Handbook of Resilience in Children*, New York: Springer.

Goldstone, J. (1991) *Revolution and Rebellion in the Early Modern World*, Berkeley, CA: University of California Press.

Goodrum, Abby A. (2005) *Impact and Analysis of Law Enforcement Activity in Academic and Public Libraries*, Chicago, IL: American Library Association.

Gordon, C. (1991) "Governmental rationality: An introduction". In G. Burchell, C. Gordon and P. Miller (eds) *The Foucault Effect: Studies in Governmentality*. Chicago, IL: University of Chicago Press.

Graham, S. (2010) *Cities under Siege: The Rise of the New Military Urbanism*, London: Verso.

Grayson, K. (2003) "Securitization and the boomerand debate: a rejoinder to Liotta and Smith-Windsor", *Security Dialogue*, 34(3): 337–343.

Grayson, K. (2008) "Human security as power/knowledge: the biopolitics of a definitional debate", *Cambridge Review of International Affairs*, 21 (3): 383–401.

Guardian (2010) "France defends Roma expulsion policy", L. Davies, 15 September 2010. [Available at http://www.guardian.co.uk/world/2010/sep/15/france-defends-roma-crackdown (accessed 9 November 2012).

Guchet, X. (2010) "La biométrie à l'école : une approche anthropologique", in A. Ceyhan and P. Piazza (eds.), *L'identification biométrique. Champs, acteurs, enjeux et controverses*, Paris: Presses de la MSH.

Guild, E. (2009) *Security and Migration in the 21st Century*, Cambridge: Polity Press.

Guillaume, X. (2011) "Resistance and the international: the challenge of the everyday", *International Political Sociology*, 5(4): 459–462.

Gunderson, L. H. (2000) "Ecological resilience – in theory and application", *Annual Review of Ecology and Systematics*, 31: 425–439.

Gurr, T. (1970) *Why Men Rebel*, Princeton, NJ: Princeton University Press.

Habermas, J. (1984) *Theory of Communicative Action.* Volume 1, Cambridge: Polity Press.

Habermas, J. (1987) *Theory of Communicative Action.* Volume 2, Boston, MA: Beacon Press.

Hacker, J. (2002) *The Divided Welfare State: The Battle over Public and Private Social Benefits in the United States*, Cambridge: Cambridge University Press.

Haftendorn, H. (1991) "The security puzzle: theory-building and discipline-building in international security", *International Studies Quarterly*, 35(1): 3–17.

Hage, G. (2003) *Against Paranoid Nationalism*, Sydney: Pluto Press.

Hall, P. (1999) "Social capital in Britain", *British Journal of Political Science*, 29(3): 417–461.

Hameiri, S. (2008) "Risk management, neo-liberalism and the securitisation of the Australian aid program", *Australian Journal of International Affairs*, 62(3): 357–371.

Hammerstad, A. (2011) "UNHCR and the securitization of forced migration", in A. Betts and G. Loescher (eds), *Refugees in International Relations*, Oxford: Oxford University Press.

Han, M. and Hua, S. (eds) (1990) *Cries for Democracy – Writings and Speeches from the 1989 Chinese Democracy Movement*, Princeton, NJ: Princeton University Press.

Handler, J. (1978) *Social Movements and the Legal System*, New York: Academic Press.

Handmer, J. W. and Dovers, S. R. (1996) "A typology of resilience: rethinking institutions for sustainable development", *Industrial & Environmental Crisis Quarterly* 9(4): 482–511.

Hansen, L. (2006) *Security as Practice. Discourse Analysis and the Bosnian War*, London: Routledge.

Hansen, L. (2010) "De-securitization, Counter-securitization, or Visual Insurgency? Exploring Security Discourses through Responses to the Muhammad Cartoons". Paper presented at the fifty-first Annual Convention of the International Studies Association, New Orleans, February 17–20.

Hansen, L. (2012) "Reconstructing desecuritisation: the normative-political in the Copenhagen School and directions for how to apply it", *Review of International Studies*, 38(3): 525–546.

Hanson-Young, S. (2010) "Gillard and Abbott locked in race to the bottom", *Press Release*, 6 July. http://greensmps.org.au/content/media-release/gillard-and-abbott-locked-race-bottom-greens.

Hardt, M. and Negri, A. (2001) *Empire*, Cambridge, MA: Harvard University Press.

Harrigan, J. and Martin, P. (2002) "Terrorism and the resilience of cities", *Economic Policy Review*, 8(2): 97–116.

Hartling, L. M. (2008) "Strengthening resilience in a risky world: it's all about relationships", *Women and Therapy*, 31(2–4): 51–70.

Hauser, S. (1999). "Understanding resilient outcomes: adolescent lives across time and generations", *Journal of Research on Adolescence*, 9(1): 1–24.

Havel, V. (1992) "The power of the powerless", in P. Wilson (ed.), *Open letters: Selected writings 1965–1990*, New York: Vintage Books.

Hayden, P. (2005) "Security beyond the state: cosmopolitanism, peace, and the role of just war theory", in M. Evans (ed.), *Just War Theory: A Reappraisal*, Edinburgh: Edinburgh University Press, pp. 157–176.

Health Canada (2003) "Learning from SARS: Renewal of public health in Canada," A report of the National Advisory Committee on SARS and Public Health. Ottawa: Health Canada.

Heilmann, E. (1991) *Des Herbiers aux fichiers informatiques: l'évolution du traitement de l'information dans la police*, doctoral thesis in information and communication science, Université de Strasbourg II.

Herington, J. (2010) "Security and the anatomy of value", Unpublished paper delivered at seventh Pan-European International Relations Conference, Stockholm, Sweden. Available athttp://stockholm.sgir.eu/uploads/Herington%20-%20Draft.pdf.

Herington, J. (2012) "The concept of security", in M. Selgelid and C. Enemark (eds), *Ethical and Security Aspects of Infectious Disease Control: Interdisciplinary Perspectives*, . Cheltenham: Ashgate Publishing,

Hobsbawm, E. (2006), "Les briseurs de machines", *Revue d'histoire moderne et contemporaine*, 53: 13–28.

Holling, C. (1973) "Resilience and stability of ecological systems", *Annual Review of Ecology and Systematics*, 4: 1–23.

Holling, C. S. (1996) "Engineering resilience versus ecological resilience", in P. Schulze (ed.). *Engineering within Ecological Constraints*, Washington, DC: National Academy Press, pp. 31–44.

Hollis, C. (2001) *Commonwealth of Australia House of Representatives Hansard*, 23 August, p. 30133.

Holm, K. (2006) "Europeanising export controls: the impact of the European code of conduct on arms exports in Belgium, Germany and Italy", *European Security*, 15(2): 213–234.

Honig, B. (2005) "Bound by law, administrative discretion and the politics of technicalities: lessons from Louis F. Post and the first Red Scare", in L. Douglas, A. Sarat and M. Umphrey (eds), *The Limits of Law*, Palo Alto, CA: Stanford University Press.

Hoogensen, G. (2012) "Security by any other name: negative security, positive security, and a multi-actor approach", *Review of International Studies,* 38(4): 836–859.

Hoogensen, G. and Stuvoy, K. (2006) "Gender, resistance and human security", *Security Dialogue,* 37(2): 207–228.

Horkheimer, M. (1974 [1947]) *Eclipse of Reason.* New York: Continuum.

Hoy, D. (2004) *Critical Resistance: From Poststructuralism to Postcritique,* Cambridge MA: MIT Press.

HREOC (2008) *Submission to the Joint Standing Committee on Migration, Inquiry into Immigration Detention in Australia.* 4 August. Available at http://www.humanrights. gov.au/legal/submissions/2008/20080829_immigration_detention.html.

Hudson, H. (2005) "Doing security as though humans matter: a feminist perspective on gender and the politics of human security", *Security Dialogue,* 36(2): 155–174.

Hughes, C. (2006) *Chinese Nationalism in the Global Era,* London: Routledge.

Human Rights Watch (2012) *France: Renewed Crackdown on Roma.* Available athttp://www.hrw.org/news/2012/08/10/france-renewed-crackdown-roma (accessed 20 November 2012).

Huysmans, J. (1998a) "The question of the limit: desecuritisation and the aesthetics of horror in political realism", *Millennium,* 27(3): 569–589.

Huysmans, J. (1998b) "Security! What do you mean? From concept to thick signifier", *European Journal of International Relations,* 4(2): 226–255.

Huysmans, J. (1998c) "Desecuritization and the aesthetics of horror in political realism", *Millennium: Journal of International Studies* 27(3): 569–589.

Huysmans, J. (2000) "The European Union and the securitization of migration", *Journal of Common Market Studies,* 38 (5): 751–777.

Huysmans, J. (2006) *The Politics of Insecurity: Fear, Migration and Asylum in the EU,* London: Routledge.

Huysmans, J. (2011) "What's in an act? On security speech acts and little security nothings", *Security Dialogue,* 42(4–5): 371–383.

Hyndman, J. and Mountz, A. (2008) "Another brick in the wall? Non-refoulement and the externalization of asylum by Australia and Europe", *Government and Opposition,* 43 (2): 249–269.

Ignatieff, M. (2004) *The Lesser Evil: Political Ethics in the age of Terror,* Toronto: Penguin Books.

Independent (2007) "Ireland deports Roma after stand-off over roundabout". C. Soares 26 July 2007. Available at http://www.independent.co.uk/news/world/europe/ireland-deports-roma-after-standoff-over-roundabout-458753.html (accessed 9 November 2012).

International Standards Organization (ISO) (2011). Available at http://www.iso.org/ (accessed: 21/05/2011).

James, M. (1991) "Economic rationalism and the liberal tradition", *Policy,* 7(3): 2–5.

Jutila, M. (2006) "Desecuritizing minority rights: against determinism", *Security Dialogue,* 37(2): 167–185.

Jonsson, S. (2010) "The ideology of universalism", *New Left Review,* 63: 115–126.

Kahan, J.H., Allen, A.C. and George, J.K. (2009) "An operational framework for resilience", *Journal of Homeland Security and Emergency Management,* 6(1): 1–49.

Kamrava, M. (1998) "Non-Democratic states and political liberalisation in the Middle East: a structural analysis", *Third World Quarterly,* 19(1): 63–85.

Kearney, S. (2010) "Gillard talks tough on border security", *Sunday Herald Sun,* July 4.

Keck, M. and Sikkink, M. (1998) *Activists beyond Borders,* Ithaca, NY: Cornell University Press.

Kersch, K. (2006) "The Supreme Court and international relations theory", *Albany Law Review*, 69: 771–799.

Klein, N. (2008) *The Shock Doctrine: The Rise of Disaster Capitalism*, New York: Metropolitan.

Klein, R., Nicholls, R.J., and Thomalla, F.(2003) "Resilience to natural hazards: how useful is this concept?", *Environmental Hazards*, 5(1–2): 35–45.

Knight, B. (2010) "New UNICEF report condemns German policy of deporting Roma children." *Deutsche Welle,* 8 July 2010, available from http://www.dw.de/new-unicef-report-condemns-german-policy-of-deporting-roma-children/a-5775224.

Knox, H. (2007) "Rites of passage: organization as an excess of flows", *Scandinavian Journal of Management,* 23: 265–284.

Kompridis, N. (2006) *Critique and Disclosure: Critical Theory Between Past and Future*, Cambridge MA: MIT Press.

Koselleck, R. (2004) "The historical-political semantics of asymmetric counterconcencepts", in *Futures Past, on the Semantics of Historical Time,* trans. K. Tribe, New York: Columbia University Press.

Koslowski, R. and Kratochwil, F. (1994) "Understanding change in international politics: the Soviet Empire's demise and the international system", *International Organization,* 48(2): 215–247.

Krause, K. and Williams, M. C. (1996) "Broadening the agenda of security studies: politics and methods", *Mershon International Studies Review*, 40(2): 229–254.

Krause, K. and Williams, M. C. (1997) "From strategy to security: foundations of critical security studies", in K. Krause and M. Williams (eds), *Critical Security Studies: Concepts and Cases*, London: UCL Press.

Kuhn, T. (1962) *The Structure of Scientific Revolutions*, Chicago, IL: University of Chicago Press.

Laclau, E. (1992) "Universalism, particularism, and the question of identity", *October*, 61: 83–90.

Laclau, E. (1996) *Emancipation(s)*, London: Verso.

Lacouette-Fougère, C. (2011) "Le projet INES aboutira-t-il? La carte nationale d'identité électronique en France : une solution à la recherche de problèmes", in A. Ceyhan and P. Piazza (eds.), *L'identification biométrique. Champs, acteurs, enjeux et controverses*, Paris: Editions de la MSH.

Lai, H. H. (2006) "Religious policies in post-totalitarian china: maintaining political monopoly over a reviving society", *Journal of Chinese Political Science*, 11(1): 55–77.

Laing, R. D. (1967) *The Politics of Experience*, Penguin: London.

Laitin, D. D. (2002). Comparative politics: the state of the subdiscipline" in I. Katznelson and H. V. Milner (eds), *Political Science: The State of the Discipline*, New York: Norton.

Lambroschini, C. (1992) "Éditorial", *Le Figaro* 23 avril.

Latour, B. (1988) *The Pasteurization of France*, Cambridge, MA: Harvard University Press.

Lee, R. M. (2005) "Resilience against discrimination: ethnic identity and other-group orientation and protective factors for Korean Americans", *Journal of Counseling Psychology*, 52(1): 36–44.

Le Figaro (2013) "Roms : Manuel Valls affiche sa fermeté", C. Cornevin, 14 March 2013. Available at http://www.lefigaro.fr/actualite-france/2013/03/14/01016-20130314 ARTFIG00647-roms-le-cri-d-alarme-et-le-message-de-fermete-de-valls.php (accessed 5 June 2013).

Lentzos, F. and Rose, N. (2009) "Governing insecurity: contingency planning, protection, resilience", *Economy and Society*, 38(2): 230–254.

Leonard, S. and Kaunert, C. (2011) "Reconceputalizing the audience in securitization theory", in T. Balzacq (ed.), *Securitization Theory: How Security Problems Emerge and Dissolve*. London, Routledge, pp. 55–76.

Lessig, L. (2006) *Code*, New York: Basic Books.

Li, H. (1999) "A brief statement of mine". Available at http://www.falundafa.ca/library/english/jw/jw9907221 e.html, accessed 4 April 2008.

Li, H. (2001) "Beyond the limits of forbearance". Available at http://www.clearwisdom.net/emh/articles/2001/1/2/6668.html, accessed 4 April 2008.

Li, H. (2007) "Further remarks on 'politics'". Available at http://www.clearwisdom.net/emh/articles/2007/2/22/82932.html, accessed 4 April 2008.

Li, R. P. Y. and Thompson, W. R. (1975) "The 'coup contagion' hypothesis", *The Journal of Conflict Resolution*, 18(1): 63–88.

Libération (2013) "Deux campements roms évacués dans la matinée", Agence France Presse. Available at http://www.liberation.fr/societe/2013/03/28/deux-campements-roms-evacues-dans-la-matinee_891944 (accessed 7 June 2013).

Lieberthal, K. G. (2004 [1995]) *Governing China: From Revolution to Reform*, 2nd ed., London and New York: W. W. Norton & Co.

Lindbom, A. and Rothstein, B. (2006). "La résilience du modèle suédois de Welfare dans l'économie mondialisée." *Revue internationale de politique comparée*, 13(3): 429–445.

Lindström, B. (2001), "The meaning of resilience", *International Journal of Adolescent Medicine and Health*, 13(1): 7–12.

Linklater, A. (1990) *Beyond Realism and Marxism: Critical Theory and International Relations*, London: Palgrave Macmillan.

Linklater, A. (1998) *The Transformation of Political Community*, Columbia, SC: University of South Carolina Press.

Lipset, S. (1970) *Political Man: The Social Bases of Politics*, London: Heinemann.

Lobel, J. (2003) "Introduction: losers, fools and prophets" ", in J. Lobel (ed.), *Success without Victory: Lost Legal Battles and the Long Road to Justice in America*, New York: New York University Press.

Longrigg, J. (1992) "Epidemics ideas and classical Athenian society", in T. Ranger and P. Slack (eds), *Epidemics and Ideas: Essays on the Historical Perception of Pestilence*. Cambridge: Cambridge University Press.

Loosemore, M., Raftery, J., Reilly, C. and Higgon, D. (2006) *Risk Management in Projects*, London: Routledge.

Los Angeles Times (2012) "France again cracks down on Roma settlements", 10 August.

Luban, D. (2007) "Preventive war and human rights", in H. Shue and D. Rodin (eds), *Preemption: Military Action and Moral Hustification*, Oxford: Oxford University Press, pp. 171–201.

Luban, D. (2008) "Lawfare and legal ethics in Guantanamo", *Stanford Law Review*, 60(6): 1981–2027.

Lundborg, T. and Vaughan-Williams, N. (2011) "Resilience, critical infrastructure, and molecular security: the excess of 'life' in biopolitics", *International Political Sociology*, 5(4): 367–383.

Luthans, F. (2002) "The need for and meaning of positive organizational behavior", *Journal of Organizational Behavior*, 23(6): 695–706.

Luthar, S. S. (1993) "Annotation: methodological and conceptual issues in research on chilhood resilience", *Journal of Child Pyschology and Psychiatry*, 34(4): 441–453.

Luthar, S. S., Cicchetu, D. and Becker, B. (2000) "The construct of resilience: a critical evaluation and guidelines for future work", *Child Development,* 71(3): 573–562.

Lynch, C. (1999) *Beyond Appeasement: Interpreting Interwar Peace Movements in World Politics*, Ithaca, NY: Cornell University Press.

Lynch, M. (2008) "Lie to me: Sanctions on Iraq, moral argument and the international politics of hypocrisy", in R. M. Price (ed.) *Moral Limit and Possibility in World Politics*, Cambridge: Cambridge University Press.

Lynn Jones, S. (1992) "The Future of International Security Studies", in D. Ball and D. Horner (eds.) *Strategic Studies in a Changing World*. Canberra: ANU SDSC.

Lyon, D. (2001). *Surveillance Society: Monitoring Everyday Life*. New York: McGraw-Hill International.

Lyon, D. (2007) *Surveillance Studies*, Boston: Polity Press.

Lyon, D. and Marukami Wood, D. (2012) "Security, surveillance and sociological analysis", *Canadian Journal of Sociology*, 49(4): 317–327.

MacKenzie, M. (2009) "Securitization and desecuritization: female soldiers and the reconstruction of women in post-conflict Sierra Leone", *Security Studies*, 18(2): 241–261.

Mahoney, J. (2000). "Path dependence in historical sociology", *Theory and Society* 29(4): 507–548.

Mahoney, J. and Thelen, K. (eds) (2010) *Explaining Institutional Change: Ambiguity, Agency, and Power*, Cambridge: Cambridge University Press.

Manne, R. (2013) "Tragedy of errors", *The Monthly*, March, pp. 18–25.

Marchand, P. (1991) *Discours de Philippe Marchand, Ministre de l'Intérieur, "Un projet global pour la securite interieure"*. Paris: Ministère de l'Intérieur, 20 novembre.

Marchetti, X. (1993) "Éditorial". *Le Figaro*, 1 avril.

Marr, D. and Wilkinson, M. (2002) *Dark Victory*, Melbourne: Black Inc.

Martin, A., van Brakel, R. and Bernhard, D. (2009) "Understanding resistance to digital surveillance: towards a multi-disciplinary, multi-actor framework", *Surveillance and Society*, 6(3): 203–212.

Marx, G. T. (1988) *Undercover: Police Surveillance in America*, Berkeley, CA: University of California Press.

Marx, G. T. (2004) *Windows into the Soul: Surveillance and Society in an Age of High Technology*, University of Chicago Press: Chicago.

Marx, G. T. (2006) "Soft surveillance: the growth of mandatory volunteerism in collecting personal information: hey Buddy can you spare a DNA?", in T. Monahan (ed.), *Surveillance and Security: Technological Politics and Power in Everyday Life*, London: Routledge.

Marx, G.T. (forthcoming) *Windows Into the Soul: Surveillance and Society in an Age of High Technology*, Chicago, IL: Universitty of Chicago Press.

Masten, A. S. (1994) "Resilience in indivudal development equals Succeful adaptation despite risk and adversity", in M. C. Wang and E. W. Gordon (eds), *Education Resilience in Inner-city America*, Hillsdale: Erlbaum.

Masten, A. S. and Powell, J. L. (2003) "A resilience framework for research, policy and practice", in S. S. Luthar (ed.), *Resilience and Vulnerability: Adaptation in the Context of Childhood Adversities*, Cambridge: Cambridge University Press.

Mathieu, L. (2002), "Rapport au politique, dimensions cognitives et perspectives pragmatiques dans l'analyse des mouvements sociaux", *Revue française de science politique*, (52)(1): 75–100.

McCarthy, J. and Zald, M. (1977) *The Trend in Social Movements in America: Professionalization and Resource Mobilization*, Ann Arbor: Center for Research on Social Organization, University of Michigan.

McDonald, M. (2010) "Lest we forget: the politics of memory and Australian military intervention", *International Political Sociology*, 4(3): 387–402.

McDonald, M. (2011) "Deliberation and resecuritization: Australia, asylum-seekers and the normative limits of the Copenhagen School", *Australian Journal of Political Science*, 46(2): 281–295.

McDonald, M. (2012) *Security, the Environment and Emancipation*, London: Routledge: 2012).

McInnes, C. and Rushton, S. (2011) "HIV/AIDS and securitization theory", *European Journal of International Relations*, 19(1): 485–509.

McKay, F., Thomas, S. and Kneebone, S. (2011) "It would be OK if they came through the proper channels: community perceptions and attitudes toward asylum seekers in Australia", *Journal of Refugee Studies*, 25(1):113–133.

McMahan, J. (2005) "Just cause for war", *Ethics and International Affairs*, 19(3): 1–21.

McMahan, J. (2009) *Killing in War,* Oxford: Oxford University Press.

McMaster, D. (2002) "Asylum-seekers and the insecurity of a nation", *Australian Journal of International Affairs*, 56(2): 279–290.

McPhail, C., Schweingruber, D. and McCarthy, J. (1998) "Policing protest in the United States: 1960–1995", in D. Della-Porta and H. Reiter (eds), *Policing Protest: The Control of Mass Demonstrations in Western Democracies*, Minneapolis, MN: University of Minnesota Press.

Merquior, J. (1980) *Rousseau and Weber: Two Studies in the Theory of Legitimacy*, London: Routledge & Kegan Paul.

Merton, R. (1957) *Social Theory and Social Structure*, New York: Basic Books.

Milliken, J. (1999) "The study of discourse in international relations: A critique of research and methods", *European Journal of International Relations*, 5(2): 225–254.

Mitchell, M. (2009) *Complexity: A Guided Tour*, Oxford: Oxford University Press.

Mitchell, T. (1990) "Everyday metaphors of power", *Theory & Society*, 19(5): 545–577.

Morozov, V. (2004) "Russia in the Baltic Sea region: desecuritization or deregionalization?", *Cooperation and Conflict*, 39(3): 317–331.

Mountz, A. (2010) *Seeking Asylum: Human Smuggling and Bureaucracy at the Border*, Minneapolis, MN: University of Minnesota Press.

Mulgan, T. (2001) *The Demands of Consequentialism*, Oxford: Oxford University Press.

Nacu, A. (2012) "From silent marginality to spotlight scapegoating? A brief case study of France's policy towards the Roma", *Journal of Ethnic and Migration Studies* 38(8): 1323–1328.

Nathan, A. (2003) "Authoritarian Resilience", *Journal of Democracy*, 14(1): 6–17.

Nathan, A., Link, P. and Zhang, L. (eds) (2001) *The Tiananmen Papers: The Chinese Leadership's Decision to Use Force against Their Own People – in Their Own Words*, New York: Public Affairs.

Neal, A. (2012) "Normalization and legislative exceptionalism: counterterrorist lawmaking and the changing times of security emergencies", *International Political Sociology*, 6: 260–276.

Neocleous, M. (2008) *Critique of Security*, Edinburgh: Edinburgh University Press.

Neocleous, M. (2011) "Inhuman security", in D. Chandler and N. Hynek (eds) *Critical Perspectives on Human Security: Rethinking Emancipation and Power in International Relations*. London: Routledge.

Neufeld, M. (1995) *The Restructuring of International Relations Theory*, Cambridge: Cambridge University Press.

Neufeld, M. (2004) "Pitfalls of emancipation and discourses of security: reflections on Canada's 'security with a human face'", *International Relations*, 18(1): 109–123.

New York Times (2010) "Italian cities plan to shut Roma camps", E. Povoledo, 3 September 2010. Available at http://www.nytimes.com/2010/09/04/world/europe/04roma.html?_ r=0 (accessed 9 November 2012).

Noiriel, G. (2001) "Les pratiques policières d'identification des migrants et leurs enjeux pour l'histoire des relations de pouvoir. Contribution à une réflexion en 'longue durée'", in G. Noiriel (ed.), *État, nation et immigration: Vers une histoire du pouvoir*, Paris: Belin.

Norris, F. H., Stevens, S. P., Pfefferbaum, B., Wyche, K. F. and Pfefferbaum, R. L. (2008) "Community resilience as a metaphor: theory, set of capacities, and strategy for disaster readiness", *American Journal of Community Psychology*, 41(1–2): 127–150.

North, D. C., Wallis, J. J. and Weingast, B. D. (2009) *Violence and Social Orders: A Conceptual Framework for Interpreting Recorded Human History*, Cambridge: Cambridge University Press.

Noun, A. and Chyba, C. (2008) "Biotechnology and biosecurity," in N. Bostrom and M. Cirkovic (eds) *Global Catastrophic Risks*, Oxford: Oxford University Press.

Nunes, J. (2012) "Reclaiming the political: emancipation and critique in security studies", *Security Dialogue*, 43(4): 345–361.

O'Brien, G. and Reid, P. (2005) "The future of UK emergency management: new wine, old skin?", *Disaster Prevention and Management*, 14(3): 353–361.

O'Brien, K. J. (1996) "Rightful resistance", *World Politics*, 49(1): 31–55.

Ollier-Malaterre, A. (2010) "Contributions of work-life and resilience initiatives to the individual/organization relationship", *Human Relations*, 63(1): 41–62.

O'Malley, P. (2010) "Resilient subjects: uncertainty, warfare and liberalism", *Economy & Society*, 39(4): 488–509.

O'Malley, P. (2011) "From risk to resilience: technologies of the self in the age of catastrophes" [unpublished paper].

Orend, B. (2002) "Justice after War", *Ethics and International Affairs*, 16(1): 43–56.

Orend, B. (2006) *The Morality of War*, Peterborough: Broadview Press.

Ownby, D. (2008) *Falun Gong and the Future of China*, Oxford: Oxford University Press.

Onuf, N. (1989) *World of Our Making*, Columbia, SC: University of South Carolina Press.

Palmer, D. (2007) *Qigong Fever: Body, Science, and Utopia in China, 1949–1999*, New York: Columbia University Press.

Paltemaa, L. and Vuori, J. (2006) "How cheap is identity talk? A framework of identity frames and security discourse for the analysis of repression and legitimization of social movements in mainland China", *Issues & Studies*, 42(3): 47–86.

Paltemaa, L. and Vuori, J. A. (2009) "Regime transition and the Chinese politics of technology: From mass science to the controlled internet", *Asian Journal of Political Science*, 17(1): 1–23.

Pape, R. A. (2012) "When duty calls: a pragmatic standard of humanitarian intervention', *International Security*, 37(1): 41–80.

Parsons, T. (1951) *The Social System*, London: Routledge and Kegan Paul.

Pasqua, C. (1993) *Intervention de M. Charles Pasqua, Ministre de l'Intérieur, à l'université d'été des jeunes RPR*. Paris, Ministère de l'Intérieur, 4 septembre.

Patterson, J. M. (2002) "Understanding family resilience", *Journal of Clinical Psychology*, 58(3): 233–246.

Peck, J., Theodore, N. and Brenner, N. (2010) "Postneoliberalism and its malcontents", *Antipode*, 41(1): 94–116.

Peck, J. and Tickell, A. (1994) "Jungle law breaks out: neoliberalism and global-local disorder", *Area* 26(4): 317–326.

Peoples, C. (2011) "Security after emancipation? Critical theory, violence and resistance". *Review of International Studies* 37(3):1113–1135.

Peoples, C. and Vaughan-Williams, N. (2010) *Critical Security Studies: An Introduction*, London: Routledge.

Perera, S. (2009) *Australia and the Insular Imagination*, London: Palgrave.

Perry, E. and Selden, M. (eds) (2003) *Chinese Society: Change, Conflict and Resistance*, 2nd ed, London: Routledge Curzon.

Petersen, K. L. (2012) "Risk analysis – A field within security studies?", *European Journal of International Relations*, 18(4): 693–717.

Pfister, U. and Suter, C. (1987) "International financial relations as part of the world-system", *International Studies Quarterly*, 31(3): 239–272.

Pheng, M. (2012) "Moulin-Galant: La question Rom". Available at http://www.mediapart.fr/journal/france/051112/dans-le-bidonville-de-moulin-galant-un-film-sur-les-roms-et-les-elus-locaux.

Pickering, S. (2011) "Common sense and original deviancy: news discourses and asylum seekers in Australia", *Journal of Refugee Studies*, 14(2): 169–186.

Piazza, P. (2004) "Septembre 1921: la première carte d'identité de Français et ses enjeux", *Genèses* 54:76–89.

Piazza, P. (2009) "Edvige et les résistances au fichage policier", *Hermès* 53:75–8.

Piazza, P. (ed.) (2011), *Aux origines de la police scientifique: Alphonse Bertillon, précurseur de la science du crime*, Paris: Karthala.

Pierson, P. (1996) "The new politics of the welfare state", *World Politics*, 48(2): 143–179.

Pieterse, J. N. (1992) *Emancipation, Modern and Postmodern*, London: Sage.

Pin-Fat, V. (2009) *Universality, Ethics and International Relations: A Grammatical Reading*, London: Routledge.

Plodinec, M. J. (2009) *Definitions of Resilience: An Analysis*, Oak Ridge, TN: Community and Regional Resilience Institute.

Polanyi, K. (1944) *The Great Transformation*, Boston, MA: Beacon Press

Porta, D. (1996) "Social movements and the state: thoughts on the policing of protest", in D. McAdam, J. McCarthy and M. Zald (eds), *Comparative Perspectives on Social Movements*, Cambridge: Cambridge University Press.

Price-Smith, A. (2009) *Contagion and Chaos: Disease Ecology and National Security in the Era of Globalization*, Cambridge MA: MIT Press.

Prozorov, S. (2005) "X/Xs: Toward a general theory of exception", *Alternatives*, 30(1): 81–112.

Pusca, A. (2010) "The 'Roma Problem' in the EU: nomadism, (in)visible architectures and violence", *Borderlands*, 9(2): 1–17.

Ratner, M., and Ray, E. (2004) *Guantanamo: What the World Should Know*, White River Junction, VT: Chelsea Green.

Refugee Council of Australia (2008) *Submission to the Joint Standing Committee on Migration, Inquiry into Immigration Detention in Australia*, August.

Remacle, E. and Martinelli, M. (2004) "CFSP initiatives on conventional arms limitations: global actorness of global responsibility?", in J. Mawdsley, J., Martinelli *et al.* (eds), *Europe and the Global Arms Agenda: Security Trade and Accountability*, BICC/DFAC Security Sector Governance and Conversion Studies, Baden-Baden: Nomos Verlagsgesellschaft.

Renaud, F. G., Birkmann, J., Damm, M. and Gallopin, G. (2010) "Understanding multiple thresholds of coupled social-ecological systems exposed to natural hazards as external shocks", *Natural Hazards*, 55(3): 749–763.

Reuters (2012) "EU says monitoring France over wave of Roma expulsions", Reuters, 10 August 2012. Available at http://www.reuters.com/article/2012/08/10/us-france-roma-eu-idUSBRE87912S20120810 (accessed 9 November 2012).

Rigby, A. (2005) "Forgiveness and reconciliation in jus post bellum", in M. Evans (ed.), *Just War theory: A Reappraisal,* Edinburgh: Edinburgh University Press.

Rodrik, D. (1997) *Has Globalization Gone too Far?* Washington: Institute for International Economics.

Roe, P. (2004) "Securitization and minority rights: conditions of desecuritization", *Security Dialogue,* 35(3): 279–294.

Roe, P. (2008a) "The 'value' of positive security", *Review of International Studies,* 34: 777–794.

Roe, P. (2008b) "Actor, audience(s) and emergency measures: securitization and the UK's decision to invade Iraq", *Security Dialogue,* 39(6): 615–635.

Roe, P. (2012a) "Is securitization a 'negative' concept? Revisiting the normative debate over normal versus extraordinary politics", *Security Dialogue,* 43(3): 249–266.

Rogers, P. (2011a) "Resilience and Civil Contingencies: Tensions in Northeast and Northwest UK (2000–2008)", *Journal of Policing, Intelligence and Counter Terrorism,* 6(2): 91–107.

Rogers, P. (2011b) "Development of resilient Australia: enhancing the PPRR approach with anticipation, assessment and registration of risks", *Australian Journal of Emergency Management,* 26(1): 54–59.

Rogers, P. (2012a) "Resilience revisited – an etymology and genealogy of a contested concept", *Climate Futures Working Paper Series,* 4.

Rogers, P. (2012b) "Rethinking resilience: surveillance, community and the UK riots", *Surveillance and Everyday Life Research Group* (First Annual Conference), University of Sydney, 20–21ˢ February, 2012.

Rogers, P. (2012c) *The Resilience of the City: Change, (Dis)Order and Disaster,* London: Ashgate.

Rogers, P. (2013a) "The rigidity trap in global resilience: Neoliberalisation through principles, standards, and benchmarks", *Globalizations,* 10(3): 383–395.

Rogers, P. (2013b) "Rethinking resilience: articulating community and the UK riots", *Politics,* 33(4): 322–333.

Rogin, M. (1967) *The Intellectuals and McCarthy: The Radical Specter,* Cambridge, MA: MIT Press.

Rogin, M. (1988) *Ronald Reagan, The Movie,* Berkeley, CA: University of California Press.

Ronel, N. and Elisha, E. (2011) "A different perspective: introducing positive criminology", *International Journal of Offender Therapy and Comparative Criminology,* 55(2): 305–325.

Ross Schneider, B. (2008) "Economic liberalization and corporate governance: the resilience of business groups in Latin America", *Comparative Politics,* 40(4): 379–397.

Rothschild, E. (1995) "What is security?", *Daedalus,* 124(3): 53–98.

Rumgay, J. (2004) "Scripts for safer survival: pathways out of female crime", *Howard Journal,* 43(4): 405–419.

Rutter, M. (1987) "Psychosocial resilience and protective mechanisms", *American Journal of Orthopsychiatry,* 57(3): 316–331.

Rutter, M. (1990) "Psychological resilience and protective mechanisms", in J. Rolf, A. S. Masten, D. Cicchetti, K. H. Nuechterlein and S. Weintraub (eds), *Risk and Protective Factors in the Development of Psychopathology,* New York: Cambridge University Press.

Rutter, M. (2006) "Implications of resilience concepts for scientific understanding", *Annals of the New York Academy of Sciences*, 1094: 1–12.

Sale, K. (2006) *La Révolte luddite : briseurs de machines à l'ère de l'industrialisation* (translated by C. Izoard) Paris: L'Échappée.

Saleh, A. (2010) "Broadening the concept of security", *Geopolitics Quarterly*, 6(4): 228–241.

Salter, M. B. (2008) "Securitization and desecuritization: dramaturgical analysis and the Canadian aviation transport security authority", *Journal of International Relations and Development*, 11(4): 321–349.

Salter, M. B. (2011) "When securitization fails: the hard case of counter-terrorism programs", in T. Balzacq (ed.), *Securitization Theory: How Security Problems Emerge and Dissolve.* Abingdon: Routledge.

Salter, M. B. and Mutlu, C. E. (eds) (2012) *Research Methods in Critical Security Studies: An Introduction*, London: Routledge.

Sarat, A. (2010) "Introduction: towards new conceptions of the relationship of law and soveriegnty under conditions of emergency", in A. Sarat (ed.) *Sovereignty, Emergency, Legality*, Cambridge: Cambridge University Press.

Schimmelfennig, F. (2005) "The community trap: liberal norms, rhetorical action and the Eastern enlargement of the European Union", in F. Schimmelfennig and U. Sedelmeier (eds), *The Politics of European Union Enlargement: Theoretical Approaches*, London: Routledge, 2005.

Schmitt, B. (2001) *A common European Export Policy for Defence and Dual-Use Items?*, Occasional Paper 25, Paris: The Institute for Security Studies, Western European Union

Schoon, I. (2006) *Risk and Resilience: Adaptations in Changing Times*, Cambridge: Cambridge University Press.

Scott, J. (1985) *Weapons of the Weak Everyday Forms of Peasant Resistance.* New Haven, CT: Yale University Press.

Scott, J. (1987) *Weapons of the Weak. Everyday Forms of Peasant Resistance*,2nd ed., New Haven, CT: Yale University Press.

Scott, J. (1990) *Domination and the Arts of Resistance: Hidden Transcripts*, New Haven, CT: Yale University Press.

Scott, J. (1992) "Experience". In J. Butler and J. W. Scott (eds) *Feminists Theorize the Political*. New York and London: Routledge.

Scott, J. (1995) "Universalism and the history of feminism", *Differences: A Journal of Feminist Cultural Studies*, 7(1): 1–14.

Searle, J. (2009) "Language and social ontology", in C. Mantzavinos (ed.), *Philosophy of the Social Sciences: Philosophical Theory and Scientific Practice*, Cambridge: Cambridge University Press.

Searle, J. (2011) *Making the Social World: The Structure of Human Civilization*, Oxford: Oxford University Press.

Seccombe, K. (2002) "Beating the odds versus changing the odds: poverty, resilience, and family policy", *Journal of Marriage and Family*, 64(2): 384–394.

Seery, M. D., Allison, H. E. and Cohen, S. R. (2010) "Whatever does not kill us: cumulative lifetime adversity, vulnerability, and resilience", *Journal of Personality and Social Psychology*, 99(6): 1025–1041.

Seymor, J. D. (2005) "Sizing up china's prisons", in B. Bakken (ed.) *Punishment, and Policing in China,* Lanham, MD: Rowman and Littlefield Publishers.

Sharp, J., Routledge, P, Philo, C. and Paddison, R. (2000) *Entanglements of Power: Geographies of Domination/Resistance*, London: Routledge.

Shepherd, L. J. (2007) "Victims, perpetrators and actors revisited", *British Journal of Politics & International Relations*, 9(2): 239–256.

Shue, V. (1994) "Legitimacy crisis in China?", in P. H. Gries and S. Rosen (eds), *State and Society in 21st-century China: Crisis, Contention and Legitimation*, London: Routledge.

Sigona, N. (2005) "Locating 'the gypsy problem'. The Roma in Italy: stereotyping, labelling and 'nomad camps'", *Journal of Ethnic and Migration Studies*, 31(4): 741–756.

Sigona, N. (2011) "The governance of Romani people in Italy: discourse, policy and practice", *Journal of Modern Italian Studies*, 16(5): 590–606.

Slater, D. (2003) "Iron Cage in an iron fist: authoritarian institutions and the personalization of power in Malaysia", *Comparative Politics*, 36(1): 81–101.

Slaughter, A.-M. (2003) "A global community of courts", *Harvard International Law Journal*, 44: 191–220.

Snow, D., Rochford, E. B, Worden, S. K., and Benford, R. D. (1986) "Frame alignment processes, micromobilization, and movement participation", *American Sociological Review*, 51(4): 464–481.

Sontag, S. (1988) *Illness as Metaphor and AIDS and Its Metaphors*, New York: Anchor Books.

Sparke, M. (2006) 'Political geography: political geographies of globalization (2) – governance' *Progress in Human Geography,* 30(2): 1–16.

St John, R., King, A., de Jong, D., Bodies-Collins, M. and Squires, S. G. (2005) "Border screening for SARS", *Emerging Infectious Diseases* 11: 6–10.

Stone, G. (2004) *Perilous Times: Free Speech in Wartime from the Seditious Act to the War on Terror*, New York: W. W. Norton.

Tanner, M. S. (2004) "China rethinks unrest", *The Washington Quarterly*, 27: 137–156.

Tarrow, S. and Tilly, C. (2006) *Contentious Politics*, New York: Paradigm Publishers.

Taureck, Rita (2006) "Securitisation theory and securitisation studies", *Journal of International Relations and Development*, 9(1): 53–61.

Thornton, P. (2002) "Framing dissent in contemporary China: irony, ambiguity and metonymy", *China Quarterly*, 171: 661–681

Tickner, A. (1992) *Gender in International Relations. Feminist Perspectives on Achieving Global Security*, New York: Columbia University Press.

Tickner, J. A. (1997) "You just don't understand: troubled engagements between feminists and IR theorists", *International Studies Quarterly*, 41(4): 611–632.

Tilly, C. (1978) *From Mobilization to Revolution*, Reading, MA: Addison-Wesley.

Tisseron, S. (2007) *La résilience*, Paris: Presses Universitaires de France.

Traini, C. (2011), "Les émotions de la cause animale: Histoires affectives et travail militant", *Politix. Revue des sciences sociales du politique*, 93(1): 69–92.

Tsing, A. (2005) *Friction: An Ethnography of Global Connection*, Princeton, NJ: Princeton University Press.

Tuan, Y.-F. (1979) *Landscapes of Fear,* New York: Pantheon Books.

Tuncer, S. (2009) *Le refus de prélèvement d'ADN: Scène d'un travail politique de dénonciation de l'ordre sécuritaire*, Master's thesis in sociology, Paris, EHESS.

Ungar, M. (2004) "A constructionist discourse on resilience", *Youth & Society*, 35(3): 341–365.

Ungar, M. (2011) "The social ecology of resilience: addressing contextual and cultural ambiguity of a nascent construct", *American Journal of Orthopsychiatry*, 81(1): 1–17.

Unger, R. (1976) *Law in Modern Society: Toward a Criticism of Social Theory*, New York: The Free Press.

Urry, J. (2009) "Aeromobilities and the global", in S. Cwerner, S. Kesselring and J. Urry (eds) *Aeromobilities,* London: Routledge.

Vale, L. and Campanella, T. (eds) (2005) *The Resilient City: How Modern Cities Recover from Disasters*, Oxford: Oxford University Press.

Van Munster, R. (2007) "Security on a shoestring: a hitchiker's guide to critical schools of security in Europe", *Security Dialogue*, 42(2): 235–243.

Vinthagen, S. and Lilja, M. (2007) "Resistance", in G. L. Andersson and K. G. Herr (eds), *Encyclopedia of Activism and Social Justice*, Thousand Oaks, CA: Sage.

Von Eye, A. and Schuster, C. (2000) "The odds of resilience", *Child Development*, 71(3): 563–66.

Vuori, J. A. (2008) "Illocutionary logic and strands of securitisation – applying the theory of securitisation to the study of non-democratic political orders", *European Journal of International Relations*, 14(1): 65–99.

Vuori, J. A. (2011a) "Religion bites: Falungong, securitization/desecuritization in the People's Republic of China", in Thierry Balzacq (ed.), *Securitization Theory: How Security Problems Emerge and Dissolve,* London: Routledge.

Vuori, J. A. (2011b) *How to Do Security with Words – A Grammar of Securitisation in the People's Republic of China*, Annales Universitatis Turkuensis B 336, Turku: University of Turku Press.

Vuori, J. A. (2014) *Critical Security and Chinese Politics: The Anti-Falungong Campaign*, London and New York: Routledge.

Wæver, O. (1989) "Conflicts of vision – visions of conflict", in O. Wæver, P. Lemaitre and E. Tromer (eds), *European Polyphony: Perspectives beyond East-West Confrontation*, London: Macmillan.

Wæver, O. (1995) "Securitization and desecuritization", in R. D. Lipschutz (ed.), *On Security,* New York: Columbia University Press, pp. 46–86.

Wæver, O. (1999) "Securitizing sectors? Reply to Eriksson", *Cooperation & Conflict*, 34(3): 334–340.

Wæver, Ole (2000) "The EU as a security actor: reflections from a pessimistic Constructivist on post-sovereign security orders", in M. Kelstrup and M. C. Williams (eds.), *International Relations Theory and the Politics of European Integration: Power, Security, and Community*, London: Routledge.

Wæver, O. (2002) "Security: a conceptual history for international relations". Paper presented at British International Studies Association Conference, London, December 16–18.

Waever O. (2003) "Securitisation: taking stock of a research programme in security studies", unpublished mansucript.

Wæver, O. (2011) "Politics, security, theory", *Security Dialogue*, 42(4–5): 465–480.

Wæver, O., Buzan, B., Kelstrup, M. and Lemaitre, P. (eds) (1993) *Identity, Migration and the New Security Agenda in Europe*, London: Pinter.

Walker, B. H., Anderies, J. M., Kinzip, A. P. and Ryan, P. (2006) "Exploring resilience in social-ecological systems through comparative studies and theory development: introduction to the special issue", *Ecology and Society* 11(1): 12–16.

Walker, B. and Meyers, J. (2004) "Thresholds in ecological and socio-ecological systems: a developing database", *Ecology and Society*, 9(2): 3–18.

Walker, J. and Cooper, M. (2011) "Genealogies of resilience. From systems ecology to the political economy of crisis adaptation", *Security Dialogue*, 42(2): 143–160.

Walker, R. B. J. (1993) *Inside/Outside: International Relations as Political Theory*, Cambridge: Cambridge University Press.

Walker, R. B. J. (2006) "Lines of insecurity: international, imperial, exceptional", *Security Dialogue*, 37: 65–82.

Walker, B. and Salt, D. (2012) "Preparing for practice: the essence of resilience thinking", in B. Walker and D. Salt (eds), *Resilience Practice: Building Capacity to Absorb Disturbance and Maintain Function*, Washington, DC: Island Press.

Walt, S. (1991) "Renaissance of security studies", *International Studies Quarterly*, 35(2): 211–239.

Walzer, M. (1977) *Just and Unjust Wars: A Moral Argument with Historical Illustrations*, 4thed., New York: Basic Books

Walzer, M. (2004) "Just and unjust occupations", *Dissent*. Available at http://www.dissentmagazine.org/article/?article=400.

Webber, J. and Macleod, C. (eds) (2010) *Between Consenting Peoples: Political Community and the Meaning of Consent*, Vancouver: UBC Press.

Weber, M. (1978) *Economy and Society: An Outline of Interpretive Sociology*, ed. Guenther Roth and Claus Wittich, Berkeley, CA: University of California Press.

Weldes, J., Laffey, M., Gusteerson, G. and Duvall, R. (1999) *Cultures of Insecurity: States, Communities, and the Production of Danger*, Minneapolis, MA: University of Minnesota Press.

Wendt, A. (1999) *Social Theory of International Politics*, Cambridge: Cambridge University Press.

White, R. (1981) *Inventing Australia.* Sydney: Allen & Unwin.

WHO (2006) *SARS – How a Global Epidemic was Stopped.* Geneva: WHO Press.

Wibben, A. (2011a) "Feminist politics in feminist security studies", *Politics & Gender*, 7(4): 590–595.

Wibben, A. (2011b) *Feminist Security Studies: A Narrative Approach*, Abingdon: Routledge.

Wilkinson, C. (2011) "The limits of spoken words: from meta-narratives to experiences of security', in T. Balzacq (ed.), *Securitization Theory: How Security Problems Emerge and Dissolve*, London: Routledge, 94–115.

Wilkinson, C. (2007) "The Copenhagen School on tour in Kyrgyzstan: is securitization theory useable outside Europe?", *Security Dialogue*, 38(5): 5–25.

Williams, M. (2003) "Words, images, enemies: securitization and international politics", *International Studies Quarterly*, 47(4): 511–531.

Williams, M. (2007) *Culture and Security: Symbolic Power and the Politics of International Security*, New York: Routledge.

Williams, M. (2011a) "Securitization and the liberalism of fear", *Security Dialogue*, 42(4–5): 453–463.

Williams, M. (2011b) "The continuing evolution of securitization theory", in T. Balzacq (ed.), *Securitization Theory. How Security Problems Emerge and Dissolve*, London, Routledge.

Willsher, K. (2012) " France clears out Roma camps, prompting criticism of Hollande", *Los Angeles Times*, 10 August, available fromhttp://articles.latimes.com/2012/aug/09/world/la-fg-france-roma-20120810.

Wilson, E. (2012) "Much to be proud of, much to be done: faith-based organizations and the politics of asylum in Australia", *Journal of Refugee Studies*, 24(3): 548–564.

Wolfers, A. (1952) "National security as an ambiguous symbol", *Political Science Quarterly*, 67(4): 481–502.

Wood, D. *et al.* (2003) "The constant state of emergency?: Surveillance after 9/11", in K. Ball and F. Webster (eds), *The Intensification of Surveillance – Crime, Terrorism and Warfare in the Information Age*, London, Pluto Press.

Wyn Jones, R. (1999) *Security, Strategy and Critical Theory*, Boulder, CO: Lynne Rienner.

Wyn Jones, R. (2005) "On emancipation: necessity, capacity and concrete utopias". In K. Booth (ed.) *Critical Security Studies and World Politics*. Boulder, CO and London: Lynne Rienner Publishers.

Wyn Jones, R. (2012) "The test of practice: An interview with Richard Wyn Jones". In S. Brincat, L. Lima and J. Nunes (eds) *Critical Theory in International Relations and Security Studies: Interviews and Reflections*. Abingdon: Routledge.

Yan Kong, T. (2006) "Globalization and labour market reform: patterns of response in Northeast Asia", *British Journal of Political Science*, 36(2): 359–383.

Zhou, H., Wan, J, Wan, J and Jia, H. (2010) "Resilience to natural hazards: a geographic perspective", *Natural Hazards*, 53(1): 21–41.

Zhao, Z. (2009) *Prisoner of the State. The Secret Journal of Zhao Ziyang*, trans. and ed. B. Pu, R. Chiang and A. Ignatius, New York, London, Toronto, Sydney: Simon & Schuster.

Zimmerer, K. (1994) "Human geography and the new ecology: the prospect and promise of integration", *Annals of the Association of American Geographers*, 84: 108–125

Zong, H. (2002) "Zhu rongji in 1999 (I)", *Chinese Law and Government*, 35(1): 53–72.

Zureik, E. and Salter, M. (eds) (2005) *Global Surveillance and Policing*. Portland, OR: Willan Publishing.

人民日报 [*Renmin ribao*] (24.7.1999) '受中共中央委托, 王兆国向各民主党派中央, 全国工商联领导人和无党派人士：   通报中央处理"法轮功"问题的文件精神' [Notification from Wang Zhaoguo Regarding the Essence of the Central Government Documents on Handling the "Falun Gong" Issue].

Index